1 MONTH OF
FREE
READING

at

www.ForgottenBooks.com

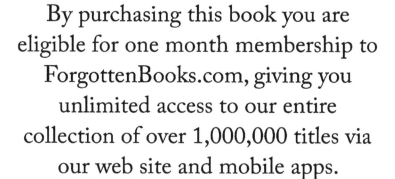

By purchasing this book you are eligible for one month membership to ForgottenBooks.com, giving you unlimited access to our entire collection of over 1,000,000 titles via our web site and mobile apps.

To claim your free month visit: www.forgottenbooks.com/free893438

ISBN 978-0-265-81380-5
PIBN 10893438

White's Grammar School Texts

SALLUST'S

CATILINE-WAR

WITH A VOCABULARY

BY

JOHN T. WHITE, D.D. Oxon.

NEW EDITION
(Fifteenth and Sixteenth Thousand.)

LONDON

LONGMANS, GREEN, AND CO.

AND NEW YORK: 15, EAST SIXTEENTH STREET.

1887

LONDON:
PRINTED BY GILBERT AND RIVINGTON, LD,
ST. JOHN'S HOUSE, CLERKENWELL ROAD, E.C.

PREFACE.

FOR some long time past it has been widely felt that a reduction in the cost of *Classical Works* used in schools generally, and more especially in those intended for boys of the middle classes, is at once desirable and not difficult of accomplishment. For the most part only portions of authors are read in the earlier stages of education, and a pupil is taken from one work to another in each successive half-year or term; so that a book needlessly large and proportionably expensive is laid aside after a short and but partial use.

In order, therefore, to meet what is certainly a want, Portions of the *Classical Writers* usually read in Schools are now being issued under the title of GRAMMAR SCHOOL TEXTS; while, at the request of various Masters, it has been determined to add to the series some of the *Gospels in Greek.*

Each TEXT is provided with a VOCABULARY of the words occurring in it. In every case the

origin of a word, when known, is stated at the commencement of the article treating of it, if connected
with another Latin, or Greek, word ; at the end of
it, if derived from any other source. Further still,
the primary or etymological meaning is always
given, within inverted commas, in Roman type,
and so much also of each word's history as is
needful to bring down its chain of meanings to
the especial force, or forces, attaching to it in
the particular " Text."

Moreover, as an acquaintance with the principles
of GRAMMAR, as well as with ETYMOLOGY, is
necessary to the understanding of a language, such
points of construction as seem to require elucida-
tion are concisely explained under the proper
articles, or a reference is simply made to that rule
in the *Public Schools Latin Primer*, or in *Parry's
Elementary Greek Grammar*, which meets the
particular difficulty. It occasionally happens, however, that more information is needed than can be
gathered from the above-named works. When
such is the case, whatever is requisite is supplied,
in substance, from Jelf's Greek Grammar, or the
Latin Grammars of Zumpt and Madvig.

LONDON : *January,* 1875.

CONTENTS.

C. SALLUSTII CRISPI

BELLUM CATILINARIUM.

———◆———

I.—1. OMNĪS homines, qui sese student præstare ceteris animalibus, summā ope niti decet vitam silentio ne transeant, veluti pecora, quæ natura prona, atque ventri obedientia, finxit. 2. Sed nostra omnis vis in animo et corpore sita : animi imperio, corporis servitio magis utimur : alterum nobis cum dîs, alterum cum beluis commune est. 3. Quò mihi rectius videtur ingenii quàm virium opibus gloriam quærere ; et, quoniam vita ipsa, quā fruimur, brevis est, memoriam nostri quàm maxume longam efficere. 4. Nam divitiarum et formæ gloria fluxa atque fragilis ; virtus clara æternaque habetur.

5. Sed diu magnum inter mortalīs certamen fuit, vine corporis, an virtute animi, res militaris magis procederet. 6. Nam et priùs quàm incipias consulto, et ubi consulueris maturè facto, opus est. 7. Ita utrumque, per se indigens, alterum alterius auxilio viget.

Sallust.   **B**

II.—1. Igitur initio reges (nam in terris nomen imperii id primum fuit) divorsi, pars ingenium, alii corpus exercebant : etiam tum vita hominum sine cupiditate agitabatur ; sua cuique satis placebànt. 2. Postea verò quàm in Asiā Cyrus, in Græciā Lacedæmonii et Athenienses cœpere urbes atque nationes subigere, lubidinem dominandi causam belli habere, maxumam gloriam in maxumo imperio putare; tum demum periculo atque negotiis compertum est in bello plurimùm ingenium posse. 3. Quòd si regum atque imperatorum animi virtus in pace ita, uti in bello, valeret, æquabiliùs atque constantiùs sese res humanæ haberent ; neque aliud aliò ferri, neque mutari ac misceri omnia cerneres. 4. Nam imperium facile his artibus retinetur, quibus initio partum est. 5. Verùm, ubi pro labore desidia, pro continentiā et æquitate lubido atque superbia invasere, fortuna simul cum moribus immutatur. 6. Ita imperium semper ad optumum quemque a minùs bono transfertur.

7. Quæ homines arant, navigant, ædificant, virtuti omnia parent. 8. Sed multi mortales, dediti ventri atque somno, indocti incultique vitam, sicuti peregrinantes, transegere ; quibus, profectò contra naturam, corpus voluptati, anima oneri fuit. Eorum ego vitam mortemque juxtà æstumo, quoniam de utrāque siletur. 9. Verùm enimvero is demum mihi vivere atque frui animā videtur, qui, aliquo negotio intentus, præclari facinoris aut artis bonæ famam quærit. Sed in magnā copiā rerum aliud alii natura iter ostendit.

III.—1. Pulchrum est bene facere reipublicæ:
etiam bene dicere haud absurdum est. Vel pace,
vel bello, clarum fieri licet : et qui fecere, et qui
facta aliorum scripsere, multi laudantur. 2. Ac
mihi quidem, tamenetsi haudquaquam par gloria
sequatur scriptorem et auctorem rerum, tamen in
primis arduum videtur res gestas scribere : primùm,
quòd facta dictis sunt exæquanda : dehinc, quia
plerique, quæ delicta reprehenderis, malivolentiâ et
invidiâ putant : ubi de magnâ virtute et gloriâ
bonorum memores, quæ sibi quisque facilia factu
putat, æquo animo accipit ; supra ea, veluti ficta,
pro falsis ducit.

3. Sed ego adolescentulus initio, sicuti plerique,
studio ad rempublicam latus sum; ibique mihi
advorsa multa fuere. Nam pro pudore, pro abs-
tinentiâ, pro virtute, audacia, largitio, avaritia vige-
bant. 4. Quæ tametsi animus aspernabatur, insolens
malarum artium, tamen, inter tanta vitia, imbecilla
ætas ambitione corruptâ tenebatur : 5. ac me, quum
ab reliquorum malis moribus dissentirem, nihilominus honoris cupido eadem [eademque], quæ
ceteros, fama atque invidia vexabat.

IV.— 1. Igitur, ubi animus ex multis miseriis
atque periculis requievit, et mihi reliquam ætatem a
republicâ procul habendam decrevi, non fuit consilium, socordiâ atque desidiâ bonum otium con-
terere ; neque verò agrum colendo, aut venando,
servilibus officiis intentum, ætatem agere : 2. sed, a
quo incepto studioque me ambitio mala detinuerat,
eòdem regressus, statui res gestas populi Romani

carptim, ut quæque memoriā digna videbantur, perscribere: eo magis, quòd mihi a spe, metu, partibus reipublicæ animus liber erat.

3. Igitur de Catilinæ conjuratione, quàm verissume potero, paucis absolvam : 4. nam id facinus in primis ego memorabile existumo, sceleris atque periculi novitate. 5. De cujus hominis moribus pauca priùs explananda sunt, quàm initium narrandi faciam.

V.—1. Lucius Catilina, nobili genere natus, magnā vi et animi et corporis, sed ingenio malo pravoque. 2. Huic ab adolescentiā bella intestina, cædes, rapinæ, discordia civilis, grata fúere; ibique juventutem suam exercuit. 3. Corpus patiens inediæ, vigiliæ, algoris, supra quàm cuique credibile est : 4. animus audax, subdolus, varius, cujus rei libet simulator ac dissimulator : 5. alieni appetens, sui profusus, ardens in cupiditatibus : satis eloquentiæ, sapientiæ parum. Vastus animus immoderata, incredibilia, nimis alta semper cupiebat. 6. Hunc, post dominationem Lucii Sullæ, lubido maxuma invaserat reipublicæ capiundæ; neque id quibus modis adsequeretur, dum sibi regnum pararet, quidquam pensi habebat. 7. Agitabatur magis magisque in dies animus ferox inopiā rei familiaris, et conscientiā scelerum ; quæ utraque his artibus auxerat, quas suprà memoravi. 8. Incitabant præterea corrupti civitatis mores, quos pessuma ac divorsa inter se mala, luxuria atque avaritia, vexabant.

9. Res ipsa hortari videtur, quoniam de moribus

civitatis tempus admonuit, suprà repetere, ac paucis instituta majorum domi militiæque—quomodo rempublicam habuerint, quantamque reliquerint ; ut paulatim immutata ex pulcherrumā pessuma ac flagitiosissuma facta sit—disserere.

VI.—1. Urbem Romam, sicuti ego accepi, condidere atque habuere initio Trojani, qui, Æneā duce, profugi sedibus incertis vagabantur ; cumque his Aborigines, genus hominum agreste, sine legibus, sine imperio, liberum atque solutum. 2. Hi postquam in una mœnia convenere, dispari genere, dissimili linguā, alius alio more viventes, incredibile memoratu est quàm facile coaluerint. 3. Sed, postquam res eorum civibus, moribus, agris aucta, satis prospera satisque pollens videbatur, sicuti pleraque mortalium habentur, invidia ex opulentiā orta est. 4. Igitur reges populique finitimi bello tentare : pauci ex amicis auxilio esse ; nam ceteri, metu perculsi, a periculis aberant. 5. At Romani, domi militiæque intenti, festinare, parare, alius alium hortari ; hostibus obviam ire ; libertatem, patriam parentesque armis tegere : pòst, ubi pericula virtute propulerant, sociis atque amicis auxilia portabant ; magisque dandis quàm accipiundis beneficiis amicitias parabant.

6. Imperium legitimum, nomen imperii regium, habebant : delecti—quibus corpus annis infirmum, ingenium sapientiā validum—reipublicæ consultabant: hi, vel ætate, vel curæ similitudine, PATRES adpellabantur. 7. Pòst, ubi regium imperium, quod initio conservandæ libertatis atque augendæ rei-

publicæ fuerat, in superbiam dominationemque con-
vortit, immutato more, annua imperia binosque imperatores sibi fecere : eo modo minume posse putabant per licentiam insolescere animum humanum.

VII.—1. Sed eā tempestate cœpere se quisque
extollere, magisque ingenium in promptu habere.
2. Nam regibus boni, quàm mali, suspectiores sunt,
semperque his aliena virtus formidolosa est. 3. Sed
civitas, incredibile memoratu est, adeptā libertate,
quantùm brevi creverit : tanta cupido gloriæ incesserat. 4. Jam primùm juventus, simul laboris ac
belli patiens erat, in castris per usum militiam
discebat : magisque in decoris armis et militaribus
equis, quàm in scortis atque conviviis, lubidinem
habebant. 5. Igitur talibus viris non labos insolitus,
non locus ullus asper aut arduus erat, non armatus
hostis formidolosus : virtus omnia domuerat. 6. Sed
gloriæ maxumum certamen inter ipsos erat : sese
quisque hostem ferire, murum adscendere, conspic:
dum tale facinus faceret, properabat : eas divitias
eam bonam famam magnamque nobilitatem putabant : laudis avidi, pecuniæ liberales, erant : gloriam
ingentem, divitias honestas, volebant. 7. Memor-
are possem quibus in locis maxumas hostium
copias populus Romanus parvā manu fuderit, quas
urbes naturā munitas pugnando ceperit, ni ea res
longius ab incepto traheret.

VIII.—1. Sed profecto Fortuna in omni re
dominatur; ea res cunctas, ex lubidine magis, quàm
ex vero, celebrat obscuratque. 2. Atheniensium
res gestæ, sicuti ego æstumo, satis amplæ magnificæ-

que fúere; verùm aliquanto minores tamen, quàm famī feruntur. 3. Sed, quia provenere ibi scriptorum magna ingenia, per terrarum orbem Atheniensium facta pro maxumis celebrantur. 4. Ita eorum, qui fecere, virtus tanta habetur, quantùm verbis eam potuere extollere præclara ingenia. 5. At populo Romano nunquàm ea copia fuit : quia prudentissimus quisque negotiosus maxume erat ; ingenium nemo sine corpore exercebat ; optumus quisque facere quàm dicere, sua ab aliis benefacta laudari quàm ipse aliorum narrare, malebat.

IX.—1. Igitur domi militiæque boni mores colebantur ; concordia maxuma, minuma avaritia erat ; jus bonumque apud eos, non legibus magis quàm naturā, valebat. 2. Jurgia, discordias, simultates, . cum hostibus exercebant : cives cum civibus de virtute certabant : in suppliciis deorum magnifici, domi parci, in amicis fideles erant. 3. Duabus his artibus, audaciā in bello, ubi pax evenerat æquitate, seque remque publicam curabant. 4. Quarum rerum ego maxuma documenta hæc habeo ; quòd sæpius vindicatum est in eos, qui contra imperium in hostem pugnaverant quique tardiùs revocati prœlio excesserant, quàm qui signa relinquere, aut pulsi loco cedere ausi erant ; 5. in pace verò, quòd, beneficiis, quàm metu, imperium agitabant, et, acceptā injuriā, ignoscere quàm persequi malebant.

X.—1. Sed, ubi labore atque justitiā respublica crevit, reges magni bello domiti, nationes feræ et populi ingentes vi subacti, Carthago æmula imperii Romani ab stirpe interiit, cuncta maria terræque patebant ; sævire Fortuna, ac miscere omnia, cœpit. 2. Qui labores, pericula, dubias atque asperas res facile toleraverant, iis otium, divitiæ optandæ aliis, oneri miseriæque fuere. 3. Igitur primò pecuniæ, deinde imperii cupido crevit : ea quasi materies omnium malorum fuere. 4. Namque avaritia fidem, probitatem, ceterasque artīs bonas subvertit ; pro his, superbiam, crudelitatem, deos neglegere, omnia venalia habere, edocuit. 5. Ambitio multos mortalīs falsos fieri subegit ; aliud clausum in pectore, aliud in linguā promptum habere ; amicitias inimicitiasque, non ex re, sed ex commodo, æstumare ; magisque vultum, quàm ingenium, bonum habere. 6. Hæc primò paulatim crescere, interdum vindicari : pòst, ubi contagio quasi pestilentia invasit, civitas immutata ; imperium, ex justissumo atque optumo, crudele intolerandumque factum.

XI.—1. Sed primò magis ambitio, quàm avaritia, animos hominum exercebat : quod tamen vitium propiùs virtutem erat. 2. Nam gloriam, honorem, imperium bonus et ignavus æque sibi exoptant : sed ille verā viā nititur ; huic quia bonæ artes desunt, dolis atque fallaciis contendit. 3. Avaritia pecuniæ studium habet, quam nemo sapiens concupivit : ea, quasi venenis malis imbuta, corpus animumque virilem effeminat ; semper infinita, insatiabilis est ; neque copiā neque inopiā minuitur. 4. Sed, postquàm L. Sulla, armis receptā republicā, ex bonis initiis malos eventūs habuit, rapere omnes, trahere. domum alius alius agros cupere ;

neque modum neque modestiam victores habere,
fœda crudeliaque in civibus facinora facere.
5. Huc accedebat quòd L. Sulla exercitum, quem
in Asiā ductaverat, quò sibi fidum faceret, contra
morem majorum, luxuriose nimisque liberaliter
habuerat ; loca amœna, voluptaria, facile in otio
ferocīs militum animos molliverant. 6. Ibi primùm
insuevit exercitus populi Romani amare, potare ;
signa, tabulas pictas, vasa cælata mirari ; ea
privatim ac publice rapere ; delubra spoliare ; sacra
profanaque omnia polluere. 7. Igitur hi milites,
postquàm victoriam adepti sunt, nihil reliqui victis
fecere. 8. Quippe secundæ res sapientium animos
fatigant : ne illi, corruptis moribus, victoriæ temper-
arent.

XII.—1. Postquam divitiæ honori esse cœpere,
et eas gloria, imperium, potentia sequebatur ;
hebescere virtus, paupertas probro haberi, in-
nocentia pro malivolentiā duci cœpit. 2. Igitur
ex divitiis juventutem luxuria atque avaritia cum
superbiā invasere : rapere, consumere ; sua parvi
pendere, aliena cupere ; pudorem, pudicitiam,
divina atque humana promiscua, nihil pensi atque
moderati habere. 3. Operæ pretium est, quum
domos atque villas cognoveris in urbium modum
exædificatas, visere templa deorum, quæ nostri
majores, religiosissumi mortales, fecere. 4. Verùm
illi delubra deorum pietate, domos suas gloriā
decorabant ; neque victis quidquam, præter injuriæ
licentiam, eripiebant. 5. At hi contrà, ignavissumi
homines, per summum scelus omnia ea sociis

adimere, quæ fortissumi viri victores reliquerant :
proinde quasi injuriam facere, id demum esset
imperio uti.

XIII.—1. Nam quid ea memorem, quæ, nisi iis
qui videre, nemini credibilia sunt : a privatis
compluribus subversos montes, maria contracta
esse.   2. Quibus mihi videntur ludibrio fuisse
divitiæ ; quippe, quas honeste habere licebat, abuti
per turpitudinem properabant.   3. Sed lubido
stupri, ganeæ, ceterique cultūs, non minor incesserat : vescendi causā terrā marique omnia exquirere ;
dormire priùs, quàm somni cupido esset ; non
famem aut sitim, neque frigus neque lassitudinem
opperiri, sed ea omnia luxu antecapere.   4. Hæc
juventutem, ubi familiares opes defecerant, ad
facinora incendebant.   5. Animus imbutus malis
artibus haud facilè lubidinibus carebat : eo profusiùs
omnibus modis quæstui atque sumptui deditus
erat.

XIV.—1. In tantā tamque corruptā civitate,
Catilina, id quod factu facillimum erat, omnium
flagitiorum atque facinorum circum se, tamquam
stipatorum, catervas habebat.   2. Nam, quicumque
impudicus, adulter, ganeo, manu ventre bona patria
laceraverat ; quique alienum æs grande conflaverat,
quo flagitium aut facinus redimeret ; 3. præterea,
omnes   undique   parricidæ,   sacrilegi,   convicti
judiciis, aut pro factis judicium timentes ; ad hoc,
quos manus atque lingua perjurio aut sanguine
civili alebat ; postremò, omnes quos flagitium,
egestas, conscius animus exagitabat ; ii Catilinæ

proxumi familiaresque erant. 4. Quòd si quis etiam a culpā vacuus in amicitiam ejus inciderat, quotidiano usu atque illecebris facilè par similisque ceteris efficiebatur. 5. Sed maxumè adolescentium familiaritates adpetebat : eorum animi molles et ætate fluxi, dolis haud difficulter capiebantur. 6. Nam, uti cujusque studium ex ætate flagrabat, aliis scorta præbere ; aliis canes atque equos mercari ; postremò, neque sumptui, neque modestiæ suæ parcere, dum illos obnoxios fidosque faceret. 8. Scio fuisse nonnullos, qui ita existumarent— juventutem, quæ domum Catilinæ frequentabat, parum honestè pudicitiam habuisse : sed ex aliis rebus magìs, quàm quòd cuiquam id compertum foret, hæc fama valebat.

XV.—1. Jam primùm adolescens Catilina multa nefanda stupra fecerat ; cum virgine nobili, cum sacerdote Vestæ, alia hujuscemodi contra jus fasque. 2. Postremò, captus amore Aureliæ Orestillæ, cujus, præter formam, nihil umquam bonus laudavit, quòd ea nubere illi dubitabat timens privignum adultum ætate, pro certo creditur, necato filio, vacuam domum scelestis nuptiis fecisse. 3. Quæ quidem res mihi in primis videtur causa fuisse facinoris maturandi. 4. Namque animus impurus, dîs hominibusque infestus, neque vigiliis neque quietibus sedari poterat ; ita conscientia mentem excitam vastabat. 5. Igitur colos exsanguis, fœdi oculi, citus modò modò tardus incessus ; prorsus in facie voltuque vecordia inerat.

XVI.—1. Sed juventutem, quam, ut suprà

diximus, illexerat, multis modis mala facinora
edocebat.   2. Ex illis testes signatoresque falsos
commodare ; fidem, fortunas, pericula vilia habere.
Pòst, ubi eorum famam atque pudorem adtriverat,
majora alia imperabat : 3. si causa peccandi in
præsens minùs suppetebat, nihilo minùs insontes,
sicuti sontes, circumvenire, jugulare : scilicet,
ne per otium torpescerent manūs aut animus,
gratuito potiùs malus atque crudelis erat.   4. Eis
amicis sociisque confisus Catilina, simul quòd æs
alienum per omnīs terras ingens erat, et quòd
plerique Sullani milites, largiùs suo usi, rapinarum
et victoriæ veteris memores, civile bellum exopta-
bant, opprimundæ reſpublicæ consilium cepit. 5. In
Italiā nullus exercitus : Cn. Pompeius in extremis
terris bellum gerebat: ipsi consulatum petenti
magna spes : senatus nihil sanè intentus : tutæ
tranquillæque res omnes : sed ea prorsus opportuna
Catilinæ.

XVII.—1. Igitur circiter Kalendas Junias, L.
Cæsare et C. Figulo consulibus, primò singulos
adpellare : hortari alios, alios tentare : opes suas,
imparatam rempublicam, magna præmia conjurationis docere. 2. Ubi satis explorata sunt, quæ
voluit, in unum omnīs convocat, quibus maxuma
necessitudo, et plurimum audaciæ. 3. Eò convenere, senatorii ordinis, P. Lentulus Sura, P.
Autronius, L. Cassius Longinus, C. Cethegus, P. et
Servius Sullæ, Servii filii, L. Vargunteius, Q.
Annius, M. Porcius Læca, L. Bestia, Q. Curius :
4. præterea ex equestri ordine, M. Fulvius Nobilior,

L. Statilius, P. Gabinius Capito, C. Cornelius : ad
hoc multi ex coloniis et municipiis, domi nobiles.
5. Erant præterea complures paulò occultiùs
consilii hujusce participes nobiles, quos magis
dominationis spes hortabatur, quàm inopia, aut alia
necessitudo. 6. Ceterùm juventus pleraque, sed
maxume nobilium, Catilinæ inceptis favebat. Quibus in otio vel magnificè vel molliter vivere copia
erat, incerta pro certis, bellum quàm pacem,
malebant. 7. Fuere item eā tempestate qui crederent M. Licinium Crassum non ignarum ejus
consilii fuisse ; quia Cn. Pompeius, invisus ipsi,
magnum exercitum ductabat, cujusvis opes voluisse
contra illius potentiam crescere ; simul confisum, si
conjuratio valuisset, facilè apud illos principem se
fore.

XVIII.—1. Sed antea item conjuravere pauci
contra rempublicam, in quibus Catilina ; de quā,
quàm verissumè potero, dicam. 2. L. Tullo M.
Lepido consulibus, P. Autronius et P. Sulla, legibus
ambitūs interrogati, pœnas dederant. 3. Pòst
paulò Catilina, pecuniarum repetundarum reus,
prohibitus erat consulatum petere, quòd intra
legitimos dies profiteri nequiverit. 4. Erat eodem
tempore Cn. Piso, adolescens nobilis, summæ
audaciæ, egens, factiosus, quem ad perturbandam
rempublicam inopia atque mali mores stimulabant.
5. Cum hoc, Catilina et Autronius circiter Nonas
Decembrīs, consilio communicato, parabant in
Capitolio Kalendis Januariis L. Cottam et L.
Torquatum consules interficere ; ipsi, fascibus

correptis, Pisonem cum exercitu ad obtinendas duas
Hispanias mittere. # # # # 6. Eā re cognitā, rursus
in Nonas Februarias consilium cædis transtulerant
7. Jam tum non consulibus modo, sed plerisque
senatoribus perniciem machinabantur. 8. Quòd ni
Catilina maturâsset pro curiā signum sociis dare,
eo die post conditam urbem Romanam pessumum
facinus patratum foret. Quia nondum frequentes
armati convenerant, ea res consilium diremit.

XIX.—1. Postea Piso in citeriorem Hispaniam
quæstor proprætore missus est, adnitente Crasso,
quòd eum infestum inimicum Cn. Pompeio cognoverat. 2. Neque tamen senatus provinciam
invitus dederat : quippe fœdum hominem a republicā procul esse volebat : simul, quia boni
complures præsidium in eo putabant : et jam tum
potentia Cn. Pompeii formidolosa erat. 3. Sed is
Piso in provinciā ab equitibus Hispanis, quos in
exercitu ductabat, iter faciens occisus est. 4. Sunt
qui ita dicant, imperia ejus injusta, superba, crudelia,
barbaros nequivisse pati : 5. alii autem, equites
illos, Cn. Pompeii veteres fidosque clientes, voluntate
ejus Pisonem adgressos ; numquam Hispanos
præterea tale facinus fecisse, sed imperia sæva
multa antea perpessos. Nos eam rem in medio
relinquemus. De superiore conjuratione satis
dictum.

XX.—1. Catilina ubi eos, quos paulò antè
memoravi, convenisse videt : tametsi cum singulis
multa sæpe egerat, tamen in rem fore credens
universos adpellare et cohortari, in abditam partem

ædium secedit ; atque ibi, omnibus arbitris procul amotis, orationem hujuscemodi habuit.

2. " Ni virtus fidesque vostra spectata mihi forent, nequiquam opportuna res cecidisset ; spes magna, dominatio, in manibus frustra fuissent : neque ego per ignaviam, aut vana ingenia, incerta pro certis captarem. 3. Sed, quia multis et magnis tempestatibus vos cognovi fortes fidosque mihi, eò animus ausus maxumum atque pulcherrumum facinus incipere : simul, quia vobis eadem, quæ mihi, bona malaque intellexi ; 4. nam idem velle atque idem nolle, ea demum firma amicitia est.

5. Sed, ego quæ mente agitavi, omnes jam antea divorsi audîstis. 6. Ceterùm mihi in dies magis animus accenditur, quum considero, quæ conditio vitæ futura sit, nisi nosmet ipsi vindicamus in libertatem. 7. Nam, postquam respublica in paucorum jus atque ditionem concessit, semper illis reges, tetrârchæ vectigales esse ; populi, nationes stipendia pendere ; ceteri omnes, strenui, boni, nobiles atque ignobiles, vulgus fuimus, sine gratiâ, sine auctoritate, his obnoxii, quibus, si respublica valeret, formidini essemus. 8. Itaque omnis gratia, potentia, honos, divitiæ apud illos sunt, aut ubi illi volunt : repulsas nobis reliquere, pericula, judicia, egestatem. 9. Quæ quousque tandem patiemini, fortissumi viri ? Nonne emori per virtutem præstat, quàm vitam miseram atque inhonestam, ubi alienæ superbiæ ludibrio fueris, per dedecus amittere ?

10. Verùm enimvero, pro deûm atque hominum

fidem ! victoria nobis in manu : viget ætas, animu:
valet : contrà illis, annis atque divitiis, omni:
consenuerunt. Tantummodo incepto opus est
cetera res expediet. 11. Etenim quis mortalium
cui virile ingenium, tolerare potest illis divitia:
superare, quas profundant in exstruendo mari' e
montibus coæquandis ; nobis rem familiarem etian
ad necessaria deesse ? illos binas, aut amplius
domos continuare ; nobis larem familiarem nusquàn
ullum esse ? 12. Quum tabulas, signa, toreumat:
emunt ; nova diruunt, alia ædificant ; postremo
omnibus modis pecuniam trahunt, vexant ; tamei
summā lubidine divitias vincere nequeunt. 13. A.
nobis domi inopia, foris æs alienum ; mala res, spe·
multo asperior: denique, quid reliqui habemus
præter miseram animam ?

14. Quin igitur expergiscimini ? En illa, iila
quam sæpe optâstis, libertas, præterea divitiæ
decus, gloria, in oculis sita sunt ! fortuna omni:
victoribus præmia posuit. 15. Res, tempus, pericula
egestas, belli spolia magnifica magis, quàm oratio
hortentur.   16. Vel imperatore vel milite m·
utimini : neque animus, neque corpus a vobi·
aberit.   17. Hæc ipsa, ut spero, vobiscum consu
agam ; nisi forte me animus fallit, et vos servir·
quàm imperare, parati estis."

XXI.—1. Postquam accepere ea homines, quibu·
mala abundè omnia erant, sed neque res, nequ·
spes bona ulla ; tametsi illis quieta movere magn:
merces videbatur, tamen postulare plerique, ut
proponeret, quæ conditio belli foret ; quæ præmi:

armis peterent; quid ubique opis aut spei haberent.
2. Tum Catilina polliceri tabulas novas, proscrip-
tionem locupletium, magistratūs, sacerdotia, rapinas,
alia omnia, quæ bellum atque lubido victorum fert.
3. Præterea esse in Hispaniā citeriore Pisonem, in
Mauritaniā cum exercitu P. Sittium Nucerinum,
consilii sui participes : petere consulatum C. Antonium, quem sibi collegam fore speraret, hominem
et familiarem, et omnibus necessitudinibus circumventum : cum eo consulem initium agendi facturum.
4. Ad hoc, maledictis increpat omnīs bonos :
suorum unumquemque nominans laudare : admon-
ebat alium egestatis, alium cupiditatis suæ, complures periculi aut ignominiæ, multos victoriæ
Sullanæ, quibus ea prædæ fuerat. 5. Postquam
omnium animos alacrīs videt ; cohortatus, ut
petitionem suam curæ haberent, conventum dimisit.

XXII.—1. Fuere eā tempestate, qui dicerent,
Catilinam, oratione habitā, quum ad jusjurandum
popularīs sceleris sui adigeret, humani corporis
sanguinem, vino permixtum, in pateris circumtulisse;
2. inde quum post exsecrationem omnes degustav-
issent, sicuti in sollemnibus sacris fieri consuevit,
aperuisse consilium suum, atque eò dictitare
fecisse, quò inter se fidi magis forent alius alii tanti
facinoris conscii. 3. Nonnulli ficta et hæc et multa
præterea existumabant ab iis, qui Ciceronis
invidiam, quæ postea orta est, leniri credebant
atrocitate sceleris eorum, qui pœnas dederant.
Nobis ea res pro magnitudine parum comperta est.

Sallust   C

XXIII.—1. Sed in eā conventione fuit Q. Curius, natus haud obscuro loco, flagitiis atque facinoribus coopertus ; quem censores senatu, probri gratiā, amoverant.   2. Huic homini non minor vanitas, quàm audacia : neque reticere, quæ audierat, neque suamet ipse scelera occultare, prorsus neque dicere, neque facere, quidquam pensi habebat.   3. Erat ei cum Fulviā, muliere nobili, vetus consuetudo : cui quum minùs gratus esset, quia inopiā minùs largiri poterat, repente glorians maria montesque polliceri cœpit : minari interdum ferro, nisi obnoxia foret ; postremò ferociùs agitare, quàm solitus erat.   4. At Fulvia, insolentiæ Curii causā cognitā, tale periculum reipublicæ haud occultum habuit ; sed, sublato auctore, de Catilinæ conjuratione quæ quõque modo audierat, compluribus narravit. 5. Ea res in primis studia hominum accendit ad consulatum mandandum   M. Tullio Ciceroni. 6. Namque antea pleraque nobilitas invidiā æstuabat, et quasi pollui consulatum credebant, si eum, quamvis egregius, homo novus adeptus foret. Sed, ubi periculum advenit, invidia atque superbia postfuere.

XXIV.—1. Igitur, comitiis habitis, consules declarantur M. Tullius et C. Antonius.   2. Quod factum primò popularīs conjurationis concusserat. Neque tamen Catilinæ furor minuebatur : sed in dies plura agitare ; arma per Italiam locis opportunis parare ; pecuniam, suā aut amicorum fide sumptam mutuam, Fæsulas ad Manlium quemdam portare, qui postea princeps fuit belli faciundi.

3. Eā tempestate plurimos cujusque generis homines adscivisse dicitur; mulieres etiam aliquot, quæ, ubi ætas tantummodo quæstui, neque luxuriæ, modum fecerat, æs alienum grande conflaverant: 4. per eas se Catilina credebat posse servitia urbana sollicitare, urbem incendere, viros earum vel adjungere sibi, vel interficere.

XXV.—1. Sed in his erat Sempronia, quæ multa sæpe virilis audaciæ facinora commiserat. 2. Hæc mulier genere atque formā, præterea viro, liberis satis fortunata fuit; literis Græcis atque Latinis docta; psallere, saltare elegantiùs, quàm necesse est probæ; multa alia, quæ instrumenta luxuriæ. 3. Sed ei cariora semper omnia, quàm decus atque pudicitia fuit: pecuniæ an famæ minùs parceret, haud facilè discerneres. 4. Sed ea sæpe antehac fidem prodiderat, creditum abjuraverat, cædis conscia fuerat; luxuriā atque inopiā præceps abierat. 5. Verùm ingenium ejus haud absurdum: posse versūs facere, jocum movere, sermone uti vel modesto, vel molli, vel procaci: prorsus multæ facetiæ multusque lepos inerat.

XXVI.—1. His rebus comparatis, Catilina nihilominus in proxumum annum consulatum petebat; sperans, si designatus foret, facilè se ex voluntate Antonio usurum. Neque interea quietus erat, sed omnibus modis insidias parabat Ciceroni. 2. Neque illi tamen ad cavendum dolus aut astutiæ deerant. 3. Namque, a prinⁱipio consulatūs sui, multa pollicendo per Fulvⁱ n, effecerat, ut Q. Curius, de quo paulò antè mⁱ ioravi, consilia Catilinæ sibi proderet. 4. Ad hoc, collegam suum Antonium pactione provinciæ perpulerat, ne contra rempublicam sentiret ; circum se præsidia amicorum atque clientium occulte habebat. 5. Postquam dies comitiorum venit, et Catilinæ neque petitio neque insidiæ, quas consulibus in Campo fecerat, prospere cessere, constituit bellum facere, et extrema omnia experiri, quoniam quæ occulte tentaverat, aspera fœdaque evenerant.

XXVII.—1. Igitur C. Manlium Fæsulas atque in eam partem Etruriæ, Septimium quemdam, Camertem, in agrum Picenum, C. Julium in Apuliam dimisit ; præterea alium alio, quem ubique opportunum sibi fore credebat. 2. Interea Romæ multa simul moliri : consuli insidias tendere, parare incendia, opportuna loca armatis hominibus obsidere : ipse cum telo esse, item alios jubere : hortari, uti semper intenti paratique essent : dies noctesque festinare, vigilare, neque insomniis neque labore fatigari. 3. Postremò, ubi multa agitanti nihil procedit, rursus intempestā nocte conjurationis principes convocat per M Porcium Læcam : 4. ibique, multa de ignaviā eorum questus, docet se Manlium præmisisse ad eam multitudinem, quam ad capiunda arma paraverat ; item alios in alia loca opportuna, qui initium belli facerent ; seque ad exercitum proficisci cupere, si priùs Ciceronem oppressisset : eum suis consiliis multùm obficere.

XXVIII.—1. Igitur, perterritis ac dubitantibus ceteris, C. Cornelius, eques Romanus, operam suam pollicitus, et cum eo L. Vargunteius, senator, constituere eā nocte paulo pòst cum armatis hominibus * * * sicuti salutatum introire ad Ciceronem, ac de improviso domi suæ imparatum confodere. 2. Curius, ubi intellegit quantum periculi consuli impendeat, propere per Fulviam dolum, qui parabatur, enuntiat. 3. Ita illi, januā prohibiti, tantum facinus frustra susceperant.

4. Interea Manlius in Etruriā plebem sollicitare, egestate simul ac dolore injuriæ novarum rerum cupidam, quòd Sullæ dominatione agros bonaque omnia amiserat; præterea latrones cujusque generis, quorum in eā regione magna copia erat; nonnullos ex Sullanis colonis, quibus lubido atque luxuria ex magnis rapinis nihil reliqui fecerant.

XXIX.—1. Ea quum Ciceroni nuntiarentur, ancipiti malo permotus—quòd neque urbem ab insidiis privato consilio longiùs tueri poterat, neque exercitus Manlii quantus, aut quo consilio foret, satis compertum habebat—rem ad senatum refert jam antea volgi rumoribus exagitatum. 2. Itaque, quod plerumque in atroci negotio solet, senatus decrevit, darent operam consules, ne quid respublica detrimenti caperet. 3. Ea potestas per senatum more Romano magistratui maxuma permittitur; exercitum parare, bellum gerere, coërcere omnibus modis socios atque civīs; domi militiæque imperium atque judicium summum habere: aliter, sine populī jussu, nulli earum rerum consuli jus est.

XXX.—1. Post paucos dies L. Sænius, senator, in senatu literas recitavit, quas Fæsulis adlatas sibi dicebat; in quibus scriptum erat, C. Manlium arma cepisse cum magnā multitudine ante diem vi. Kalendas Novembrīs. 2. Simul, id quod in tali re solet, alii portenta atque prodigia nuntiabant; alii conventūs fieri, arma portari, Capuæ atque in Apuliā servile bellum moveri. 3. Igitur, senati decreto, Q. Marcius Rex Fæsulas, Q. Metellus Creticus in Apuliam circumque loca, missi—ii utrique ad urbem imperatores erant, 4. impediti ne triumpharent calumniā paucorum, quibus omnia honesta atque inhonesta vendere mos erat—5. sed prætores, Q. Pompeius Rufus Capuam, Q. Metellus Celer in agrum Picenum; iisque permissum, uti pro tempore atque periculo exercitum compararent. 6. Ad hoc, si quis indicavisset de conjuratione, quæ contra rempublicam facta erat, præmium servo libertatem et sestertia centum; libero impunitatem ejus rei, et sestertia ducenta; 7. itemque, uti gladiatoriæ familiæ Capuam et in cetera municipia distribuerentur pro cujusque opibus; Romæ per totam urbem vigiliæ haberentur, iisque minores magistratūs præessent.

XXXI.—1. Quibus rebus permota civitas, atque immutata urbis facies: ex summā lætitiā atque lasciviā, quæ diuturna quies pepererat, repente omnīs tristitia invasit: festinare, trepidare; neque loco nec homini cuiquam satis credere; 2. neque bellum gerere, neque pacem habere; suo quisque metu pericula metiri. 3. Ad hoc, mulieres, quibus, reipublicæ magnitudine, belli timor insolitus incesserat, adflictare sese; manūs supplices ad cœlum tendere; miserari parvos liberos; rogitare; omnia

pavere ; superbiā atque deliciis omissis, sibi patriæ-
que diffidere.

4. At Catilinæ crudelis animus eadem illa
movebat, tamen etsi præsidia parabantur, et ipse
lege Plautiā interrogatus ab L. Paullo. 5. Postremò,
dissimulandi causā atque sui expurgandi, sicuti
jurgio lacessitus foret, in senatum venit. 6. Tum
M. Tullius consul, sive præsentiam ejus timens sive
irā commotus, orationem habuit luculentam atque
utilem reipublicæ ; quam postea scriptam edidit.
7. Sed, ubi ille adsedit, Catilina, ut erat paratus ad
dissimulanda omnia, demisso voltu, voce supplici
postulare a Patribus cœpit ne quid de se temere
crederent : eā familiā ortum, ita ab adolescentiā
vitam instituisse, ut omnia bona in spe haberet :
ne æstumarent sibi patricio homini, cujus ipsius
atque majorum plurima beneficia in plebem
Romanam essent, perditā republicā opus esse, quum
eam servaret M. Tullius, inquilinus civis urbis
Romæ. 8. Ad hoc maledicta alia quum adderet,
obstrepere omnes, hostem atque parricidam vocare.
9. Tum ille furibundus : " Quoniam quidem circumventus," inquit, " ab inimicis præceps agor, incendium meum ruinā restinguam."

XXXII.—1. Dein se ex curiā domum proripuit.
Ibi multa secum ipse volvens, quòd neque insidiæ
consuli procedebant, et ab incendio intellegebat
urbem vigiliis munitam, optumum factu credens
exercitum augere ac, priùs quàm legiones scrib-
erentur, antecapere quæ bello usui forent ; nocte
intempestā cum paucis in Manliana castra profectu

est. 2. Sed Cethego atque Lentulo, ceterisque quorum cognoverat promptam audaciam, mandat, quibus rebus possent, opes factionis confirment, insidias consuli maturent, cædem, incendia, aliaque belli facinora parent : sese propediem cum magna exercitu ad urbem accessurum.

XXXIII.—1. Dum hæc Romæ geruntur, C. Manlius ex suo numero ad Marcium Regem mittit, cum mandatis hujuscemodi : 2. " Deos hominesque testamur, imperator, nos arma neque contra patriam cepisse, neque quò periculum homini faceremus, sed uti corpora nostra ab injuriā tuta forent ; qui miseri, egentes, violentiā atque crudelitate feneratorum plerique patriæ, sed omnes famā atque fortunis, expertes sumus : neque cuiquam nostrum licuit, more majorum, lege uti neque, amisso patrimonio, liberum corpus habere ; tanta sævitia feneratorum atque prætoris fuit. 3. Sæpe majores vostrum, miseriti plebis Romanæ, decretis suis inopiæ opitulati sunt : ac novissume, memoriā nostrā, propter magnitudinem æris alieni, volentibus omnibus bonis, argentum ære solutum est. 4. Sæpe ipsa plebes, aut dominandi studio permota, aut superbiā magistratuum, armata a patribus secessit. 5. At nos non imperium neque divitias petimus, quarum rerum causā bella atque certamina omnia inter mortalīs sunt, sed libertatem, quam nemo bonus, nisi cum animā simul, amittit. 6. Te atque senatum obtestamur consulatis miseris civibus ; legis præsidium, quod iniquitas prætoris eripuit, restituatis : neve nobis eam necessitudinem im-

ponatis, ut quæramus, quonam modo ulti maxume
sanguinem nostrum pereamus."

XXXIV.—1. Ad hæc Q. Marcius respondet : si
quid ab senatu petere vellent, ab armis discedant,
Romam supplices proficiscantur : eā mansuetudine
atque misericordiā senatum populumque Romanum
semper fuisse, ut nemo umquam ab eo frustra
auxilium petiverit.

2. At Catilina ex itinere plerisque consularibus,
præterea optumo cuique, literas mittit : se falsis
criminibus circumventum, quoniam factioni inimic-
orum resistere nequiverit, fortunæ cedere, Mas-
siliam in exsilium proficisci ; non quòd sibi tanti
sceleris conscius ; sed uti respublica quieta foret,
neve ex suā contentione seditio oriretur. Ab his
longè divorsas literas Q. Catulus in senatu recitavit,
quas sibi nomine Catilinæ redditas dicebat : earum
exemplum infra scriptum.

XXXV.—1. " L. Catilina Q. Catulo S. Egregia
tua fides, re cognitā, gratam in magnis periculis
fiduciam commendationi meæ tribuit. 2. Quam
ob rem defensionem in novo consilio non statui
parare ; satisfactionem ex nullā conscientiā de culpā
proponere decrevi, quam, me dius Fidius, veram
licet cognoscas. 3. Injuriis contumeliisque con-
citatus, quòd, fructu laboris industriæque meæ
privatus, statum dignitatis non obtinebam, publicam
miserorum causam pro meā consuetudine suscepi :
non quin æs alienum meis nominibus ex pos-
sessionibus solvere possem, quum alienis nominibus
liberalitas Orestillæ, suis filiæque copiis, persolveret

sed quòd non dignos homines honore honestatos videbam, meque falsā suspicione alienatum sentiebam. 4. Hoc nomine satis honestas, pro meo casu, spes reliquæ dignitatis conservandæ sum sequutus. 5. Plura quum scribere vellem, nuntiatum est vim mihi parari. 6. Nunc Orestillam commendo tuæque fidei trado : eam ab injuriā defendas, per liberos tuos rogatus. Haveto."

XXXVI.—1. Sed ipse paucos dies commoratus apud C. Flaminium Flammam in agro Arretino, dum vicinitatem antea sollicitatam armis exornat, cum fascibus atque aliis imperii insignibus in castra ad Manlium contendit. 2. Hæc ubi Romæ comperta sunt, senatus Catilinam et Manlium hostes judicat ; ceteræ multitudini diem statuit, ante quam sine fraude liceret ab armis discedere, præter rerum capitalium condemnatis ; 3. præterea decernit, uti consules delectum habeant ; Antonius cum exercitu Catilinam persequi maturet ; Cicero urbi præsidio sit.

4. Eā tempestate mihi imperium populi Romani multo maxume miserabile visum est : cui quum ad occasum ab ortu solis omnia domita armis paterent ; domı otium atque divitiæ, quæ prima mortales putant, adfluerent ; fuere tamen cives qui seque remque publicam obstinatis animis perditum irent. 5. Namque, duobus senati decretis, ex tantā multitudine neque præmio inductus conjurationem patefecerat, neque ex castris Catilinæ quisquam omnium discesserat : tanta vis morbi, uti tabes, plerosque civium animos invaserat.

XXXVII.—1. Neque solùm illis aliena mens erat, qui conscii conjurationis ; sed omnino cuncta plebes, novarum rerum studio, Catilinæ incepta probabat. 2. Id adeo more suo videbatur facere. 3. Nam semper in civitate, quibus opes nullæ sunt, bonis invident, malos extollunt ; vetera odere, nova exoptant ; odio suarum rerum mutari omnia student ; turbā atque seditionibus sine curā aluntur, quoniam egestas facile habetur sine damno. 4. Sed urbana plebes, ea vero præceps ierat multis de causis. 5. Primùm omnium, qui ubique probro atque petulantiā maxume præstabant ; item alii per dedecora patrimoniis amissis ; postremò omnes quos flagitium aut facinus domo expulerat ; ii Romam, sicuti in sentinam, confluxerant ; 6. deinde, multi memores Sullanæ victoriæ, quòd, ex gregariis militibus alios senatores videbant, alios ita divites, uti regio victu atque cultu ætatem agerent, sibi quisque, si in armis forent, ex victoriā talia sperabant ; 7. præterea, juventus, quæ in agris manuum mercede inopiam toleraverat, privatis atque publicis largitionibus excita urbanum otium ingrato labori prætulerat. 8. Eos atque alios omnīs malum publicum alebat. Quò minùs mirandum est homines egentīs, malis moribus, maxumā spe, reipublicæ juxta ac sibi consuluisse. 9. Præterea, quorum victoriā Sullæ parentes proscripti, bona erepta, jus libertatis imminutum erat, haud sane alio animo belli eventum exspectabant. 10. Ad hoc quicumque aliarum atque senati partium erant, conturbari rempublicam, quàm minùs valere ipsi, malebant. 11. Id adeo malum multos post annos in civitatem reverterat.

XXXVIII.—1. Nam, postquam, Cn. Pompeio et M. Crasso consulibus, tribunicia potestas restituta est, homines adolescentes, summam potestatem nancti, quibus ætas animusque ferox, cœpere senatum criminando plebem exagitare; dein, largiundo atque pollicitando, magis incendere; ita ipsi clari potentesque fieri. 2. Contra eos summā ope nitebatur pleraque nobilitas, senati specie, pro suā magnitudine. 3. Namque, uti paucis absolvam, per illa tempora quicumque rempublicam agitavere honestis nominibus—alii, sicuti populi jura defenderent, pars, quò senati auctoritas maxuma foret— bonum publicum simulantes pro suā quisque potentiā certabant: neque modestia neque modus contentionis erat: utrique victoriam crudeliter exercebant.

XXXIX.—1. Sed, postquam Cn. Pompeius ad bellum maritimum atque Mithridaticum missus est, plebis opes imminutæ, paucorum potentia crevit. 2. Ei magistratūs, provincias, aliaque omnia tenere: ipsi innoxii, florentes, sine metu ætatem agere; ceteros judiciis terrere, quò plebem in magistratu placidiùs tractarent. 3. Sed, ubi primùm dubiis rebus novandis spes oblata est, vetus certamen animos eorum adrexit. 4. Quòd si primo prœlio Catilina superior aut æquā manu discessisset, profecto magna clades atque calamitas rempublicam oppressisset; neque illis, si victoriam adepti forent, diutiùs eā uti licuisset, quin defessis et exsanguibus, qui plus posset, imperium atque libertatem extorqueret. 5. Fuere tamen extra conjurationem complures, qui ad Catilinam initio profecti sunt : in his A. Fulvius, senatoris filius ; quem retractum ex itinere parens necari jussit. 6. Eisdem temporibus Romæ Lentulus, sicuti Catilina præceperat, quoscumque moribus aut fortunā novis rebus idoneos credebat, aut per se aut per alios sollicitabat; neque solùm cives, sed cujusquemodi genus hominum, quod modò bello usui foret.

XL.—1. Igitur P. Umbreno cuidam negotium dat, uti legatos Allobrogum requirat, eosque, si possit, impellat ad societatem belli ; existumans, publice privatimque ære alieno oppressos, præterea, quòd naturā gens Gallica bellicosa esset, facilè eos ad tale consilium adduci posse. 2. Umbrenus, quòd in Galliā negotiatus erat, plerisque principibus notus erat, atque eos noverat : itaque sine morā, ubi primùm legatos in foro conspexit, percunctatus pauca de statu civitatis, et quasi dolens ejus casum, requirere cœpit, quem exitum tantis malis sperarent. 3. Postquam illos videt queri de avaritiā magistratuum, accusare senatum, quòd in eo auxilii nihil esset ; miseriis suis remedium mortem exspectare : " at ego," inquit, " vobis, si modò viri esse voltis rationem ostendam, quā tanta ista mala effugiatis." 4. Hæc ubi dixit, Allobroges in maxumam spem adducti Umbrenum orare, uti sui misereretur : nihil tam asperum, neque tam difficile, quin cupidissumè facturi essent, dum ea res civitatem ære alieno liberaret. 5. Ille eos in domum D. Bruti perducit quòd foro propinqua, neque aliena consilii, propter Semproniam ; nam tum Brutus ab Romā aberat. 6. Præterea Gabinium arcessit, quò major auctoritas sermoni inesset. Eo præsente conjurationem aperit ; nominat socios, præterea multos cujusque generis innoxios, quò legatis animus amplior esset ; dein eos pollicitos operam suam dimittit.

XLI.—1. Sed Allobroges diu in incerto habuere quidnam consilî caperent. 2. In alterā parte erat æs alienum, studium belli, magna merces in spe victoriæ : at in alterā majores opes, tuta consilia, pro incertā spe certa præmia. 3. Hæc illis volventibus, tandem vicit fortuna reipublicæ. 4. Itaque Q. Fabio Sangæ, cujus patrocinio civitas plurimùm utebatur, rem omnem, uti cognoverant, aperiunt. 5. Cicero, per Sangam consilio cognito, legatis præcipit, ut studium conjurationis vehementer simulent, ceteros adeant, bene polliceantur, dentque operam, uti eos quàm maxume manifestos habeant.

XLII.—1. Eisdem ferè temporibus in Galliā citeriore atque ulteriore, item in agro Piceno, Bruttio, Apuliā, motus erat. 2. Namque illi, quos antea Catilina dimiserat, inconsultè ac veluti per dementiam cuncta simul agere : nocturnis consiliis, armorum atque telorum portationibus, festinando, agitando omnia, plus timoris quàm periculi effecerant. 3. Ex eo numero complures Q. Metellus Celer prætor ex senatūs consulto, causā cognitā, in vincula conjecerat ; item in ulteriore Galliā C. Murena, qui ei provinciæ legatus præerat.

XLIII.—1. At Romæ Lentulus cum ceteris, qui

principes conjurationis erant, paratis—ut videbantur
—magnis copiis, constituerant, uti, Catilina in
agrum Fæsulanum quum venisset, L. Bestia tribunus
plebis, concione habitā, quereretur de actionibus
Ciceronis, bellique gravissumi invidiam optumo
consuli imponeret ; eo signo, proxumā nocte cetera
multitudo conjurationis suum quisque negotium
exsequerentur. 2. Sed ea divisa hoc modo dice-
bantur : Statilius et Gabinius uti cum magnā manu
duodecim simul opportuna loca urbis incenderent,
quò tumultu facilior aditus ad consulem ceterosque,
quibus insidiæ parabantur, fieret : Cethegus Ciceronis januam obsideret, eum vi adgrederetur, alius
autem alium : sed filii familiarum, quorum ex
nobilitate maxuma pars, parentes interficerent ;
simul, cæde et incendio perculsis omnibus, ad
Catilinam erumperent. 3. Inter hæc parata atque
decreta Cethegus semper querebatur de ignaviā
sociorum : illos dubitando et dies prolatando
magnas opportunitates corrumpere ; facto, non
consulto, in tali periculo opus esse ; seque, si pauci
adjuvarent, languentibus aliis, impetum in curiam
facturum. 4. Naturā ferox, vehemens, manu
promptus, maxumum bonum in celeritate putabat.

XLIV.—1. Sed Allobroges, ex præcepto Ciceronis,
per Gabinium ceteros conveniunt ; ab Lentulo,
Cethego, Statilio, item Cassio, postulant jusjurandum,
quod signatum ad civīs perferant : aliter haud facilè
eos ad tantum negotium impelli posse. 2. Ceteri
nihil suspicantes dant : Cassius semet eò brevi
venturum pollicetur, ac paulo ante legatos ex urbe

proficiscitur. 3. Lentulus cum eis T. Volturcium quemdam, Crotoniensem, mittit, uti Allobroges, priùs quàm domum pergerent, cum Catilinā, datā et acceptā fide, societatem confirmarent. 4. Ipse Volturcio literas ad Catilinam dat, quarum exemplum infrà scriptum est : " Quis sim, ex eo, quem ad te misi, cognosces. 5. Fac cogites, in quantā calamitate sis, et memineris te virum esse ; consideres, quid tuæ rationes postulent ; auxilium petas ab omnibus, etiam ab infimis." 6. Ad hoc, mandata verbis dat : Quum ab senatu hostis judicatus sit, quo consilio servitia repudiet ? in urbe parata esse, quæ jusserit : ne cunctetur ipse propiùs accedere.

XLV.—1. His rebus ita actis, constitutā nocte, quā proficiscerentur, Cicero per legatos cuncta edoctus L. Valerio Flacco et C. Pomptino prætoribus imperat, uti in ponte · Mulvio per insidias Allobrogum comitatūs deprehendant : rem omnem aperit, cujus gratiā mittebantur : cetera, uti facto opus sit, ita agant permittit. 2. Illi, homines militares, sine tumultu præsidiis collocatis, sicuti præceptum erat, occultè pontem obsidunt. 3. Postquam ad id loci legati cum Volturcio venere, et simul utrimque clamor exortus est ; Galli, citò cognito consilio, sine morā prætoribus se tradunt. 4. Volturcius primò, cohortatus ceteros, gladio se a multitudine defendit ; dein, ubi a legatis desertus est, multa priùs de salute suā Pomptinum obtestatus, quòd ei notus erat, postremò timidus, ac vitæ diffidens, veluti hostibus, sese prætoribus dedit.

λ

XLVI.—1. Quibus rebus confectis, omnia propere per nuntios consuli declarantur. 2. At illum ingens cura atque lætitia simul occupavere. Nam lætabatur, conjuratione patefactā, civitatem periculis ereptam esse : porro autem anxius erat, in maxumo scelere tantis civibus deprehensis, quid facto opus ; pœnam illorum sibi oneri, impunitatem perdundæ reipublicæ, credebat. 3. Igitur, confirmato animo, vocari ad sese jubet Lentulum, Cethegum, Statilium, Gabinium, item Q. Cæparium quemdam, Tarracinensem, qui in Apuliam ad concitanda servitia proficisci parabat. 4. Ceteri sine morā veniunt : Cæparius, paulo antè domo egressus, cognito indicio, ex urbe profugerat. Consul Lentulum, quòd prætor erat, ipse manu tenens perducit ; reliquos cum custodibus in ædem Concordiæ venire jubet. 5. Eò senatum advocat, magnāque frequentiā ejus ordinis Volturcium cum legatis introducit : Flaccum prætorem scrinium cum literis, quas a legatis acceperat, eòdem adferre jubet.

XLVII.—1. Volturcius interrogatus de itinere, de literis, postremò quid, aut quā de causā, consilii habuisset, primò fingere alia, dissimulare de conjuratione ; pòst, ubi fide publicā dicere jussus est, omnia, uti gesta erant, aperit : paucis antè diebus a Gabinio et Cæpario socium adscitum nihil ampliùs scire, quàm legatos : tantummodo audire solitum ex Gabinio, P. Autronium, Servium Sullam, L. Vargunteium, multos præterea in eā conjuratione esse. 2. Eadem Galli fatentur ; ac Lentulum dissimulantem coarguunt, præter literas, sermonibus.

quos habere solitus : ex libris Sibyllinis, regnum
Romæ tribus Corneliis portendi : Cinnam atque
Sullam antea; se tertium, cui fatum foret urbis
potiri : præterea ab incenso Capitolio illum esse
vigesimum annum, quem sæpe ex prodigiis haru-
spices respondissent bello civili cruentum fore.
3. Igitur, perlectis literis, quum priùs omnes signa
sua cognovissent, senatus decernit, uti abdicato
magistratu Lentulus itemque ceteri in liberis
custodiis haberentur. 4. Itaque Lentulus P.
Lentulo Spintheri, qui tum ædilis, Cethegus Q.
Cornificio, Statilius C. Cæsari, Gabinius M. Crasso,
Cæparius (nam is paulo antè ex fugā retractus erat)
Cn. Terentio senatori traduntur.

XLVIII.—1. Interea plebes, conjuratione patefactā, quæ primò, cupida rerum novarum, nimis
bello favebat, mutatā mente, Catilinæ consilia
exsecrari, Ciceronem ad cœlum tollere : veluti ex
servitute erepta gaudium atque lætitiam agitabat ;
2. namque alia belli facinora prædæ magis, quàm
detrimento fore ; incendium vero crudele, im-
moderatum, ac sibi màxume calamitosum putabat ;
quippe cui omnes copiæ in usu quotidiano et cultu
corporis erant.

3. Post eum diem, quidam L. Tarquinius ad
senatum adductus erat, quem ad Catilinam pro-
ficiscentem ex itinere retractum aiebant. 4. Is
quum se diceret indicaturum de conjuratione, si
fides publica data esset, jussus a consule, quæ sciret,
edicere, eadem fere, quæ Volturcius, de paratis
incendiis, de cæde bonorum de itinere hostium,

senatum edocet : præterea, se missum a M. Crasso, qui Catilinæ nuntiaret, ne Lentulus, Cethegus, alii ex conjuratione deprehensi terrerent ; eòque magis properaret ad urbem accedere, quò et ceterorum animos reficeret, et illi faciliùs e periculo eriperentur. 5. Sed ubi Tarquinius Crassum nominavit, hominem nobilem, maxumis divitiis, summā potentiā, alii, rem incredibilem rati ; pars, tametsi verum existumabant, tamen, quia in tali tempore tanta vis hominis leniunda, quàm exagitanda videbatur, plerique Crasso ex negotiis privatis obnoxii, conclamant indicem falsum esse, deque eā re postulant uti referatur. 6. Itaque, consulente Cicerone, frequens senatus decernit Tarquinii indicium falsum videri ; eumque in vinculis retinendum, neque ampliùs potestatem faciundam, nisi de eo indicaret, cujus consilio tantam rem mentitus esset. 7. Erant eo tempore qui æstumarent, illud a P. Autronio màchinatum, quò faciliùs, adpellato Crasso, per societatem periculi reliquos illius potentiā tegeret. 8. Alii Tarquinium a Cicerone immissum aiebant, ne Crassus, more suo, suscepto malorum patrocinio, rempublicam conturbaret. 9. Ipsum Crassum ego postea prædicantem audivi tantam illam contumeliam sibi ab Cicerone impositam.

XLIX.—1. Sed eisdem temporibus Q. Catulus et C. Piso, neque gratiā, neque precibus, neque pretio, Ciceronem impellere potuere, uti per Allobroges aut alium indicem C. Cæsar falsò nominaretur. 2. Nam uterque cum illo gravīs inimicitias exercebant ; Piso obpugnatus in judicio repetundarum, propter cujusdam Transpadani supplicium injustum; Catulus ex petitione pontificatūs odio incensus, quòd, extremā ætate, maxumis honoribus usus, ab adolescentulo Cæsare victus discesserat. 3. Res autem opportuna videbatur; quòd privatim egregiā liberalitate, publicè maxumis muneribus grandem pecuniam debebat. 4. Sed, ubi consulem ad tantum facinus impellere nequeunt, ipsi singulatim circumeundo atque ementiundo, quæ se ex Volturcio aut Allobrogibus audîsse dicerent, magnam illi invidiam conflaverant, usque eò, ut nonnulli equites Romani, qui præsidii causā cum telis erant circum Concordiæ, seu periculi magnitudine seu animi mobilitate impulsi, quò studium suum in rempublicam clarius esset, egredienti ex senatu Cæsari gladio minitarentur.

L.—1. Dum hæc in senatu aguntur, et dum legatis Allobrogum et Tito Volturcio, comprobato eorum indicio, præmia decernuntur; liberti, et pauci ex clientĭbus Lentuli, divorsis itineribus, opifices atque servitia in vicis ad eum eripiendum sollicitabant, partim exquirebant duces multitudinum, qui pretio rempublicam vexare soliti erant; 2. Cethegus autem, per nuntios, familiam atque libertos suos, exercitatos [in audaciam], orabat grege facto cum telis ad sese irrumperent. 3. Consul, ubi ea parari cognovit, dispositis præsidiis, ut res atque tempus monebat, convocato senatu, refert, quid de his fieri placeat, qui in custodiam traditi erant. 4. Sed eos, paulo antè, frequens senatus judicaverat, contra rempublicam fecisse. Tum D. Junius Silanus, primus sententiam rogatus, quòd eo tempore consul designatus erat, de his qui in custodiis tenebantur, præterea de L. Cassio, P. Furio, P. Umbreno, Q. Annio, si deprehensi forent, supplicium sumendum decreverat: isque postea, permotus oratione C. Cæsaris, pedibus in sententiam Tiberî Neronis iturum se dixerat, qui de eā re, præsidiis additis, referundum censuerat. 5. Sed Cæsar, ubi ad eum ventum, rogatus sententiam a consule, hujuscemodi verba loquutus est.

LI.—1. "Omnīs homines, Patres Conscripti, qui de rebus dubiis consultant, ab odio, amicitiā, irā, atque misericordiā vacuos esse decet. 2. Haud facilè animus verum providet, ubi illa obficiunt; neque quisquam omnium lubídiñi simul, et usui paruit. 3. Ubi intenderis ingenium, válet: si lubídô possidet, ea dominatur, animus nihil valet. 4. Magna mihi copia memorandi, Patres Conscripti, qui reges atque populi, irā aut misericordiā impulsi, malè consuluerint: sed ea malo dicere, quæ majores nostri contra lubidinem animi recte atque ordine fecere. 5. Bello Macedonico, quod cum rege Perse gessimus, Rhodiorum civitas magna atque magnifica, quæ populi Romani opibus creverat, infida atque advorsa nobis fuit: sed postquam, bello confecto, de Rhodiis consultum est, majores nostri, ne quis divitiarum magis quàm injuriæ causā bellum inceptum diceret, impunitos dimisere. 6. Item bellis Punicis omnibus, quum sæpe Carthaginienses et in pace et per inducias multa nefaria facinora fecissent, numquam ipsi per occasioner talia fecere : magis quid se dignum foret, quàm quid in illis jure fieri posset, quærebant.

7. Hoc item providendum est, Patres Conscripti, ne plus valeat apud vos P. Lentuli et ceterorum scelus, quàm vostra dignitas ; neu magis iræ vostræ, quàm famæ, consulatis. 8. Nam si digna pœna pro factis eorum reperitur, novum consilium adprobo : sin magnitudo sceleris omnium ingenia exsuperat, iis utendum censeo, quæ legibus comparata sunt. 9. Plerique eorum, qui ante me sententias dixerunt, compositè atque magnificè casum reipublicæ miserati sunt : quæ belli sævitia esset, quæ victis acciderent, enumeravere ; rapi virgines, pueros ; divelli liberos a parentium complexu ; matres familiarum pati, quæ victoribus collibuissent ; fana atque domos exspoliari ; cædem, incendia fieri ; postremò, armis, cadaveribus, cruore atque luctu omnia compleri. 10. Sed, per deos immortalis ! quò illa oratio pertinuit ? an, uti vos infestos conjurationi faceret ?   Scilicet quem res tanta atque tam atrox non permovit, eum oratio accendet ! 11. Non ita est : neque cuiquam mortalium injuriæ suæ parvæ videntur : multi eas graviùs æquo habuere. Sed aliis alia licentia, Patres Conscripti. 12. Qui demissi in obscuro vitam · habent, si quid iracundiā deliquere, pauci sciunt ; fama atque fortuna pares sunt : qui magno imperio præditi in excelso ætatem agunt, eorum facta cuncti mortales novere. 13. Ita in maxumā fortunā minuma licentia est : neque studere, neque odisse, sed minumè irasci decet : 14. quæ apud alios iracundia dicitur, in

Imperio superbia atque crudelitas adpellatur. 15. Equidem ego sic æstumo, Patres Conscripti, omnīs cruciatūs minores, quàm facinora illorum, esse : sed plerique mortales postrema meminere, et, in hominibus impiis, sceleris eorum obliti de pœnā disserunt, si ea paulo severior fuit.

16. D. Silanum virum fortem atque strenuum certè scio, quæ dixerit, studio reipublicæ dixisse, neque illum in tantā re gratiam aut inimicitias exercere ; eos mores, eam modestiam viri cognovi. 17. Verùm sententia non mihi crudelis—quid enim in talīs homines crudele fieri potest ?—sed aliena a republicā nostrā videtur. 18. Nam profecto aut metus aut injuria te subegit, Silane, consulem designatum, genus pœnæ novum decernere. 19. De timore supervacaneum est disserere, quum præsenti diligentiā clarissumi viri consulis tanta præsidia sint in armis. 20. De pœnā possumus equidem dicere id, quod rês habet ; in luctu atque miseriis mortem ærumnarum requiem, non cruciatum, esse ; eam cuncta mortalìum mala dissolvere ; ultrà neque curæ neque gaudio locum esse. 21. Sed, per deos immortalīs, quamobrem in sententiam non addidisti, uti priùs verberibus in eos animadverteretur ? 22. An, quia lex Porcia vetat ? at aliæ leges item condemnatis civibus animam non eripi, sed exsilium permitti, jubent. 23. An, quia gravius est verberari, quàm necari ? quid autem acerbum, aut grave nimis in homines tanti facinoris convictos ? 24. Sin quia levius est, quî convenit in minore negotio legem timere, quum eam in majore neglexeris ?

· 25. At enim quis reprehendet quòd in parricidas reipublicæ decretum erit ? Tempus, dies, fortuna, cujus lubido gentibus moderatur. 26. Illis meritò accidit, quidquid evenerit : ceterùm vos, Patres Conscripti, quid in alios statuatis, considerate. 27. Omnia mala exempla ex bonis orta sunt. Scilicet, ubi imperium ad ignaros, aut minùs bonos pervenit, novum illud exemplum ab dignis et idoneis ad indignos et non idoneos transfertur. 28. Lacedæmonii devictis Atheniensibus triginta viros imposuere, qui rempublicam eorum tractarent. 29. Ei primò cœpere pessumum quemque et omnibus invisum indemnatum necare : ea populus lætari et meritò dicere fieri. 30. Pòst, ubi paulatim licentia crevit, juxtà bonos et malos lubidinose interficere, ceteros metu terrere. 31. Ita civitas servitute oppressa stultæ lætitiæ gravīs pœnas dedit. 32. Nostrā memoriā victor Sulla quum Damasippum et alios hujusmodi, qui malo reipublicæ creverant, jugulari jussit, quis non factum ejus laudabat? homines scelestos, factiosos, qui seditionibus rempublicam exagitaverant, meritò necatos aiebant. 33. Sed ea res magnæ initium cladis fuit. Nam, uti quisque domum aut villam, postremò aut vas aut vestimentum alicujus, concupiverat, dabat operam, uti in proscriptorum numero esset. 34. Ita illi, quibus Damasippi mors lætitiæ fuerat, pòst paulo ipsi trahebantur : neque priùs finis jugulandi fuit, quàm Sulla omnīs suos divitiıs explevit. 35. Atque hæc ego non in M. Tullio, neque his temporibus, vereor : sed in magnā civitate multa et varia ingenia sunt. 36. Potest, alio tempore, alio consule, cui item exercitus in manu, falsum aliquid pro vero credi : ubi hoc exemplo per senati decretum consul gladium eduxerit, quis illi finem statuet, aut quis moderabitur?

37. Majores nostri, Patres Conscripti, neque consili neque audaciæ umquam eguere ; neque superbia obstabat quò minùs aliena instituta, si modo proba erant, imitarentur. 38. Arma atque tela militaria ab Samnitibus, insignia magistratuum ab Tuscis pleraque sumpserunt; postremò, quod ubique apud socios aut hostīs idoneum videbatur, cum summo studio domi exsequebantur : imitari quàm invidere bonis malebant. 39. Sed eodem illo tempore Graeciæ morem imitati verberibus animadvertebant in civīs, de condemnatis summum supplicium sumebant. 40. Postquam respublica adolevit, et multitudine civium factiones valuere, circumveniri innocentes, alia hujuscemodi fieri, cœpere ; tum lex Porcia aliæque leges paratæ sunt, quibus legibus exsilium damnatis permissum est. 41. Hanc ego causam, Patres Conscripti, quò minùs novum consilium capiamus, in primis magnam puto. 42. Profectò virtus atque sapientia major in illis fuit, qui ex parvis opibus tantum imperium fecere, quàm in nobis, qui ea bene parta vix retinemus.

43. Placet igitur eos dimitti, et augeri exercitum Catilinæ? Minume. Sed ita censeo : publicandas eorum pecunias, ipsos in vinculis habendos per municipia, quæ maxumè opibus valent ; ne quis de eis postea ad senatum referat, neve cum populo

agat : qui aliter fecerit, senatum existumare eum contra rempublicam et salutem omnium facturum."

LII.—1. Postquam Cæsar dicendi finem fecit, ceteri verbo, alius alii, variè adsentiebantur : at M. Porcius Cato, rogatus sententiam, hujuscemodi orationem habuit.

2. " Longè mihi alia mens est, Patres Conscripti, quum res atque pericula nostra considero, et quum sententias nonnullorum mecum ipse reputo. 3. Illi mihi disseruisse videntur de pœnā eorum, qui patriæ, parentibus, aris atque focis suis, bellum paravere : res autem monet cavere ab illis magis quàm quid in illos statuamus consultare. 4. Nam cetera maleficia tum persequare, ubi facta sunt ; hoc, nisi provideris ne accidat, ubi evenit, frustra judicia implores ; captā urbe, nihil fit reliqui victis. 5. Sed, per deos immortalis ! vos ego adpello, qui semper domos, villas, signa, tabulas vestras pluris, quàm rempublicam, fecistis : si ista, cujuscumque modi sint, quæ amplexamini, retinere, si volup-tatibus vestris otium præbere voltis, expergiscimini aliquando, et capessite rempublicam. 6. Non agitur de vectigalibus, non de sociorum injuriis : libertas et anima nostra in dubio est.

7. Sæpenumero, Patres Conscripti, multa verba in hoc ordine feci ; sæpe de luxuriā atque avaritiā nostrorum civium questus sum, multosque mortalīs eā causā advorsos habeo ; 8. qui mihi atque animo meo nullius umquam delicti gratiam fecissem, haud facilè alterius lubidini malefacta condonabam. 9. Sed, ea tametsi vos parvi pendebatis, tamen

respublica firma ; opulentia neglegentiam tolerabat.
10. Nunc verò non id agitur, bonisne an malis
moribus vivamus ; neque quantum aut quàm
magnificum imperium populi Romani sit : sed, hæc
cujuscumque modi videntur, nostra an, nobiscum
unà, hostium futura sint. 11. Hìc mihi quisquam
mansuetudinem et misericordiam nominat ? Jam
pridem equidem nos vera rerum vocabula amisimus ;
quia bona aliena largiri liberalitas, malarum rerum
audacia fortitudo vocatur : eo respublica in extremo
sita est. 12. Sint sane, quoniam ita se mores
habent, liberales ex sociorum fortunis, sint miseri-
cordes in furibus ærarii : ne illis sanguinem nostrum largiantur, et, dum paucis sceleratis parcunt,
bonos omnīs perditum eant.

13. Bene et composite C. Cæsar paulo antè in
hoc ordine de vitā et morte disseruit, falsa, credo,
existumans ea, quæ de inferis memorantur ; diverso
itinere malos a bonis loca tetra, inculta, fœda atque
formidolosa habere. 14. Itaque censuit pecunias
eorum publicandas, ipsos per municipia in custodiis
habendos ; videlicet timens, ne, si Romæ sint, aut
a popularibus conjurationis, aut a multitudine
conductā, per vim eripiantur. 15. Quasi vero mali
atque scelesti tantummodo in urbe et non per
totam Italiam sint ; aut non ibi plus possit audacia,
ubi ad defendendum opes minores sint. 16. Quare
vanum equidem hoc consilium, si periculum ex illis
metuit : sin in tanto omnium metu solus non timet,
eo magis refert mihi atque vobis timere. 17. Quare,
quum de P. Lentulo ceterisque statuetis, pro certc

habetote, vos simul de exercitu Catilinæ et de omnibus conjuratis decernere. 18. Quanto vos attentiùs ea agetis, tanto illis animus infirmior erit : si paululum modò vos languere viderint, jam omnes feroces aderunt.

19. Nolite existumare, majores nostros armis rempublicam ex parvā magnam fecisse. 20. Si ita res esset, multo pulcherrumam eam nos haberemus : quippé sociorum atque civium, præterea armorum atque equorum, major nobis copia, quàm illis. 21. Sed alia fuere, quæ illos magnos fecere, quæ nobis nulla sunt; domi industria, foris justum imperium, animus in consulendo liber, neque delicto neque lubidini obnoxius. 22 Pro his nos habemus luxuriam atque avaritiam ; publicè egestatem, privatim opulentiam ; laudamus divitias, sequimur inertiam ; inter bonos et malos discrimen nullum ; omnia virtutis præmia ambitio possidet. 23. Neque mirum ; ubi vos separatim sibi quisque consilium capitis, ubi domi voluptatibus, hìc pecuniæ, aut gratiæ, servitis : eò fit, ut impetus fiat in vacuam rempublicam.

24. Sed ego hæc omitto. Conjuravere nobilissumi cives patriam incendere : Gallorum gentem infestissumam nomini Romano ad bellum arcessunt : dux hostium supra caput est : 25. vos cunctamini etiam nunc, quid intra mœnia adprehensis hostibus faciatis ? 26. Misereamini censeo—deliquere homines adolescentuli, per ambitionem—atque etiam armatos dimittatis. 27. Ne, ista vobis mansuetudo et misericordia, si illi arma

ceperint, in miseriam convortet. 28. Scilicet res
aspera est ; sed vos non timetis eam. Immo verò
maxumè ; sed inertiā et mollitiā animi, alius alium
exspectantes cunctamini, dîs immortalibus confisi,
qui hanc rempublicam in maxumis sæpe periculis
servavere. 29. Non votis, neque suppliciis muliebri-
bus auxilia deorum parantur : vigilando, agendo,
bene consulendo prospera omnia cedunt : ubi so-
cordiæ te atque ignaviæ tradideris, nequiquam deos
implores ; irati infestique sunt. 30. Apud majores
nostros, T. Manlius Torquatus bello Gallico filium
suum, quòd is contra imperium in hostem pugna-
verat, necari jussit ; atque ille egregius adolescens immoderatæ fortitudinis morte pœnas dedit :
31. vos de crudelissumis parricidis quid statuatis
cunctamini ? Videlicet vita cetera eorum huic
sceleri obstat. 32. Verùm parcite dignitati Lentuli,
si ipse pudicitiæ, si famæ suæ, si dîs aut hominibus
umquam ullis pepercit : 33. ignoscite Cethegi
adolescentiæ, nisi iterum patriæ bellum fecit.
34. Nam quid ego de Gabinio, Statilio, Cæpario
loquar ? Quibus si quidquam umquam pensî fuisset,
non ea consilia de republicâ habuissent. 35. Postremò, Patres Conscripti, si mehercule peccato locus
esset, facilè paterer vos ipsā re corrigi, quoniam
verba contemnitis ; sed undique circumventi sumus.
Catilina cum exercitu faucibus urget : alii intra
mœnia, in sinu urbis, sunt hostes : neque parari,
neque consuli quidquam occultè potest : quò magis
properandum.

36. Quare ita ego censeo : quum nefario consilio

sceleratorum civium respublica in maxuma pericula venerit, iique indicio T. Volturcii et legatorum Allobrogum convicti confessique sint cædem, incendia, alia fœda atque crudelia facinora, in civīs patriamque paravisse, de confessis, sicuti de manifestis rerum capitalium, more majorum, supplicium sumendum."

LIII.—1. Postquam Cato adsedit, consulares omnes itemque senatūs magna pars sententiam ejus laudant, virtutem animi ad cœlum ferunt; alii alios increpantes timidos vocant; Cato magnus atque clarus habetur; senati decretum fit, sicuti ille censuerat.

2. Sed mihi multa legenti, multa audienti, quæ populus Romanus, domi militiæque, mari atque terrā, præclara facinora fecit, forte lubuit adtendere quæ res maxume tanta negotia sustinuisset. 3. Sciebam sæpenumero parvā manu cum magnis legionibus hostium contendisse : cognoveram parvis copiis bella gesta cum opulentis regibus ; ad hoc, sæpe fortunæ violentiam toleravisse ; facundiā Græcos, gloriā belli Gallos ante Romanos fuisse. 4. Ac mihi multa agitanti constabat paucorum civium egregiam virtutem cuncta patravisse, eoque factum, uti divitias paupertas, multitudinem paucitas superaret. 5. Sed postquam luxu atque desidiā civitas corrupta est, rursus respublica magnitudine suā imperatorum atque magistratuum vitia sustentabat ; ac, veluti effetā parente, multis tempestatibus haud sane quisquam Romæ virtute magnus fuit. 6. Sed, memoriā meā ingenti virtute,

divorsi moribus, fuere viri duo, M. Cato et C. Cæsar;
quos quoniam res obtulerat, silentio præterire non
fuit consilium, quin utriusque naturam et mores,
quantùm ingenio possem, aperirem.

LIV.—1. Igitur iis genus, ætas, eloquentia, propè
æqualia fuere; magnitudo animi par, item gloria,
sed alia alii. 2. Cæsar beneficiis ac munificentiã
magnus habebatur; integritate vitæ Cato. Ille
mansuetudine et misericordiã clarus factus: huic
severitas dignitatem addiderat. 3. Cæsar dando,
sublevando, ignoscendo; Cato nihil largiundo
gloriam adeptus est. In altero miseris perfugium,
in altero malis pernicies: illius facilitas, hujus
constantia, laudabatur. 4. Postremò, Cæsar in
animum induxerat laborare, vigilare; negotiis
amicorum intentus sua neglegere; nihil denegare,
quod dono dignum esset; sibi magnum imperium,
exercitum, novum bellum exoptabat, ubi virtus
enitescere posset. 5. At Catoni studium modestiæ,
decoris, sed maxumè severitatis erat. Non divitiis
cum divite neque factione cum factioso, sed cum
strenuo virtute cum modesto pudore cum innocente
abstinentiã certabat: esse, quàm videri, bonus
malebat: ita, quo minùs gloriam petebat, eo magis
sequebatur.

LV.—1. Postquam, ut dixi, senatus in Catonis
sententiam discessit, consul optumum factu ratus
noctem, quæ instabat, antecapere, ne quid eo spatio
novaretur, triumviros, quæ supplicium postulabat,
parare jubet: 2. ipse, dispositis præsidiis, Lentulum
in carcerem deducit: idem fit ceteris per prætore'

3. Est in carcere locus, quod Tullianum adpellatur, ubi paululum descenderis ad lævam, circiter duodecim pedes humi depressus. 4. Eum muniunt undique parietes atque insuper camera, lapideis fornicibus juncta : sed incultu, tenebris, odore fœda atque terribilis ejus facies est. 5. In eum locum postquam demissus est Lentulus, [vindices rerum capitalium] quibus præceptum erat, laqueo gulam fregere. 6. Ita ille patricius, ex clarissumā gente Corneliorum, qui consulare imperium Romæ habuerat, dignum moribus factisque suis exitum vitæ invenit. De Cethego, Statilio, Gabinio, Cæpario, eodem modo supplicium sumptum est.

LVI.—1. Dum ea Romæ geruntur, Catilina ex omni copiā, quam et ipse adduxerat et Manlius habuerat, duas legiones instituit; cohortīs pro numero militum complet : 2. deinde, ut quisque voluntarius aut ex sociis in castra venit, æqualiter distribuerat ; ac brevi spatio legiones numero hominum expleverat, quum initio non amplius duobus millibus habuisset. 3. Sed ex omni copiā circiter pars quarta erat militaribus armis instructa; ceteri, ut quemque casus armaverat, sparos aut lanceas, alii præacutas sudes, portabant. 4. Sed, postquam Antonius cum exercitu adventabat, Catilina per montīs iter facere, ad urbem modo modo in Galliam versus castra movere; hostibus occasionem pugnandi non dare ; sperabat propediem sese habiturum, si Romæ socii incepta patravissent. 5. Interea servitia repudiabat, cujus initio ad eum magnæ copiæ concurrebant, opibus conjurationis fretus; simul alienum suis rationibus existumans videri causam civium cum servis fugitivis com-municavisse.

LVII.—1. Sed, postquam in castra nuntius pervenit Romæ conjurationem patefactam, de Lentulo, Cethego, ceteris, quos suprà memoravi, supplicium sumptum, plerique, quos ad bellum spes rapinarum aut novarum rerum studium illexerat, dilabuntur; reliquos Catilina per montīs asperos magnis itineribus in agrum Pistoriensem abducit eo consilio, uti per tramites occultè perfugerent in Galliam. 2. At Q. Metellus Celer cum tribus legionibus in agro Piceno præsidebat, ex difficultate rerum eadem illa existumans, quæ suprà diximus, Catilinam agitare. 3. Igitur, ubi iter ejus ex per-fugis cognovit, castra propere movet, ac sub ipsis radicibus montium consedit, quà illi descensus erat in Galliam properanti. 4. Neque tamen Antonius procul aberat; utpote qui magno exercitu locis æquioribus expeditus impeditos in fugā sequeretur. 5. Sed Catilina, postquam videt montibus atque copiis hostium sese clausum, in urbe res adversas, neque fugæ neque præsidii ullam spem; optumum factu ratus in tali re fortunam belli tentare statuit cum Antonio quamprimum confligere. Itaque, concione advocatā, hujuscemodi orationem habuit.

LVIII.—1. "Compertum ego habeo, milites, verba virtutem non addere; neque ex ignavo strenuum neque fortem ex timido exercitum ora-tione imperatoris fieri. 2. Quanta cujusque animo audacia naturā aut moribus inest, tanta in bello

Sallust. E

patere solet : quem neque gloria neque pericula excitant, nequiquam hortere ; timor animi auribus obficit. 3. Sed ego vos, quò pauca monerem, advocavi ; simul uti causam consilii aperirem.

4. Scitis equidem, milites, socordia atque ignavia Lentuli quantam ipsi cladem nobisque adtulerit ; quōque modo, dum ex urbe præsidia opperior, in Galliam proficisci nequiverim. 5. Nunc quo in loco res nostræ sint, juxtà mecum omnes intellegitis. 6. Exercitūs hostium duo, unus ab urbe, alter a Galliā, obstant : diutiùs in his locis esse, si maxumè animus ferat, frumenti atque aliarum rerum egestas prohibet. 7. Quocumque ire placet, ferro iter aperiundum est. 8. Quapropter vos moneo, uti forti atque parato animo sitis ; et, quum prœlium inibitis, memineritis, vos divitias, decus, gloriam, præterea libertatem atque patriam in dextris vostris portare. 9. Si vincimus, omnia nobis tuta erunt, commeatūs abundè, coloniæ atque municipia patebunt : sin metu cesserimus, eadem illa advorsa fient : 10. neque locus, neque amicus quisquam teget, quem arma non texerint. 11. Præterea, milites, non eadem nobis et illis necessitudo impendet : nos pro patriā, pro libertate, pro vitā certamus ; illis supervacaneum est pugnare pro potentiā paucorum. 12. Quò audaciùs adgredimini, memores pristinæ virtutis. 13. Licuit nobis, cum summā turpitudine, in exsilio ætatem agere : potuistis nonnulli Romæ, amissis bonis, alienas opes exspectare. 14. Quia illa fœda atque intoleranda viris videbantur, hæc sequi decrevistis. 15. Si hæc relinquere voltis,

audaciā opus est : nemo, nisi victor, pace bellum mutavit. 16. Nam in fugā salutem sperare, quum arma, quibus corpus tegitur, ab hostibus averteris, ea verò dementia est. 17. Semper in prœlio eis maxumum est periculum, qui maxumè timent: audacia pro muro habetur.

18. Quum vos considero, milites, et quum facta vostra æstumo, magna me spes victoriæ tenet. 19. Animus, ætas, virtus vostra me hortantur ; præterea necessitudo, quæ etiam timidos fortīs facit. 20. Nam multitudo hostium ne circumvenire queat, prohibent angustiæ. 21. Quòd si virtuti vostræ fortuna inviderit, cavete, inulti animam amittatis ; neu capti potiùs sicuti pecora trucidemini, quàm virorum more pugnantes cruentam atque luctuosam victoriam hostibus relinquatis."

LIX.—1. Hæc ubi dixit, paululum commoratus signa canere jubet atque instructos ordines in locum æquum deducit : dein, remotis omnium equis, quò militibus, exæquato periculo, animus amplior esset, ipse pedes exercitum, pro loco atque copiis, instruit. 2. Nam, uti planities erat inter sinistros montīs, et ab dextrā rupes aspera, octo cohortīs in fronte constituit : reliqua signa in subsidio artiùs collocat. 3. ·Ab eis centuriones omnīs lectos, et evocatos, præterea ex gregariis militibus optumum quemque armatum, in primam aciem subducit. C. Manlium in dextrā, Fæsulanum quemdam in sinistrā parte curare jubet : ipse cum libertis et colonis propter aquilam adsistit, quam, bello Cimbrico, C. Marius in exercitu habuisse dicebatur.

4. At ex alterā parte C. Antonius, pedibus æger, quòd prœlio adesse nequibat, M. Petreio legato exercitum permittit. 5. Ille cohortīs veteranas, quas tumulti causā conscripserat, in fronte, post eas ceterum exercitum in subsidiis, locat. Ipse equo circumiens, unumquemque nominans adpellat, hortatur, rogat, uti meminerint, se contra latrones inermīs, pro patriā, pro liberis, pro aris atque focis suis, certare. 6. Homo militaris, quòd ampliùs annos triginta tribunus, aut præfectus, aut legatus, aut prætor cum magnā gloriā fuerat, plerosque ipsos factaque eorum fortia noverat : ea commemorando militum animos accendebat.

LX.—1. Sed ubi, rebus omnibus exploratis, Petreius tubā signum dat, cohortīs paulatim incedere jubet; idem facit hostium exercitus. 2. Postquam eò ventum est, unde a ferentariis prœlium committi posset, maxumo clamore cum infestis signis concurrunt; pila omittunt; gladiis res geritur. 3. Veterani, pristinæ virtutis memores, comminus acriter instare : illi haud timidi resistunt : maxumā vi certatur. 4. Interea Catilina cum expeditis in primā acie versari, laborantibus succurrere, integros pro sauciis arcessere, omnia providere, multùm ipse pugnare, sæpe hostem ferire; strenui militis et boni imperatoris officia simul exsequebatur. 5. Petreius, ubi videt Catilinam, contrà ac ratus erat, magnā vi tendere, cohortem prætoriam in medios hostīs inducit; eos perturbatos atque alios alibi resistentes interficit; ¹ᵒinde utrimque ex lateribus adgreditur. 6. Manlius

et Fæsulanus in primis pugnantes cadunt. 7. Catilina postquam fusas copias seque cum paucis
relictum videt, memor generis atque pristinæ
dignitatis in confertissumos hostes incurrit ibique
pugnans confoditur.

LXI.—1. Sed, confecto prœlio, tum verò cerneres,
quanta audacia, quantaque animi vis fuisset in
exercitu Catilinæ. 2. Nam fere, quem quisque
pugnando locum ceperat, eum, amissā animā,
corpore tegebat. 3. Pauci autem, quos cohors
prætoria disjecerat, paulo divorsiùs, sed omnes
tamen advorsis volneribus conciderant. 4. Catilina
verò longè a suis inter hostium cadavera repertus
est, paululum etiam spirans, ferociamque animi,
quam habuerat vivus, in voltu retinens. 5. Postremò, ex omni copiā, neque in prœlio neque in
fugā quisquam civis ingenuus captus est; 6. ita
cuncti suæ hostiumque vitæ juxtà pepercerant.
7. Neque tamen exercitus populi Romani lætam
aut incruentam victoriam adéptus erat : nam
strenuissimus quisque aut occiderat in prœlio, aut
graviter volneratus discesserat. 8. Multi autem,
qui de castris visundi aut spoliandi gratiā pro-
cesserant, volventes hostilia cadavera, amicum alii,
pars hospitem aut cognatum reperiebant : fuere
item qui inimicos suos cognoscerent. 9. Ita variè
per omnem exercitum lætitia, mæror, luctūs atque
gaudia agitabantur.

VOCABULARY.

ABBREVIATIONS.

a. *or* act. . .	active.
abbrev.. . .	abbreviation.
abl.	ablative.
acc.	accusative.
acc. to . . .	according to.
adj.	adjective.
adv.	adverb.
c = cum . .	with.
cf. = confer	compare.
comm. gen.	. common gender.
comp. . . .	{ compar tive degree.
conj.. . . .	conjunction.
contr. . . .	contracted.
dat.	dative.
decl.. . . .	declension.
def. defect. .	defective.
dem. demonstr.	demonstrative.
dep.. . . .	deponent.
desid.. . .	desiderative.
dissyll.. . .	dissyllable.
distr. . . .	distributive.
esp.. . . .	especially.
etym. . . .	etymology.
f.	feminine.
folld. follg.	{ followed, fol- lowing.
fr.	from.
freq.. . . .	frequentative.
fut.. . . .	future.
gen.. . . .	genitive.
gov.. . . .	governing.
Gr.	Greek.
Hist. Inf. .	Historic Infinitive.
imperf.. . .	imperfect.
impers.. . .	impersonal.
inch.. . . .	inchoative.
ind. *or* indic..	indicative.
indecl. . . .	indeclinable.
indef. . . .	indefinite.
inf. *or* infin. .	infinitive.
intens.. . .	intensive.
interj. . . .	interjection.
interrog. . .	interrogative.

irr. *or* irreg. . .	irregular.
m.	masculine.
n. *or* neut.. .	neuter.
nom. . . .	nominative.
num. . . .	numeral.
obsol. . . .	obsolete.
opp.. . . .	{ opposed, oppos- ite.
ord.	ordinal.
p..	page.
P. *or* part. .	participle.
pa.	participial adj.
pass. . . .	passive.
perf.. . . .	perfect.
pers.. . . .	person, personal.
pluperf. . .	pluperfect.
plur.. . . .	plural.
pos.	positive degree.
poss. . . .	possessive.
prep. . . .	preposition.
pres.. . . .	present.
prob.. . . .	probably.
pron. . . .	pronoun.
q.v.	quod vide.
[§] . . .	{ paragraph in Public Schools Latin Primer.
rel.	relative.
Sans.. . . .	Sanscrit.
semi-dep.. .	semi-deponent.
sing. . . .	singular.
subj.. . . .	subjunctive.
subst., substt.	{ substantive, substantives.
sup.	{ superlative, supine.
trisyll. . . .	trisyllable.
t. t.	technical term.
uncontr.. .	uncontracted.
v. a.	verb active.
v. dep. . . .	verb deponent.
v. n.	verb neuter.
voc.	vocative.
=	equal to.

N.B.—The figures before v. a., v. dep., and v. n., denote the conjugation of the verb.

Where the etymology is not given, the word is of very uncertain or unknown origin.

Such forms and meanings of words as do not belong to the text, are not inserted in the Vocabulary.

VOCABULARY.

[N.B.—*Roman numerals denote the chapter, Arabic figures the section.*]

1. **A**, abbrev. of Aulus.

2. **ă**; see ab.

ăb (**ā, abs**), prep. gov. abl.: 1. *From, away from.*—2. *On the side of, in the direction of.* —3. *At, on, in.*—4. Of the agent: *By* [akin to Gr. ἀπ-ό; Sans. *ap-a*].

abdĭcātus, a, um, P. perf. pass. of abdico :—abdicato magistratu, Abl. Abs. [§ 125, b], xlvii. 3.

ab-dĭco, dĭcāvi, dĭcātum, dĭcāre, 1. v. a. [ăb, "from"; dĭco, "to proclaim"] ("To proclaim" one's self removed "from" anything; hence) Political t. t.: *To give up, resign, lay down, abdicate* an office.—Pass.: ab-dĭcor, dĭcātus sum, dĭcāri.

abdĭtus, a, um, 1. P. perf. pass. of abdo.—2. Pa.: *Hidden, concealed, secret.*

ab-do, dĭdi, dĭtum, dĕre, 3. v. a. [ăb, "away"; do, "to put"] ("To put away *or* remove"; hence) *To hide, conceal.*—Pass.: ab-dor, dĭtus sum, di.

ab-dūco, duxi, ductum, dūcĕre, 3. v. a. [ăb, "away"; dūco, "to lead"] *To lead away* or *off.*

ab-jūro, jūrāvi, jūrātum, jūrāre, 1. v. a. [ăb, "away from"; jūro, "to swear"] ("To swear away from" one's self; hence) *To deny on oath.*

ăb-ŏrĭgĭn-es, um, m. plur. [ăb, "from"; ŏrĭgo, ŏrĭgĭn-is, "a beginning, commencement"] ("Those from the beginning"; hence) *The original or native inhabitants* of a country ; *the Aborigines;*—at vi. 1 the term is applied to the earliest inhabitants of Italy.

ab-solvo, solvi, sŏlūtum, solvĕre, 3. v. a. [ăb, "from"; solvo, "to loose"] ("To loose from" something; hence) Of a statement, etc.: *To bring to a conclusion ; to conclude, finish;*—at iv. 3 without nearer Object ; so, also, at xxxviii. 3.

abstĭnent-ĭa, ĭæ, f. [abstĭnens, abstĭnent-is, "abstaining" from what is wrong]

("An abstaining" from what is wrong; hence) *Moderation, self-restraint.*

ab-sum, fŭi, esse, v. n. [ăb, "away, away from"; sum, "to be"] 1. *To be away* or *away from; to be absent.*—2. *To be at a distance, to be distant.*—3. With *ab: To be,* or *keep, at a distance from* dangers, etc.; vi. 4.—4. *To be wanting.*

ab-surdus, surda, surdum, adj. [ăb, in "intensive" force; surdus, "deaf"; hence, "deaf *or* not listening" to a thing; hence, "without understanding"] *In a high degree without understanding, senseless, stupid, absurd:*—bene dicere haud absurdum est, *to speak well is by no means senseless,* i. e. to be eloquent is no contemptible thing; iii. 1; where *bene dicere* is the subject of *est* [§ 140, 1. (1)], and *absurdum* is the attributive complement [§ 93, (2)].

ăbund-e, adv. [abund-us, "copious, abundant"] ("After the manner of the *abundus*"; hence) *Copiously, abundantly, in abundance.*

ăb-ūtor, ūsus sum, ūti, 3. v. dep. [ăb, denoting "reversal"; ūtor, "to use"] *To put to a wrong use, misuse, misemploy, abuse:*—as this verb governs both an Acc. and an Abl., either *eas* or *eis* is

to be supplied after *abuti* at xiii. 2.

ac; see atque.

ac-cēdo, cessi, cessum, cēd-ĕre, 3. n. [for ad-cēdo; fr. ăd, "to *or* towards"; cēdo, "to go"] 1. *To go to* or *towards; to draw near, approach.*—2. With accessory notion of augmentation: a. *To be added.*—b. Impers.: **accedebat,** *It was added;*—at xi. 5 the subject of *accedebat* is the follg. sentence introduced by the adv. *quòd* [Notes on Syntax, p. 149, F, *b*, (5)].

ac-cen-do, di, sum, dĕre, 3. v. a. ("To set fire to"; hence) *To inflame* a person *or* the mind; *to kindle, set on fire, arouse,* etc.—Pass.: **ac-cendor,** sus sum, di [for ad-candor; fr. ăd, "to"; root CAN, akin to Gr. κάω, καίω, "to burn, set fire to"].

acceptus, a, um, P. perf. pass. of accipio.

accessūrus, a, um, P. fut. of accedo;—at xxxii. 2 supply *esse* with *accessurum* [§ 158].

ac-cĭdo, cĭdi, no sup., cĭdĕre, 3. v. n. [for ad-cădo; fr. ăd, "upon"; cădo, "to fall"] ("To fall upon"; hence) 1. With Dat. of person: *To happen* to or *befall* one.—2. *To take place. happen, occur,* etc.

ac-cĭpĭo, cēpi, ceptum, cĭpĕre, 3. v. a. [for ad-capio; fr. ăd, "to"; căpĭo, "to take"] ("To take to" one's self; hence) 1. *To receive.*—2. Mentally: *To learn, hear,* etc.;—at vi. 1 without nearer Object.—Pass.: ac-cĭpĭor, ceptus sum, cĭpi.

accipiundus, a, um, Gerundive of accipio.—Observe the Gerundive Attraction in accipiundis beneficiis, vi. 5.

ac-cūs-o, āvi, ātum, āre, 1. v. a. [for ad-caus-o; fr. ăd, "to"; caus-a, "a judicial process"] ("To bring to a judicial process"; hence, "to accuse"; hence) *To complain of* or *against* a person, etc.; *to bring charges against, blame,* etc.

ăc-erbus, erba, erbum, adj. [root AC, whence ăc-ŭo, "to sharpen, make pointed"] ("Sharpened"; hence, "sharp, pointed"; hence, "harsh" to the taste; hence) Of things: *Harsh, bitter, rigorous, severe.*

ăc-ĭes, ĭei, f. [id.] ("An edge *or* sharp edge"; hence) Military t. t.: 1. *Order* or *line of battle:*—prima acies, *the first* or *front line, the van;* lx. 4.—2. *An army in order of battle.*

ăcr-ĭter, adv. [ăcer, acr-is, "sharp"; hence, "strong, vigorous"] ("After the manner of the *acer*"; hence) *Strongly, vigorously, with vigour,* etc.

ac-tĭo, tĭōnis, f. [for ag-tio; fr. ăg-o, "to do, act"] ("A doing," etc.; hence) 1. *An action, deed, act, proceeding.*—2. *A public action* or *act.*

actus, a, um, P. perf. pass. of ago.

ăd, prep. gov. acc.: 1. *To, towards.*—2. *Up to.*—3. *At, by, near to.*—4. *In answer* or *reply to.*—5. *In addition to, besides.*—6. With Gerunds or Gerundives: *For, for the purpose of, to, in order to.*

addĭtus, a, um, P. perf. pass. of addo.

ad-do, dĭdi, dĭtum, dĕre, 3. v. a. [ăd, "to"; do, "to put"] ("To put to *or* on to"; hence) 1. *To add.*—2. *To add to* by way of increase; *to augment, increase.*—Pass.: ad-dor, dĭtus sum, di.

ad-dūco, duxi, ductum, dūcĕre, 3. v. a. [ăd, "to"; dūco, "to lead"] 1. *To lead* or *bring to* or *up to; to bring up* to a place, etc.—2. *To bring into* or *over to* a certain plan, feeling, act, etc.—Pass.: ad-dūcor, ductus sum, dūci.

adductus, a, um, P. perf. pass. of adduco.

adduxĕram, pluperf. ind. of adduco.

1. ăd-ĕo, adv. [prob. for ăd-ĕom; fr. ăd, "to *or* up to"; ĕom (= ĕum), old masc. acc.

sing. of pron. is] ("To, *or* up to, this"; hence) Used enclitically with pron., in order to give prominence to something previously stated (xxxvii. 2. 11), or something following: *Indeed, in fact, in truth.*

2. ăd-ĕo, īvi *or* ĭi, ĭtum, īre, v. a. [ăd, "to"; eo, "to go"] *To go to* or *up to, to approach* a person, *etc.*, for the purpose of accosting him, *etc.*; xli. 5.

ădeptus, a, um, P. perf. of adipiscor;—at vii. 8 in pass. force; *Having been obtained:* adeptā libertate, Abl. Abs. [§ 125].

ad-fĕro (af-), tŭli, lātum, ferre, v. a. irr. [ăd, "to"; fĕro, "to bear, bring," *etc.*] 1. *To bring* or *take to* a person or place;—at xxx. 1 with Dat. of person;—at xlvi. 5 with Adv. of place.—*2. To produce, cause, occasion* something to one; lviii. 3.—Pass.: ad-fĕror, lātus sum, ferri.

adflic-to (afflic-), tāvi, tātum, tāre, 1. v. a. intens. [for adflig-to; fr. adflīg-o, "to dash to the ground"; hence, "to cast down" mentally, "to grieve," *etc.*] With Person. pron. in reflexive force: *To grieve, vex,* or *disquiet one's self; to be plunged in,* or *feel, great trouble* or *affliction;*— at xxxi. 3 adflictare is the Hist. Inf. [§ 140, 2].

ad-flŭo (af-), fluxi, fluxum, flŭĕre, 3. v. n. [ăd, "to *or* up to"; flŭo, "to flow"] ("To flow to *or* up to"; hence) With accessory notion of abundance: *To flow* or *stream to one,* etc.; *to come to one in abundance;* xxxvi. 4.

ad-grĕdĭor (ag-), gressus sum, grĕdi, 3. v. dep. [for ad-grădĭor; fr. ăd, "to"; grădĭor, "to step"] ("To step to"; hence) With accessory notion of hostility: 1. With Acc. of person: *To attack, fall upon, assault, assail* a person, *etc.*—2. Without nearer Object: *To advance to the attack, to make an attack.*

adgressus, a, um, P. perf. of adgredior;—at xix. 4 supply esse with adgressos [§ 158].

ăd-ĭgo, ēgi, actum, ĭgĕre, 3. v. a. [for ăd-ăgo; fr. ăd, "to"; ăgo, "to drive"] ("To drive" cattle, *etc.*, "to" a place; hence) *To drive, urge, force, bring,* etc., a person *to* some act, state of mind, *etc.* —Phrase: Adigere aliquem ad jusjurandum, *To put one to an oath, to make* or *force one to take an oath, to bind one by an oath;* xxii. 1.

ăd-ĭmo, ēmi, emptum, ĭmĕre, 3. v. a. [for ăd-ĕmo; fr. ăd, "to"; ĕmo, "to take"] ("To take to" one's self from another; hence)

With Acc. of thing and Dat. of person [§§ 96; 106, (3)]: *To take away* something *from* one; *to strip* or *deprive* one *of* something;—at xii. 5 ad-imere is the Hist. Inf. [§ 140, 2].

ăd-ĭpiscor, eptus sum, ĭpisci, 3. v. dep. [for ăd-ăpiscor; fr. ăd, in "strengthening force"; ăpiscor, "to lay hold of"] (" To lay hold of"; hence, "to arrive at, reach"; hence) *To obtain, get, acquire,*

ădĭ-tus, tūs, m. [ADI, root of adeo, "to go to"] (" A going to"; hence) *Means* or *liberty of approach; access.*

ad-jungo, junxi, junctum, jungĕre, 3. v. a. [ăd, "to"; jungo, "to join"] (" To join to"; hence) With Acc. and Dat. of person : *To attach* or *bind* a person to one's self *as a friend, to make* a person *one's friend;* xxiv. 4.

ad-jŭvo, jūvi, jūtum, jŭvāre, 1. v. n. [ăd, "without force"; juvo, "to help"] *To help; to give help, aid,* or *assistance.*

adlātus (allātus), a, um, P. perf. pass. of adfĕro;—at xxx. 1 supply esse with ad-latns [§ 158].

ad-mŏnĕo, mŏnŭi, mŏnĭtum, mŏnēre, 2. v. a. [ăd, "without force"; moneo, "to remind"] *To remind* one, or *put* one *in mind of* or *about* something;—at xxx. 4 with

Acc. of person and Gen. of thing;—at vi. 9 with ellipse of Acc. of person and folld. by de.

adnĭtens, ntis, P. pres. of adnĭtor:—adnitente Crasso, Abl. Abs. [§ 125], xix. 1.

ad-nĭtor (an-), nīsus *or* nixus sum, nīti, 3. v. dep. [ăd, "at, against, upon"] (" To lean against *or* upon"; hence) *To exert one's self, strive, use one's endeavours,* etc.

ădŏlesc-ens, entis, (P. pres. of adolesco, " to grow up"; used as) adj. *Growing up, not yet come to full growth, young;* xxxviii. 1.—As Subst.: *A young man,* between the years of 15 or 17 and 30, or even till near 40, according as a person appeared more or less vigorous, or as spoken of in relation to older persons.

ădŏlescent-ĭa, ĭæ, f. [ădŏlescens, ădŏlescent-is, "a young man"] (" The state of the *adolescens*"; hence) *Youth, youthful age, early years.*

ădŏlescent-ŭlus, ŭli, m. dim. [id.] *A very young man, quite a youth, a mere youth;* —at xlix. 2 Sallust calls Cæsar "adolescentulus," although he was then 33, or acc. to some 35, years of age; cf. adolescens at end.

ădŏlē-sco, ădŏlēvi (rarely ădŏlŭi), ădultum, ădŏlescĕre, 3. v. n. inch. [ădŏlĕ-o, "to cause to grow up"; in pass.

or neut. force, " to be caused to grow up, to grow up "] (" To grow up "; hence) *To increase, become greater, be augmented*, etc.; li. 40.

ădŏlēvi, perf. ind. ᴏf adolesco.

adpellātus (appellātus), a, um, P. perf. pass. of adpello: —adpellato Crasso, Abl. Abs. [§ 125], xlviii. 7.

ad-pello (ap-), pellāvi, pellātum, pellāre, 1. v. a. [ăd, "to "; pello (v. a. 3.), "to drive *or* move "] (In reflexive force : " To move *or* bring one's self to " a person in order to address him ; hence) 1. *To address, speak to, accost.*—2. *To entreat, request, beg.*—3. *To complain of, accuse, impeach*, etc.—4. *To name, mention by name.*—5. a. With double Acc. [§ 99]: *To call, name* an Object that which is denoted by the second Acc.—b. In Pass. with Nom. [§ 87, D, a] : *To be called or named;* vi 6; lv. 3

adpĕtens (appĕtens), ntis, 1. P. pres. of adpeto.—2. Pa.: With Gen. [§ 132] : *Striving after, eager for, grasping at, covetous of.*

ad-pĕto (ap-), pĕtīvi *or* pĕtĭi, pĕtītum, pĕtĕre, 3. v. a. [ăd, "to *or* towards "; pĕto, "to seek *or* go to "] (" To seek *or* go to *or* towards ";

hence) *To strive after, seek out, long for.*

ad-prĕhendo (ap-), prĕhendi, prĕhensum, prĕhendĕre, 3. v. a. [ăd, "without force "; prehendo, "to seize "] *To seize, lay hold of.*—Pass. : ad-prĕhendor, prehensus sum, prehendi.

adprĕhensus (apprehensus), a, um, P. perf. pass. of adprehendo.

ad-prŏbo (ap-), prŏbāvi, prŏbātum, prŏbāre, 1. v. a. [ăd, in "strengthening " force ; prŏbo, "to approve "] *To approve, approve of, assent to*, etc.

adrexi, perf. ind. of adrĭgo.

ad-rĭgo (ar-), rexi, rectum, rĭgĕre, 3. v. a. [for ad-rĕgo ; fr. ăd, "up "; rĕgo, in meaning of "to keep straight "] (" To keep straight up "; hence, "to set up, erect "; hence) Of the mind as Object : *To incite, rouse, encourage,* etc.

ad-scendo (a-), scendi, scensum, scendĕre, 3. v. a. [for ad-scando ; fr. ăd, "up "; scando, "to mount *or* climb "] *To mount or climb up, to ascend.*

adscī-sco (asci-), vi, tum, scĕre, 3. v. a. inch. (ascĭ-o, "to take to one's self knowingly ; to receive, admit "] 1. a. With double Acc. : *To receive, admit, take, adopt* one as that denoted by second Acc.—b. In Pass. constr.: With Nom.: *To be received, etc.,* as something. — **2.** *To take, draw, win over, attach* a person to one's self, *etc.*— Pass.: adscī-scor, tus sum, sci.

adscītus (ascītus), a, um, P. perf. pass. of adsciscor.—As the pass. voice of verbs governing two accusatives becomes Copulative, adscitum at xlvii. 1 is folld. by acc., inasmuch as it is in attribution to the acc. se, which must be supplied as the subject of the Inf. *scire* [§ 142: Notes to Syntax, p. 134, D; § 158].

adscīvisse (ascīvisse), perf. inf. of adscisco.

adsēdi, perf. ind. of adsīdo.

ad-sent-ī-or, adsensus sum, adsentīri, 3. v. dep. n. [ăd, "in accordance with"; sentĭ-o, "to think"] ("To think in accordance with"; hence, as a result) *To give* or *express assent, to assent.*

ad-sĕquor (as-), sĕquūtus sum, sĕqui, 3. v. dep. [ăd, "up to"; sĕquor, "to follow"] ("To follow up to"; hence) *To gain, obtain, attain.*

ad-sīdo (as-), sēdi, no sup., sīdĕre, 3. v. a. [ăd, "without force"; sīdo, "to seat one's self, sit down"] Of an orator who had concluded his speech: *To sit down, resume one's seat.*

ad-sisto (as-), stĭti, no sup., sistĕre, 3. v. n. [ăd, "without force"; sisto (neut.), "to place one's self, stand," *etc.*] ("To place one's self"; hence) Milit. t. t.: *To take up one's post* or *station; to station* or *post one's self;*—at lix. 3 adsistit is the Hist. pres.

ad-sum (as-), fŭi, esse, v. n. [ăd, "at"; sum, "to be"] ("To be at" a place, *etc.;* hence) **1.** With Dat.: *To be present at.*—**2.** Alone: *To be present, to be here;*—at lii. 18 aderunt implies 'will be at the gates of Rome.'

ad-tendo (at-), tendi, tentum, tendĕre, 3. v. a. [ăd, "to *or* towards"; tendo, "to bend"] ("To bend, direct, *etc.,* to *or* towards"; hence) Mentally: *To mark, consider, observe, attend to;*—at liii. 2 folld. by clause as Object.— N.B. In the above force this verb is sometimes folld. by animum, animos, *or* animo.

ad-tĕro (at-), trīvi, trītum, tĕrĕre, 3. v. a. [ăd, "against"; tĕro, "to rub"] ("To rub" one thing "against" another; hence) *To destroy, waste, weaken, impair.*

ad-trīvĕram, pluperf. ind. of adtĕro.

adtulĕrim, perf. subj. of adfĕro.

ădulter, ĕri, m. *An adulterer.*

ădul-tus, ta, tum, adj. [for adol-tus; fr. adol-esco, " to grow up "] With Abl. denoting age : *Grown up*.—At xv. 2 some editions have adulta ætate, Abl of quality [§ 115].

ad-vĕnĭo, vēni, ventum, vĕnīre, 4. v. n. [ăd, "to"; venio, "to come"] 1 In pres. tenses : *To come to* or *towards* a person or thing, *to advance,* etc.—2. In perf. tenses : *To have come to,* etc. ; *to arrive, be present.*

adven-to, tāvi, tātum, tāre, 1. v. n. intens. [advĕn-ĭo, " to come to *or* towards "] 1. In pres. tenses : *To come to* or *towards* a person, etc. ; *to approach, draw near.*—2. In perf. tenses : *To have come to,* etc. ; *to arrive, be present.*

ad-vŏco, vŏcāvi, vŏcātum, vŏcāre, 1. v. a. [ăd, "to"; vŏco, "to call"] *To call* or *summon to* a person or place ; —at xlvi. 5 with Acc. of person and Adv. of place ;—at lviii. 3 with Acc. of person alone, and folld. by quŏ c. Subj.

advor-sus (adver-), a, um, adj. [for advort-sus; fr. advort-o (= advert-o), "to turn to *or* towards" a person or thing; hence) 1. *Turned to* or *towards ; with the face* or *front towards :*—advorsa vulnera (*wounds turned towards* the foe ; i. c.) *wounds in front*

of the body ; lxi. 3.—2. With Dat. [§ 106, 3] : *Unfavourable, unpropitious, adverse.*— 3. *Hostile, in hostile opposition, opposed.*

æd-es, is, f. ("The burning *or* shining thing"; hence) 1. Sing. : With reference to the altar : *A temple.*—2. Plur. : With reference to the hearth : *A dwelling, house,* etc. [prob. akin to αἴθ-ω, "to burn"].

æd-ĭ-fĭc-o, āvi, ātum, āre, 1. v. a. [for æd-ĭ-făc-o; fr. æd-es, "an abode"; (i) connecting vowel ; FAC, root of facio, "to make"] ("To make an abode"; hence) *To build, construct, erect.*

æd-īlis, īlis, m. [æd-es; see ædes] ("One pertaining to *ædes*"; hence) *An ædile,* a Roman magistrate, who was not eligible for office till he had attained the age of thirty-seven years. The Ædiles were four in number; two being styled Plebeian Ædiles, the other two Curule Ædiles. The former were first created A.U. 260, as assistants of the Tribunes of the people. The latter were originally chosen from the Patricians, A.U. 387, for the purpose of performing certain public games for which the Plebeian Ædiles of that year had refused to make preparations. They were allowed, amongst other privileges, the use of the Curule chair—the official chair, inlaid with ivory—and from this circumstance obtained their distinctive name. The main business of the Ædiles was to superintend the public buildings and works, to see that private edifices did not become ruinous and so cause danger, and to undertake the general supervision of the public markets, taverns, etc.

æger, gra, grum, adj. *Ill, suffering, sick, diseased,* etc.

æmüla, æ; see æmülus.

æm-ülus, üla, ülum, adj. [akin to ïm-ïtor, "to imitate"] ("That imitates, that vies with," another; hence) In a bad sense : *Envious, jealous.*—As Subst. : **æmüla**, æ, f. *A female rival,* as one that is envious, *etc.,* of another;—at x. 1 applied to Carthage.

Ænēas, æ, m. *Æneas;* the mythic son of Anchises, a Trojan prince, and the goddess Venus. He was the ancestor of the Romans, and after death was worshipped under the title of Jupiter Indiges;—Ænēā duce, Abl. Abs. [§ 125, *a*] [*Alvelas*].

æquäbïl-ïter, adv. [æquäbïl-is, in force of "uniform, equable"] ("After the manner the *æquabilis*"; hence) *niformly, in a uniform way r manner, equably, without Sallust.*

change, etc.—Comp. : æquäbïl-ïus ; (Sup. does not occur).

æquäbïlïus, comp. adv.; see æquabiliter.

æquä-lis, le, adj. [æqu(a) -o, "to equal"] ("That equals"; hence) *Equal;*—at liv. 1 æqualia, nom. neut. plur., is predicated of the three sing. subst. genus, ætas, eloquentia [§ 92, 2, *a*].

æquäl-ïter, adv. [æquäl-is, "equal"] ("After the manner of the *æquālis*"; hence) *Equally, in equal proportions.*

æqu-e (dissyll.), adv. [æqu-us, "equal"] ("After the manner of the *æquus*"; hence) *Equally, alike.*

æquïor, us ; see æquus.

æqu-ïtas, ïtätis, f. [æqu-us, "just"; also, "equable"] ("The quality of the *æquus*"; hence) 1. *Just or equitable conduct; justice.*—2. *Equable conduct; moderation; calmness, equanimity.*

æquum, i ; see æquus.

æquüs, a, um, adj. ("Pertaining to one" kind, nature, *etc.;* hence) 1. Of place : *Level, even, plain,* etc.—2. *Favourable, advantageous.*—3. *Equal :*— æquä manu discēdēre, *to come off* from battle (*with equal hand,* i. e.) *on equal terms or with a drawn engagement,* xxxix. 4.—4. *Quiet, calm, composed.*—Adverbial

F

expression: æquo animo (*with a quiet mind*, i. e.) *quietly, calmly, composedly*, iii. 2.—5. Morally: Of things: *Reasonable, right, fair, proper.*—As Subst.: æquum, i, n. *That which is reasonable, right,* etc.; li. 11.—Comp.: æqu-ĭor [akin to Sans. *ekas*, "one "].

ærarĭum, ĭi; see ærarius.

ær-ārĭus, ārĭa, ārĭum, adj. [æs, ær-is, "copper, bronze"; hence, as made of it, "money"] *Of* or *belonging to money.*—As Subst.: ærarium, ĭi, n. ("A thing—here, place—belonging to money"; hence) At Rome: *The* public *treasury* in the temple of Saturn.

ærumna, æ, f. *Great trouble, hardship, distress, tribulation,* etc.

æs, æris, n.: 1 *Copper, bronze.*—2. *Money:*—æs alienum (*the money of another;* i. e.) *a sum owed, debt;* xiv. 2 [akin to Sans. *ayas*, "iron"].

æs-tŭmo (-tĭmo), tŭmāvi, tŭmātum, tŭmāre, 1.v.a. [prob. for ær-tŭmo; fr. æs, ær-is, "money"] ("To calculate the money value of a thing"; hence) 1. *To estimate, value, put a value upon, weigh,* etc. —2. *To reckon, think, deem,* etc.

æstŭ-o, āvi, ātum, āre, 1. v. n. [æstus, uncontr. gen. æstŭ-is, "heat"] ("To have *æstus*"; hence, "to be hot";

hence) *To burn, be inflamed* with envy, etc.

æ-tas, tātis, f. [for æv-tas; fr. æv-um, "life"] ("The state of *ævum*"; hence) 1. *Life-time, life.*—2. *A* particular *time* or *season of life, age.*—3. *Old* or *advanced age.*

æt-ernus, erna, ernum, adj. [contr. fr. ætāt-ernus; fr. ætas, ætāt-is, "time"] ("Pertaining to *ætas*"; hence, with accessory notion of duration) *Everlasting, eternal.*

agendi, agendo, Gerunds in di and do fr. ago.

ăg-er, ăgri, m.: 1. *A field, land.*—2. Plur.: a. *The fields, the country.*—b. *Lands, fields, landed property.*—3. *Territory, district.*—4. Plur.: *Lands, territories* of a state [akin to Sans. *aj-ras*, Gr. ἀγ-ρός; cf. English *acre*].

ăgĭtando, Gerund in do fr. agito.

ăg-ĭto, ĭtāvi, ĭtātum, ĭtāre, 1. v. a. freq. [ag-o, "to set in motion"] ("To set in constant motion"; hence) 1. a. *To disquiet, torment, torture, vex, trouble, agitate.*—b. *To attack* or *assail* with reproaches, insults, etc.;—at xxiii. 3 supply eam as the Object of agitare [§ 158].—2. *To turn over* in the mind, *ponder, revolve,* etc.—3. *To deliberate upon, design, devise, plot,* etc.—4. *To intend, purpose,* etc.—**5. a.** *To be occupied with; to employ* or *engage one's self in* or *about* something.—**b.** With a Subst. as a circumlocution for the verb akin to such subst.: agitare gaudium atque lætitiam (xlviii. 1) = gaudere atque lætari, *to rejoice and to be exceedingly delighted:*—so, also, in pass. construction: lætitia, mæror, luctus atque gaudia agitabantur (lxi. 9) = lætābantur, *they were exceedingly delighted;* mærebant, *they mourned;* lugēbant, *they sorrowed;* gaudēbant, *they rejoiced.*—**6.** Of life, time, *etc.*: *To pass, spend.*—Pass.: ăgĭtor, ĭtātus sum, ĭtāri.

ăgo, ēgi, actum, ăgĕre, 3. v. a. ("*To set, or* put, in motion"; hence) **1.** *To drive,* whether actually or figuratively.—**2.** *To do, transact, perform,* etc.;—at xlii. 2 agere is the Hist. Inf. [§ 140, 2].—**3. a.** *To discuss, treat of, deliberate about,* etc.—**b.** With cum populo and without nearer Object: *To ∪reat with,* or *address, the people,* li. 43.—**4.** Of time, life, *etc.: To pass, spend,* etc.;—at xxxix. 2 agere is the Hist. Inf. [§ 140, 2].—**5. a.** *To plead* a cause, *etc., bring* an action, *maintain* a suit, in a court of law.—**b.** Pass.: (a) With thing as Subject: (*To be in suit* or *in*

question; hence, apart from judicial matters) *To come in question, to be debated,* etc.; lii. 10.—(b) Impers.: agitur, *It is debated, the question arises,* lii. 6.—Pass.: ăgŏr, actus sum, ăgi [ἄγω].

agr-estis, este, adj. [ager, agr-i, in plur. "the country"] ("Of *or* belonging to the country"; hence, as opp. to the refinement of cities) *Rustic, boorish, uncultivated, barbarous.*

aio, v. defect.: With Objective clause: *To assent, affirm, maintain* that something is, is done, *etc.* [akin to Sans. root AH, for AGH, "to say, speak"].

ălăcer, cris, cre, adj. Of the mind: *Eager, roused, excited,* etc.

alg-or, ōris, m. [alg-ĕo, "to be cold"] *Cold, the cold.*

ălĭ-bi, adv. [alĭ-us, "another"] *At another place, elsewhere:*—alii alibi, *some here, others there,* lx. 5.

ălĭēnātus, a, um, P. perf. pass. of alieno.

ălĭēn-o, āvi, ātum, āre, 1. v. a. [aliēn-us, "belonging to another"] ("*To make*" something "*alienus*"; hence, of property, "to transfer, alienate" from one's self; hence) *To alienate* or *estrange* from public favour, *etc.:*—r falsā suspicione alienatr

F 2

sentiebam, *I perceived that I was alienated* from public favour (i. e. *was neglected* or *discarded*) *from* (= in consequence of) *a false suspicion* respecting me, xxxv. 3 : supply esse with alienatum [§ 158]; *falsā suspicione* is Abl. of cause [§ 111].

ălĭēnum, i; see alienus.

ălĭ-ēnus, ēna, ēnum, adj. [ălĭ-us, "another"] 1. *Of*, or *belonging to, another ; another's.*—As Subst.: alienum, i, n. *That which is another's, another's property*, etc.; v. 5 : in plur., at xii. 2.—**2.** Of the mind, *etc.*: *Hostile, estranged, unfriendly.*—**3.** With Gen.: *Unsuitable, unfavourable, inconvenient for :*—neque aliena consilii, *and not unsuitable* (i. e. *very suitable* or *convenient) for consultation*, xl. 5.—**4.** With Dat.: *Perilous, dangerous, hurtful, injurious to ;* lvi. 5.—**5.** Wi.h ab : *Foreign to, not in accordance with ;* li. 17.

ălĭ-o, adv. [ălĭ-us, "another"] *In another way :*—aliud alio *one thing in one direction, another thing in another direction ;* ii. 3.

ălĭqu-ando, adv. [aliqu-i, "some"] ("At some time"; hence) In admonitions, entreaties, *etc.: At length, at last, now ;* lii. 2.

ălĭquant-o, adv. [aliquant-us, "some, considerable"] ("After the manner of the *aliquantus*"; hence) With Comp. adj.: *Some, much, a little.*

ălĭ-qui, qua, quod (Gen.: ălĭcūjus; Dat.: ălĭcui; Plur.: ali-qui, quæ, qua), indef. pron. adj. [ălĭ-us; qui (indefinite pron.), "any "] ("Another be it any"; hence) *Some.*

ălĭ-quis, quid (Gen. : ălĭcūjus; Dat. : ălĭcui; Fem. Sing. and Neut. Plur. not used), indef. pron. subst. [ălĭ-us; quis] *Some one, somebody, any one ; something.*—Neut. with Gen. of 1st or 2nd decl. : *Something of = some.*

ălĭ-quot, indef. num. adj. plur. indecl. [ălĭ-us, "another," plur. "other, others"; quot, "as many as"] ("Others, as many as" they may be; hence) *Some; several; a few, not many.*

ăl·ĭter, adv. [ăl-is, old form of ălĭus, "another"] ("After the manner of the *alius*"; hence) 1. *In another manner, otherwise.*—**2.** *In any other case, otherwise, else.*

ăl-ĭus, ĭa, ĭud (Gen.: ălĭus; Dat.: ălĭi), adj.: 1. *Another :* —Plur.: *Other.*—As Subst.:a. alius, m. sing. *Another person, another.*—b. aliud, n. sing. *Another thing.*—c. alĭi, m. plur. *Other persons, others.*—dalia, n. plur.: (a) *Other* *things.*—(b) *Other houses;* xx. 12.—2. *Of another kind, different;* lii. 2.—3. Distributively, whether as pron. or subst.: a. alius . . . alius, *one . . . another:*—alius alio more viventes, *living one in one way, another in another way,* i. e. each in a different way, vi. 2: alia alii, *of one kind to the one, of another kind to the other,* i. e. of a *different kind to each,* liv. 1.—b. alii . . . pars, *some . . . others.*—See, also, alibi, alio, and pars [akin to ἄλλος].

allātus, a, um, P. perf. pass. of adfĕro.

Allobrŏgos, um, m. plur. ("People of another land") *The Allobroges,* a people of Gallia Narbonensis [Celtic word].

ăl-o, ŭi, ĭtum *and* tum, ĕre, 3. v. a. *To nourish, maintain, sustain, support.*—Pass.: ălor, tus *and* (later) ĭtus sum, i. [akin to Gr. ἀλ-θω, " to make to grow "].

al-ter, tĕra, tĕrum (Gen.: alterĭus; Dat.: altĕri), adj. [akin to ăl-ĭus, " another "] I. *One, another; the one,* or *the other* of two.—As Subst.: alter, m. sing. *Another person, another.*—2. Distributively, whether as adj. or subst.: alter . . . alter, *one . . . another; the one . . . the other.*

al-tus, ta, tum, adj. [ăl-o, " to nourish "] (" Nourished, increased by nourishment "; hence) *High, lofty,* whether actually or figuratively.—As Subst.: alta, ōrum, n. plur. *Lofty,* or *grand, things ;* v. 5.

amb-ĭtĭo, ĭtĭōnis, f. [amb-io, " to go round "; hence, " to canvass " for an office by going round to the voters] (" A canvassing " for votes in a lawful manner; hence) *A desire* or *longing for honour; ambition.* See ambĭtus.

amb-ĭtus, ĭtus, m. [id.] *A canvassing* for votes, esp. with bribery or by other unlawful means, prohibited by severe laws. See ambitio.

ămĭc-ĭtĭa, ĭtĭæ, f. [ămĭc-us, " a friend "] (" The quality of the *amicus* "; hence) *Friendship.*

1. **ăm-ĭcus,** ĭca, ĭcum, adj. [am-o, " to love "] *Loving, friendly, kind.*—As Subst.: ăm-ĭcus, i, m. *A friend.*

2. **ămĭcus,** i; see 1. amicus.

ămīsi, perf. ind. of amitto.

ămissus, a, um, P. perf. pass. of amitto.

ă-mitto, mīsi, missum, mittĕre, 3. v. a. [ă, " from "; mitto, " to let go "] (" To let go from one; to let slip "; hence) *To lose.*—Pass.: ă-mittor, missus sum, mitti.

ăm-o, āvi, ātum, āre, 1. v. a. *To love :*—in a bad sense, *t* *intrigue,* etc., *with ;*—at xi. 6 without nearer Object [akin to Sans. root KAM, "to love "].

ăm-œnus, œna, œnum, adj. [perhaps ăm-o, "to love "] (" Loved "; hence) *Delightful, pleasant, agreeable,* etc.

ăm-or, ōris, m. [ăm-o, "to love "] *Love,* both in a good and bad sense.

āmōtus, a, um, P. perf. pass. of amoveo.

ā-mŏvĕo, mōvi, mōtum, mŏvēre, 2. v. a. [ā, " away "; mŏvĕo, "to move"] 1. *To move away, remove.*—2. *To remove* or *expel* from an order, etc.; xxiii. 1.—Pass.: **ā-mŏvĕor,** mōtus sum, mŏvēri.

āmōvĕram, pluperf. ind. of amoveo.

amplexor, ātus sum, āri, 1. v. dep. intens. [for amplectsor; fr. amplect-or, " to embrace"] 1. *To embrace.*— 2. *To value, be fond of, love, esteem.*

amplĭor, us; see amplus.

amplĭus, comp. adv. [adverbial neut. of amplĭor, " great, comprising much "] 1. *More, beyond, further, besides, in addition,* etc.—2. With Abl. of thing compared [§ 124]: *More than, above, beyond.*— 3. As a mere adverbial modification of time, number, *etc.,* without influencing the construction of the case to which it is attached: amplĭus annos

triginta, *for thirty years,* (and) *more,* or *above thirty years,* where annos is Acc. of " Duration of time," lix. 6 [§ 102, (1)]; binas aut amplĭus domos, *two houses or more,* where domos is the nearer Object : — after continuare, xx. 11.

am-pl-us, a, um, adj. [am, " around "; pl·ĕo, "to fill "] (" Filled around "; hence) 1. *Of large extent, extensive, ample.*—2. Of courage : *Great,* etc. ☞ Comp.: ampl-ĭor.

an, conj. [prob. a primitive word] Introducing the second half of a disjunctive interrogation, or a clause implying doubt: 1. *Or, or whether.*— 2. With the first half of the interrogation not expressed, but to be supplied from preceding context: *Or, or rather, or indeed.*—3. In indirect questions : ne . . . an, *whether . . . or,* lii. 10.

an-cep-s, an-cĭpĭt-is, adj [for an-capit-s; fr. an (= ambi), "around, round about "; căput, capĭt-is, " a head "] (" Having heads round about " one, *i. e.* before and behind ; hence, " two-headed "; hence) *Double, twofold;*—at xxix. 1 anceps malum refers to the malum both within and outside of the city.

angust-Iœ, ĭarum, f. plur. [angust-us, "narrow "] (" The

state of the *angustus*"; hence)
A defile or *pass* in the mountains.

ăn-ĭma, ĭmæ, f. ("That which breathes *or* blows"; hence, "air, a breath"; hence) 1. *Life.*—2. *The rational soul* or *nature* of man, *mind* [akin to Sans. root AN, "to breathe *or* blow"].

ănĭmadvertĕrētur ; see animadverto, no. 2, b.

ănĭm-adverto, adverti, adversum, advertĕre, 3. v. a. [ănĭm-us, "the mind"; adverto, "to turn towards"] ("To turn the mind towards" a thing; hence, "To mark, observe, notice"; hence, with accessory notion of the consequence resulting from marking, *etc.*, a fault or crime) 1. *To chastise, punish.*—2. Judicial t. t.: a. With in c. Acc. of person, and without Acc. of nearer Object : *To inflict punishment on* some one ; li. 39.—b. Impers. Pass.: folld. by in c. Acc.: animadverteretur, *Punishment should be inflicted upon,* li. 21.—Pass.: ănĭm-advertor, adversus sum, adverti.

ănĭm-al, ālis, n. [ănĭm-a, "life"] ("A thing pertaining to *anima*"; hence) *A living being.*

ăn-ĭmus, ĭmi, m. ("That which blows *or* breathes"; hence, "vital power, life";

hence, "the rational soul, *or* intellectual principle," in man ; hence) 1. *Mind.*—2. *Intellect, reason.*—3. *Courage, spirit;*— at lviii. 8 forti (atque parato) animo is Abl. of quality [§ 115] [akin to Sans. root AN, "to breathe"].

Annĭus, ĭi, m. *Annius* (*Quintus*) ; a Roman senator, one of Catiline's accomplices ; xvii. 3.   He escaped being taken (l. 4) ; but what subsequently became of him is not known.

an-nus, ni, m. ("That which goes round, a circuit"; hence) Of time : *A year;*—at lix. 6 triginta annos is the Acc. of "Duration of time" [§ 102, (1)] [akin to Sans. AM, "to go"; *am-ati*, "time"; also to Gr. ἔν-ος = ἐν-ιαυτός, "a year"].

ann-ŭus, ŭa, ŭum, adj. [ann-us, "a year"] ("Of, *or* belonging to, *annus*"; hence) *Annual, lasting a year, of a year's duration.*

ante, adv. *and* prep.: 1. Adv. : *Before, previously.*— 2. Prep. gov. acc. : a. *Before.* —b. To denote superiority *or* precedence : *Before, above, superior to :*—ante aliquem esse, *to be before,* i. e. *to surpass* or *excel any one,* liii. 3. —c. Ante folld. by dies, etc., and an ordinal adj. gives the date of the day denoted by such ordinal: ante diem vi.

Kalendas Novembrīs, *on the sixth day before the Calends of November;* here ante governs Calendas, and diem is Acc. of time [akin to Sans. *ati,* "beyond"; Gr. ἀντί, "over against"].

ant-ĕā, adv. [prob. for ant-eam; fr. an-te, "before"; eam, acc. sing. fem. of pron. is, "this, that"] ("Before this *or* that time") *Formerly, previously, in previous* or *past time.*

antĕ-căpĭo, cēpi, captum, căpĕre, 3. v. a. [ante, "before" in time; căpĭo, "to take"] 1. *To take beforehand; to preoccupy;* [§ 140, 2].—**2.** *To anticipate.*

ante-hac, adv. [prob. for ante-hanc; fr. ante, "before" in time; hanc, fem. acc. sing. of hic, "this"] ("Before this"; hence, with reference to time past) *Formerly, previously,* etc.

Antōnius, ĭi, m. *Antonius (Caius);* Cicero's colleague in the consulship; xxiv. 1. See also what is said respecting him at xxi. 3.

anxĭus, ĭa, ĭum, adj. [for ang-sĭus; fr. ang-o, "to squeeze"; hence, "to torment"] ("Tormented"; hence) *Anxious, troubled, solicitous.*

ă-pĕr-ĭo, ŭi, tum, īre, 4. v. a. ("To uncover, lay bare"; hence) 1. *To open.*—**2.** *To ʳe, reveal, make known*

a plan, *etc.*—**3.** *To set forth, state.*—**4.** Of a road, way, etc.: *To lay open,* i. e. to make free from impediments. — Pass.: **ă-pĕr-ĭor,** tus sum, īri [prob. for ab-pĕr-ĭo; fr. ăb, denoting "reversal"="English un-"; root PER, akin to Sans. root VRE or VAR, "to cover"].

ăpĕrĭundus, a, um, Gerundive of aperio;—at lviii. 7 aperiundum is used in attributive construction, and has the force of necessity attaching to it [§ 144, 2].

ap-ud, prep. gov. acc. [prob. ap-ĭo or ăp-o, "to lay hold of"] ("Laying hold of"; hence) 1. *With, near to.*— **2.** With Acc. of name of person : *At the house of, with;* xxxvi. 1.—**3.** *Among, with* persons, amongst, *etc.,* whom something occurs, *etc.:*—apud majores nostros, *among our ancestors,* i. e. *in the time of our ancestors,* lii. 30; apud vos, *with you,* li. 7.

Apūlĭa, æ, f. *Apulia* (now *Puglia*) *;* a province of Southern Italy, between the Apennines and the Adriatic Sea.

ăquĭl-a, læ, f. ("The quick, or rapid, one" ("An eagle"; hence) The figure of *an eagle,* as the principal standard of a Roman legion [akin to Gr. ὠκ-ύς, "swift"; Sans. *ásu,* "quickly"].

ăr-a (old form ăs-a), æ, f.

("A seat *or* raised place"; hence) *An elevation for sacred purposes;* i. e. *an altar* [prob. akin to Sans. root âs, "to sit"].

ar-bĭ-ter, tri, m. ("One who goes to" something in order to hear or see; hence) *A looker-on, eye-witness, witness* [ar (old form of ad), "to"; root BI, akin to βῆ-μι, "to go": bē-to, bī-to, "to go"].

ar-ces-so, sīvi, sītum, sĕre, 3. v. a. [for ar-ced-so; fr. ar (= ad), "to"; cēd-o, "to go"] (In causative force: "to cause to go, *or* come, to" one; hence) *To call, summon, send for,* etc.;—at lx. 4 arcessere is Hist. Inf. [§ 140, 2].

ardens, ntis : 1. P. pres. of ardeo.—2. Pa.: *Fiery, hot, eager, impetuous.*

ardĕo, arsi, arsum, ardēre, 2. v. n.: 1. *To be on fire, burn, blaze.*—2. *To be inflamed, excited,* etc., by any passion, etc.

ardŭus, a, um, adj.: 1. *Steep.*—2. *High, lofty.*—3. *Difficult arduous* [akin to Sans. *úrdva,* Gr. ὀρθός, "erect"].

arg-entum, enti, n. ("Silver"; hence) *Silver-money;* —at xxxiii. 3 the expression argentum ære solutum est refers to the Valerian Law (carried by Q. Valerius Flaccus,

B.C. 46), by which it was decreed that debts should be cancelled by the payment of an *as* for a *sestertius,* i. e. of one-fourth part. See sestertius [akin to Sans. *raj-atam,* "silver," as "the shining thing"; fr. root RAJ, "to shine"; cf. ἀργ-ὔρος].

ar-ma, mōrum, n. plur. ("Things adapted" to any purpose; hence, "implements"; hence) *Arms, weapons* [prob. ἄρ-ω, "to adapt"].

armātus, a, um, P. perf. pass. of armo.

arm-o, āvi, ātum, āre, 1. v. a. [arm-a, "arms"] *To furnish with arms or weapons; to arm.* —Pass.: arm-or, ātus sum, āri.

ăr-o, āvi, ātum, āre, 1. v. a. *To plough* [ἀρ-όω].

Arrēt-īnus, ina, īnum [for Arrētĭ-īnus; fr. Arrētĭ-um; "Arretium" (now "Arezzo"), a large town of Etruria] *Of, or belonging to, Arretium; Arretine.*

ar-s, tis, f.: 1. *Art, skill,* etc.—2. *Manner,* or *mode, of acting; practice* [either akin to ἄρ-ω, "to join," and so, "a joining"; or fr. ăr-o, "to plough," and so "a ploughing," as the earliest and most important act of skill].

art-e, adv. [art-us, "close"] 1. *Closely.*—2. In Comp. to mark a very high degree: *Very closely;* lix. 2. ☞

Comp.: art-ĭus; (Sup.: art-issĭme).

artīs=artes acc. plur. of ars.

artĭus, comp. adv.; see arte.

Asĭa, æ, f. *Asia,* i. e. 1. Asia, as such.—2. Asia Minor.

asper, ĕra, ĕrum, adj.: 1. *Rough, rugged.*—2. *Cruel, bitter.*—3. Of circumstances, etc.: *Perilous, dangerous, adverse, calamitous, critical.* ☞ Comp.: aspĕr-ĭor; (Sup.: asper-rĭmus).

aspĕrĭor, us; see asper.

a-spernor, spernātus sum, spernāri, 1. v. dep. [ā (= ăb), "away from"; spernor, "to spurn"] ("To spurn away from" one's self; hence) *To disdain, scorn, despise.*

astūt-ĭa, ĭæ, f. [astūt-us, "sagacious," also, "cunning"] ("The quality of the *astutus*"; hence) 1. *Sagacity, skill, dexterity, adroitness.*—2. *Cunning, subtlety, craftiness.*

ăt, conj. *But, yet* [akin to Sans. *atha,* Gr. ἀτ-άρ, "but"].

(Ăthēn-ĭensis, ĭense, adj. [Athen-æ, "Athens"; the chief city of Attica in Northern Greece] "Of, *or* belonging to, Athens; Athenian."—As Subst.) Athenienses, ĭum, m. plur. *The Athenians;*—at li. 28 the words devictis Atheniensibus refer to the overthrow of the Athenians 'he Lacedæmonians at the close of the third Peloponnesian War, when they were compelled to demolish the fortifications of their city, throw down the Long Walls which connected it with the Piræus, and to submit to the Thirty Tyrants.

at-que (contr. ac), conj [for ad-que; fr. ăd, denotiṇʒ "addition"; quĕ, "and"] 1. *And also; and.*—2. With comparative adjectives, or words expressing dissimilarity, difference, contrariety, *etc.:* *Than, to:*—contra ac, *otherwise than, contrary to what,* lx. 5.—3. After words denoting similarity, *etc.:* *As, with.* —4. After simul : *As.*

ătrōc-ĭtas, ĭtātis, f. [atrox, atrōc-is, "fierce"] ("The quality of the *atrox*"; hence) *Fierceness, atrocity, atrociousness.*

ătr-ox, ōcis, adj. [prob. ater, atr-i, "black"] ("Pertaining to *ater*"; hence, "hideous"; hence) *Atrocious, horrible, terrible.*

attent-e, adv. [attent-us, "attentive"] ("After the manner of the *attentus*"; hence) *Attentively, carefully, diligently.* ☞ Comp.: attent-ĭus; (Sup. : attent-issĭme).

attentĭus, comp. adv.; see attente.

auc-tor, tōris, m. [for aug-tor; fr. aug-ĕo, "to produce"]

("He who produces"; hence, "a father"; hence) 1. *An originator, executor, performer, doer,* etc.—2. *A reporter, informant, narrator.*

auctŏr-ĭtas, ĭtātis, f. [auctor, "a producer"] ("The quality, *etc.,* of the *auctor*"; hence, "a producing" of a thing; hence) 1. *Weight* of character, *influence, authority.* —2. Political t. t. : *The will* or *authority* of the Senate.— 3. Of things: *Importance, weight,* etc.

auctus, a, um, P. perf. pass. of augeo;—at vi. 3 aucta is used by the figure Zeugma with moribus, though it belongs only in reality to civibus and agris. Render : *Increased in (number of) citizens, refined* (where it represents exculta) *in manners, enlarged in territory.*

audāc-ĭa, ĭæ, f. [audax, audāc-is, "daring, bold"] ("The quality of the *audax*"; hence) 1. In a good sense : *Boldness, courage, bravery.*— 2. In a bad sense : *Audacity, presumption, shamelessness,* etc.;—at xviii. 4 summæ audaciæ is Gen. of quality [§ 128].

audācĭus, comp. adv.; see audacter.

audac-ter, adv. [audax, audāc-is, "bold"] *Boldly.* ☞ Comp.: audāc-ĭus; (Sup.: audac-issĭme).

aud-ax, ācis, adj. [aud-ĕo, "to dare"] *Daring ;* i. e. a. In a good sense : *Bold, courageous.*—b. In a bad sense : *Bold, audacious.*

audĕo, ausus sum, audēre, 2. v. semi-dep. *To dare,* or *venture,* to do something.

aud-ĭo, īvi *or* ĭi, ītum, īre, 4. v. a. ("To give ear to"; hence) 1. *To hear :*—folld. by Acc. of part. pres. in concord with a subst. to denote that one's self, *etc.,* hears the person, *etc.,* who is the Object of the verb, doing, *etc.,* the thing pointed out by such part.; xlviii. 9.—2. *To listen* or *hearken to; to examine into, make enquiry about.*—Pass. : aud-ĭor, ītus sum, īri [akin to αὖs (= οὖs), αὐτ-ός, "ear"].

augendus, a, um, Gerundive of augeo.

augĕo, auxi, auctum, augēre, 2. v. a. *To increase, augment.* —Pass. : **augĕor,** auctus sum, augēri [akin to αὐξάνω].

Aulus, i, m. *Aulus ;* ι Roman prænomen.

Aurēlĭa, æ, f. *Aurelia ;* a Roman female name.

aur-is, is, f. [for aud-is ; fr. aud-ĭo, "to hear"] ("The hearing thing"; hence) *The ear.*

ausus, a, um, P. perf. of audeo.

aut, conj. *Or :*—aut aut, *either . . . or.*

aut-em, conj.: **1.** *But, on the other hand, yet, however, nevertheless.* — **2.** *Besides, further, moreover* [akin to αὐτ-άρ].

Autronǐus, ǐi, m. *Autronius* (*Publius*), with the cognomen of *Pætus*; a Roman who was an active accomplice of Catiline. After the suppression of the conspiracy he was brought to trial, and entreated Cicero with many tears to undertake his defence, pleading their early friendship, and their having been colleagues in the quæstorship. His request was refused; while further all his friends withdrew from him. Upon being found guilty he went into banishment in Epīrus.

auxǐl-ǐum, ǐi, n. [probably obsolete auxil-is (= aug-silis), "increasing," fr. aug-eo, "to increase"] ("The quality, *or* state, of the *auxǐlis*"; hence) *Help, aid, assistance;*—at vi. 5 and lii. 29, in plur.: at vi. 5 the expression auxilia portare, *to carry help,* is unusual; the ordinary term is auxilium ferre.

ăvār-ǐtǐa, ǐtǐæ, f. [ăvār-us, "covetous"] ("The quality of the *avarus*"; hence) *Covetousness, avarice.*

ăvertĕrim, perf. subj. of averto;—at lviii. 16 this tense is used as a modified perf. ind.

ā-verto, verti, versum, vertĕre, 3. v. a. [ā (=ab), "away"; verto, "to turn"] *To turn away.*

ăv-ĭdus, ĭda, ĭdum, adj. [ăv-ĕo, "to desire earnestly"] With Gen. [§ 132]: *Earnestly desiring or desirous of; eager for.*

barbărus, i, m. [barbarus (adj.), "barbarian"] *A barbarian.*

bellǐc-ōsus, ōsa, ōsum, adj. [bellǐc-us, "warlike"] *Very warlike, martial.*

b-ellum, elli, n. [old form dŭ-ellum; fr. dŭ-o, "two"] ("A contest, *etc.*, between two parties"; hence) **1.** *War, warfare.*—**2.** *A combat, fight, engagement, battle.*

bēl-ŭa, ŭæ, f. *A beast, wild beast* [prob. akin to θήρ, "a wild animal"].

bĕn-ĕ, adv. [obsol. bĕn-us = bŏn-us, "good"] ("After the manner of the *benus*"; hence) *In a good way or manner, well:* —bene pollicēri, *to promise well,* i. e. *to make large promises,* xli. 5: bene consulendo, *by consulting well,* i. e. *by adopting good counsels or plans,* lii. 29.

bĕnĕ-făcǐo (or, as two words, bene facio), fēci, factum, făcĕre, 3. v. n. [bĕnĕ, "well"; facǐo, "to do"] ("To do well to" a person;

hence) With Dat. [§ 106, (3)]: *To do well* or *good to; to benefit.*

běně-făc-tum, ti, n. [id.] ("A thing well done or performed"; hence) *A good* or *honourable action, an heroic deed.*

běně-fĭc-ĭum, ĭi, n. [for bene-fac-ium; fr. bene, "well"; fac-io, "to do"] ("A doing good *or* well"; hence) *Kindness, favour, service, benefit.*

Bestĭa, æ, m. [bestĭa, "a beast"] *Bestia (Lucius Calpurnius);* a Roman senator who joined in the conspiracy of Catiline; xvii. Bestia is called by Sallust (xliii. 1) "Tribune of the people"; but it seems he was at that time merely Tribune elect, and held office in the following year. It was agreed amongst the conspirators that he should make a complaint in the Senate against Cicero; and that a rising should take place on the following night. Cicero's vigilance effectually defeated this plan.

bĭ-ni, næ, na, num. distrib. adj. plur. [bī = bis, "twice"] ("Pertaining to *bi*"; hence) 1. *Two apiece* or *for each.*— 2. *Two.*

bŏna, orum; bŏni, orum; bŏnum, i; see bonus.

1. bŏnus, a, um, adj.: 1. *Good,* in the fullest meaning of the word.—As Subst.: bonus, i, m. *A good and honourable man.*—2. *Upright, honest, virtuous,* etc.—As Subst.: a. bŏnum, i, n. *Goodness, uprightness, probity,* etc.—b. bŏni, orum, m. plur. *The good, the virtuous.*—3. *Brave, gallant, active.*—As Subst.: bŏnus, i, m. *A brave,* etc., *man.*—4. *Good* or *serviceable* for something.—As Subst.: bŏnum, i, n: a. *Advantage, profit,* etc.—b. *The public good, advantage* or *weal.*—5. *Wealthy, rich.*—As Subst.: bŏna, ōnum, n. plur. *Wealth, riches, goods, property, fortune.*—6. Of leisure: *Valuable, important,* etc. ☞ (Comp.: melior); Sup.: optŭmus *or* optĭmus.

2. bŏnus, i; see 1. bonus.

brěv-is, e, adj. *Short.*—Adverbial Abl.: brěvi, *In a short time, shortly* [akin to βραχύς].

Bruttĭ-us, a, um, adj. [Bruttĭ-i, "The Bruttĭi"; the inhabitants of the most Southern part of Italy] *Of,* or *belonging to, the Bruttii :*—ager Bruttius, *the country* or *territory of the Bruttii.*

Brūtus, i, m. [brūtus, "stupid, dull"] *Brutus (Decimus Junius);* a Roman Patrician descended from L. Junius Brutus, who feigned stupidity to escape death at the han

Tarquinius Superbus. During his absence from Rome his wife Sempronia received the ambassadors of the Allobroges at her house as mentioned in chapter xl.

C, abbrev. of Caius.

căd-ăvĕr, āvĕris, n. [căd-o, "to fall dead"] ("That which falls dead"; hence) *A dead body, corpse, carcase.*

cădo, cĕcĭdi, cāsum, cădĕre, 3. v. n.: 1. *To fall, fall down.*—2. *To fall dead, die.* —3. *To fall out, happen, come to pass,* esp. in an unexpected manner [akin to Sans. root ÇAD, "to fall"].

cæd-es, is, f. [cæd-o, "to slay"] *A killing* or *slaying; slaughter.*

cælātus, a, um, P. perf. pass. of cælo.

cæl-o, āvi, ātum, āre, 1. v. a. [cæl-um, "a chisel *or* burin" of an engraver] ("To employ the cælum on something"; hence) *To engrave* in relief, *to emboss,* etc.—Pass.: cæl-or, ātus sum, āri.

Cæpārĭus, ĭi, m. [cæparius, "a dealer in onions"] *Caparius (Quintus),* a native of Terracina, and one of Catiline's accomplices. He was strangled in the Tullianum; lv. 6.

Cæsar, ăris, m. ("Hairy One") *Cæsar;* a cognomen in the Julian family at Rome:

1. Lucius Julius Cæsar: consul B.C. 63 in conjunction with C. Marcius Figulus. He voted for the death of the Catilinarian conspirators, amongst whom was Lentulus, the husband of his own sister; xvii.—2. Caius Julius Cæsar, the conqueror of Britain, and subsequently the first Roman Emperor. At the time of the conspiracy he was Prætor elect; and it was into his charge that Statilius was given; xlvii. 4 [akin to Sans. keça, "hair"].

Caius, i, m. *Caius;* a Roman prænomen; abbreviated C.

călămĭtas, ātis, f. *Misfortune, injury, mishap, disaster, calamity.*

călămĭt-ōsus, ōsa, ōsum, adj. [for călămĭtāt-ōsus; fr. călămĭtas,călămĭtāt-is,"calamity"] ("Full of *calamitas*"; hence) *Very calamitous, destructive, ruinous, or disastrous;*—at xlviii. 2 folld. by Dat. [§ 106, (3)].

călumnĭa, ĭæ, f. *Trickery, intrigue, artifice,* etc.

cămĕra, æ, f. *A vault, arched roof, arch* [καμάρα].

Cămers, tis, adj. *Of,* or *belonging to, Camerinum* (now *Camerino*), a town of Umbria in Italy.—As Subst.: **Cămers**, tis, m. *A man of Camerinum.*

campus, i, m.: 1. *An even place, a plain, a field.*—2.

The Campus Martius; a large grassy plain in Rome on the banks of the Tiber, originally the property of the Tarquinii, after whose expulsion it was dedicated to Mars ;—whence its name. It was used by the Romans for games, exercises, purposes of recreation, and military drill ; and was also the place where the Comitia Curiata were held ; xxvi. 5. [prob. akin to Gr. κῆπος, " a garden "].

căn-is, is, comm. gen. *A dog* [akin to Sans. çvan; Gr. κύων, κύν-ος, " a dog "; Germ. hun-d; Eng. " houn-d "].

căno, cĕcĭni, cantum, cănĕre, 3. v. n. (" To utter *or* produce melodious notes; to sound, sing, play "; hence) Of signals : With instrument or signal as Subject : *To be sounded* or *given*; lix. 1 [akin to Sans. root CAMS, " to praise, to relate "].

căp-esso (-isso), essīvi *or* essĭi, essītum, essĕre, 3. v. a. desid. [căp-ĭo, " to take "] (" To take, catch at, *or* seize eagerly"; hence) Of the state, public affairs, *etc.* : *To undertake, engage in, occupy one's self with,* in a zealous or earnest manner.

căpĭo, cēpi, captum, căpĕre, 3. v. a. : 1. *To take, lay hold of, etc.* :—capere arma, *to take up arms,* xxvii. 4.—2. a. Of a city, *etc.* : *To take* by force of arms, *to capture.*—b. Of persons : *To take prisoner* in battle, *etc.*—3. Of a design, plan, *etc.*: *To take up, form, frame, entertain.*—4. *To ensnare, catch,* etc., by wiles, artifices, *etc.*—5. Of love : *To captivate, enchain,* etc., a person.—6. Of an office, the state, *etc.*: *To take upon one's self, undertake, enter upon* the management of, *etc.* —Pass.: **căpĭor,** captus sum, căpi.

căpĭt-ālis, āle, adj. [căput, căpĭt-is, " the head "; hence, " the life "] (" Relating to *caput*"; hence) Law t. t.: *Capital, involving the forfeiture of life.*

Căpĭt-o, ōnis, m. [căput, căpĭt-is, " a head "] (" One with a large head ") *Capito* (*Publius Gabinius*); a Roman knight, one of Catiline's accomplices; xvii. 3. He was strangled in prison. Cicero, in his orations against Catiline (iii. 3 sqq. : iv. 6), calls him P. Gabinius Cimber.

Căpĭtōlĭum, ĭi, n. *The Capitol:* the temple of Jupiter at Rome built on the summit of Mons Saturnius or Tarpeius. Hither the new Consuls were conducted with great pomp by the Senate and people on the first day of January in each year, when they offered up their vows and sacrificed, each of them, an ox to Jupiter: after this they entered on their office; see Kalendæ. The Capitol was burnt on three occasions: viz.: 1. B.C. 83, during the troubles consequent upon the struggle between Sylla and Marius; after which it was rebuilt by Sylla and dedicated by Catŭlus. It is to this destruction of it that Sallust refers at xlvii. 2.—2. A.D. 70, by the soldiers of Vitellius. Vespasian rebuilt it.—3. A.D. 80, in the brief reign of Titus, during a conflagration that raged at Rome for three days and three nights. Domitian re-erected it in a very magnificent way.—N.B. Capitolium is not used in the present work in the meaning of the Capitoline Hill.

căpĭundus (căpĭendus), a, um, Gerundive of capio.

cap-to, tāvi, tātum, tāre, 1. v. a. intens. [cap-ĭo, "to seize"] ("To strive to seize, to catch at," *etc.; hence) To strive after, endeavour or seek to obtain, grasp at.*

captus, a, um, P. perf. pass. of capio.

Căpŭa, æ, f. *Capua* (now the village of *Santa Maria); the chief city of Campania, noted for its luxury;—at xxx. 2 Capuæ* is Gen. of name of a town, in sing. number of 1st decl. [§ 121, B, *b*]: at xxx. 9 is Acc. of motion to a place [§ 101].

carcer, ĕris, m. ("An enclosed place"; hence) *A prison* [Sicilian κάρκἄρ-ον, akin to ἕρκ-ος, and Lat. arc-eo].

căr-ĕo, ŭi, ĭtum, ēre, 2. v. n. ("To shear *or* be shorn"; hence) With Abl. [§ 119, b.]: *To be without, to do without.*

carp-tim, adv. [carp-o, "to pluck"] ("By a plucking"; hence) *In separate or small portions; separately, piecemeal.*

Carthāgĭnĭenses, ĭum; see Carthago.

Carthāgo, ĭnis, f. ("New Town") *Carthage; a city of Northern Africa, long the rival of Rome, and represented as having been built by Dido, after she had fled from Tyre. It was destroyed by Scipio Africanus the Younger at the close of the third Carthaginian War, B.C. 146.—Hence* **Carthāgĭn-ĭensis, ĭense, adj.** *Of, or belonging to, Carthage; Carthaginian.— As* Subst.: **Carthāgĭnĭenses, ĭum, m. plur.** *The people of Carthage, the Carthaginians.*

că-rus, ra, rum, adj.: With Dat. [§ 106, (3)]: *Beloved by, dear or precious to, esteemed or regarded by.* ☞ Comp. cār-ĭor [for cam-rus; akin to Sans. root KAM, "to love"].

Casslus, ĭi, m. [cass-es, "a hunting-net"] ("One pertaining to *casses;* One with a hunting-net"] *Cassĭus;* a Roman name; see Longīnus.

castra, ōrum, n. plur. *A camp* or *encampment,* as containing several soldiers' tents or huts [prob. for skad-trum; akin to Sans. root SKAD, "to cover"].

că-sus, sūs, m. [for cad-sus; fr. cad-o, "to fall"; hence, "to fall out, happen"] ("A falling out *or* happening"; hence) 1. *Chance, accident,* etc.—2. *A misfortune, mishap, calamity, adverse* or *unfortunate state* or *condition.*

caterva, æ, f.: 1. *A band* or *crowd* of persons.—2. *A military troop, company,* etc.

Cătĭlīna, æ, m. *Catiline* (*Lucius Sergius);* a descendant of an ancient patrician family which had become impoverished. His character, as drawn by Sallust, presents a loathsome picture of extravagance, vice, and the deepest crimes. He was engaged in two conspiracies against his country. The first, as briefly described in xviii., took place B.C. 65, and proved wholly unsuccessful, apparently through his precipitancy. The second was in the year of Cicero's consulship, B.C. 63; and it is this which Sallust describes in this present work.—Hence Cătĭlīn-ārĭus, ārĭa, ārĭum, adj. *Of,* or *belonging to, Catiline; Catilinarian, Catiline-.*

Cătĭlīnārĭus, a, um; see Catilina.

Căt-o, ōnis, m. [căt-us, "sharp, intelligent"] ("Sharp *or* Intelligent One") *Cato* (*Marcus Porcius);* a great-grandson of Cato the Censor. He is generally known as Cato Uticensis from his having killed himself at Utica after the battle of Thapsus (B.C. 46), when Scipio Metellus, disregarding his advice, was signally routed, and all Africa, Utica excepted, submitted to Cæsar.

Cătŭlus, i, m. [cătŭlus, "a cub, whelp"] *Catulus* (*Quintus);* a Roman senator, who read in the Senate a letter which he had received from Catiline after the outbreak of the conspiracy, and which is given in ch. xxxv.

causa, æ, f.: 1. *A cause, reason :*—eā causā, *for that reason, on that account.*—2. Adverbial Abl., folld. by Gen. or Gerund in di: *For the sake* or *purpose of.*—3. *A cause* in law, *a law-suit.*

căvendum, Gerund in dum fr. caveo.

căvĕo, cāvi, cautum, căvēre, 2. v. n.: 1. *To be on* one's, etc., *guard; to take heed, care, or precaution; to be cautious; to beware.*—**2.** Folld. by ab : *To be on* one's, etc., *guard* against, *to beware of.*—**3.** With simple Subj., ne being omitted [§ 154]; (in this construction only in imperat.): *To take heed that, to beware lest.*

cecidissem, pluperf. subj. of cado.

cēd-o, cessi, cessum, cēdĕre, 3. v. n.: **1.** *To go, go along.* —**2.** *To go away, retire, depart, withdraw.*—**3.** *To turn out, issue, eventuate, result.* —**4.** With Dat.: *To yield, give way, submit to* [Gr. root χαδ, whence χάζομαι (i. e. χάδ-σομαι), "to retire"].

cĕlĕbr-o, āvi, ātum, āre, 1. v. a. [cĕlĕber, cĕlĕbr-is, "renowned"] ("To make *celeber*"; hence) *To render renowned* or *famous; to celebrate.*

Celer, ĕris, m. [celer, "swift"] *Celer;* a cognomen of Quintus Metellus; see Metellus.

cĕlĕr-ĭtas, ĭtātis, f. [cĕler, "quick"] ("The quality of the *celer*"; hence) *Swiftness, speed, quickness, celerity;*— at xliv. 4 of quickness of action.

censĕo, ŭi, um, ēre, 2. v.a. ("To reckon *or* count"; hence) **1.** *To be of opinion, reckon, consider,* etc.;—at lii. 26 folld.

by simple Subj. [§ 154].—**2.** Political t. t.: With Objective clause: **a.** *To vote that* or *for.* —**b.** Of the Senate : *To decree, resolve, ordain.*

cens-or, ōris, m. [cens-ĕo, "to value, *or* assess" property] ("One who values " property; hence) *A Censor.* The Censors were Roman magistrates, who originally had the charge of the people so far only as their property was concerned, and who classified them according to the value of their possessions. Gradually however they attained a power which extended to the superintendence of morals and conduct in general. They also let out the public tolls, made contracts for the erection or repairs of public edifices, and procured victims for the public sacrifices. At first the Censors, who were two in number, were elected for five years : but afterwards a law was passed that they should be chosen every five years, but continue in power only for a year and a half.

censŭĕram, pluperf. ind. of censeo.

centum, num. adj. indecl. *A hundred* [akin to Sans. *çatan;* Gr. ἔκατον].

centŭrĭ-o, ōnis, m. [centŭrĭ-a, "a century" or division of troops in the Roman armies, originally, though not always, containing 100 men] ("One having—*i. e.* commanding—a *centuria*") *A centurion.*

cēpĕrim, perf. subj. of capio.

cerno, crēvi, crētum, cernĕre, 3. v. a. ("To separate or sift"; hence) *To see, perceive,* whether by the eye or the mind;—at lxi. 1 the second person sing. of Subj. mood (cerneres) is used indefinitely in the force of the Eugl. "one"; French, "on" [root CER or CER; akin to Gr. κρί-νω; Sans. root KRI, "to separate"].

certā-men, mǐnis, n. [cert(a)-o, "to contend"] ("That which contends"; hence) 1. *A contest, fight, battle, engagement,* etc.—2. *A contest, dispute,* etc.

cert-e, adv. [cert-us, "sure"] ("After the manner of the *certus*"; hence) *Surely, assuredly, certainly* :—certe scio, *I know assuredly* or *certainly, I am sure* or *convinced.*

cer-to, tāvi, tātum, tāre, 1. v. n. intens. [fr. CER, root of cerno, in force of "to fight"] 1. a. *To fight, contend, struggle.* —b. Impers. Pass.: certatur, (*It is fought,* i. e.) *The battle is waged;* Hist. pres.—2. *To contend, struggle, put forth efforts* for one's own purposes. —3. With cum : In a good sense : *To vie with, to emulate,* etc.; ix. 2.

cer-tus, ta, tum, adj. [fr. CER-, root of cer-no, "to decide"] ("Decided"; hence) *Sure, certain.* — As Subst.: certum, ǐ, n. *A certainty* ;— at xvii. 6 in plur. :—pro certo, *for* or *as a certainty,* xv. 2, etc.

cētĕra, ōrum; cĕtĕri, ōrum; see cētĕrus.

ceterum, adv. [adverbial neut. acc. of ceterus, "the rest"] ("As to the rest *or* what remains"; hence, "in other respects, otherwise"; hence) 1. *Besides, moreover.—* 2. *But, yet, notwithstanding, still.*

c-ētĕr-us, a, um, adj.: 1. Sing. (rare): *The rest* or *remainder of* that denoted by the subst. to which it is in attribution.—2. Plur.: *The rest of* that denoted by the subst. to which it is in attribution; *the remaining, the other.* —As Subst.: a. cĕtĕri, ōrum, m. plur. *The rest of* or *the remaining persons; the rest, the others.*—b. cētĕra, ōrum, n. plur. *The rest of* or *the remaining things* [prob. demonstr. particle ce; Sans. pron. itar-a, "the other"].

Cĕthēgus, i, m. *Cethegus* (*Caius*); one of Catiline's accomplices. The part assigned to him by Lentulus, under whose orders he was placed, was the attempted murder of Cicero; xliii. 2. He was one of those who were strangled in the Tullianum; lv. 6.

Cicer-o, ōnis, m. [cicer, "a chick-pea "] (" One having a *cicer*": i. e. either marked with a spot resembling one, or skilled in raising this species of pulse) *Cicero* (*Marcus Tullius*); the greatest of the Roman orators and writers, born at Arpīnum, 3rd January, B.C. 106; murdered by the soldiers of Mark Antony, B.C. 43. He was consul B.C. 63 in conjunction with C. Antonius (xxiv.1), and by his prompt and decisive measures saved Rome from the terrible consequences that would have ensued had Catiline's conspiracy proved successful.

Cimbr-Icus, Ĭca, Ĭcum, adj. [Cimbr-i, "the Cimbri," a people of Northern Germany, who in conjunction with the Teutŏnes invaded the South of Europe and defeated six Roman generals and their armies. They were conquered by Marius, B.C. 101, in the Raudii Campi, near Verona] *Of*, or *pertaining to, the Cimbri ; Cimbric : —* bellum Cimbricum, *the Cimbric war* (lix. 3); see above.

Cinna, æ, m. *Cinna* (*Lucius Cornelius*); a Roman patrician, who was consul B.C. 87, and was unconstitutionally deposed from his consulate by the senate. Hereupon he fled from Rome and raised an army with which he invested it by land, while Marius, returning from Africa, blockaded it on the sea-side. Upon the capture of the city the friends of Sulla were ruthlessly massacred; see Marius and Sulla.

circ-Ĭter, adv. [circ-us, " a circle "] With words denoting time *or* number : *About, near, much about, not far from.—* N.B. An Abl. or Acc. is often found in connexion with circiter, but independent of it as to construction.

circum, adv. *and* prep. [adverbial acc. of circus, "a ring "] (" In a ring "; hence) 1. Adv.: *Around, round about;* xxx.—**2.** Prep. gov. acc.: *Around, round about, all round.*

circum-eo, (circŭ-), īvi *or* ĭi, Ĭtum, īre, v. a. [circum, " around "; ĕo, " to go "] *To go around.*

circumeundo, Gerund in do fr. circumeo.

circum-fĕro, tŭli, lātum, ferre, 3. v. a. [circum, " around "; fĕro, " to carry "] *To carry around.*

circumĭens, ĕuntis, P. pres. of circumeo.

circumtŭlisse, perf. inf. of circumfĕro.

circum-vĕnĭo, vēni, ventum, vĕnīre, 4. v. a. [circum, " around "; vĕnĭo, " to come "]

("To come around"; hence) 1. *To surround, encompass;—* at lviii. 20 without Acc. of nearer Object.—2. With accessory notion of hostility: *To surround, beset.*—3. *To oppress, beset, distress,* etc.—4. *To circumvent, deceive, cheat, defraud.* — Pass.: circumvĕnĭor, ventus sum, vĕnīri.

circumventus, a, um, P. perf. pass. of circumvenĭo.

cĭ-ter, tra, trum, adj. [for cis-ter; fr. cis, "on this side"] *On this side, hither.* ☞ Comp.: cĭtĕr-ĭor; (Sup.: cĭtĭmus).

cĭtérĭor, us; see cĭter.

cĭt-o, adv. [cĭt-us, "quick"] ("After the manner of the *citus*"; hence) *Quickly, soon, speedily.*

cĭ-tus, ta, tum, adj. [cĭ-ĕo, "to put in motion"] ("Put in motion"; hence) *Quick, rapid.*

cīv-ĭlis, īle, adj. [cīv-is, "a citizen"] *Of, or pertaining to, a citizen or to citizens; civil.*

1. cīvis, is, comm. gen. ("A dweller"; hence) 1. *A citizen,* as a dweller in a city.—2. *A fellow-citizen, fellow-countryman;* xliv. 1 [akin to Sans. root KSHI, "to dwell"].

2. cīvīs = cives, acc. plur. of 1. civis.

cīv-ĭtas, ĭtātis, f. [civ-is, "a citizen"] ("The condition of a *civis*"; hence, "citizenship"; hence) 1. *A state, commonwealth.—*2. *The people of a state, citizens.*

clā-des, dis, f. ("A breaking" to pieces; hence) 1. *Injury, mischief, disaster,* etc.; xxxix. 4.—2. *Slaughter, massacre,* etc. [κλά-ω, "to break"].

clămor, ōris, m. [clām-o, "to cry out"] *Outcry, clamour, shout,* etc.

clārissĭmus, a, um, sup. adj.; see clārus.

clā-rus, ra, rum, adj. [akin to clŭ-ĕo, "to hear"] ("Heard"; hence) 1. *Celebrated, renowned, famous, illustrious.—*2. *Evident, manifest, clear, plain,* etc. ☞ (Comp.: clār-ĭor); Sup.: clārissĭmus.

clau-do, si, sum, dĕre, 3. v. a. ("To shut" something that is open, "to close"; hence) 1. *To shut, enclose, encompass, surround.*—2. *To shut up, conceal, keep close* in the breast, etc.; x. 5.—Pass.: claudor, sus sum, di [akin to κλεί-ω, "to shut"].

clausus, a, um, P. perf. pass. of claudo.

clĭ-ens, entis, comm. gen. [for clu-ens, which is also found; fr. clŭ-ĕo, "to hear"] ("The hearing one"; hence) 1. At Rome: *A client.*—2. Of foreign nations: *A retainer, dependant, adherent.*

Cn., abbrev. of Cneius.

Cneĭus, ĭi, m. *Cneius;* a Roman prænomen.

cŏæquandus, a, um, Gerundive of coæquo.

cŏ-æquo, æquāvi, æquātum, æquāre, 1. v. a. [co (= cum), "with"; æquo, "to make equal *or* even"] ("To make" one thing "equal *or* even" with another; hence) *To even, level.*

cŏ-ălesco, ălŭi, ălĭtum, ălescĕre, 3. v. n. [co (= cum), "together"; alesco, "to grow"] ("To grow together"; hence) *To unite in one body; to become united, join together firmly.*

cŏălŭĕrim, perf. subj. of coalesco.

cŏ-argŭo, argŭi, no sup., argŭĕre, 3. v. a. [co (= cum), in "strengthening" force; argŭo, "to convict"] *To convict, prove guilty.*

cœl-um, i, n. ("The hollow *or* vaulted thing"; hence) *Heaven, the heavens, the sky:* —ad cœlum tollere *or* ferre, (to *lift or bear to the heavens;* i. e.) *to exalt or extol to the skies;* xlviii. 1; liii. 1 [akin to κοῖλ-ος, "hollow"].

cœp-i (pres. cœpĭo, *etc.,* ante-class.), isse, v. def. a. and n. [contr. fr. co-apĭo; fr. co. (= cum), in "intensive" force; ap-io, "to lay hold of"] 1. *To begin.* — 2. With pres. inf. as a circum-

locution for the imperf. ind. of such inf., with the concomitant notion of some duration; pollicēri cœpit = pollicebātur; see polliceor.

cŏ-ercĕo, ercŭi, ercĭtum, ercēre, 2. v. a. [for co-arcĕo; fr. co (= cum), in "intensive" force; arcĕo, "to enclose"] ("To enclose wholly"; hence) *To restrain, check, curb, keep within bounds,* etc.

cōg-ĭto, ĭtāvi, ĭtātum, ĭtāre, 1. v. a. [contr. fr. cŏ-ăgĭto; fr. co (= cum), in "augmentative" force; ăgĭto, "to revolve,"* etc.,* in the mind] 1. *To revolve thoroughly; to weigh or ponder well; to think.*—2. *To plan, purpose, meditate.*

co-gnă-tus, ta, tum, adj. [co (= cum), "with"; gnascor (= na-scor), "to be born"] ("Born with" another; hence) *Connected by birth, related by blood.*—As Subst.: **cognātus,** i, m. *A blood-relation, kinsman,* either on the father's or the mother's side.

cognĭtus, a, um, P. perf. pass. of cognosco.

co-gnosco, gnōvi, gnĭtum, gnoscĕre, 3. v. a. [co (= cum), in "augmentative" force; gnosco (= nosco), "to become acquainted with"] ("To become acquainted with on all sides"; hence) 1. *To become thoroughly acquainted* *with, learn, ascertain.*—2. In perf. tenses: *To have know-ledge of, to know.*—3. *To recognize* a person or thing already known; lxi. 8.—4. *To examine* or *investigate* judic-ially a case, *etc.*, at law.—Pass.: co-gnoscor,gnītus sum, gnosci.

cognōvĕram, cognōvĕrim, pluperf. ind. and subj. of cognosco.

cŏhors, tis, f. ("An enclosed place"; hence, "a multitude enclosed," *etc.*, in a place; hence) *A cohort;* the tenth part of a Roman legion.

cŏhortātus, a, um, P. perf. of cŏhortor.

cŏhortīs = cohortes, acc. plur. of cohors.

cŏ-hortor, hortātus sum, hortāri, 1. v. dep. [co (= cum), in "strengthening" force; hortor, "to exhort"] *To ex-hort earnestly; to encourage, animate.*

cŏlendo, Gerund in do fr. colo.

col-lēg-a, æ, m. [for con-lēg-a; fr. con (= cum), "to-gether with"; lĕg-o, "to choose"] ("One chosen to-gether with *or* at the same time with" another; hence) *A partner in office, a col-league.*

col-lībet (col-lŭbet, con-lŭbet), lībŭit, lībĭtum est, v. impers. [con (= cum), in "strengthening" force; lĭbet, "it pleases"] With Dat. [§ 106, (3)] *It pleases,* or *is agree-able to.* — N. B. Impersonal verbs sometimes take a neut. pron. sing. as Subject; but at li. 9 a neut. plur. (quæ) is used, and the verb is in 3rd pers. plur.

collĭbuissent, 3. pers. plur. pluperf. subj. of collĭbet.

collŏcātus, a, um, P. perf. pass. of colloco.

col-lŏco, lŏcāvi, lŏcātum, lŏcāre, 1. v. a. [for con-lŏco; fr. con (= cum), in "intensive" force; lŏco, "to place"] *To place, post,* or *station* any-where.—Pass.: col-lŏcor, lŏc-ātus sum, lŏcāri.

cŏlo, cŏlŭi, cultum, cŏlĕre, 3. v. a. ("To abide *or* dwell, in" a place; hence) 1. *To till,* or *cultivate,* the ground. —2. Morally: *To cultivate, attend to, practise,* etc.—Pass.: cŏlor, cultus sum, cŏli.

cŏlōn-ĭa, ĭæ, f. [colōn-us, "a colonist"] ("A thing pertaining to a *colonus*"; hence) *A colony.*

cŏl-ōnus, ōni, m. [col-o, "to inhabit"] ("An inhabit-ant"; hence) *An inhabitant of a colony, a colonist.*

cŏlor, ōris, m. ("Colour"; hence) *Natural colour, com-plexion.*

cŏmĭtā-tus, tūs, m. [com-it(a)-or, "to accompany, attend "] ("An accompanying, attending"; hence) *A retinue, train, suite,* etc.;—at xlv. 1 in plur.

cŏm-I-tĭum, tĭī, n. [com (= cum), "together" : I, root of eo, "to go"] ("A going, *or* coming, together"; hence, "the comitium," *i. e.* the place for the assembling of the Romans when voting by Curiæ; hence) Plur.: *The Comitia,* i. e. the assembly of the Romans for the election of magistrates, *etc.*

commĕă-tus, tūs, m. (com-mĕ(a)-o, "to go to and fro"] ("A going to and fro"; hence, "a caravan, train," *etc.;* hence) *Provisions, supplies,* etc., as brought by a caravan, *etc.*

commĕmŏrando, Gerund in do fr. commemoro.

com-mĕmŏro, mĕmŏrāvi, mĕmŏrātum, mĕmŏrāre, 1. v. a. [com (= cum), in "augmentative" force; mĕmŏro, "to mention"] *To make mention of, recount, speak of, relate.*

commendă-tĭo, tĭōnis, f. [commend(a)-o, "to commend, recommend"] ("A commending," etc.; hence) *Commendation, recommendation.*

com-mendo, mendāvi, mendātum, mendāre, 1. v. a. [for com-mando; fr. com (= cum), in "augmentative" force; mando, "to commit"] ("To

commit, *or* entrust, thoroughly"; hence) *To commit, entrust, confide, commend* a person to one's care, *etc.*

com-mĭnus (cō-), adv. [com (= cum), "together"; mănus, "hand"] ("Hands together"; hence) *Hand to hand, in close fight* or *contest, at close quarters.*

commĭsĕram, pluperf. ind. of committo.

com-mitto, mīsi, missum, mittĕre, 3. v. a. [com (= cum), "together"; mitto, "to cause to go"] ("To cause to go together"; hence) 1. Of battle : *To engage in, join, commence.* —2. With Dat. [§ 106, (3)]: *To trust, entrust.*—Pass.: committor, missus sum, mitti.

commŏd-o, āvi, ātum, āre, 1. v. a. [commŏd-um, "advantage"] ("To give to another for his advantage," etc.; hence) *To give, supply, furnish,* etc.;—at xvi. 2 commodare is the Hist. Inf. [§ 140, 2].

commŏd-um, i, n. [commŏdus, "convenient"; "advantageous"] ("A convenient thing; an advantageous thing"; hence) 1. *A convenient condition, convenience.* —2. *Advantage, profit, benefit.*

commŏrātus, a, um, P. perf. of commoror.

com-mŏror, mŏrātus sum, mŏrāri, 1. v. dep. [com (= cum), in "strengthening"

force; mŏror, "to delay"]
*To stop, stay, sojourn, tarry,
linger;*—at xxxvi. 1 folld. by
Acc. of Duration of Time
[§ 102, (1)].

commŏtus, a, um, P. perf.
pass. of commoveo.

com-mŏvĕo, mōvi, mōtum,
mŏvēre, 2. v. a. [com (= cum),
in "intensive" force; moveo,
"to move"] ("To move greatly
or violently"; hence) *To rouse,
excite,* etc. — Pass.: com-
mŏvĕor, mōtus sum, mŏvēri.

commūnĭcātus, a, um, P.
perf. pass. of communico:—
communicato consilio, Abl.
Abs. [§ 125], xviii. 5.

commūn-ĭco, ĭcāvi, ĭcātum,
ĭcāre, 1. v. a. [commūn-is,
"common"] ("To do, *or* have,
in common" with another;
hence) 1. *To communicate,
impart.*—2. With cum: *To
share with,* etc.—Pass.: com-
mūn-ĭcor, ĭcātus sum, ĭcāri.

com-mūnis, mūne, adj. [com
(= cum), "together"; munis,
"serving"] ("Serving together"; hence) *Common.*

compărătus, a, um, P. perf.
pass. of comparo.

com-păro, părāvi, părātum,
părāre, 1. v. a. [com (= cum),
"together"; păro, "to bring
or put"] ("To bring, *or* put,
together"; hence) 1. *To make
or get ready, prepare.*—2. *To
provide,* etc.—Pass.: com-
păror, părātus sum, părāri.

com-pĕr-ĭo, i, tŭm, īre, 4.
v. a. [com (= cum), in "augmentative" force; root PER,
akin -to per-ior, "to pass
through"] ("To go, *or* pass,
through" a thing; hence) *To
find out accurately; to ascertain, discover, learn;*—at ii. 2
compertum est has for its
Subject the clause, in bello . . .
posse [§ 156, (3)].—Pass.:
com-pĕr-ĭor, tus sum, īri.

compertus, a, um, P. perf.
pass. of comperio.—Phrases:
a. Compertum aliquid habere
(*to have something found out
or ascertained;* i. e.) *to have
found out or ascertained something;*—at xxix. 1 compertum
is in attribution to the clause,
neque exercitus . . . foret; at
lviii. 1 to the clause verba,
virtutem non addere.—b. Compertum est, *etc.,* alicui (*it has
been ascertained,* etc., *by some
one;* i. e.) *some one has ascertained,* etc.

com-plĕo, plēvi, plētum,
plēre, 2. v. a. [com (= cum),
in "augmentative" force;
plĕo, "to fill"] 1. *To fill completely or entirely; to fill up;*
—sometimes with Abl. [§ 119,
b].—2. Military t. t.: *To
make* an army or a division of
it *of the full number, to fill
up, complete.*—Pass.: com-
plĕor, plētus sum, plēri.

complexus, ūs, m. [for com-
plect-sus; fr. complect-or, "t‹

embrace"] ("An embracing"; hence) *An embrace.*

com-plūres, plūra (and, sometimes, plūrĭa), adj. [com (= cum), in "augmentative" force; plūres, "very many"] *Very many, several.*—As Subst.: m. *Very many, or several, persons.*

compŏsĭt-e, adv. [compŏsĭt-us, in force of "fitly ordered," etc.] ("After the manner of the *compositus*"; hence) *In a fit, or well ordered, way; skilfully,* etc.

comprŏbātus, a, um, P. perf. pass. of comprobo.

com-prŏbo, prŏbāvi, prŏbātum, prŏbāre, 1. v. a. [com (= cum), in "intensive" force; probo, "to approve of"] ("To approve of" something "thoroughly"; *to assent to,* etc.; hence) *To prove, attest, establish, confirm.*—Pass.: comprŏbor, ātus sum, āri.

con-cēdo, cessi, cessum, cēdĕre, 3. v. a. [con (= cum), in "intensive" force; cēdo, "to yield"] *To yield, give up, resign one's self or itself;* xx. 7.

concessi, perf. ind. of concēdo.

con-cĭdo, cĭdi, no sup., cĭdĕre, 3. v. n. [for con-cădo; fr. con (= cum), in "augmentative" force; cădo, "to fall"] ("To fall utterly"; hence, "to fall to the ground, fall *or* tumble down"; hence) *To fall* in battle.

concĭ-o, ōnis, f. [concĭ-o *or* concĭ-ĕo, "to collect together, assemble"] ("A collecting together, assembling"; hence) 1. *An assembly, meeting.*—2. *A speech, harangue* before a public assembly.

concĭtandus, a, um, Gerundive of concito.

concĭtātus, a, um, P. perf. pass. of concito.

concĭ-to, tāvi, tātum, tāre, 1. v. a. [conci-eo, "to rouse"] 1. *To rouse greatly.*—2. *To rouse, stir up, instigate to a revolt,* etc.; xlvi. 3.—3. *To excite, stir up, exasperate,* etc. —Pass.: concĭ-tor, tātus sum, tāri.

con-clāmo, clāmāvi, clāmātum, clāmāre, 1. v. a. [con (=cum), in "intensive" force; clāmo, "to cry out"] *To cry out aloud; to exclaim, shout out.*

1. **concord-ĭa, ĭæ,** f. [concors, concord-is, "with the same *or* like hearts"; hence, "united" in sentiment or feeling, etc.] ("The quality of the *concors*"; hence) 1. *Unanimity, harmony, concord.*—2. Personified as a goddess: *Concord;*—at xlix. 4 supply templum *or* ædem before Concordiæ [§ 127, *a*].

2. **Concordĭa, æ;** see 1. concordia, no. 2.

con-cŭpi-sco, cŭpīvi *or* cŭpĭi, cŭpītum, cŭpiscĕre, 3. v. a. inch. [con (= cum), in "intensive" force; cŭpĭ-o, "to desire"] *To become very desirous of; to long for, strive after, covet.*

concupīvĕram, concŭpīvi, pluperf. and perf. ind. of concupisco.

con-curro, curri (rarely cŭcurri), cursum, currĕre, 3. v. n. [con (= cum), "together"; curro, "to run"] 1. *To run together* or *in a body.—2. To flock in crowds*, etc.—3. Military t. t.: *To rush together* or *to meet one another* in battle; *to join battle, fight.*

concussĕram, pluperf. ind. of concutio.

con-cŭtĭo, cussi, cussum, cŭtĕre, 3. v. a. [for con-quătĭo; fr. con (= cum), in "intensive" force; quătĭo, "to shake"]("To shake violently"; hence) *To terrify, alarm, agitate*, etc.—Pass.: con-cŭtĭor, cussus sum, cŭti.

condemnātus, a, um, P. perf. pass. of condemno.—As Subst.: condemnāti, ōrum, m. plur. *The condemned.*

con-demno, demnāvi, demnātum, demnāre, 1. v. a. [for con-demno; fr. con (= cum), in "strengthening" force; damno, "to condemn"] With Gen. of charge [§ 133]: *To condemn, sentence on a charge of, to convict of;* xxxvi. 3.—Pass.: con-demnor, demnātus sum, demnāri.

condĭdi, perf. ind. of condo.

cond-ĭtĭo, ĭtĭonis, f. [cond-o, "to put together"] ("A putting together"; hence) 1. *State*, or *condition*, of a person or thing.—2. *An agreement, terms, conditions.*

condĭtus, a, um, P. perf. pass. of condor.

con-do, dĭdi, dĭtum, dĕre, 3. v. a. [con (= cum), "together"; do, "to put"] ("To put together"; hence) Of a city, state, etc.: *To build, found.*—Pass.: con-dor, dĭtus sum, di.

con-dōno, dōnāvi, dōnātum, dōnāre, 1. v. a. [con (= cum), in "strengthening" force; dono, "to give"] ("To give, make a present of" something; hence) Of an offence, crime, etc.: *To pardon, forgive, condone.*

con-dūco, duxi, ductum, dūcĕre, 3. v. a. [con (= cum), "together"; dūco, "to lead"] ("To lead together"; hence, in business matters, "to take to one's self by hiring"; i. e.) *To hire.*—Pass.: con-dūcor, ductus sum, dūci.

conductus, a, um, P. perf. pass. of conduco.

confectus, a, um, P. perf. pass. of confĭcĭo:—confecto proelio, *when the battle was over*, lxi. 1: Abl. Abs. [§ 125].

confertissŭmus, a, um; see confertus.

confer-tus, ta, tum, adj. [for conferc-tus; fr. conferc-io, "to cram, *or* press close, together"] ("Crammed, *or* pressed close, together"; hence) *Crowded together, in a close body:*—in confertissumos hostes, (*into the enemy most crowded together;* i.e.) *into the thickest (part) of the enemy,* lx. 6. ☞ (Comp.: confert-ĭor); Sup.: confert-issŭmus.

confessus, a, um, P. perf. of confiteor;—at li. 36 supply eis with confessis [§ 158].

con-fĭcĭo, fēcĭ, fectum, fĭcĕre, 3. v. a. [for con-făcĭo; fr. con, in "augmentative" force; facio, "to make"] ("To make thoroughly"; hence) 1. *To execute, effect, complete, accomplish.*—2. *To bring to an end,* etc.—Pass.: con-fĭcĭor, fectus sum, fĭci.

con-fīdo, fisus sum, fīdĕre, 3. v. a. *and* n. semi-dep. [con (= cum), in "intensive" force; fīdo, "to trust"] With Objective clause: 1. Act.: *To be persuaded,* or *confident, that;* xvii. 7.—2. Neut.: *To rely upon, trust to, confide in,* etc.:—with Dat. [§ 106, (3)] xvi. 4; lii. 28.

confirmātus, a, um, P. perf. pass. of confirmo:—confirmato animo, Abl. Abs. [§ 125], xlvi. 3.

con-firm-o, āvi, ātum, āre, ¹. v. a. [con (= cum), in "aug-mentative" force; firm-us, "strong"] ("To make very strong"; hence) 1. *To strengthen,* whether actually or figuratively. — 2. Of an alliance, confederacy, etc.: *To ratify, confirm.*—3. *To encourage, make bold,* etc.:—confirmare animum, (*to encourage one's mind;* i. e.) *to take heart* or *courage.*—Pass.: con-firm-or, ātus sum, āri.

confīsus, a, um, P. perf. of confīdo;—at xvii. 6 supply esse with confisum, which is in that place a verb [§ 158].

con-fĭtĕor, fessus sum, fĭtēri, 2. v. dep. [for con-fateor; fr. con (= cum), in "augmentative" force; fateor, "to own"] *To own, confess, allow, acknowledge.*

con-flīgo, flixi, flictum, flīg-ĕre, 3. v. n. [con (= cum), "together"; flīgo, "to dash"] ("To dash together"; hence) *To come,* or *enter, into conflict; to engage, contend.*

con-flo, flāvi, flātum, flāre, 1. v. a. [con (= cum), "together"; flo, "to blow"] ("To blow together"; hence, "to bring about, cause, effect"; hence) 1. Of debt: *To incur, contract.*—2. Of ill-will, *etc.: To kindle, inflame, stir up, excite,* etc.

con-flŭo, fluxi, no sup., flŭĕre, 3. v. n. [con (= cum), "together"; flŭo, "to flow"]

(Of liquids: "To flow to-gether"; hence) Of persons: *To flow, flock,* or *crowd to-gether.*

con-fŏdĭo, fŏdi, fossum, fŏdĕre, 3. v. a. [con (= cum), in "intensive" force; fŏdĭo, " to dig "] ("To dig tho-roughly"; hence) *To run,* or *pierce, through; to trans-fix.*—Pass.: con-fŏdĭor, fossus sum, fŏdi.

conjēcĕram, pluperf. ind. of conjicio.

con-jĭcĭo, jēci, jectum, jĭcĕre, 3. v. a. [for con-jăcĭo; fr. con (= cum), in "augmentative" force; jăcĭo, "to cast "] *To throw, cast,* etc.:—in vincula conjicere, *to throw into prison,* xlii. 3.

conjŭrā-tĭo, tĭōnis, f. [con-jur(a)-o, "to swear together"; hence, "to conspire, plot "] 1. *A conspiracy, plot.*—2. *A band,* or *body, of conspirators.*

conjŭrātus, a, um, P. perf. pass. of conjūro.—As Subst.: conjurāti, ōrum, m. plur. *Conspirators.*

con-jūro, jūrāvi, jūrātum, jūrāre, 1. v. a. *and* n. [con (= cum), "together"; juro, "to swear "] ("To swear to-gether"; hence) In bad sense: 1. Act.: With Inf.: *To con-spire to do,* etc.; lii. 24.—2. Neut.: *To form a plot* or *conspiracy; to plot, conspire;* xviii. 1

conscĭent-ĭa, ĭæ, f. [con-sciens, conscient-is, "being conscious "] 1. *Consciousness.* —2. *Conscience.*

con-scĭ-us, a, um, adj. [con (= cum), "with "; scĭ-o, "to know "] 1. *Knowing,* or *con-scious of,* something with another; *privy* or *accessory to, aware of;*—at xxii. 2; xxv. 4 with Gen. [§ 132] 2. a. *Knowing* something *with* or *within one's self, con-scious of something;* — at xxxiv. 2 with Gen. of thing and Dat. of person [§§ 132; 107].—b. *Conscious of guilt* (rare in this meaning, and mostly poetical); xiv. 3.

con-scrībo, scripsi, scrip-tum, scrībĕre, 3. v. a. [con (= cum), "together"; scrībo, "to write "] ("To write to-gether" in a list, *etc.;* hence) 1. Of soldiers (whose names were written down in a list, on their taking the military oath): *To enrol, enlist, levy.*— 2. Of enrolment in a particular class of citizens: *To enrol, appoint, choose, select.*— Pass.: con-scrībor, scriptus sum, scrībi.

conscripsĕram, pluperf. ind. of conscrībo.

conscriptus, a, um, P. perf. pass. of conscrībo.—As Subst.: conscripti, ōrum, m. plur. *The enrolled ;*—a term originally given to such Romans as

Brutus enrolled amongst the Senate to fill up the places of those whom Tarquin the Proud had put to death. See Patres Conscripti in pater.

consēdi, perf. ind. of con-sīdo.

con-sĕnesco, sĕnŭi, no sup., sĕnescĕre, 3. v. n. [con (= cum), in "strengthening" force; sĕnesco, "to grow old"] ("To become old"; hence) *To become weak, infirm, enfeebled.*

consĕnŭi, perf. ind. of con-senesco.

conservandus, a, um, Gerundive of conservo.

con-servo, servāvi, servātum, servāre, 1. v. a. [con (= cum), in "strengthening" force; servo, "to keep"] ("To keep thoroughly"; hence) *To keep safe or unharmed, to preserve.*

con-sīd-ĕro, ĕrāvi, ĕrātum, ĕrāre, 1. v. a.: 1. *To look closely at, examine, inspect.*— 2. *To observe* with the mind, *consider, think attentively of,* etc.;—at xx. 6 folld. by clause as Object.

con-sīdo, sēdi, sessum, sīdĕre, 3. v. n. [con (= cum), "together"; sīdo, "to sit down"] ("To sit down together"; hence) Of troops, etc.: *To encamp, pitch a camp, take up a station or position.*

consĭlĭum, ĭi, n.: 1. *De-*liberation, consultation, counsel.—2. *A plan, purpose, design.*—3. *Prudence, discretion.*—4. *A meeting* for deliberation; *a council,* etc.

conspexi, perf. ind. of con-spicio.

con-spĭcĭo, spexi, spectum, spĭcĕre, 3. v. a. [for con-spĕcĭo; fr. con (= cum), in "augmentative" force; spĕcĭo, "to see"] *To see, behold, observe.*—Pass.: con-spĭcĭor, spectus sum, spĭci.

constābat; see consto.

constant-er, adv. [constans, constant-is, in force of "uniform, harmonious"] ("After the manner of the *constans*"; hence) *Uniformly, harmoniously, consistently.* ☞ Comp. constant-ĭus.

constant-ĭa, ĭæ, f. [constans, constant-is, in force of "firm, constant"] ("The quality of the *constans*"; hence) *Firmness, constancy, steadfastness, consistency,* etc.

constĭtŭĕram, pluperf. ind. of constituo;—at xliii. 1 constituerant has for its Subject Lentulus cum ceteris = Lentulus et ceteri.

con-stĭtŭo, stĭtŭi, stĭtūtum, stĭtŭĕre, 3. v. a. [for con-statuo; fr. con (= cum); statŭo, "to place"] 1. [con, "together"] ("To place, or set, together"; hence) *To draw up* an army or fleet in order of battle.—2. [con, in "augmentative" force]: a. *To put, place, set, station.*—b. *To fix, appoint, etc.*—c. *To resolve, determine, decide, etc.* —Pass.: con-stĭtŭor, stĭtūtus sum, stĭtŭi.

constĭtūtus, a, um, P. perf. pass. of constituo.

con-sto, stĭti, stātum, stāre, 1. v. n. [con (= cum), in "augmentative" force; sto, "to stand"] ("To stand firm"; hence) Of facts, reports, etc.: *To be established, certain, clear, evident.*—Impers.: constabat, *It was evident*, etc.; with clause as Subject [§ 157].

consŭē-sco, vi, tum, scĕre, 3. v. n. inch. [consŭĕ-o, "to be accustomed"] *To accustom one's self:*—In perf. tenses, *To have accustomed one's self*, i. e. *to be accustomed* or *wont*.

consŭē-tūdo, tūdĭnis, f. [for consuet-tūdo, fr. consŭĕt-us, "accustomed"] ("The state, or quality, of the *consuetus*"; hence) 1. *Custom, habit, use, usage.*—2. *Familiarity, intimacy.*

consŭēvi, perf. ind. of consuesco.

consul, ŭlis, m. *A consul;* one of the two chief magistrates of the Roman state, chosen annually after the expulsion of the kings.

consŭl-āris, āre, adj. [con- sul, "a consul"] *Of*, or *belonging to, a consul* or *the consuls; consular.*—As Subst.: consŭlaris, is, m. *One who has been consul; a man of consular rank*, etc.

consŭl-ātŭs, ātūs, m. [id.] *The office of consul; the consulship* or *consulate.*

consŭlendo, Gerund in do fr. consŭlo.

consŭlo, ŭi, tum, ĕre, 3. v. n. *and* a.: 1. Neut.: a. *To take counsel, deliberate, consult.*—Impers. Pass.: consultum est, *It was deliberated*, i. e. *there was a deliberation.* —b. With Dat.: *To take counsel for* some person or thing; *to have regard for, take measures for, consult for.* —2. Act.: a. Political t. t.: *To take counsel with* the competent authorities, *to consult* them;—at xlviii. 6 consulente Cicerone is Abl. Abs. [§ 125]: after consulente supply senatum [§ 158].—b. *To take counsel about* or *deliberate upon* something; *to consider* something; lii. 35.—Pass.: consŭlor, consultus sum, consuli.

consul-to, tāvi, tātum, tāre, 1. v. a. *and* n. intens. [consŭl-o, "to take counsel"] ("To take great counsel"; hence) 1. Act.: With Acc. of thing: *To take counsel about* or *deliberate upon* something; *to con-*

sider something ;—at lii. 3 with clause as Object.—2. Neut.: a. *To consult, deliberate, take counsel,* etc. ; —at li. 1 with de.—b. With Dat. of thing : *To consult for,* etc. ; vi. 6.

consul-tum, ti, n. [consŭl-o, "to determine upon"] ("That which is determined upon "; hence) *A resolution, decree:*— Sĕnāti *or* Sĕnātūs consultum (or as one word senatuscon- sultum), *a decree of the senate.*

consultus, a, um, P. perf. pass. of consŭlo ;—at xliii. 3 consulto is the Abl. Neut. dependent on opus ; see opus.

con-sŭmo, sumpsi, sump- tum, sūmĕre, 3. v. a. [con (= cum), in "intensive" force ; sūmo, "to take "] ("To take wholly *or* completely "; hence, "to consume, devour "; hence) *To waste, squander,* etc. ;—at xii. 2 consumere is the Hist. Inf. [§ 140, 2], and has no Object depending on it.

contăg-ĭo, ĭōnis, f. [con- tingo, "to come in contact " with some object, through true root CONTAG] ("A com- ing in contact"; hence, in bad sense, "contagion"; hence) Morally: *Contagion, pollution, infection,* etc.

con-temno, tempsi, tem- ptum, temnĕre, 3. v. a. [con (= cum), in "augmentative"

force ; temno, "to despise "] *To despise greatly; to dis- dain, make light of, con- temn.*

con-tendo, tendi, tentum, tendĕre, 3. v. n. [con (= cum), in "augmentative" force ; tendo] 1. [tendo, "to stretch "] ("To stretch with all one's might; to strain"; hence) a. *To make an effort or endeavour; to exert one's self, strive, endeavour.*—b. With notion of hostility : *To strive, contend, struggle,* etc. —2. [tendo, "to bend one's way "] *To bend one's way,* or *proceed, eagerly,* etc.

conten-tĭo, tĭōnis, f. [for contend-tĭo ; fr. contend-o, " to contend "] 1. *A contend- ing, striving, exertion, effort.* —2. *A contention, contest, dispute, controversy, strife.*

con-tĕro, trīvi, trītum, tĕrĕre, 3. v. a. [con (= cum), in "augmentative" force ; tero, "to rub, bruise," *etc.*] (To rub *or* bruise greatly "; hence, "to diminish by rub- bing, wear away"; hence) Of time, *etc.*: In a bad sense : *To waste, consume.*

contĭnent-ĭa, ĭæ, f. [con- tĭnens, continent-is, in force of "restraining the passions, moderate "] ("The state *or* condition of the *continens*"; hence) *Self-restraint, modera- tion,* etc.

contĭnŭ-o, āvi, ātum, āre, 1. v. a. [continu-us, "joined together, continuous"] ("To make *continuus*"; hence) *To join together, connect, unite*, etc.

contra, adv. *and* prep. : 1. Adv. : a. *Against, on the contrary.*—b. *On the other hand.*—2. Prep. gov. acc. : a. *Against.*—b. *In opposition to, contrary to.*

contractus, a, um, P. perf. pass. of contrăho.

con-trăho, traxi, tractum, trăhĕre, 3. v. a. [con (= cum), "together"; trăho, "to draw"] ("To draw together"; hence) *To narrow, lessen, contract,* etc. —Pass. : **con-trăhor**, tractus sum, trăhi.

contŭmēl-ĭa, ĭæ, f. [con-tŭmesco, through obsol. adj. contŭmēl-us, "swelling greatly"] ("The quality of the *contumelus*"; hence) *Insult, affront, contumely.*

con-turbo, turbāvi, turb-ātum, turbāre, 1. v. a. [con (= cum), in "augmentative" force; turbo, "to throw into confusion"] *To throw into utter confusion; to disorder,* etc.—Pass. : **con-turbor**, turb-ātus sum, turbāri.

con-vĕnĭo, vēni, ventum, vĕnīre, 4. v. n. *and* a. [con (= cum), "together"; venio, "to come"] 1. Neut. : a. *To come together, assemble.*—b. ("To

fit with, in, *or* to" something; hence) Impers. : **convĕnit,** *It is fit, becoming, suitable, proper or seemly.*—2. Act. : *To go to one in order to address him,* etc.; *to meet,* etc.

conven-tĭo, tĭōnis, f. [con-vĕn-ĭo, "to come together"] ("A coming together"; hence) 1. *A meeting, assembly.*—2. *An agreement, compact, covenant,* etc.

conven-tŭs, tūs, m. [id.] (id.) *A meeting, assembly.*

convictus, a, um, P. perf. pass. of convinco.

con-vinco, vīci, victum, vincĕre, 3. v. a. [con (= cum), in "augmentative" force; vinco, "to overcome"] ("To overcome completely"; hence) 1. *To convict, prove guilty,* etc.;—at lii. 36 with Abl. of cause [§ 111].—2. With Abl. of charge : *To convict, prove or find guilty of.*—Pass. : **convincor**, victus sum, vinci.

con-vīv-ĭum, ĭi, n. [con (= cum), "together"; vīv-o, "to live"] ("A living together"; hence) *A feast, banquet, entertainment.*

convŏcātus, a, um, P. perf. pass. of convoco.

con-vŏco, vŏcāvi, vŏcātum, vŏcāre, 1. v. a. [con (= cum), "together"; vŏco, "to call"] *To call together; to convene, convoke.*—Pass. : **con-vŏcor**, vŏcātus sum, vŏcāri.

Sallust.

H

con-vorto, vorti, vorsum, vortĕre, 3. v. n. [con (= cum), in "strengthening" force; vorto (= verto), "to turn"] Of things as Subject: *To turn itself, change, be or become changed*, etc.

cŏ-ŏpĕrĭo, ŏpĕrŭi, ŏpertum, ŏpĕrīre, 4. v. a. [co (= cum), in "augmentative" force; operio, "to cover"] ("To cover entirely"; hence) *To cover over, load, overwhelm* with infamy, *etc.*—Pass.: cŏ-ŏpĕrĭor, ŏpertus sum, ŏpĕrīri.

cŏŏpertus, a, um, P. perf. pass. of cooperio.

cŏ-p-ĭa, ĭæ, f. [contr. fr. co-op-ia; fr. co (= cum), in "augmentative" force; ops, ŏp-is, "means," *etc.*] ("The thing pertaining to *ops*"; hence) 1. Sing.: a. *Plenty, abundance.*—b. *Abundance = large number;*—at lii. 20 the sentence will be, fully, major nobis copia est, quàm illis erat. — c. *Ability, power, means;*—at xvii. 6 folld. by Inf.—d. *A force, forces, body of troops, troops;* lvi. 3.—2. Plur.: a. *Forces, troops.*—b. *Resources, supplies.*

1. Cornēlĭus, ĭi, m. *Cornelius* (*Caius*); a Roman knight, one of Catiline's accomplices; xvii. 4. In conjunction with L. Vargunteius he undertook to attempt the murder of Cicero; xxviii. 1.

2. Cornēlĭus, ĭi, m. *Cornelius;* the name of a Roman *gens* or house, reckoning amongst its members many distinguished men and women; —tribus Corneliis, *to three (of the) Cornelii,* xlvii. 2; see also, Cinna, Lentulus, and Sulla.

Corn-ĭ-fĭc-ĭus, ĭi, m. [for Corn-i-fac-ius; fr. corn-u, "a horn"; (i) connecting vowel; fac-io, "to make"] ("One pertaining to the making of horns; Horn-maker") *Cornificius* (*Quintus*); a Roman senator to whose custody Cethegus was committed; xlvii. 4. In the year B.C. 66 he had been Prætor, and in B.C. 64, the year before the conspiracy, he had been a candidate for the Consulshiph at the same time as Cicero, but lost his election.

corp-us, ŏris, n. ("That which is made *or* formed"; hence) *The body* [akin to Sans. root KLIP, "to make"].

correptus, a, um, 1. P. perf. pass. of corripio.—2. Pa.: *Corrupt, depraved, etc.;* iii. 4.

cor-rĭgo, rexi, rectum, rĭgĕre, 3. v. a. [for con-rĕgo; fr. con (= cum), in "augmentative" force; rĕgo, "to make straight"] ("To make straight"; hence) *To amend, make better, correct.*—Pass.: cor-rĭgor, rectus sum, rĭgi.

cor-rĭpĭo, rĭpŭi, reptum, rĭpĕre, 3. v. a. [for con-răpĭo; fr. con (= cum), in "augmentative" force; răpĭo, "to seize"] ("To seize violently"; hence) *To seize upon*, etc.—Pass.: cor-rĭpĭor, reptus sum, rĭpi.

cor-rumpo, rūpi, ruptum, rumpĕre, 3. v. a. [for con-rumpo; fr. con (= cum), in "augmentative" force; rumpo, "to break"] ("To break completely"; hence, "to destroy, bring to nought"; hence) Morally: *To corrupt, seduce, mislead*, etc.—Pass.: cor-rumpor, ruptus sum, rumpi.

corruptus, a, um, P. perf. pass. of corrumpo.

Cotta, æ, m. *Cotta* (*Lucius*); a consul, whom Catiline, in his first conspiracy, had sought to kill; xviii. 5; see Catilina.

Crassus, i, m. [crassus, "thick"] *Crassus* (*Marcus Licinius*); a Roman senator, remarkable for his vast wealth; xlviii. 5. It was into his charge that Gabinius was given by the Senate; lvii. 4. He was suspected of complicity in Catiline's first conspiracy, and was accused by Tarquinius in the senate of being engaged in the second; xlviii. 5. In B.C. 60 he united with Pompey and Cæsar in forming the first triumvirate. He was defeated in an engagement with the Parthians, B.C. 53, in which he lost his son. Subsequently, being induced by Surenas, the Parthian general, to come to an interview, he was murdered by some unknown hand.

crēdens, ntis, P. pres. of credo.

crēd-ĭbĭlis, ĭbĭle, adj. [crēd-o, "to believe"] *That may* or *can be believed; credible;*—at v. 3 with Dat. [§ 107, *d*].

crēd-ĭtum, ĭti, n. [crēd-o, "to lend" on loan] ("That which is lent"; hence) *A loan.*

crē-do, dĭdi, dĭtum, dĕre, 3. v. n. *and* a.: 1. Neut.: a. With Dat. [§ 106, (3)]: *To put faith* or *confidence in; to trust to* or *confide in;*—at xxxi. 1 credere is the Hist Inf. [§ 140, 2].—b. With Dat. of person [§ 106, (3)]: *To trust* one in his declarations, *to give* one *credence, to believe* one.— c. Inserted parenthetically in a clause, like puto, opīnor, and Gr. οἶμαι: *I believe, think, suppose, imagine;* lii. 13.—2. Act.: a. With Acc. of thing: *To believe, credit, hold* or *admit as true;* xxxi. 7.—b. With Objective clause: *To suppose, think, imagine, that* etc.; xxiii. 6, *etc.*—c. Pass. ·

With Inf.: *To be believed* or *regarded; to be held* as doing something; xv. 2.—d. With second Acc.: *To suppose, regard, consider* some person or thing as being that which is denoted by second Acc.; xxxix. 6 [akin to Sans. prefix *çrat*, "faith"; do (akin to Sans. root DHÂ), "to put"].

crē-sco, vi, tum, scĕre, 3. v. n. *To increase;*—at x. 6 crescere is the Hist. Inf. [§ 140, 2].

Crēt-ĭcus, ĭci, m. [Crēt-a, "Crete," now "Candia"; an island in the Eastern part of the Mediterranean Sea] ("One belonging to Crete") *Creticus;* a cognomen of Q. Metellus, who reduced Crete under the Roman power, B.C. 67—65. For this success he obtained a triumph, B.C. 62; see urbs.

crēvĕrim, crēvi, perf. subj. and ind. of cresco.

crī-men, mĭnis, n. ("The separating *or* sifting thing"; hence, "a judicial investigation"; hence) *A charge, accusation*, etc. [prob. akin to Sans. root KRÎ, "to separate"; whence also CRE, CER, roots of cerno, "to sift," *etc.*].

crīmĭnando, Gerund in do fr. criminor.

crīmĭn-or, ātus sum, āri, 1. v. dep. [crīmen, crīmĭn-is, "an accusation"] *To bring an accusation* or *charge* against; *to accuse, calumniate*, etc.

Crispus, i, m. [crispus, "curled"; of persons, "with curly hair, curly-headed"] *Crispus;* a Roman cognomen; see Sallustius.

Crŏtōn-ĭensis, ĭensis, m. [Croto, Crŏtōn-is, "Croto or Crotona" (now "Crotone"); a town on the east coast of Bruttium] *A man*, or *inhabitant, of Croto or Crotona.*

crŭcĭā-tus, tūs, m. [cruci(a)o, "to torture"] *Torture, torment.*

crūd-ēlis, ēle, adj. ("Wrathful"; hence) *Cruel.* (Comp.: crūdēl-ĭor); Sup.: crūdēl-issĭmus [prob. akin to Sans. root KRUDH, "to be wrathful"].

crūdēl-ĭtas, ĭtātis, f. [crūdēl-is, "cruel"] ("The quality of the *crudelis*"; hence) *Cruelty.*

crūdēl-ĭter, adv. [id.] ("After the manner of the *crudelis*"; hence) *Cruelly.*

crŭ-entus, enta, entum, adj. [prob. akin to cru-or, "blood"] *Bloody, blood-stained*, etc.

crŭ-or, ōris, m. *Blood.*

cuiquam, dat. sing. of quisquam.

cuique, cūjusque, dat. and gen. sing. of quisque.

cūjusquĕmŏdi; see modus.

culp-a, æ, f. ["A deed, action"; hence, in a bad sense)

A crime, fault [akin to Sans. root KLIP, "to make"].

cul-tŭs, tūs, m. [for col-tus, fr. cŏl-o, "to cultivate"] ("Culture"; hence) 1. *Manner* or *mode of living.*—2. *Luxury, wantonness, luxurious habits,* etc. — 3. *Dress, clothing.*

cum, prep. gov. abl. *With;* —written after relative and personal pronouns; *e. g.* quibuscum, secum, *etc.* [akin to Sans. *sam;* Gr. ξύν, σύν].

cunc-tor, tātus sum, tāri, 1. v. dep. *To delay, linger, hesitate, doubt* [akin to Sans. root CANK, "to fluctuate, doubt"].

cunctus, a, um (most frequently plur.), adj. [contr. fr. conjunctus, P. perf. pass. of conjungo, "to join together or unite"] ("United together"; hence) *All.*—As Subst.: cuncta, ōrum, n. plur. *All things.*

cŭpĭd-e, adv. [cupid-us, "eager"] *Eagerly, zealously.* 𝕾𝕲 (Comp.: cŭpĭd-ĭus); Sup.: cŭpĭd-issĭme.

cŭpĭdissĭme; see cupide.

cŭpĭd-ĭtas, ĭtātis, f. [cŭpĭd-us, "desirous"] ("The quality of the *cupidus*"; hence) 1. *Longing desire, eagerness.*— 2. *Passionate desire, ruling propensity* or *passion.*—3. *Covetousness, cupidity, avarice.*

cŭp-ĭdo, ĭdĭnis, f. [cŭp-ĭo,

"to desire"] ("A desiring"; hence) *Desire, longing,* etc.

cŭp-ĭdus, ĭda, ĭdum, adj. [id.] With Gen. [§ 132]: *Desirous of, eager for,* etc.

cŭp-ĭo, īvi or ĭi, ītum, ĕre, 3. v. a.: 1. *To long,* or *wish, for; to desire.*—2. In a bad sense: *To have an eager desire for, to covet;*—at xi. 4 cupere is the Hist. Inf. [§ 140, 2].—3. With Inf.: *To long,* or *be eager, to do, etc.* [akin to Sans. root KUP, "to become excited"].

cūr-a, æ, f. [for cær-a; fr. cær-o, old form of quær-o, "to seek"] ("The seeking thing"; hence, with accessory notion of trouble) 1. *Care, carefulness, attention.* — 2. *Care, anxiety, solicitude, apprehension,* etc.

cūrĭa, æ, f. *The Senate-house.*

Cŭrĭus, ĭi, m. *Curius (Quintus);* one of the accomplices of Catiline. He sent word, through Fulvia, to Cicero, of the design that was formed for his assassination; xxviii. 2.

cūr-o, āvi, ātum, āre, 1. v. a. [cur-a, "care"] 1. *To care for, look* or *attend to.*—2. Without Object: *To take,* or *be in, charge;* lix. 3.—3. Political t. t.: Of the state: *To take charge of, administer, manage.*

custŏdĭ-a, æ, f. [custŏdĭ-o,

"to guard"] ("A guarding, keeping guard"; hence) *A watching, guard, custody :*—libera custodia, *free custody,* i. e. custody under some person's charge and not in the public prison;—at xlvii. 3 in plur.

cus-tos, tōdis, comm. gen. *A guard, keeper* [akin to κυθ, root of κεύθ-ω, "to cover, to hide"].

Cȳrus, i, m. *Cyrus,* surnamed the "Elder," son of Cambȳses, a Persian noble, and Mandāne, daughter of Astyages, king of Media. Upon arriving at man's estate he dethroned his grandfather, and transferred the empire from the Medes to the Persians, B.C. 559. [κῦρος, "supreme power;" akin to Sans. *çura,* "a hero."]

D., abbrev. of Decimus.

Dămăsippus, i, m. *Damasippus;* an agnomen of Lucius Junius Brutus, a zealous and cruel adherent of Marius. When the younger Marius was reduced to despair by the blockade of Præneste, B.C. 82, he resolved that his principal enemies should not survive him. Accordingly he contrived to despatch a letter to Brutus Damasippus (at that time Prætor Urbanus), wherein he desired the latter to summon the Senate and procure the assassination of four of their number : viz. P. Antistius, C. Papirius Carbo, L. Domitius, and Scævŏla the Pontifex Maximus. This was done, and the dead bodies of the four senators were thrown into the Tiber. In the same year Brutus Damasippus was defeated by Sulla, and being made prisoner was put to death [Δαμάσιππος, "Horsetamer"].

damnătus, a, um, P. perf. pass. of damno.—As Subst.: **damnăti,** ōrum, m. plur. *Condemned persons, criminals.*

damn-o, āvi, ātum, āre, 1. v. a. [damn-um, in the meaning of "a penalty"] ("To bring a penalty upon"; hence) *To condemn.* — Pass. : **damn-or,** ātus sum, āri.

dam-num, ni, n. ("The subduing, *or* damaging, thing"; hence) *Hurt, harm, damage, injury, loss* [akin to Sans. root DAM (whence also Gr. δαμ-άω, Lat. dŏm-o), "to tame"].

dando, Gerund in do fr. do; liv. 3.

dandus, a, um, Gerundive of do; vi. 5.

dătus, a, um, P. perf. pass. of do.

dē, prep. gov. abl.: 1. *From, away from.*—2. *Out of, forth from.*—3. *For, on account of, because of.*—4. *About, con-*

cerning, respecting.—5. With neut. adj.: To form an adverbial expression; *e. g.* de improviso, *on a sudden, suddenly;* xxviii. 1.

de-běo, būi, bǐtum, bēre, 2. v. a. [contr. fr. dē-hǎběo; fr. dē, "from"; hǎběo, "to have"] ("To have, *or* hold, from" a person; hence) 1. *To owe.*—2. With Inf.: *To be bound to* do, *etc.; I,* etc., *ought to do, etc.*

Děcem-ber, bris, m. ("Ten-time *or* period") *December;* the tenth month of the Roman year, reckoning from March, which was originally the first month.—As Adj.: *Of December* [decem, "ten"; ber = Sans. *vár-a,* Persian *bár,* "time *or* period"].

Děcembrĭs = Decembres, acc. plur. of December as adj.

dē-cerno, crēvi, crētum, cernēre, 3. v. a. *and* n. [dē, in "strengthening" force; cerno, "to determine"] 1. Act.: a. *Of* the senate, *etc.*: (a) *To determine, decide, decree;*—at l. 4 with Objective clause. —(b) *To give* or *assign by a decree, to vote* or *decree* something to some one; l. 1.—b. *Of* persons in general: *To resolve, determine;*—at iv. 1 with Objective clause; at xxxv. 2 with Inf.—2. Neut.: a. *Of* the senate, *etc.*: *To determine, decide, decree;*—

at xxxvi. 3 folld. by uti and Subj.; at xxix. 2 folld. by simple Subj.—b. Impers. Pass.: decretum erit, *It shall have been decreed,* i. e. *a decree shall have been made;* li. 25.—Pass.: dē-cernor, crētus sum, cerni.

děc-et, ŭit, no sup., ēre, 2. v. n. impers. *(It) is becoming, fitting, proper, suitable,* etc.; —at i. 1 and li. 1 with clause as Subject;—at li. 13 with Inf. as Subject [§ 157; see, also, Notes to Syntax, p. 149 *b,* (1); (2)] [akin to Sans. root DIÇ; Gr. δείκ·νῡμι, "to show, to distinguish"].

Děcĭmus, i, m. [děcĭmus, "tenth"] *Decimus;* a Roman prænomen.

dē-clāro, clārāvi, clārātum, clārāre, 1. v. a. [de, denoting "completely"; clāro, "to make clear"] ("To make quite clear"; hence) *To announce, declare, proclaim* one as elected to an office;—at xxiv. 1 in Pass., folld. by a Nom. [§ 93, (2)].—Pass.: dē-clāror, clārātus sum, clārāri.

děcŏr-o, āvi, ātum, āre, 1. v. a. [děcus, děcŏr-is, "an ornament"] *To ornament, adorn, decorate.*

děcŏr-us, a, um, adj. [děcor, děcŏr-is, "gracefulness"] ("Having *decor*"; hence) *Graceful, beautiful, elegant, decorated,* etc.

dēcrē-tum, ti, n. [decerno, "to decree"; through true root DECRE] ("That which is decreed"; hence) *A decree, ordinance.*

dēcrētus, a, um, P. perf. pass. of decerno.

dēcrēvēram, dēcrēvi, pluperf. and perf. ind. of decerno.

dĕc-us, ŏris, n. [dec-et, "it is becoming"] ("That which is becoming"; hence) 1. *Honour, dignity.*—2. *Moral dignity, virtue.*

dē-dĕcus, dĕcŏris, n. [dē, in "negative" force; dĕcus, "that which is becoming"] ("That which is unbecoming" to one; hence) 1. *Disgrace, dishonour, shame.* — 2. *A vicious action, a shameful or disgraceful deed or act.*

dēdĭtus, a, um, P. perf. pass. of dedo.

dē-do, dĭdi, dĭtum, dĕre, 3. v. a. [dē, "away from"; do, "to put"] ("A putting away from" one's self; hence) 1. *To give up* to one; *to surrender.*—2. Pass. in reflexive force: Of the mind as Subject: *To give up, surrender,* or *abandon itself* to some course, etc. — Pass.: dē-dor, dĭtus sum, di.

dē-dūco, duxi, ductum, dūcĕre, 3. v. a. [dē; dūco, "to lead"] 1. [dē, "down"] With in c. Acc.: *To lead down, conduct,* or *bring* into a place.

—2. [dē, "away"] *To lead away* or *off,* etc.

dēfendendum, Gerund in dum fr. defendo.

de-fendo, fendi, fensum, fendĕre, 3. v. a. [dē, "away from"; obsol. fendo, "to beat or strike"] ("To beat or strike away from" one; hence) *To protect, defend;*—at xxxv 6 the Subj. (defendas) is used to express a wish or desire, like the Gr. Optative [fendo is akin to Sans. root HAN, "to strike"].

dēfen-sĭo, sĭonis, f. [for defend-sĭo; fr. defend-o, "to defend"] ("A defending"; hence) *Defence, protection.*

dēfessus, a, um, P. perf. of defetiscor.—As Subst.: de-fessi, ōrum, m. plur. *Men utterly wearied* or *tired out.*

dē-fētiscor, fessus sum, fĕtisci, 3. v. dep. [for defătiscor; fr. dē, in "augmentative" force; fătiscor, in force of "to grow weary, become exhausted"] *To grow utterly weary, to become quite tired out.*

dē-fĭcĭo, fēci, fectum, fĭcĕre, 3. v. n. [for de-făcĭo; fr. dē, "away from"; făcĭo, "to make"] ("To make one's self away from" a thing; hence) *To fail, fall short, be wanting.*

dē-gusto, gustāvi, gustātum, gustāre, 1. v. a. [dē, in "strengthening" force; gusto, "to taste"] 1. *To taste,* whether solids or liquids.—2. Of liquids alone: *To taste, take a taste* or *small quantity of.*

dĕ-hinc, adv. [dē, "from"; hinc, "hence"] ("From hence"; hence) In time: *After this, next, afterwards, then.*

dein; see deinde.

dĕ-inde (abbrev. dein), adv. [de, "from inde, "thence"] ("From thence"; hence) 1. Of succession: *Afterwards, next in order, after that.*—2. Of time: *In the next place, afterwards, after that.*

1. dēlec-tus, tūs, m. [for de-legtus; fr. dēlīgo, "to choose out"; through root DELEG; see deligo] ("A choosing out or selecting"; hence) Of soldiers: *A levy.*

2. dēlectus, a, um, P. perf. pass. of dēlīgo.—As Subst.: dēlecti, ōrum, *Chosen,* or *selected, persons;* vi. 6.

dē-līciæ, ārum, f. plur. [dēlīcĭ-o, "to allure"] ("That which allures"; hence) *Delight, pleasure, luxury.*

dē-lictum, ti, n. [dēliqu-tum (trisyll); fr. deli(n)qu-o, "to do wrong"] ("That which is done wrong"; hence) *A fault, offence, crime.*

dē-līgo, lēgi, lectum, līgĕre. 3. v. a. [for dē-lĕgo; fr. dĕ, "from"; lĕgo, "to choose"] ("To choose from" a number, whether greater or smaller; hence) *To choose out, select.*—Pass.: dē-līgor, lectus sum, līgi.

dē-linquo, līqui, lictum, linquĕre, 3. v. a. *and* n. [dē, denoting "completeness"; linquo, "to leave"] (1. Act.: "To leave quite or entirely"; perhaps found only once.)—2. Neut.: *To commit a fault* or *offence, do wrong, transgress;* lii. 26;—at li. 12 folld. by Acc. of neut. pron. as "Acc. of Respect"].

dēlīqui, perf. ind. of dē-linquo.

dēlū-brum, bri, n. [dēlū-"to wash out, cleanse ("That which brings abou' effects a cleansing"; h' *A temple, shrine,* as a pl moral cleansing or exp'

dēment-ĭa, ĭæ, f. [. dement-is, "out of one's m.. *⁄* ("The state of the *demens* te hence) 1. *Insanity, madness.* —2. *Foolishness, folly.*

dēmissus, a, um, 1. P. perf. pass. of demitto.—2. Pa.: a. Of the countenance, *etc.: Downcast, turned towards the ground, looking downwards,* etc.—b. *Lowly, humble, unassuming.*

dē-mitto, mīsi, missum, mittĕre, 3. v. a. [dē, "down"; mitto, "to suffer, or allow, to go"] ("To suffer, or allov to go down"; hence) *To* down, lower. — Pass.: dē-mittor, missus sum, mitti.

dēmum, adv.: 1. Enclitically with pronouns: *Especially, indeed;* ii. 9, *etc.*—2. With tum: *Then at length, then indeed;* ii. 2 [a lengthened form of particle dem in idem, tandem, *etc.*, and akin to Gr. δή].

dē-nĕgo, nĕgāvi, nĕgātum, nĕgāre, 1. v. a. [de, in "augmentative" force; nĕgo, "to deny"] ("To deny thoroughly"; hence) *To reject, refuse, deny* a request, *etc.*

dēnī-que, adv. [for deinque; fr. dĕin, "then"; quĕ, "and"] ("And then"; hence) 1. *At length, at last.*—2. In a climax: *In short, in a word, briefly.*

dē-prĕhendo, prĕhendi, prĕhensum, prĕhendĕre, 3. v. a. [dē, "away"; prĕhendo, "to take"] ("To take, or snatch, away"; hence) 1. *To seize upon, catch, overtake.* — 2. *To detect, find out, discover* any one, especially in doing what is wrong.—Pass.: dē-prĕhendor, prĕhensus sum, prĕhendi.

dēprĕhensus, a, um, P. perf. pass. of deprehendo.

dēpressus, a, um, P. perf. pass. of deprĭmo.

dē-prĭmo, pressi, pressum, primĕre, 3. v. a. [for de-prĕmo; fr. dē, "down"; premo, "to

press"] ("To press down"; hence) *To sink deep in the ground.* — Pass. : dē-prĭmor, pressus sum, prĭmi.

de-scendo, scendi, scensum, scendĕre, 3. v. n. [for dē-scando; fr. dē, "down"; scando, "to climb"] ("To climb down"; hence) *To come,* or *go, down; to descend;*—at lv. 3 the second person sing. of the perf. subj. (descenderis) is used in an indefinite force; see cerno.

descen-sus, sūs, m. [for descend-sus; fr. descend-o, "to descend"] ("A descending"; hence) *A descending way, road, etc.; a descent.*

dē-sĕro, serŭi, sertum, serĕre, 3. v. a. [dē, in "negative" force; sĕro, "to join"] ("To disjoin; to undo *or* sever" one's connexion with some object; hence) *To forsake, abandon, desert.*—Pass.: dē-sĕror, sertus sum, sĕri.

dēsertus, a, um, P. perf. pass. of desĕro.

dēsĭd-ĭa, ĭæ, f. [dēsĭd-ĕo, "to sit down idle"] ("A sitting down idle"; hence) *Idleness, inactivity, slothfulness.*

dēsignātus, a, um, P. perf. pass. of designo.

dē-signo, signāvi, signātum, signāre, 1. v. a. [dē, "off *or* away" from something; signo, "to mark"] ("To mark off," *etc.;* "to mark out"; hence) 1. *To appoint, or nominate,* a person to an office.—2. Part. perf. pass.: Political t. t.: *Elect;*—applied to a person elected to an office, but who has not yet entered upon it.

dē-sum, fŭi, esse, v. n. [dē, "away from"; sum, "to be"] ("To be away from"; hence) *To fail; to be wanting or lacking.*

dē-tĭnĕo, tĭnŭi, tentum, tĭnēre, 2. v. a. [for dē-tĕnĕo; fr. dē, "away"; tĕnĕo, "to hold"] *To hold away* or *off; to keep away* or *back; to detain.*

dētrĭ-mentum, menti, n. [dētĕro, "to rub off," through true root DETRI] ("That which is rubbed off"; hence) *Loss, hurt, damage, injury, detriment.*

deûm (= deorum), gen. plur. of deus; xx. 10.

dĕus, i, m. *A god, deity* [akin to Gr. θεός; Sans. *deva,* "a god"].

dēvictus, a, um, P. perf. pass. of dēvinco.

dē-vinco, vīci, victum, vincĕre, 3. v. a. (dē, denoting "completeness"; vinco, "to conquer"] *To conquer completely; to vanquish, subdue, reduce,* etc.—Pass.: dē-vincor, victus sum, vinci.

dex-ter, tra, trum, adj. *Right* as opposed to "left";

on the right-hand side; to, or *on, the right.*—As Subst.: dextra, æ, f. *The right hand* [akin to Sans. *daksh-a;* Gr. δέξ-ιος, δεξ-ιτερός].

dicendi, Gerund in di fr. dico.

dīco, dixi, dictum, dīcĕre, 3. v. a. ("To show, *or* point out," by speaking; hence) 1. a. *To speak, say, state, mention, report;*—at xvi. 1 without follg. Object;—at li. 5 folld. by Objective clause, bellum (esse) inceptum;—so at li. 29 by fiĕri (*sc.* ea) merīto.—b. Pass.: (a) *To be said, mentioned, reported;* lix. 3.—(b) Impers.: dictum est, *It has been said, spoken,* etc.;—at xix. 4 with satis dictum supply est, *it has been spoken enough; i. e. enough has been said.*—2. a. *To pronounce, deliver* a speech, etc.—b. Without follg. Object: *To speak, be a speaker,* etc.:—bene dicere, *to speak well* or *be a good speaker,* iii. 1.—3. a. With second Acc.: *To call* something that which is denoted by the second Acc.—b. Pass. folld. by Nom. [§ 93, 2]: *To be called* something; li. 14.—Pass.: dīcor, dictus sum, dīci [akin to Gr. δείκ-νυμι, and Sans. root DIC, "to show"].

dic-tum, ti, n. [dīc-o, "to speak"] ("That which is spoken"; hence) 1. *A saying* or *statement—*2. *A word.*

dictus, a, um, P. perf. pass. of dīcor.

dī-es, ēi, m. (in Sing. sometimes f.) *A day;*—at xxxvi. 1 dies is the Acc. of Duration of Time [§ 102, (1)]; cf., also, xxvii. 2, dies noctesque.— Phrases: a. in dies (acc. plur.), or as one word (indies), *day by day, daily.*—b. dies noctesque, *days and nights,* or *day and night,* i. e. *continually, unceasingly, uninterruptedly,* xxvii. 2; see above.—c. Ante diem vi. Kalendas Novembris; see ante, no. 2, c. [akin to Sans. *div,* " heaven, a day "].

dif-fīcilis, fīcīle, adj. [for dis-făcīlis; fr. dis, in " negative " force; facilis, " easy "] *Not easy, hard, difficult.*

difficul-tas, tātis, f. [difficul (old form of diffīcīlis), " difficult "] (" The state or condition of the *difficul*"; hence) *Difficulty, difficult* or *dangerous position* of affairs, etc.

difficul-ter, adv. [id.] (" After the manner of the *difficul*"; hence) *With difficulty:*—haud difficulter, *without difficulty, easily.*

diffīdens, ntis, P. pres. of diffīdo.

dif-fīdo, fīsus sum, fīdĕre, 3. v. n. semi-dep. [for dis-fido; fr. dis, in " negative " force; fido, " to trust "] With Dat. [§ 106, 3]: *To be mistrustful,*

to feel mistrust, to despair about a matter, *etc.;*—at xxxi. 3 diffīdere is the Hist. Inf. [§ 140, 2].

dign-ĭtas, ĭtātis, f. [dign-us, " worthy "] (" The quality of the *dignus*"; hence, "worthiness "; hence) *Dignity, rank, honour.*

dig-nus, na, num, adj. (" Shown, pointed out "; hence) 1. a. *Worthy.*—As Subst.: digni, ōrum, m. plur. *Worthy persons.*—b. With Abl. [§ 119, (a)]: *Worthy of.* —2. Of things: a. *Suitable, fit, fitting, proper.*—b. With Abl. [§ 119, (a)]: *Suitable to,* etc. [fr. same source as dico; see dico].

dī-lābor, lapsus sum, lābi, 3. v. dep. [dī (= dis), " in different directions "; lābor, " to glide "] (" To glide in different directions *or* away"; hence) Of persons: *To slip away, disperse, be scattered,* etc.

dīlĭgent-ĭa, ĭæ, f. [diligens, diligent-is, " diligent "] (" The quality of the *diligens*"; hence) *Carefulness, attentiveness, earnestness, diligence.*

dī-mitto, mīsi, missum, mittĕre, 3. v. a. [dī (= dis), " apart "; mitto, " to send "] (" To send apart " from one; hence) 1. *To send about, in different directions* or *to different parts.*—2. Of an

assembly: *To break up, dissolve, dismiss.*—3. *To send away; to let go, dismiss, free, release.*—Pass.: dĭ-mittor, missus sum, mitti.

dĭrēmi, perf. ind. of dirimo.

dĭr-ĭmo, ēmi, emptum, ĭmĕre, 3. v. a. [for dĭs-ĕmo; fr. dis, "apart"; ĕmo, "to take"] ("To take apart"; hence, "to part, separate"; hence) *To frustrate, destroy, bring to nought, put an end to.*

dĭ-rŭo, rŭi, rŭtum, rŭĕre, 3. v. a. [dī (= dis), "apart"; ruo, "to dash down"] ("To separate by dashing down"; hence) Of buildings: *To throw* or *pull down, to demolish, destroy.*

dîs, dat. *and* abl. plur. of dĕus.

dis-cēdo, cessi, cessum, cēdĕre, 3. v. n. [dis, "apart"; cēdo, "to go"] ("To go apart"; hence) 1. *To go away, depart:*—ab armis discēdĕre, *to depart from arms,* i. e. *to lay down one's arms.*—2. *To come off* in a certain way, whether in battle or a civil contest.—3. a. *To go away* to a place.—b. Political t. t.: With in alicujus sententiam, (*To go away to,* i. e.) *go* or *pass over to some one's opinion, to adopt some one's views,* etc.

dis-cerno, crēvi, crētum, cernĕre, 3. v. a. [dis, "apart"; cerno, "to separate"] ("To separate apart"; hence) Mentally: *To distinguish, decide, discern;*—at xxv. 3 the second pers. sing. (of the imperf.) Subj.—discernĕres—is used in an indefinite force; see cerno.

disco, dĭdĭci, no sup., discĕre, 3. v. a. ("To be shown" how to do, etc., something; hence) *To learn* [akin to Gr. δείκ-νῡμι, Sans. root DIÇ, "to show"; cf. dico].

discord-ĭa, ĭæ, f. [discors, discord-is, "disagreeing"] ("The quality of the *discors*"; hence) *Discord, dissension, variance.*

discrĭ-men, mĭnis, n. [for discre-men; fr. discerno, "to separate," through true root DISCRE] ("That which separates *or* divides"; hence, "an intervening space; a separation *or* division"; hence) *Distinction, difference.*

disjēcĕram, pluperf. ind. of disjicio.

dis-jĭcĭo, jēci, jectum, jĭcĕre, 3. v. a. [for dis-jăcĭo; fr. dis, "in different directions"; jăcĭo, "to throw"] ("To throw in different directions"; hence) Military t. t.: *To scatter, disperse, rout* the enemy.

dis-par, păris, adj. [dis, in "negative" force, like English "un-"; par, "equal"] ("Ur-equal "; hence) *Unlike, dissimilar, different :*—dispări genere, *of different race,* Abl. of quality [§ 115], vi. 2.

dis-pŏno, pŏsŭi, pŏsĭtum, pōnĕre, 3. v. a. [dis, "in different directions "; pōno, "to place "] ("To place in different directions "; hence) Of troops, *etc. : To set in order, to draw up, post, station, dispose.*—Pass. : dispōnor, pŏsĭtus sum, pōni.

dispŏsĭtus, a, um, P. perf. pass. of dispono.

dis-sentĭo, sensi, sensum, sentīre, 4. v. n. [dis, denoting "opposition *or* difference "; sentĭo, "to think "] *To think differently, differ in opinion, dissent.*

dis-sĕro, sĕrŭi, sertum, sĕrĕre, 3. v. a. *and* n. [dis, "asunder "; sĕro, in force of "to plant "] ("To plant asunder *or* apart "; hence, "to fix in " the ground, *etc.,* at certain distances; to set asunder "; hence) 1. Act. : *To treat of, narrate, recount, etc.*—2. Neut. : *To argue, treat, discuss.*

dissĕrŭisse, perf. ind. of dissĕro.

dis-sĭmĭlis, sĭmĭle, adj. [dis, in "negative " force; sĭmĭlis, "like "] *Unlike, dissimilar;*—at vi. 2 dissimili linguā is Abl. of quality [§ 115].

dissĭmŭlandi, Gerund in di fr. dissimulo.

dissĭmŭlandus, a, um, Gerundive of dissimulo.

dissĭmŭlā-tor, tōris, m. [dissimul(a)-o, "to dissemble "] *A dissembler, concealer.*

dissĭmŭl-o, āvi, ātum, āre, 1. v. a. [for dissĭmĭl-o; fr. dissĭmĭl-is, "unlike "] ("To represent (a thing as) unlike or different from " what it really is; hence) 1. *To feign, dissemble, put a false face on, etc.*—2. Without Object : *To dissemble;* xxxi. 5 ; xlvii. 1.

dis-solvo, solvi, sŏlūtum, solvĕre, 3. v. a. [dis, "asunder "; solvo, "to loosen "] ("To loosen asunder "; hence) Of troubles, ills, *etc. : To put an end to.*

dis-trĭbŭo, trĭbŭi, trĭbūtum, trĭbŭĕre, 3. v. a. [dis, denoting "amongst " persons; trĭbŭo, "to give "] ("To give amongst " several persons; hence) *To divide, divide out, distribute.*—Pass. : dis-trĭbŭ-or, trĭbūtus sum, trĭbŭi.

dĭ-tĭo, tĭōnis, f. [prob. for de-tio; fr. do, "to put," through root DE] ("A putting " one's self under another; hence, with reference to the person under whom one places one's self) *Dominion, sway, rule, authority.*

dĭu, adv. [old abl. form of dies, " a day "] 1. *For a long* *time ; a long while, long.*—2. Comp.: dĭūtĭus, *Longer, any longer.*

dĭūtĭus, comp. adv. ; see diu.

dĭū-turnus, turna, turnum, adj. [dĭu, "for a long time "] (" Of, *or* belonging to, *diu* "; hence) *Of long duration, long, prolonged ;*—at xxxi. 1 diuturna quies, *long rest,* refers to the fact that from the time of Sulla, B.C. 79, down to the time of which Sallust treats, B.C. 63, a space of about 16 years, there had been a cessation of civil discord ; see Sulla.

dĭ-vello, velli, vulsum, vellĕre, 3. v. a. [dī (= dis), "asunder"; vello, "pluck "] *To pluck* or *tear asunder ; to tear away, separate by force.* — Pass.: dĭ-vellor, vulsus sum, velli.

dĭv-es, ĭtis, adj. *Rich, wealthy.*—As Subst. m. *A rich* or *wealthy man* [akin to Sans. root DIV, "to shine "].

dĭ-vĭdo, vīsi, vīsum, vĭdĕre, 3. v. a. (" To part asunder "; hence, "to divide, separate"; hence) *To divide out ; distribute, etc.*—Pass. : dĭ-vĭdor, vīsus sum, vĭdi [dī (= dis), "apart"; root VID, probably akin to Sans. root BHID, "to part *or* divide "].

dĭv-īnus, īna, īnum, adj. [dĭv-us, "a deity "] (" Of, *or* belonging to, a deity "; hence) *Divine, sacred.*—As Subst. :

dĭvīna, ōrum, n. plur. *Divine,* or *sacred, things.*

dĭvīsus, a, um, P. perf. pass. of divido ;—at xliii. 2 supply esse with divisa.

dĭvĭt-ĭæ, ĭārum, f. plur. [dīves, dĭvĭt-is, "rich "] (" Things pertaining to the *dives* "; hence) *Riches, wealth ;*—at xlviii. 5 maximis divitiis is Abl. of quality [§ 115].

dĭvors-e, adv. [divors-us, "separate "] *Apart, in a scattered way.* ☞ Comp.: dĭvors-ĭus ; (Sup.: divorsissĭme).

dĭvorsĭus, comp. adv. ; see divorse.

dĭvor-sus, sa, sum, adj. [for divort-sus ; fr. divort-o (= divert-o), "to turn away, *or* in a different direction "] (" Turned away *or* in a different direction "; hence) 1. a. *Apart, separate, single, alone ;*—at xx. 5 in adverbial force, *separately, individually.* —b. Of things: *Contrary, opposite,* in their nature, *etc. ;* v. 8.—2. a. *Different, various.* —b. *Different, unlike, dissimilar.*—c. *Of a different nature, kind,* or *sort.*

do, dĕdi, dătum, dăre, 1. v. a.: 1. *To give* in the fullest sense of the word ; *to grant, appoint, furnish,* etc.—2. Of a province as Object: *To give, assign ;* xix. 2.—Pass. : dor, dătus sum, dări [akin to δω, root of δί-δω-μι; and to Sans. root DÁ].

dŏc-ĕo, ŭi, tum, ēre, 2. v. a. [akin to dīc-o, "to say"] 1. With Objective clause: *To show, state, inform* a person, *that*; xxvii. 4.—2. With Acc. of thing: *To tell* a person of, *to set forth*, etc.; xvii. 1.— Pass.: dŏc-ĕor, tus sum, ēri [from same root as dico; see dico].

doctus, a, um: 1. P. perf. pass. of dŏcĕo.—2. Pa.: *Well taught, learned, skilled, versed*, etc., in *or* in doing something;—at xxv. 2 docta has a threefold construction; viz. it is folld. by " Abl. of Respect" [§ 116], literis; by Inf. [§ 140, 4] psallĕre, *etc.*; by "Acc. of Respect" [§ 100] alia.

dŏc-ŭmentum, ŭmenti, n. [doc-eo, "to teach"] ("That which teaches"; hence) 1. *A lesson, example*, etc.—2. *A proof.*

dŏlens, ntis, P. pres. of doleo.

dŏl-ĕo, ŭi, ĭtum, ēre, 2. v. a. *To grieve at* or *over; to deplore*; xl. 2.

dŏl-or, ōris, m. [dŏl-ĕo, "to grieve"] ("That which grieves"; hence) With Objective Gen. [§ 132]: *Grief, mortification, vexation, anger at* or *on account of* something; xxviii. 4.

dŏlus, i. m.: 1. *Guile, craft, deceit, trick*, etc.—2. *A stratagem*, used in one's own defence; *address*; xxvi. 2.

domi; see dŏmus.

dŏmĭnandi, Gerund in di fr. dominor.

dŏmĭnā-tĭo, tĭōnis, f. [domin(a)-or, "to rule"] ("A ruling"; hence) 1. *Rule, power.*—2. In a bad sense: *Unrestricted power, tyranny, despotism.*

dŏmĭn-or, ātus sum, āri, 1. v. dep. [domin-us, "a lord or master"] ("To be a *dominus*"; hence) 1. *To rule, bear rule* or *sway* whether actually or figuratively.—2. Of fortune as Subject: *To be mistress, possess absolute power.*

dŏmĭtus, a, um, P. perf. pass. of domo.

dŏm-o, ŭi, ĭtum, āre, 1. v. a. ("To tame"; hence) *To subdue, vanquish.* — Pass.: dŏm-or, ĭtus sum, āri [akin to Sans. root DAM, Gr. δαμ-άω, "to tame"].

dŏmum; see domus.

dŏmus, i *and* ūs, f.: 1. *A house, dwelling-house, abode.* —Particular expressions: a. Gen.: dŏmi [§ 121, B. *a*], *At home*, i. e. at one's own house;—at xxviii. 1 the pron. suæ is put in attribution to it.—b. Acc.: dŏmum, after verbs of motion [§ 101]: *To the house, homewards.*—**2.** *Native place, country, home.* —Particular expressions : a. Gen. : **dŏmi** [§ 121. B. *a*], *In one's own country*, etc. ; xvii. 4.—b. **dŏmi militiæque,** *At home and abroad.*—c. Acc. : **dŏmum,** after verbs of motion [§ 101], *Homewards, to one's, etc., own country; * xliv. 3 [δόμος].

dōnum, ni, n. [for dā-num, fr. DA, root of do, " to give "] (" That which is given "; hence) *A gift, present.*

dormĭo, īvi *or* ĭi, ītum, īre, 4. v. n. *To sleep* [akin to δρα, a root of Gr. δαρ-θάνω; and to Sans. root DRÂ *or* DRAI, " to sleep "].

dŭbĭtando, Gerund in do fr. dubito.

dŭb-ĭto, ĭtāvi, ĭtātum, ĭtāre, 1. v. n. intens. [obsol. dub-o, fr. dŭo, "two "] (" To move two ways; to vibrate to and fro"; hence) *To doubt; to be in doubt or hesitation; to hesitate.*

dŭbĭum, ĭi ; see dubius.

dŭbĭus, ĭa, ĭum, adj. [obsol. dŭb-o, " to move two ways, vibrate to and fro "; fr. dŭo, "two "] (" Vibrating to and fro"; hence) 1. *Doubtful, uncertain.*—As Subst.: **dŭbĭum,** ĭi, n. *Doubt, a state of doubt.* —2. *Critical, perilous, difficult, precarious.*—As Subst. : **dubĭum,** ĭi, n. *Danger, peril :*

—in dubio, *in danger or peril, at stake ;* lii. 6.

dŭ-cent-i, æ, a, num. adj. plur. [du-o, "two "; cent-um, " a hundred "] *Two hundred.*

dūc-o, duxi, ductum, dūc-ĕre, 3. v. a. : 1. *To lead, conduct.*—**2.** With pro: *To hold, deem, consider, regard as* something.—Pass. : **dūc-or,** tus sum, i [akin to Sans. root DUH, " to lead out "].

duc-to, tāvi, tātum, tāre, 1. v. a. intens. [duc-o, " to lead "] 1. *To lead, conduct,* etc.—**2.** *To lead, be the leader of, command; * xix. 3.

dum, conj. [akin to diu] 1. *While, whilst, during the time that* [§ 152, II, (2)]:—dum is used at times with the present indic. of a past event ; so, dum hæc geruntur; xxxiii. 1, *etc.; * cf. [§ 153, *a*, (2)].—**2.** [§ 152, I, 4] *Provided that ;* v. 6, *etc.*

dŭ-o, æ, o, num. adj. plur. *Two* [δύο].

dŭŏ-dĕcim, num. adj. plur. indecl. [for dŭo-dĕcem; fr. dŭo, "two "; decem, " ten "] (" Two and ten ") *Twelve.*

dux, dŭcis, comm. gen. [= duc-s; fr. duc-o, " to lead "] 1. *A leader.*—**2.** *A general, chief.*

ĕ ; see ex.

ĕa, fem. nom. sing. ; neut. nom. and acc. plur. of is.

ĕădem, fem. nom. sing.; nom. and acc. plur. of idem.

ĕasdem, fem. acc. plur. of idem.

ē-dīco, dixi, dictum, dīcĕre, 3. v. a. [ē (= ex), "out"; dīco, "to speak"] ("To speak out" something; hence) To make known, declare, tell, disclose, etc.

ē-do, dĭdi, dĭtum, dĕre, 3. v. a. [ē (= ex), "out or forth"; do, "to put"] ("To put out or forth"; hence) Of a speech, writing, etc.: To publish, give to the world, etc.; xxxi. 6.

ē-dŏcĕo, dŏcŭi, doctum, dŏcēre, 2. v. a. [ē (= ex), in "intensive" force; dŏcĕo, "to teach"] 1. To teach thoroughly, to instruct.—2. With Acc. of person and Acc. of thing: a. To teach a person, or instruct a person in, something; xvi. 1. —b. To apprise or inform a person of something; to make known, or disclose, something to a person; xlviii. 4.—3. Pass.: With Acc. of thing: To be apprised, or informed, of something; xlv. 1 [see Notes to Syntax, p. 134, III, C].

ēdoctus, a, um, P. perf. pass. of ēdŏcĕo.

ē-dūco, duxi, ductum, dūcĕre, 3. v. a. [ē (= ex), "out"; dūco, in force of "to draw"] Of a sword as Object: To draw out or forth from the scabbard; li. 36.

ef-fēmĭn-o, āvi, ātum, āre, 1. v. a. [for ex-fēmĭn-o; fr. ex, denoting "change"; fēmĭn-a, "a woman"] ("To change into a woman"; hence) To render effeminate, enervate.

ef-fēt-us, a, um, adj. [for ex-fēt-us; fr. ex, in "strengthening" force; fēt-o (of birds), "to lay eggs"] ("That has laid eggs"; hence, "that has brought forth" young; hence) Exhausted, worn out, by bearing;—at liii. 5 effetā parente is Abl. Abs [§ 125, a].

ef-fĭcĭo, fēci, fectum, fĭcĕre, 3. v. a. [for ex-făcĭo; fr. ex, "out"; făcĭo, "to make"] ("To make, or work, out"; hence) 1. With double Acc.: To render something, or make something to be, that which is denoted by the second Acc.; i. 3.—2. Pass.: With Nom. as Complement [§ 93, 2]: To be rendered or made; xiv. 4.— 3. To bring about, bring to pass, effect, etc.;—at xxvi. 3 folld. by ut c. Subj.—4. To cause, produce, etc., xlii. 2.—Pass.: ef-fĭcĭor, fectus sum, fĭci.

ef-fŭgĭo, fŭgi, fŭgĭtum, fŭgĕre, 3. v. a. [for ex-fŭgĭo; fr. ex, "out from"; fŭgĭo, "to flee"] ("To flee out from"; hence) To flee from, escape, etc.; xl. 3.

ĕgens, tis: 1. P. pres. of ĕgĕo.—2. Pa.: Needy, necessitous, destitute.

ĕg-ĕo, ŭi, no sup., ĕre, 2.
v. n.: 1. *To be in need; to be
needy,* or *destitute.*—2. With
Gen. [§ 119, 1]: *To be without, to be destitute or devoid
of, to be deficient in* [akin to
ἀχ-ήν, "needy"].

ĕges-tas, tātis, f. [for egent-
tas; fr. ĕgens, egent-tis, "being
in need"] ("The state of the
egens"; hence) 1. *Need, deep
poverty, indigence, destitu-
tion, a destitute condition.*
—2. With Objective Gen. :
Want or *need of* something;
a deficiency in something.

ēgi, perf. ind. of ago.

ĕgo, Gen. mĕi (plur. nos),
pers. pron.: 1. *I.*—2. Strengthened by suffix met : *I myself*
[akin to Gr. ἐγώ ; Sans.
aham].

ĕgrĕdĭens, ntis, P. pres. of
ēgrĕdĭor.

ĕ-grĕdĭor, gressus sum,
grĕdi, 3. v. dep. [for ē-grădĭor;
fr. ē (= ex), "out"; grădĭor
"to step"] ("To step out"
hence) *To come out* or *forth*
from a place, *etc.*

ĕ-grĕg-ĭus, ĭa, ĭum, adj. [ē
(= ex), "out of"; grex, greg-
is, "a flock"] ("That is
(chosen) out of the flock";
hence) *Excellent, eminent,
famous, remarkable, etc.*

ĕgressus, a, um, P. perf.
of ēgrĕdĭor.

eisdem, dat. *and* abl. plur.
of idem.

ēlĕgan-ter, adv. [for ēlĕg-
ant-ter; fr. ēlĕgans, ēlĕgant-
is, "elegant"] ("After the
manner of the *elegans*";
hence) *Elegantly, tastefully,
gracefully,* etc. ☞ Comp.:
ēlĕgant-ĭus; (Sup.: ēlĕgant-
issĭme).

ēlĕgantĭus, comp. adv.; see
eleganter.

ēlŏquent-ĭa, ĭæ, f. [ēlŏquens,
ēlŏquent-is, "eloquent"] ("The
quality of the *eloquens*";
hence) *Eloquence.*

ĕ-mentĭor, mentītus sum,
mentīri, 4. v. dep. [ē (= ex),
"without force"; mentĭor,
"to lie, *or* speak falsely,
about"] *To lie,* or *speak
falsely, about; to state falsely,
give a false colour to;*—at xlix.
4 ementiundo quæ, *etc.* =
ementiundo ea, quæ, *etc.*

ēmentĭundo (= ēment-
ĭendo), Gerund in do fr.
ēmentĭor.

ĕmo, ēmi, emptum, ĕmĕre,
3. v. a. [ĕmo, "to take"] ("To
take" to one's self in exchange
for money; hence) *To buy,
purchase.*

ĕ-mŏrĭor, mortŭus sum,
mŏri, 3. v. dep. [ē (= ex), in
"augmentative" force; mŏr-
ĭor, "to die"] *To die quite*
or *utterly; to die out and
out.*

en, interj. [§ 138] *Lo! behold! see!* [ἤν].

ĕnim, conj. *For.*

ĕnim-vĕro (sometimes written separately enim vero), adv. [enim, "truly"; vero, "truly"] *To be sure, certainly, indeed, in truth, assuredly.*

ēnĭte-sco, ēnĭt-ŭi, no sup., ēnĭte-scĕre, 3. v. n. [enite-o, "to shine out or forth"] *To shine forth; to be conspicuous or distinguished.*

ē-nŭmĕro, nŭmĕrāvi, nŭmĕrātum, nŭmĕrāre, 1. v. a. [ē (= ex), in "strengthening" force; nŭmĕro, "to reckon"] ("To reckon completely or thoroughly"; hence) *To reckon, or count, up; to enumerate.*

ē-nuntĭo, nuntĭāvi, nuntĭātum, nuntĭāre, 1. v. a. [ē (= ex), "out"; nuntio, "to tell"] ("To tell out"; hence) *To divulge, disclose, reveal,* etc.

1. ĕo, masc. *and* neut. abl. sing. of is.

2. ĕo, adv. [prob. for eom (=eum), old acc. sing. masc. of pron. is, "this, that"] 1. Of place: *To that place, thither, there.—*2. Of amount *or* degree: *To such an amount* or *degree; to that extent,* etc. :— usque eo, ut (folld. by Subj.), *even to such a degree, that,* etc.; xlix. 4.—3. Of cause *or* reason: *a.* Referring to what precedes: *On that account, therefore.—b.* Referring to what follows: *For this reason, on the following account :—*eo . . . quo, *for the following*

reason . . . . (viz.) *in order that;* xlviii. 4.

3. ĕo, with comparative degree; see is.

4. ĕo, īvi *or* ĭi, ĭtum, īre v. n. *To go;—*at xxxvi. 4 folld. by Supine in um [§ 141, 5]: so, lii. 12;—at vi. 5 ire is the Hist. Inf. [§ 140, 2] [root I, akin to Sans. root I, Gr. *ἰ-έναι,* "to go"].

1. ĕōdem, masc. *and* neut. abl. sing. of īdem.

2. ĕōdem, adv. [for eomdem (=eundem), old acc. masc. sing. of idem, "the same"] 1. *To the same place.—*2. *To the same matter,* or *point; to the same subject,* etc.

ĕos, masc. acc. plur. of is.

ĕosdem, masc. acc. plur. of idem.

ĕqu-ĕ-s, ĭtis, m. [for equ-i-(t)s; fr. ĕqu-us; I, root of eo, "to go"] ("The horse-going one"; hence) 1. *A horseman.—*Plur.: *Cavalry.—*2. *A* (Roman) *knight,* whose horse was furnished by the state.

ĕqu-ester, tris, estre, adj. [equ-us, "a horse"] ("Pertaining to a horse"; hence) *Equestrian,* i. e. of the knights.

ĕ-quĭdem, adv. [e = demonstrative particle ce; quidem, "indeed"] *Indeed, truly.*

ĕqu-us, i, m. *A horse:—*equo (abl.), *on his horse,* or *on horseback;* lix. 5 [akin to Gr. ἵκκος (= ἵππος), and Sans. açva].

ēreptus, a, um, P. perf. pass. of eripio.

ērĭpĭendus, a, um, Gerundive of eripio.

ē-rĭpĭo, rĭpŭi, reptum, rĭpĕre, 3. v. a. [for ē-răpĭo; fr. ē (= ex), "away"; răpĭo, "to snatch"] 1. *To snatch, tear,* or *wrest away.*—2. With Acc., and Dat. of person (Dat. of disadvantage) [§ 107]: *To snatch* or *take away* from; *to deprive* one *of;* xii. 4: so in Pass. constr. with Dat. only; li. 22.—3. With Abl. *or* ex: *To deliver* or *set free from;* xlvi. 2; xlviii. 1.—4. *To rescue,* etc., *from custody;* lii. 14, where it is folld. by ā and Abl. of agent.—Pass.: ē-rĭpĭor, reptus sum, rĭpi.

ē-rumpo, rūpi, ruptum, rumpĕre, 3. v. n. [ē (= ex), "out"; rumpo, "to break"] *To break out; to burst* or *sally forth; to rush out.*

et, conj. *And:*—et . . . et, *both . . . and* [akin to Gr. ἔτι, "moreover"; Sans. *ati,* "much, exceedingly"].

ĕt-ĕnim, conj., introducing a corroborative clause or one containing the reason of the preceding statement [et, "and"; enim, "truly"] *And truly, for truly, for.*

ĕtĭam, conj. [akin to et] 1. *And too, and furthermore; likewise, also, besides.* — 2. *Even.*

Etrūrĭa, æ, f. *Etruria* (now *Tuscany);* a country of central Italy.

et-si, conj. [et, "even"; si, "if"] *Even if, although;* see tamen.

e-vĕnĭo, vēni, ventum, vĕnīre, 4. v. n. [ē (= ex), "out"; vĕnĭo, "to come"] ("To come out"; hence) *To turn out, issue, happen, occur, take place, come to pass.*

ēvĕn-tus, tūs, m. [ēvĕn-ĭo, "to turn out, issue"] ("That which turns out *or* issues"; hence) *Issue, result, termination.*

ēvŏcātus, a, um, P. perf. pass. of ēvŏco.—As Subst.: ēvŏcātus, i, m. *An evocatus;* i.e. *a veteran* (Roman) *soldier,* who had served his time and was called out to do duty on some emergency; such an one was exempted from all the drudgery of the military service.

ē-vŏco, vŏcāvi, vŏcātum, vŏcāre, 1. v. a. [ē (= ex), "out"; vŏco, "to call"] *To call out* or *forth, to summon.* —Pass.: ē-vŏcor, vŏcātus sum, vŏcāri.

ex (ē), prep. gov. abl.: 1. Of place: *Out of, away from:* —ex ĭtĭnĕre, (*out of the journey,* i. e.) *during* or *on the journey;* xxxiv. 2.—2. *From, through, by reason of, in consequence of.* — 3. *To* denote a transition *from,* or *out of,* one state, *etc.,* to another.—4. *Out of, arising out of* some circumstance, *etc.*—5. *According to, in accordance or conformity with.*—6. Of time : a. *After, immediately or directly after.*—b. *From, from the time of, since.*—7. Specifying a multitude from which a thing, *etc.,* is taken, or of which it forms a part : *Out of, of :*—ex alterā parte, (*out of the other party* or *side,* i. e.) *on the other side,* lix. 4 [Gr. ἐξ].

ex-ædĭfĭco, ædĭfĭcāvi, ædĭfĭcātum, ædĭfĭcāre, 1. v. a. [ex, denoting "completeness"; ædĭfĭco, "to build"] ("To build completely"; hence) *To build up, erect, construct.*—Pass.: **ex-ædĭfĭcor,** ædĭfĭcātus sum, ædĭfĭcāri.

exæquandus, a, um, Gerundive of exæquo.

exæquātus, a, um, P. perf. pass. of exæquo.

ex-æquo, æquāvi, æquātum, æquāre, 1. v. a. [ex, denoting "completeness"; æquo, "to make equal"] ("To make quite equal to *or* level with" something; hence) *To place on a level* or *equality; to make perfectly equal.*—Pass.: **ex-æquor,** æquātus sum, æquāri.

exăgĭtandus, a, um, Gerundive of exăgĭto.

ex-ăgĭto, ăgĭtāvi, ăgĭtātum, ăgĭtāre, 1. v. a. [ex, "without force"; ăgĭto, "to drive about"] ("To drive about, pursue, chase," *etc.;* hence) 1. *To rouse up, to exasperate,* etc.—2. Mentally : *To disturb, disquiet, harass, torment,* etc.—3. *To stir up, urge on, excite.*—Pass.: **ex-ăgĭtor,** ăgĭtātus sum, ăgĭtāri.

ex-cēdo, cessi, cessum, cēdĕre, 3. v. n. [ex, "out *or* forth"; cēdo, "to go"] *To go out, forth, or away; to depart, withdraw,* etc.

excel-sus, sa, sum, adj. [for excell-sus; fr. excell-o, "to raise up"] ("Raised up", hence) *Elevated, high, lofty.*—As Subst. : **excelsum,** i, n. *An elevated* or *lofty position, a high station.*

ex-cĭo, cīvi *or* cĭi, cĭtum, īre, 4. v. a. [ex, "out *or* forth"; cĭo, "to make to go"; hence, "to call"] ("To call out *or* forth"; hence) Mentally : *To rouse, excite,* etc.—Pass.: **ex-cĭor,** cĭtus sum, īri.

excĭ-to, tāvi, tātum, tāre, 1. v. a. intens. [excĭ-o, "to call forth"] ("To call forth"; hence, "to raise" a thing; hence, "to rouse, excite") *To rouse, excite, spur on, stimulate.*

excĭtus, a, um, P. perf. pass. of excio.

exemplum, i, n.: 1. *An example* in the widest acceptation of the word.—2. Of a letter : *A transcript, copy.*

ex-ercĕo, ercŭi, ercĭtum, ercēre, 2. v. a. [for ex-arceo ; fr. ex, " out "; arceo, " to enclose "] (" To keep *or* drive out of an enclosure " ; hence, " to drive on ; to keep busy *or* at work " ; hence, " to employ "; hence) 1. *To exercise*, whether in a proper or figurative force.—2. *To practise.*—3. *To occupy, employ.*

exercĭtātus, ta, tum : 1. P. perf. pass. of exercito.—2. Pa. : *Trained, practised*, etc.

exerc-ĭto, ĭtāvi, ĭtātum, ĭtāre, 1. v. a. freq. [exerc-eo, " to exercise."] *To exercise diligently* or *frequently.*—Pass.: **exerc-ĭtor**, ĭtātus sum, ĭtāri.

exerc-ĭtus, ĭtūs, m. [exercĕo, " to exercise "] (" Exercise "; hence) *An army*, as a trained and disciplined body of men.

ex-istĭmo (-istumo), ĭstĭmāvi, ĭstĭmātum, ĭstĭmāre, 1. v. a. [for ex æstĭmo; fr. ex, " without force "; æstĭmo, " to think "] 1. With double Acc.: *To think, deem, consider* a person or thing to be that which is denoted by the second Acc.—2. With Objective clause: *To think, consider, be of opinion that*, etc.

existumo, āre; see existĭmo.

exĭ-tus, tūs, m. [exĕo, " to go out," through true root EXI] (" A going out "; hence) *End, close, termination.*

ex-opto, optāvi, optātum, optāre, 1. v. a. [ex, in " augmentative " force ; opto, " to wish for "] *To wish*, or *long, for greatly; to desire intensely* or *eagerly.*

ex-ŏrĭor, ortus sum, ŏrīri, 3. *and* 4. v. dep. [ex, " up "; ŏrĭor, " to rise "] *To rise up, arise.*

ex-orno, ornāvi, ornātum, ornāre, 1. v. a. [ex, " without force "; orno, " to equip "] *To equip, fit out, furnish.*

exortus, a, um, P. perf. of exŏrĭor.

ex-pĕd-ĭo, īvi *or* ĭi, ītum, īre, 4. v. a. [ex, " out of "; pes, pĕd-is, " the foot "] (" To get the foot out of " a snare, etc.; hence, " to extricate, set free "; hence) *To put in order, arrange, set right.*

expĕdī-tus, ta, tum, adj. [expĕdĭ-o, " to set free "] (" Set free " from something ; hence) 1. *Unencumbered.*—2. *Without baggage, light-armed.* —As Subst. : expĕdīti, ōrum, m. plur. *Light-armed troops* or *soldiers.*

ex-pello, pŭli, pulsum, pellĕre, 3. v. a. [ex, " out "; pello, " to drive "] *To drive out* or *away.*

experg-iscor, experrectua sum, expergisci, 3. v. dep. [experg-o, "to awaken"] ("To be awakened, become awake"; hence) *To wake up; to rouse or bestir one's self,* etc.

ex-pĕrĭor, pertus sum, pĕr-īri, 4.v.dep.[ex, "thoroughly"; obsol. pĕrĭor, "to go *or* pass through"; hence, " to try "] (" To try thoroughly"; hence) *To try, attempt, have recourse to.*

ex-pers, pertis, adj. [for ex-pars ; fr. ex, implying "negation"; pars, "a part"] ("Having no part" in a thing; hence) With Gen. or Abl. [§ 119, b.] : *Destitute,* or *devoid, of.*

explānandus, a, um, Gerundive of explāno.

ex-plăno,plānāvi,plānātum, plānāre, 1. v. a. [ex, " out "; plano, " to flatten "] (" To flatten *or* spread out "; hence) *To make plain* or *clear, to explain.*

ex-plĕo, plēvi,plētum,plēre, 2. v. a. [ex, in "strengthening force"; plĕo, " to fill "] (" To fill up, fill full "; hence) 1. *To fill up* with the regular number, *complete,* etc.—2. *To satisfy, sate, glut* a longing or one who longs.

explēvi, perf. ind. of expleo.

explōrātus, a, um, P. perf. pass. of exploro.

ex-plōro, plōrāvi, plōrātum,

plōrāre, 1. v. a. [ex, in "intensive" force; plōro, "to call out"] ("To call out greatly *or* aloud "; hence, as a result) 1. *To search out, seek to discover, ascertain.*— 2. Military t. t. : *To spy out, reconnoitre, ascertain* or *learn* by scouts.—Pass. : **ex-plōror,** plōrātus sum, plōrāri.

expŭlĕram, pluperf. ind. of expello.

expurgandus, a, um, Gerundive of expurgo :—sui expurgandi, *of exculpating himself* [§ 148].

ex-purgo, purgāvi, purgātum, purgāre, 1. v. a. [ex, in "augmentative" force; purgo, " to cleanse "] ("To cleanse quite *or* thoroughly "; hence) *To clear of a charge, exculpate, vindicate.*

ex-quĭro, quīsīvi, quīsītum, quīrĕre, 3. v. a. [for ex-quæro; fr. ex, " very much "; quæro, " to seek for "] (" To seek for very much"; hence) *To search or seek out;*—at xiii. 3 exquirere is the Hist. Inf. [§ 140, 2].

ex-sanguis, sangue, adj. [ex, denoting "negation *or* opposition " to the force of the word to which it is prefixed ; sanguis, "blood"] ("Bloodless"; hence) 1. *Deadly* or *ghastly pale, wan.* —2. *Utterly feeble* or *enfeebled, exhausted.*

exsĕcra-tĭo, tĭōnis, f. [ex-sĕcr(a)-or, "to take a solemn oath," containing imprecations in case of its infringement] ("A taking a solemn oath," etc.; hence) *A solemn oath* containing imprecations in case of its infringement.

ex-sĕcr-or, ātus sum, āri, 1. v. a. [for ex-săcror; fr. ex, in "intensive" force; sacr-o, "to devote to destruction"] ("To devote greatly to destruction"; hence) *To curse greatly, to execrate;*—at xlviii. 1 exsecrari is the Hist. Inf. [§ 140, 2].

ex-sĕquor, sĕquūtus sum, sĕqui, 3. v. dep. [ex, denoting "to the end *or* close"; sĕquor, "to follow"] ("To follow to the end"; hence) *To follow up, carry out, execute, accomplish.*

exsĭl-ĭum, ĭi, n. [for exsŭlĭum; fr. exsul, exsŭl-is, "an exile"] ("The condition, *or* state, of an *exsul*"; hence) *Banishment, exile.*

ex-specto, spectāvi, spectātum, spectāre, 1. v. a. [ex, "very much"; specto, "to look out"] ("To look out very much" for a thing; hence) 1. *To wait for, await, expect.*—2. *To look, hope,* or *long for; to desire.*

ex-spŏlĭo, spŏlĭāvi, spŏlĭātum, spŏlĭāre, 1. v. a. [ex, in "intensive" force; spŏlĭo, "to spoil"] (*To spoil, pillage,* or *plunder utterly.*—Pass.: ex-spŏlĭor, spŏlĭātus sum, spŏlĭāri.

exstinctus, a, um, P. perf. pass. of exstinguo.

ex-stinguo, stinxi, stinctum, stinguĕre, 3. v. a. [ex, "without force"; stinguo, "to extinguish"] *To extinguish, quench, put out.*

exstrŭendus, a, um, Gerundive of exstruo.

ex-strŭo, struxi, structum, strŭĕre, 3. v. a. [ex, "quite, thoroughly"; strŭo, "to build"] ("To build quite or thoroughly"; hence) *To build over, cover with buildings.*

ex-sŭpĕro, sŭpĕrāvi, sŭpĕrātum, sŭpĕrāre, 1. v. a. [ex, "upwards"; sŭpĕro, "to go or pass over"] ("To go or pass over upwards"; hence, "to rise above, surmount"; hence) *To surpass, exceed.*

ex-ter (-tĕrus), tĕra, tĕrum, adj. [ex, "out"] 1. Pos.: *On the outside, outward.*—2. Sup.: a. Of place: ("Outermost"; hence) *Furthest, most distant.* —b. Of time, etc.: (a) *Latest, last.*—(b) *The last part* or *close of* that denoted by the subst. to which it is in attribution; xlix. 2.—c. *Extreme* in quality or degree.—As Subst.: (α) extrēmum, i, n. *An extremity, a dangerous* or *critical state* or *position;* lii. 11. —(β) extrēma, ōrum, n. plur.

Extremities, most violent measures, etc.; xxvi. 5.

ex-tollo, no perf. nor sup., tollĕre, 3. v. a. [ex, "up"; tollo, "to lift *or* raise"] ("To lift *or* raise up"; hence) *To exalt, extol.*

ex-torquĕo, torsi, tortum, torquēre, 2. v. a. [ex, "out *or* away"; torqueo, "to twist"] ("To twist out *or* away"; hence) With Dat. of person: *To wrest away from.*

extrā, prep. gov. acc. [contr. fr. extĕrā, abl. sing. fem. of exter *or* extĕrus, "outward"] ("On the outward part of"; hence, "outside of"; hence) 1. *Beyond; out,* or *outside, of.*—2. *Besides, in addition.*

extrēmus, a, um; see exter.

Făb-ĭus, ĭi, m. [fab-a, "a bean"] ("One pertaining to beans") *Fabius;* a Roman name.

fac, pres. imperat. of facio.

făcĕt-ĭæ, ĭārum, f. plur. [făcĕt-us, "witty"] ("The state *or* quality of the *facetus*"; hence) *Wittiness, wit, humour,* etc.

făc-ĭes, ĭēi, f. [prob. fr. făc-ĭo, "to make"] ("Make, form, figure"; hence) 1. *Face, visage, countenance.*—2. *Look, appearance, aspect.*

făcĭl-e, adv. [facil-is, "easy"] *Easily, with ease.* ☞ Comp.: făcĭl-ĭus.

făc-ĭlis, ĭle, adj. [făc-ĭo, "to do"] ("That may, *or* can, be done"; hence) *Easy, devoid of difficulty;*—at iii. 2 folld. by Supine in u [§ 141, 6]. ☞ (Comp.: făcĭl-ĭor); Sup.: făcil-ĭmus.

făcĭl-ĭtas, ĭtātis, f. [facil-is, "courteous"] ("The quality of the *facilis*"; hence) *Courtesy, affability.*

făcĭlĭus, comp. adv.; see facile.

făcĭllĭmus, a, um, sup. of facilis;—at xiv. 1 folld. by Supine in u [§ 141, 6].

făc-ĭnus, ĭnŏris, n. [făc-ĭo, "to do"] ("A thing done"; hence) 1. In a good sense: *An act, action, deed;* vii. 6, etc.—2. In bad sense: a. *A bad deed, evil act, crime.*—b. Of persons: *An instrument of crime,* etc., *an evil doer,* etc.

făcĭo, fēci, factum, făcĕre, 3. v. a. and n. ("To cause to be"; hence) 1. Act.: a. *To make* in the widest acceptation of the term:—iter facere, (*to make a march;* i.e.) *to march,* xix. 3; bellum facere, *to make* (i.e. *to enter upon* or *begin*) *a war;* xxiv. 2, *etc.;* binos imperatores facere, *to make* (i.e. *to appoint* or *create*) *two commanders,* i.e. two consuls, vi. 7.—b. With double Acc.: *To make* a person or thing that which is denoted by the second Acc.;

lii. 19; lviii. 19.—c. (a) With Subj. alone : *To cause, bring about* or *to pass*, etc., *that :* —fac (*cause that;* i. e.) *take care*, or *see, that;* xliv. 5. —(b) Impers. Pass. : **factum** (est), *It was brought*, or *it came, to pass;*—at liii. 4 folld. by eo, as Abl. of thing : *It came to pass from that* or *therefrom;* see is.—d. *To do, perform*, an action, *etc.;*—at viii. 4 supply ea (*sc.* facta) after fecère.—e. Of a bad action : *To commit, perpetrate*, etc. ; xv. 1, *etc.*—f. Without follg. Acc. : *To do*, etc.;—at viii. 5 facère is dependent on malebat.—2. Neut. : With adv. : *To do, act, deal* in the way denoted by the adv.; li. 43, *etc.*—Pass. : fīo, factus sum, fīĕri ; see fīo [akin to Sans. root BHŬ, "to be," in causative force].

făcĭundus, a, um (= faciendus), Gerundive of facio.

fac-tĭo, tĭōnis, f. [făc-ĭo, "to take part" with one] ("A taking part" with one; hence) *A* political *party; a side, faction.*

factĭ-ōsus, ōsa, ōsum, adj. [contr. fr. factĭōn-ōsus; fr. factio, faction-is, "faction"] ("Full of *factio*"; hence) *Factious, full of party-spirit, seditious.*—As Subst. : factĭ-ōsus, i, m. *A factious person, a partisan*, etc.

factu, Supine in u fr. facio.

fac-tum, ti, n. [fac-io, "to do"] ("That which is done"; hence) *A deed, action, act.*

factūrus, a, um, P. fut. of facio.

factus, a, um, P. perf. pass. of facio;—at xxi. 8; xliii. 3, and li. 43 supply esse with facturum ;—for facto opus see opus;—at x. 6 supply est with factum ; cf., also, viii. 4.

făcund-ĭa, ĭæ, f. [făcundus, "eloquent "] ("The quality of the *facundus*"; hence) *Eloquence.*

Fæsŭlæ, ārum, f. plur. *Fæsulæ* (now *Fiesole*); a city of Etruria:—Fæsulas, *to Fæsulæ*, Acc. of place "whither" [§ 101]; xxvii. 1 ; xxx. 3 :— Fæsulis, *from Fæsulæ*, Abl. of place "whence" [§ 121. C]. —Hence, **Fæsŭlānus**, āna, ānum, adj. *Of*, or *belonging to, Fæsulæ; Fæsulan.*

Fæsŭlānus, a, um, adj.; see Fæsŭlæ.

fallāc-ĭa, ĭæ, f. [fallax, fallāc-is, "deceitful "] ("The quality of the *fallax*"; hence) 1. *Deceitfulness, deceit.*—2. *A trick, artifice, stratagem.*

fallo, fĕfelli, falsum, fallĕre, 3. v. a. ("To cause to fall *or* stumble"; hence) *To deceive, trick, dupe, cheat* [akin to Gr. σφάλλω; and to Sans. root SPHAL, "to tremble," in causative force.

fals-o, adv.[fals-us, "false"] ("After the manner of the *falsus*"; hence) *Falsely.*

fal-sus, sa, sum, adj. [for fall-sus; fr. fall-o, "to deceive"] ("Deceptive"; hence) 1. *False, untrue.*—2. *False, insincere, deceptive ;* x. 5.

fāma, æ, f. ("That which is spoken *or* said"; hence) 1. *A report, rumour.*—2. *Fame, character.*—3. *Reputation, renown* [φήμη].

fă-mes, mis, f. [for fagmes] ("That which eats *or* is voracious"; hence) *Hunger* [akin to Gr. φαγ-εῖν; and Sans. root BHAKSH, "to eat"].

fămĭl-ĭa, ĭæ, f. [for famulia; fr. famul-us, "a servant"] ("The thing pertaining to the *famulus*"; hence) 1. *A household establishment ; servants, domestics, slaves.* — 2. Of gladiators : *A family,* i. e. *a body, company,* etc., under the same "lanista," *i. e.* "trainer *or* teacher."—3. *A family* regarded as part of a "gens," *i. e.* "a clan *or* house" ; xxxi. 7 ;—at xli. 2 in plur.

1. **fămĭlĭ-āris,** āre, adj. [fămĭlĭ-a, "a family"] 1. *Of, or belonging to, a family :*—res familiaris, (*effects pertaining to a family ;* i. e.) *property,* etc.—2. *Intimate, friendly, on good terms, fa-miliar.*—As Subst. : **fămĭlĭār-is,** is, m. *An intimate friend.*

2. **fămĭlĭāris,** is ; see 1. familiaris.

fămĭlĭār-ĭtas, ĭtātis, f. [familiar-is, "an intimate friend"] ("The state, *or* condition, of the *familiaris*" *,* hence) *Intimate friendship, intimacy.*

fă-num, ni, n. [f(a)-or, "to speak"] ("A thing spoken"; hence) *A temple, sanctuary, fane* dedicated to a deity by a set form of words or consecration.

fas, n. indecl. *Divine law.*

fasc-is, is, m. (1. "A bundle.") — 2. Plur. : *The fasces ;* i. e. a bundle of rods, in each of which was an axe, carried by the lictors before the consuls, or other chief magistrates possessing the power of life and death. The plur. is used because several rods (each of which was itself "a bundle") were bound up together [akin to Sans. root BADH, "to bind"].

fătĕor, fassus sum, fătēri, 2. v. dep. [akin to f(a)or, "to speak"] *To own, acknowledge, confess.*

fătīgo, āvi, ātum, āre, 1. v. a. : 1. *To weary, tire, exhaust, fatigue.*—2. *To harass, plague, torment,* etc.

fă-tum, ti, n. [f(a)-or, "to speak"] ("That which is

spoken "; hence) *Destiny, fate.*

fauc-es, ium, f. plur. ("The eating *or* swallowing thing"; hence) *The jaws* [akin to Sans. root BHAKSH, "to eat"].

făvĕo, făvi, fautum, făvēre, 2. v. n. With Dat. [§ 106, (3); *or* § 107]: *To be well-disposed* or *favourable to; to favour.*

Fĕbrŭ-ărĭus, ārĭi, m. [febrŭ-um, " expiation, atonement "] ("The thing — here, month —pertaining to *februum*"; hence) *February,* i. e. the month of expiation, so called from the great festival of expiation and lustration being celebrated on the 15th day of it.

fĕnĕrā-tor, tŏris, m. [fener(a)-o, "to lend on interest"] ("One who lends on interest"; hence) In bad sense: *A money-lender, usurer.*

fĕre, adv.: 1. *Nearly, almost, much about.*—2. *For the most part, generally, in general, commonly.*

fĕrent-ărĭus, ārĭi, m. [fĕrens, fĕrent-is, " carrying "] ("One pertaining to *ferens*") *A ferentarius;* a light-armed soldier who is said to have derived his name from carrying with him on the campaign javelins *or* darts; while the *funditor* or "slinger" would find his means of attack in the stones which he would obtain near the battle-field.

fĕrĭo, no perf. nor sup., īre, 4. v. a.: 1. *To strike.*—2. *To smite, slay, kill;*—at lx. 4 ferire is the Hist. Inf. [§ 140, 2].

fĕro, tŭli, lātum, ferre, v. a.: 1. *To bear, carry, bring,* whether actually or figuratively;—at xxi. 2 fert has a compound subject, viz. bellum atque lubido; as however it is in the sing., it shows that its subject represents a simple idea, not two distinct ones.— 2. *To report, relate, make known,* etc.—3. With ellipse of personal pron. and in reflexive force: Of the mind as Subject: (*To move itself;* i. e.) *To be disposed, inclined,* etc.; lviii. 5 [akin to Gr. φέρω, also to Sans. root BHṚI; tŭl-i is formed fr. root TUL or TOL, whence tol-lo, lā-tum = tlā-tum, akin to τλάδ-ω].

fĕrōc-ĭa, ĭæ, f. [fĕrox, fĕrōc-is, " fierce "] ("The quality of the *ferox*"; hence) *Fierceness, wild boldness, untamed spirit.*

fĕrōc-ĭter, adv. [id.] ("After the manner of the *ferox*"; hence) In a bad sense: *Fiercely, savagely, insolently.* ☞ Comp.: fĕrōc-ĭus; (Sup.: fĕrōc-issĭme).

fĕrōcĭus, comp. adv.; see ferociter.

fĕrox, ōcis, adj. : 1. In a good sense : *Spirited, bold, courageous.*—2. In a bad sense : *Fierce, violent, head-strong.* ☞ Comp. : fĕroc-ĭor.

fer-rum, ri, n. : 1. *Iron.*—2. *An iron implement* of any kind ; esp. *a sword.*

fĕr-us, a, um, adj. ("Wild" ; hence) Of persons, etc. : *Un-cultivated, barbarous, savage,* etc. [akin to θήρ, Æolic φήρ, "a wild animal"].

festīnando, Gerund in do fr. festīno.

festīno, āvi, ātum, āre, 1. v. n. *To make haste ; to hasten,* etc.

fictus, a, um : 1. P. perf. pass. of fingo.—2. Pa. : a. Of things : *Feigned, fictitious, false.*—b. Of persons : *False, dissembling.*

fĭd-ēlis, ēle, adj. [fĭd-es, "faith"] ("Pertaining to *fides*" ; hence) *Faithful.*

fĭd-es, ĕi, f. [fĭd-o, "to trust"] 1. *Trust,* in a person or thing, *confidence, faith.*—2. *Credit.*—3. *Fidelity, faith-fulness.*—4. *Good faith, sin-cerity.*—5. *A promise, en-gagement, word.*—6. *A given promise* of protection or secur-ity ; *guardian care, protection, security :* — fides publica, *a public promise of security,* etc. ; *i. e.* security or pro-tection promised in the name of the state, *etc. ;* xlvii. 1. —7. *Credibility, trustworthi-ness, truth.*

Fīd-Ius, ĭi, m. [fīd-es, "truth"] ("One pertaining to *fides*") *Fidius ; i. e.* the god of truth ; a surname of Jupiter,—always connected with deus or medius (*i. e.* particle me—see me, no. 2. —dius = deus) ; sometimes written as one word medius-fidius ; in this connexion used as a form of strong asseveration :—*by the god of truth ; most assuredly ; most un-doubtedly.*

fĭdūc-ĭa, ĭæ, f. [obsol. fĭdūc-us, *or* fĭdux (= fiduc-s), "trusting"] ("The quality of the *fiducus* or *fidux*" ; hence) *Confidence, reliance, assurance.*

fĭd-us, a, um, adj. [fīd-o, "to trust"] *Trusty, faithful :* —sometimes with Dat. [§ 106, (3)].

Fĭgŭlus, i, m. [fĭgŭlus, "a potter"] *Figulus (Caius) ;* a Roman consul, colleague of Lucius Cæsar ; xvii. 1.

fīlĭa, æ, f. [akin to filius] *A daughter.*

fīlĭus, ĭi, m. ("One caused to be" ; hence) *A son* [akin to Sans root BHŪ, "to be," in causative force].

fingo, finxi, fictum, fingĕre, 3. v. a. : 1. *To form, fashion, make.*—2. *To imagine, sup-*

pose.—3. *To feign, invent* or *make up falsely, pretend,* etc. — Pass. : **fingor,** fictus sum, fingi [prob. akin to θιγ, root of θιγ-γάνω, "to touch"].

fī-nis, nis, m. [probably for fid-nis, fr. findo, "to divide," through root FID] ("The dividing thing"; hence, "a boundary, limit"; hence) *An end.*

fin-ĭtĭmus, ĭtĭma, ĭtĭmum, adj. [fin-is; see finis] ("Pertaining to a *finis*"; hence) *Bordering upon, adjoining, neighbouring.*

fīo, factus sum, fĭĕri, v. pass. irreg.; see facio : 1. *To be made.*—2. *To become.*—3. *To happen* or *come to pass; to be brought about; to take place.*—4. Impers.: Perf. Inf. : factum (esse), *that it came to pass, that it was brought about.*

fir-mus, ma, mum, adj. ("Bearing"; hence, "firm"; hence) 1. *Strong, powerful.* —2. *Steadfast, steady, firm* [either for fer-mus, fr. fĕr-o, "to bear"; or akin to Sans. root DHRI, "to bear"].

Flaccus, i, m. [flaccus, "flabby"; of persons, "flap-eared"] *Flaccus* (*Lucius Valerius*); one of the Roman praetors at the date of Catiline's conspiracy; xlv. 1.

flāgĭtĭ-ōsus, ōsa, ōsum, adj. [flagiti-um, "a disgraceful act"] ("Full of *flagitium*"; hence) *Very shameful* or *disgraceful; infamous, flagitious.*

flāgĭt-ĭum, ĭi, n. [flāgĭt-o, "to demand *or* desire earnestly"] ("A demanding, *etc.,* earnestly some bad thing"; hence) 1. *A disgraceful, shameful,* or *infamous act.*—2. Of persons : *A profligate, scoundrel, villain.*—3. *Shame, disgrace.*

flāg-ro, rāvi, rātum, rāre, 1. v. n. ("To burn *or* be on fire"; hence) Of persons : *To be inflamed* or *burn* with passion, *etc.* [akin to Gr. φλέγ-ω, "to burn"; Sans. root BHRÂJ, "to shine"].

Flāmĭn-ĭus, ĭi, m. [flāmen, flāmĭn-is, "a flamen *or* priest" of some particular deity] ("One pertaining to a *flamen*") *Flaminius,* a Roman name; see Flamma.

Flamma, æ, m. [flamma, "a flame"] *Flamma* (*Caius Flaminius*); a friend of Catiline, at whose house the latter stayed for some days after his flight from Rome; xxxvi. 1.

florens, ntis : 1. P. pres. of floreo.—2. Pa.: *Flourishing, prosperous, in repute; eminent, distinguished.*

flōr-ĕo, ŭi, no sup., ēre, 2. v. n. [flos, flor-is, "a flower"] ("To flower"; hence) *To be in a flourishing* or *prosperous* *condition; to flourish; to be eminent, distinguished,* or *conspicuous.*

fluxus, a, um, adj. [for flugv-sus; fr. fluo, "to flow," through root FLUGV] ("Flowing"; hence) 1. *Careless, remiss, negligent.*—2. *Fleeting, transient, frail, perishable.*

fŏc-us, i, m. *A fire-place, hearth.*

foed-us, a, um, adj. [akin to foet-ĕo, "to stink"] ("Stinking"; hence) 1. *Foul, filthy.*—2. *Detestable, abominable.*—3. *Horrible, ugly, ghastly.*

fore, fut. inf. of sum.

forem (= essem), imperf. subj. of sum.

fŏr-is, adv.: 1. *Out of doors, out of the house, abroad,* etc.—2. *In public life,* etc. [akin to Gr. θύρ-α, Sans. *dvâr,* or *dvâr-a*].

for-ma, mæ, f. [for fer-ma; fr. fĕr-o] ["That which is borne," etc.; hence) 1. *Form* in the widest sense of the word; *shape, figure.*—2. *A fine form; beauty, personal charms,* etc.

formīd-o, ĭnis, f. [formīd-o, "to fear"] ("A fearing"; hence) *Fear, dread, terror.*

formīdŏl-ōsus, ōsa, ōsum, adj. [prob. for formīdĭn-ōsus; fr. formīdo, formīdĭn-is, "fear"] ("Full of *formido*"; hence) *Productive of great fear; terrible, dreadful, formidable.*

fornix, ĭcis, m. *An arch; a vault.*

for-s, tis, f. [probably for fer-s; fr.fer-o] ("A bringing";—"that which brings"; hence) *Chance, casualty, hap.*—Adverbial expression: Forte (abl.), *By chance* or *accident; perchance.*

forte; see fors.

for-tis, te, adj. *Brave, bold, courageous.* ☞ (Comp.: fort-ĭor); Sup.: fort-issĭmus [for fer-tis, fr. fĕr-o; and so, "bearing, that bears"; hence, "strong"; hence, as a result, "brave," etc.; or akin to Sans. root DHRISH, "to be courageous"].

fort-ĭtūdo, ĭtūdĭnis, f. [fort-is, "brave"] ("The quality of the *fortis*"; hence) 1. *Bravery, valour, intrepidity.*—2. *Firmness* of spirit, *fortitude,* etc.

fort-ūna, ūnæ, f. [fors, fort-is, "chance"] ("That which appertains to *fors*"; hence) 1. *Chance, hap, luck, fortune,* whether good or bad.—2. Plur.: *Possessions, property, fortune,* etc.; xxxiii. 2.—3. Personified: *Fortune* as a goddess; viii. 1.—4. *State, condition, circumstances.*

fortūnā-tus, ta, tum, adj. [fortūn(a)-o, "to make fortunate"] ("Made fortunate"; hence] *Happy, lucky, fortunate.*

fŏr-um, i, n. ("A market-place") At Rome: *The forum;* a long open space between the Capitoline and Palatine Hills, surrounded by porticoes and the shops of bankers, *etc.* Here the public assemblies of the people were held, justice administered, and public business in general transacted. Sometimes it is called Forum Romanum [usually considered akin to foris and foras, and also "that which is out of doors"; but prps. rather akin to Gr. root τορ (whence τόρ-ος, "a passage"), and so, "that which has a passage through it *or* is passed through"].

frăg-ĭlis, ĭle, adj. [frango. "to break," through root FRAG] ("That which may, *or* can be broken"; hence) *Perishable, frail,* etc.

frango, frēgi, fractum, frangĕre, 3. v. a. *To break* [akin to Gr. ῥήγνυμι, and Sans. root BHANJ, "to split, break"].

fraus, fraudis, f. ("A being deceived"; hence) *Injury, detriment, damage:* — sine fraude, *without injury,* etc.; *i.e.* without incurring punishment; xxxvi. 2.

frēgi, perf. ind. of frango.

frēquens, ntis, adj. Of persons: *In great numbers, numerous.*

frēquent-ĭa, ĭæ, f. [frēquens, frēquent-is, "numerous"] ("The state, *or* condition, of the *frequens*"; hence) *A numerous* or *full assembly, a full meeting;* —at xlvi. 5 strengthened by magna.

frēquent-o, āvi, ātum, āre, 1. v. a. [frēquens, frēquent-is, "frequent"] ("To do as the *frequens*" does; hence) *To visit frequently, to resort to habitually, to frequent.*

frē-tus, ta, tum, adj. ("Supported" by something; hence) With Abl. [§ 119, (a)]: *Relying,* or *depending, upon; trusting to* [akin to Sans. root DHRI, "to support"].

frīg-us, ŏris, n. [frīg-ĕo, "to be cold"] *Cold, coldness.*

fro-ns, ntis, f.: 1. *The forehead* or *brow.*—2. Of troops: *The front, fore-part, front line;* lix. 2 [akin to Sans. bhrū, Gr. ὀ-φρύ-s].

fruc-tus, tūs, m. [for frugvtus; fr. fru-or, "to enjoy," through root FRUGV] ("An enjoying"; hence, "fruit, produce," as that which is enjoyed; hence) Of toil, *etc.: Fruit, reward, recompense.*

frū-mentum, menti, n. [frū-or, "to eat"] ("The thing eaten"; hence) *Corn, grain.*

frŭor, fructus sum, frŭi, 3. v. dep. With Abl. [§ 119, *a*]: *To enjoy* [root FRU *or* FRUG, akin to Sans. root BHUJ, "to enjoy"].

frustra, adv. [akin to fraudo] ("In a deceived manner"; hence) *Without effect, in vain, to no purpose.*

fŭg-a, æ, f. [fŭg-ĭo, "to flee"] *Flight.*

fŭgĭ-tīvus, tīva, tĭvum, adj. [fŭgĭ-o, "to flee"] ("Fleeing, fleeing away"; hence) Of slaves: *Runaway, fugitive;* lvi. 5.

Fulv-ĭa, ĭæ, f. [fulv-us, "tawny"] ("Tawny One") *Fulvia;* a noble Roman lady of bad character, who was on terms of familiarity with Curius, one of Catiline's associates. On becoming acquainted with the plot, she gave such information of it to Cicero as enabled him to save the state.

Fulv-ĭus, ĭi, m. [id.] (id.) *Fulvius;* 1. See Nobilior.—2. Aulus Fulvius, the son of a senator, whom his father put to death for having set out from Rome to join Catiline; xxxix. 5.

fund-o, fūdi, fūsum, fundĕre, 3. v. a. ("To pour out"; hence) Milit. t. t.: *To rout, put to flight, overthrow.*—Pass.: **fund-or**, fūsus sum, fundi [root FUD, akin to χύ-σις, "a pouring out"; χέω, "to pour out"].

fūr, fūris, comm. gen. *A thief* [akin to Gr. φώρ, Sans. CHOB, "a thief"].

fŭr-ĭbundus, ĭbunda, ĭb[um, adj. [fur-o, "to rag[e] *Raging greatly, full of* or *wrath, wrathful, furio[us]*

fŭr-or, ōris, m. [fŭr-o, rage"] *Rage, fury, madn[ess]*

fūsus, a, um, P. perf. [p] of fundo.

fŭtūrus, a, um, P. fu[turus of] sum.

Găbīnĭus, ĭi, m. *Gabin[ius]* see Capito.

Galli, ōrum, m. plur.: 1. *Galli* or *Gauls.*—Hence, **Gall-ĭa**, ĭæ, f. *The countr[y of]* the *Galli; Gaul:* (a) Ga[ul] citerior (or Cisalpin[a]), *Hit[her]* (or *Cisalpine*) *Gaul;* i.[e.] Gaul on the Italian side of [the] Alps; xlii. 1: so, also, G[allia] alone at lvii. 3.—(b) Ga[ul] ulterior (or Transalpina) *F[ur]ther* (or *Transalpine*) *Ga[ul]* i. e. Gaul beyond the Al[ps] xlii. 3. — b. **Gall-ĭcus**, ĭcum, adj. *Of, or belonging [to]* the *Galli; Gallic.*—2. [The] Allobroges who belonged [to] the Gallic nation are called [by] the generic term of Ga[lli,] *Gauls*, at xlvii. 2, etc.

Gallĭa, æ; **Gallĭcus**, a, u[m;] see Galli.

gā-nĕa, nĕæ, f. ("The thi[ng] pertaining to devouring[";] hence) *An eating-house, coo[k-]shop, tavern* [akin to Sa[ns.] root GHAS, "to devour"].

gănĕ-o, ōnis, m. [gane[o]

"a tavern"] ("One with—*i.e.* frequenting—a*ganea*"; hence) *A frequenter of taverns; a glutton, gourmand, reveller,* etc.

gaud-Ĭum, ĭi, n. [gaud-eo, "to rejoice"] *Joy, gladness, delight.*

gen-s, tis, f. [gĕn-o, "to beget"] ("A begetting"; that which is begotten; hence) 1. *A race* of persons.—2. *A nation.*—3. At Rome : *A clan,* or rather *house,* containing within it several familiæ, *i. e.* families *or* branches.

gĕnus, ĕris, n. ("Birth"; hence) 1. *A race, stock, family.* —2. *Birth, descent.*—3. *Kind, sort* [γένος].

gĕro, gessi, gestum, gĕrĕre, 3. v. a. ("To bear, carry"; hence) 1. *To do, perform, carry on.*—2. Of war : *To wage.*—3. Of affairs, *etc.* : a. *To conduct, carry on, manage,* etc.—b. Pass. : *To happen, take place, be done :*—res gestæ, (*things that have happened;* i. e.) a. *Events* or *occurrences* generally.—b. In war : *Exploits, noble deeds,* etc.—Pass. : **gĕror**, gestus sum, gĕri.

gestus, a, um, P. perf. pass.)f gero.

glădĭātŏr-Ĭus, Ĭa, Ĭum, adj. [glădĭātor, glădĭātŏr-is, "a gladiator"] *Of,* or *belonging to, a gladiator* or *to gladiators.*

glădĭus, Ĭi, m. *A sword.*

glōr-Ĭa, Ĭæ, f. [akiu to clārus, "illustrious"] *Glory, renown, fame.*

glōrĭ-or, ātus sum, āri, 1. v. dep. [glori-a, "boasting"] *To glory, boast, vaunt, pride one's self, brag.*

Græci, ōrum, m. plur. *The Greeks.*—Hence, a. **Græc-us**, a, um, adj. *Of,* or *belonging to, the Greeks; Greek, Grecian.*—b. **Græc-Ĭa**, Ĭæ, f. *The country of the Greeks, Greece.* [Γραικοί].

Græcĭa, æ; **Græcus**, a, um ; see Græci.

grandis, e, adj. *Great, large, huge, vast.*

grāt-Ĭa, Ĭæ, f. [grāt-us, "pleasing"] ("The quality of the *gratus*"; hence) 1. *Favour, esteem, regard, kindness,* shown by another to one's self; *credit, influence.*—2. *Favour* shown by one's self to another ; *courtesy, kindness :* —alicui gratiam delicti facere, (*to make a favour of a fault to any one ;* i. e.) *to overlook the fault of any one, to allow a fault in any one, to extend indulgence to any one for the commission of a fault.*— Adverbial Abl. followed by Gen., Gerund in di, *or* Gen. with Gerundive : ("In favour of"; hence) *For the sake,* or *purpose, of; on account of.*

grātŭĬt-o, adv. [gratuit-us,

"done without reward," *etc.*]
("After the manner of the *gratuitus*"; hence) *Without reward* or *profit; for nought, gratuitously.*

grātus, ta, tum, adj. *Dear, pleasing, delightful;*—at v. 2 grata, nom. neut. plur., is predicated of the fem. substt. cædes, rapīnæ, discordia, inasmuch as they are things without life [§ 92, 2, *a*] [prob. akin to χαίρω(root χαρ), "to rejoice"].

grăvĭor, us ; see gravis.

1. **grăvīs** = gravēs, acc. plur. of 2. gravis.

2. **grăv-īs**, e, adj. ("Heavy" in weight; hence) 1. Of war : *Severe.*—2. Of punishment : *Heavy, severe.*—3. Of enmity : *Bitter, severe.* ☞ (Comp.: grăv-ĭor); Sup.: grav-issĭmus [prob. akin to βαρ-ύς; Sans. *gur-u*, for original *gar-u*].

grăvissĭmus, a, um ; see gravis.

grăv-ĭter, adv. [grav-is, "heavy, severe "] ("After the manner of the *gravis*"; hence) *Heavily, severely*, etc. ☞ Comp.: grăv-ĭus; Sup.: grăv-issĭme.

grăvĭus, neut. adj. and comp. adv.; see gravis and grăvĭter.

grĕg-ārĭus, ārĭa, ārĭum, adj. [grex, grĕg-is, "a flock "] ("Of, or belonging to, a *grex*"; hence) *Of the common sort, common:*—miles gregarius, *a common soldier, a private.*

grex, grĕgis, m. ("A flock " of animals ; hence) *A troop, band, body* of persons:—grege facto, (*a troop having been made* or *formed ; i. e.*) *in a body*; l. 2; Abl. Abs. [§ 125].

gŭl-a, æ, f. [akin to glu-tio, "to swallow "] ("The swallowing thing "; hence) *The gullet, throat.*

hăbendus, a, um, Gerundive of habeo.

hăb-ĕo, ŭi, ĭtum, ēre, 2. v. a. and n. : 1. Act. : a. *To have*, in the widest sense of the word.—b. *To hold* or *possess.* —c. Of a speech, *etc.*: *To deliver, utter*, etc.—d. (a) With second Acc.: *To hold, account, deem, reckon, regard* an object as being that which is denoted by the second Acc. —(b) With Objective clause and pro : *To hold, account,* etc., *as* something *that* something, *etc.*; lii. 17.—(c) Pass. : *To be held, accounted, deemed,* etc. : habēri probro, (*to be held for a disgrace; i. e.*) *to be accounted* or *deemed a disgrace* [§ 107], xii. 1. —e. With Personal pron., or Pass., in reflexive force: *To hold* or *keep himself, itself*, etc., in a certain state ; i. e., *to be constituted, circumstanced,* or *situated; to be;* ii. 3; vi. 3.—f. Pass., folld. by adj. as predicate or complement: *To exhibit itself as being of a certain kind, etc.;* i. 4.—g. Of a watch, etc. : *To keep, maintain,* etc.—h. *To treat,* etc., in a certain way; xi. 5.—j. (a) *To have, hold,* or *keep* in a certain state, *etc.;* xlvii. 3.—(b) *To hold, regard,* or *look upon* in any light, *etc.* —k. With Part. perf. pass. as a second predicate (a circumlocution for the perf. act. of the part.) *To have hold* or *possess* something as completed or finished :—compertum ego habeo verba, *etc.,* I *have ascertained* (or *learned*) *that words,* etc.; here the clause verba virtutem non addere is a substantival one [§ 156, (3)] and forms the first predicate of habeo, while compertum is in concord with that clause and forms the second predicate of the verb; lviii. 1.—2. Neut.: *To be;* xli. 1: cf. Gr. ἔχω in same force.—Pass. : **hăb-ĕor,** ĭtus sum, ēri [prob. akin to ἅπ-τομαι, "to lay hold of"; also to ăp-ĭo, *or* ăp o, "to seize *or* grasp"].

hăbētōte, 2. pers. plur. fut. imperat. of hăbĕo.

hăbĭtūrus, a, um, P. fut. of habeo.

hăbĭtus, a, um, P. perf. pass. of habeo.

hăruspex, spĭcis, m. *An haruspex;* a diviner who foretold future events from an inspection of the entrails of victims offered in sacrifice.

haud, adv.: 1. *Not at all, by no means; not, no.*—2. Imparting a directly opposite meaning to the word to which it is joined :—haud facile, (*not easily;* i. e.) *with difficulty;* haud quāquam, or as one word haudquāquam, (*not by any means;* i. e.) *by no means.*

haud-quāquam; see haud.

hĕbe-sco, no perf. nor sup., scĕre, 3. v. n. inch. [hĕbĕ-o, "to be blunt"; hence, "to be dull," etc.] *To become dull, dim,* or *faint.*

1. **hic,** hæc, hoc (Gen. hūjus; Dat. huic), pron. dem. *This* person *or* thing: 1. As Subst.: a. Sing.: (a) hic, m. *This man, he.*—(b) hoc, n. *This thing, this.*—b. Plur.: (a) hi, m. *These persons* or *men.*—(b) hæc, n. *These things.* —2. hoc, adverbial Abl.: *On this account, for this reason* [akin to Sans. pronominal root ı, aspirated; with c (= ce), demonstrative suffix].

2. **hic,** adv. [1. hic] *In this place, here.*

hic-ce, hæc-ce, hoc-ce, pron. adj. [1. hic, "this"; demonstrative particle ce, rendering the pron. more emphatic] *This . . . here, this very* or *present :* for hujuscemodi, see modus.

Hispani, ōrum, m. plur. *The Hispani* or *Spaniards.*

Hence, a. **Hispān-ĭa**, ĭæ, f. *The country of the Hispani, Spain:*—duæ Hispaniæ (xviii. 5), *the two Spains,* i. e. Hispania Ulterior, *Further Spain,* or Spain beyond the Ibērus (Ebro); Hispania Citerior, *Hither Spain,* or Spain on this side the Iberus (Ebro); cf., also, xix. 1.—**b.** **Hispān-us,** a, um, adj. *Of,* or *belonging to, the Hispani; Spanish.*

hŏ-mo, mĭnis, comm. gen. : 1. *A human being, a person; a man, woman.*—**2.** Plur. : *Men, persons* [prob. akin to Sans. root BHŪ, "to be," and so, "the being"; usually referred to humus, "the ground," and so, "the one pertaining to the ground"].

hŏnestātus, a, um, P. perf. pass. of honesto.

hŏnest-e, adv. [honest-us, "honourable"] ("After the manner of the *honestus*"; hence) *Honourably, with honour.*

hŏnest-o, āvi, ātum, āre, 1. v. a. [id.] ("To render *honestus*"; hence) *To honour, raise to honour, dignify.*— Pass. : **hŏnest-or,** ātus sum, āri.

hŏnes-tus, ta, tum, adj. [for honos-tus; fr. honos (= honor), "honour"] ("Furnished, *or* provided, with honour"; hence) *Honourable.*

hŏnor (hŏnos), ōris, m. : 1. *Honour, respect, esteem,* etc. — **2.** *A* public *honour; official dignity, office, post,* etc.

hor-tor, tātus sum, tāri, 1. v. dep. *To strongly urge; to incite, instigate, urge on; to exhort, advise,* etc. [perhaps akin to ὄρ-νυμι, "to rouse"].

hos-pes, pĭtis, m. ("The one seeking to eat"; and in Pass. force, "the one sought for the purpose of eating *or* being entertained"; hence) 1. *A visitor, friend, guest.*—**2.** *An entertainer; a host* [perhaps for hos-pit-s; akin to Sans. root GHAS, "to eat"; pĕt-o, "to seek"].

host-īlis, īle, adj. [host-is, "an enemy"] *Of,* or *belonging to, an enemy; hostile.*

hos-tis, tis, comm. gen. ("The eating one"; hence, "a stranger *or* foreigner" entertained as a "guest"; hence) *An enemy,* or *foe,* of one's country.—Plur. : *The enemy* [prob. akin to Sans. root GHAS, "to eat"].

hūc, adv. [for hoc, adverbial neut. acc. of hic, "this"] 1. *To this place, hither.*—**2.** *To this, hereto:*—huc accedebat, *hereto it was added;* xi. 5.

hūjuscĕmŏdi, **hūjusmŏdi;** see mŏdus.

hūm-ānus, āna, ānum, adj. [for homin-anus; fr. homo, homin-is, "a man"] *Of,* or *belonging to, a man; human.*

—As Subst.: **hŭmāna**, ōrum, n. plur. *Human things.*

humi; see humus.

hŭm-ŭs, i, f.: 1. *The ground, soil, earth.*—2. Adverbial Gen. of place: **humi** [§ 121, B, *b*], a. *On the ground.*—b. *Into or in the ground;* lv. 3 [akin to χαμ-αί, "on the ground"].

ĭ-bi, adv.: 1. *In that place; there.*—2. *Thereupon, then.*—3. *Therein, in that matter or those matters,* etc. [akin to Sans. pronominal root ɪ, with suffix bi].

id; see is.

ĭ-dem, ĕădem, ĭdem (Gen. ējusdem; Dat. ĕīdem), pron. dem. [pronominal root ɪ; suffix dem] ("That, *or* the very, person *or* thing"; hence) *The same:*—ĕōdem tempŏre, *at the same time* (xviii. 4), Abl. of time "when" [§ 120]: —idem qui, *etc., the same as, the same with.*—As Subst.: a. Masc.: *The same man* or *person.*—b. Neut.: (a) Sing.: *The same thing.*—(b) Plur.: *The same things.*

Ĭdōnĕus, a, um, adj. *Fit, suitable, convenient;*—sometimes with Dat. [§ 106, (3)]. —As Subst.: **Ĭdōnĕi**, ōrum, m. plur. *Suitable,* or *fit, persons.*

Ig-ĭtur, adv. [probably for ic-itus; ig = ic, fr. pronominal root ɪ; suffix itus] ("From this" thing; henec) *Therefore.*

i-gnārus, gnāra, gnārum, adj. [for in-gnārus; fr. in, "not"; gnārus, "knowing"] ("Not *gnarus*"; hence) 1. *Ignorant, unversed.*—As Subst.: **ignāri**, ōrum, m. plur. *Ignorant,* or *unversed, persons.*—2. With Objective Gen. [§ 132]: *Ignorant of, unacquainted with.*

ignāv-ĭa, ĭæ, f. [ignāv-us "inactive"; also, "cowardly"] ("The quality of the *ignāvus*"; hence) 1. *Inactivity, laziness, sloth, indolence.*—2. *Cowardice.*

i-gnāvus, gnāva, gnāvum, adj. [for in-gnāvus; fr. ĭn, "not"; gnavus, "busy, diligent"] ("Not *gnavus*"; hence) 1. *Inactive, lazy, slothful, indolent.*—As Subst.: **ignāvus**, i, m. *An indolent,* etc., *person.*—2. *Cowardly, dastardly.* —As Subst.: **ignāvus**, i, m. *A coward.*

i-gnōbĭlis, gnōbĭle, adj. [for in-gnōbĭlis; fr. ĭn, "negative" particle; gnōbĭlis (= nobĭlis), "well known"] ("Not *nobilis*"; hence, "unknown"; hence) 1. *Unknown to fame, obscure, not renowned.*—2. *Low, ignoble.*

i-gnōmĭn-ĭa, ĭæ, f. [for in-gnōmĭn-ia; fr. ĭn, in "negative" force; gnōmen (= nō-men), gnōmĭn-is, "a name"] ("A being without—*or* a depriving one of — a (good) name"; hence) *Loss of good name, disgrace, ignominy.*

ignoscendo, Gerund in do fr. ignosco.

i-gnosco, gnōvi, gnōtum, gnoscĕre, 3. v. n. [for in-gnosco; fr. ĭn, in "negative" force; gnosco (= nosco), "to know"] ("Not to know"; hence, with reference to a fault, crime, etc.) 1. *To pardon, forgive;*—at ix. 5 alone; so, rare.—**2.** With Dat. [§ 106, (3)]: *To pardon, extend pardon to;* lii. 33.

il-le, la, lud (Gen. illīus; Dat. illi), demonstr. pron. [for is-le; fr. is] *That* person *or* thing.—As Subst. : Of both numbers and all genders: *That person* or *thing ; he, she, it ; they,* etc.

illĕc-ĕbra, ĕbræ, f. [for illac-cbra; fr. ĭllĭcĭo, "to entice," through its root ILLĀC] ("That which brings about the enticing"; hence) *Enticement, allurement.*

illexĕram, pluperf. ind. of illicio.

il-lĭcĭo, lexi, lectum, lĭcĕre, 3. v. a. [for in-lacio; fr. in, "into"; lacio, "to allure"] ("To allure into" a place; hence) *To entice, allure.*

imbēcillus, a, um, adj. *Weak, feeble,* whether physically *or* mentally.

im-bŭ-o, bŭi, būtum, bŭĕre, 3. v. a. [for in-bi-o; fr. in, "in"; BI, root of bĭ-bo, "to drink"] (In causative force; "to cause

to drink in"; hence) *To imbue.*—Pass. : **im-bŭ-or,** būtus sum, bŭi.

imbūtus, a, um, P. perf. pass. of imbuo.

ĭm-ĭtor, ĭtātus sum, ĭtāri, 1. v. dep. ("To make like"; hence) *To imitate* [root ĭM, akin to μιμ-έομαι].

im-mĭnŭo, mĭnŭi, mĭnūtum, mĭnŭĕre, 3. v. a. [for in-minuo; fr. ĭn, "without force"; minuo, "to lessen"] 1. *To lessen, diminish, abridge.*—**2.** *To subvert, destroy,* etc.—Pass. : **im-mĭnŭor,** mĭnūtus sum, mĭnŭi.

immĭnūtus, a, um, P. perf. pass. of imminuo.

immissus, a, um, P. perf. pass. of immitto.

im-mitto, mīsi, missum, mittĕre, 3. v. a. [for in-mitto; fr. in, "against"; mitto, "to send"] ("To send against"; hence) *To set* or *urge on; to incite, instigate.*—Pass. : **immittor,** missus sum, mitti.

immo, adv. *Yea, yes, indeed, certainly, by all means.*

im-mŏdĕrātus, mŏdĕrāta, mŏdĕrātum, adj. [for in-mŏdĕrātus; fr. in, "not"; mŏdĕrātus, "moderate"] ("Not *moderatus*"; hence) *Excessive, unrestrained, immoderate.*—As Subst.: **immŏdĕrāta,** ōrum, n. plur. *Immoderate things,* etc. ; v. 5.

im-mortālis, mortāle, adj. [for in-mortālis; fr. in, "not";

mortālis, "mortal"] *Immortal, undying.*

immūtātus, a, um, P. perf. pass. of immūto.

im-mŭto, mūtāvi, mūtātum, mūtāre, 1. v. a. [for in-mūto; fr. ĭn, "without force"; mūto, "to change"] *To change, alter.*—Pass.: im-mŭtor, mūtātus sum, mūtāri.

im-părātus, părāta, părātum, adj. [for in-paratus; fr. ĭn, "not"; părātus, "prepared"] *Not prepared, unprepared.*

im-pĕd-ĭo, īvi *or* ĭi, ītum, īre, 4. v. a. [for in-pĕd-ĭo; fr. in, "in"; pes, pĕd-is, "the foot"] ("To get the foot in" something; hence, "to shackle," *etc. ;* hence) *To hinder, prevent, impede;*—at xxx. 4 folld. by ne c. Subj.; see 1. ne.—Pass.: im-pĕd-ĭor, ītus sum, īri.

impĕdītus, a, um : 1. P. perf. pass. of impedio.—2. Pa. : *Hindered, obstructed, encumbered, etc.*—As Subst. : impĕdīti, ōrum, m. plur. *Men, or persons, encumbered with baggage or hindered by the difficulties of their way, etc. ;* lvii. 4.

im-pello, pŭli, pulsum, pellĕre, 3. v. a. [for in-pello; fr. in, "against"; pello, "to drive"] ("To drive, *or* push, against"; hence) 1. *To impel, urge, instigate.*—2. *To per-*suade, induce.—Pass : im-pellor, pulsus sum, pelli.

im-pendĕo, no perf. nor sup., pendēre, 2. v. n. [for in-pendeo; fr. ĭn, "over"; pendĕo, "to hang"] With Dat. [§ 106, *a*]: *To hang or impend over.*

impĕrā-tor, tōris, m. [imper(a)-o] *A commander,* esp. *a commander-in-chief;*—at vi. 7 bini imperatores = bini consules.

impĕr-ĭum, ĭi, n. [impĕr-o, "to command"] 1. *A command, order.*—2. *Authority, power.*—3. *Dominion, empire, rule, sovereignty.*

im-pĕro, pĕrāvi, pĕrātum, pĕrāre, 1. v. n. *and* a. [for in-păro; fr. in, "upon"; păro, "to put"] ("To put (a matter, *etc.*) upon" one; hence) 1. Neut.: *To command, order, enjoin, bid;*—at xx. 17 used alone; at xlv. 1 folld. by Dat. of person [§ 106,(4)]and uti c. Subj.—2. Act.: With Acc. of thing demanded: *To demand or require* something of one; xvi.2.

impĕt-us, ūs, m. [impĕt-o, "to fall upon, *or* attack"] 1. *An attack, assault, onset.*—2. *Impetuosity, violence, force.*

im-pĭus, pĭa, pĭum, adj. [for in-pĭus; fr. in, "not"; pius, "holy"] *Unholy, wicked, impious. — As* Subst. : impĭi, orum, m. plur. *Wicked persons, the wicked.*

im-plŏro, plōrāvi, plōrātum, plōrāre, 1. v. a. [for in-ploro; fr. ĭn, "upon"; plōro, "to bewail"; hence, "to cry out aloud"] ("To cry out aloud upon" a person; hence) *To beg, beseech, entreat, invoke, implore;*—at lii. 29 implores (2 pers. sing. subj. pres.) is used in an indefinite force; see cerno.

impōno, pŏsŭi, pŏsĭtum, pōnĕre, 3. v. a. [for in-pōno; fr. in, "upon"; pōno, "to put"] ("To put upon"; hence) With Acc. of thing and Dat. of person [§§ 96 : 106, *a*]: 1. *To lay* something *upon* one; xliii. 1.—2. *To impose* or *lay* (a necessity, etc.) *on* or *upon* one; xxxiii. 6.—3. Of an affront, etc.: *To put, cast,* or *inflict upon;*—at xlviii. 9 in pass. constr.; where esse is to be supplied with impositam [§ 158].—4. *To set* some one, etc., *over* others as a commander, etc.; li. 28.

impŏsĭtus, a, um, P. perf. pass. of impono.

im-prōvīsus, prōvīsa, prōvīsum, adj. [for in-prōvīsus; fr. ĭn, "not"; prōvīsus, "foreseen"] ("Not foreseen"; hence) *Unexpected.*—Adverbial expression:—de improviso, *unexpectedly, suddenly.*

im-pŭdīcus, pŭdīca, pŭdīc-um, adj. [for in-pŭdīcus; fr. in, "not"; pŭdīcus, "chaste"] ("Not *pudicus*"; hence) *Un-*

chaste, immodest, lewd.*—As Subst.: impŭdīcus, i, m. *An unchaste person, a profligate.*

impulsus, a, um, P. perf. pass. of impello.

impūn-ĭtas, ĭtātis, f. [im-pūn-is, "unpunished"] ("The state, *or* condition, of the *impunis*"; hence) *Freedom, or safety, from punishment; impunity.*

im-pūnī-tus, ta, tum, adj. [for in-pūnītus; fr. ĭn, "not"; pŭnī-o, "to punish"] *Not punished, unpunished.*

im-pūrus, pūra, pūrum, adj. [for in-pūrus; fr. ĭn, "not"; pūrus, "clean, pure"] ("Not *purus*"; hence) Morally: *Un-clean, abandoned, impure.*

Ĭn, prep. gov. abl. *or* acc.: 1. With Abl.: a. *In.*—b. *In the case of.*—c. Of time: *In, in the course of, during.*—d. *Among, with.*—Phrase: in primis, *among* or *with the first,* i. e. *especially, principally,* etc. — e. Of divisions, etc.: *In, on.*—2. With Acc.: a. *Into.*—b. Of time: (a) *Unto, until.*—(b) *For:*—iu dies, (*for days,* i. e.) *daily, day by day.*—(c) *At.*—c. *Against.*—d. *Towards.*—e. *With reference* or *regard to; as to, respecting.*—f. *On, upon.*—g. *According to, after* [Gr. *ἐν*].

in-cēdo, cessi, cessum, cēd-ĕre, 3. v. n. [ĭn, "in"; cēdo, "to go"] ("To go in *or* along"; hence) 1. Military t. t.: *To move forwards, advance, march.*—2. Of abstract Subject: *To come or happen to; to befall; to attack, seize;*—at xxxi. 3 with follg. Dat. [§ 106, *a*];—at xiii. 3 alone.

incend-ĭum, ĭi, n. [incend-o, "to burn"] *A burning, conflagration.*

in-cen-do, di, sum, dĕre, 3. v. a. ("To put fire in *or* into"; hence) 1. *To set on fire, burn.*—2. *To inflame* with any passion; *to incite, excite, fire, rouse,* a person;—at xxxviii. 1 supply eam (= plebem) after incendere.—3. *To ruin, destroy.*—Pass.: **in-cen-dor,** sus sum, di [for in-can-do; fr. in, "in *or* into"; root CAN, akin to κά-ω, "to burn"].

incensus, a, um, P. perf. pass. of incendo.

incep-tum, ti, n. [for incaptum; fr. incipio, "to begin," through its true root INCAP] ("That which is begun"; hence) 1. *A commencement, beginning.*—2. *An undertaking, attempt, design.*

inceptus, a, um, P. perf. pass of incipio.

in-certus, certa, certum, adj. [in "not"; certus, "sure"] 1. *Not sure, uncertain, doubtful.* —As Subst.: **incertum,** i, n. *An uncertainty:*—in incerto, *in an uncertainty, in doubt.*—

2. Of things: *Uncertain, unsettled.*—As Subst.: incerta, ōrum, n. plur. *Uncertain things.*

incessĕram, pluperf. ind. of incēdo.

inces-sus, sūs, m. [for inced-sus; fr. incēd-o, "to walk along"] *A walking along; pace, step, gait,* etc.

in-cĭdo, cĭdi, cāsum, cĭdĕre, 3. v. n. [for in-cădo; fr. in, "into"; cădo, "to fall"] ("To fall into"; hence) With in and Acc. of thing: *To fall into;* xiv. 4.

in-cĭpĭo, cēpi, ceptum, cĭpĕre, 3. v. a. [for in-căpĭo; fr. in, "in"; căpĭo, "to take"] ("To take in" hand; hence) 1. *To begin, commence.*—2. Of an action: *To undertake,* etc. —Pass.: **in-cĭpĭor,** ceptus sum, cĭpi.

in-cĭto, cĭtāvi, cĭtātum, cĭtāre, 1. v. a. [in, "without force"; cĭto, "to set in rapid motion"] ("To set in rapid motion, urge forward"; hence) *To urge* or *spur on; to incite,* etc.

inconsult-e, adv. [inconsult-us, "indiscreet"] ("After the manner of the *inconsultus*"; hence) *Indiscreetly, inconsiderately, rashly.*

in-crēdĭbĭlis, crēdĭbĭle, adj. [in, "not"; crēdĭbĭlis, "to be believed"] *Not to be believed, incredible, extraordinary;*—at vi. 2; vii. 3 folld. b-

Supine in u [§ 141, 6].—As Subst. : **incredibilia**, um, n. plur. *Incredible, etc., things.*

incrĕpans, ntis, P. pres. of increpo.

in-crĕpo, crĕpŭi, crĕpĭtum, crĕpāre, 1.v. a. [ĭn, "against"; crĕpo, "to clatter," *etc.*] (" To clatter against "; hence) 1. *To blame* or *upbraid loudly; to chide, reprove, etc.*—2. *To inveigh against, attack, etc.*

in-crŭentus, crŭenta, crŭentum, adj. [ĭn, "not"; crŭentus, "bloody"] (" Not *cruentus*"; hence) *Bloodless.*

1. **in-cultus**, cultūs, m. [ĭn, "not"; cultus, "civilization"] (" A not having *cultus*"; hence, "absence, *or* want, of the decencies of life "; hence) *Want of cleanliness, filth, etc.*

2. **in-cultus**, culta, cultum, adj. [ĭn, "not"; cultus, "tilled"] (" Not *cultus*"; hence) 1. Of places : *Untilled, uncultivated, waste.*—2. Of persons : *Uncivilized, unpolished, rude, etc.*

in-curro, curri *and* cŭcurri, cursum, currĕre, 3. v. n. [ĭn, "against"; curro, "to run"] (" To run against"; hence) With accessory notion of hostility : *To rush against* or *upon ;*—at lx. 7 folld. by in c. Acc.

i-n-de, adv. [probably fr. pronominal root ɪ; with n, epenthetic; de, suffix] (" From that" thing; hence) 1. *From that place* or *quarter, thence.* —2. Of time : a. *After that.* —b. *Thereupon, then.*

in-demnā-tus, ta, tum, adj. [for in-damnā-tus; fr. ĭn, "not"; damn(a)-o, "to condemn"] *Not condemned, uncondemned, without trial.*

index, ĭcis, comm. gen. [for indic-s; fr. indĭc-o, "to make known"] (" One who makes (a thing) known *or* gives information "; hence) *An informer, etc.*

indĭcātūrus, a, um, P. fut. of indico.

indĭc-ĭum, ĭi, n. [indĭc-o, "to make known"] (" A making known"; hence) 1. *Disclosure, discovery* of a plot, *etc.*—2. *Evidence, information* about a plot, *etc.*

in-dĭco, dĭcāvi, dĭcātum, dĭcāre, 1. v. a. [in, "without force"; dĭco, "to make known"] 1. *To make known, show, indicate, etc.*—2. Without Object : *To give information* or *evidence ;* xlviii. 4, where esse is to be supplied with indicaturum.

indĭge-ns, ntis, adj. [indĭgĕ-o, "to need"] (" Needing"; hence) *Poor, needy, indigent.*

in-dignus, digna, dignum, adj. [in, "not"; dignus, "worthy"] *Unworthy ;* — sometimes with Abl. [§ 119, *a*].—As Subst.: **indigni,** ōrum, m. plur. *Unworthy persons.*

in-doctus, docta, doctum, adj. [ĭn, "not"; doctus, "taught"] ("Not *doctus*"; hence) *Untaught, ignorant.*

induciæ (or **indutĭæ**), ārum, f. plur. *A temporary cessation of hostilities; an armistice, truce.*

in-dūco, duxi, ductum, dūc-ĕre, 3. v. a. [in, "into"; dūco, "to lead"] 1. *To lead into* or *among;*—at lx. 5 folld. by in c. Acc.—2. With in animum, (*To bring into the mind;* i. e.) With Inf.: *To resolve, determine,* etc., *to do,* etc., liv. 4.—3. *To move, excite, rouse, persuade, prevail upon, induce.*—Pass.: **in-dūc-or,** ductus sum, dūci.

inductus, a, um, P. perf. pass. of indūco.

industrĭ-a, æ, f. [industri-us, "industrious"] ("The state, *or* condition, of the *industrius*"; hence) *Diligence, assiduity, industry.*

ĭn-ĕd-ĭa, ĭæ, f. [in, "not"; ĕd-o, "to eat"] *A not eating; a fasting, an abstaining from* or *going without food.*

ĭn-ĕo, īvi *or* ĭi, ĭtum, īre, v. a. irreg. [in, "into"; ĕo, "to go"] ("To go into"; hence) Of battle: *To enter into; to take part,* or *join, in.*

1. **ĭn-erm-ĭs,** e, adj. [for in-arm-is; fr. in, "not"; arm-a,

"arms"] *Without arms* or *weapons; unarmed.*

2. **ĭnermīs** = inermes, acc. plur. of 1. inermis.

ĭnert-ĭa, ĭæ, f. [ĭners, ĭnert-is, "inactive"] ("The quality of the *iners*"; hence) *Inactivity, idleness, laziness.*

infĕrus, a, um, adj.: 1. Pos.: *That is below* or *underneath; nether, low.*—As Subst.: **infĕri,** orum, m. plur.: a. *The inhabitants of the world below, the dead.*—b. *The lower world.*—2. Sup.: *Lowest,* whether in place or rank. — As Subst.: **infĭmi,** ōrum, m. plur. *The lowest people, the rabble, the dregs of the populace.* 🖙 (Comp.: infer-ior); Sup.: infĭmus (or īmus) [sometimes referred to ĭn, "in"; with suffix ĕrus, with f inserted as a digamma; sometimes to the Sans. *adhara,* "lower"].

infestissimus, a, um; see infestus.

in-fes-tus, ta, tum, adj. [for in-fe(n)d-tus; fr. in, "without force"; obsol. fend-o, "to strike"] ("Striking"; hence) 1. *Hostile, inimical.*— 2. *Bitter* in feeling.—3. With Dat. [§ 106, 3]: *Hostile,* etc., *to.* 🖙 (Comp.: infĕst-ĭor); Sup.: infest-issĭmus.

in-fīdus, fīda, fīdum, adj. [in, "not"; fīdus, "faithful"] *Faithless, unfaithful.*

infĭmi, ōrum; see infĕrus.

in-fīnī-tus, ta, tum, adj. [in, "not"; fīnĭ-o, "to limit, bound"] 1. *Without limit, boundless, unbounded, infinite.*

infirmior, us; see infirmus.

in-firmus, firma, firmum, adj. [in, "not"; firmus, "strong"] *Not strong, weak, infirm.* ☞ Comp.: infirm-ĭor (Sup.: infirm-issĭmus).

infrā, prep. gov. acc. and adv. [contr. fr. infĕrā, fem. abl. sing. of infĕrus, "below"] 1. Prep.: *Below,* i. e.: a. Of locality: *Lower down than.* —b. Of size or height: *Less than.*—2. Adv.: Of order, succession, etc.: *Below.*

in-gĕn-ĭum, ĭi, n. [ĭn, "in"; gĕn-o = gign-o, in pass. "to be born"] ("A being born in" one; hence, "that which is inborn"; hence) 1. *Natural disposition* or *character.*—2. *Natural capacity* or *ability, parts, genius.*

in-gens, gentis, adj. [in, "not"; gens, "a race or kind"] ("That is not of its race or kind"; hence) 1. *Vast, immense, huge.*—2. *Great, mighty, strong, powerful.*

ingĕn-ŭus, ŭa, ŭum, adj. [in, "in"; GEN, root of gigno, in pass. "to be born"] ("In-born"; i.e. "native, indigenous, not foreign"; hence) Of persons: *Free-born, born of free parents,* who have never been slaves.

in-grātus, grāta, grātum, adj. [in, "not"; grātus, "thankful"; also "pleasing"] 1. Of persons: *Unthankful, ungrateful.*—2. Of things: *Displeasing, unwelcome, unpleasant.*

in-hŏnestus, hŏnesta, hŏnestum, adj. [ĭn, "not"; honestus, "honourable"] ("Not honestus"; hence) *Dishonourable, disgraceful, shameful.*

ĭnĭbĭtĭs, 2. pers. plur. fut. ind. of ĭnĕo.

ĭnĭmĭc-ĭtĭa, ĭtĭæ, f. [ĭnĭmĭc-us, "unfriendly"] ("The state of the inimicus"; hence) *Unfriendliness, enmity.*

1. ĭn-ĭmīcus, ĭmīca, ĭmīc-um, adj. [for ĭn-ămīcus; fr. in, "not"; ămīcus, "friendly"] *Unfriendly, hostile, inimical.*—As Subst.: ĭn-ĭmīc-us, i, m. *A (private) enemy* or *foe.*

2. ĭnĭmīcus, i; see 1. ĭn-ĭmīcus.

ĭnīqu-ĭtas, ĭtātis, f. [ĭnīqu-us, "unjust"] ("The quality of the iniquus"; hence) *Injustice.*

ĭnĭ-tĭum, tĭi, n. [ĭnĕo, "to go into" a place; hence, "to enter upon, begin," through root INI] *A beginning, commencement:*—in initio, or simply initio, *in the beginning, in the first place, at first.*

injŭrĭ-a, æ, f. [injŭrĭ-us, "injurious"] ("The thing

pertaining to the *injurius*"; hence) *Unjust* or *wrongful conduct, injustice; a wrong, injury,* etc.

in-justus, justa, justum, adj. [in, "not"; justus, "just"] 1. *Unjust.*—2. *Wrongful.*

in-nŏcens, nŏcentis, adj. [in, "not"; nŏcens, "hurtful"] 1. *Not hurtful, harmless.*—2. *Blameless, guiltless, innocent.*—As Subst. comm. gen.: *An innocent, etc., person.*

innŏcent-ĭa, ĭæ, f. [innŏcens, innŏcent-is, "innocent"] ("The quality of the *innŏcens*"; hence) *Innocence.*

in-nox-ĭus, ĭa, ĭum, adj. [in, "not"; nox-a, "harm, hurt"] ("Not pertaining to *noxa*"; hence) 1. In Act. force: ("Harmless, innoxious"; hence) *Guiltless, blameless, innocent.*—As Subst.: **innoxĭus,** ĭi, m. *An innocent person,* i. e. at xl. 6 one unconnected with the conspiracy.—2. In pass. force: *Unharmed, unhurt, uninjured;* xxxix. 2.

Ĭnŏp-ĭa, ĭæ, f. [ĭnops, ĭnŏp-is, "without means"] ("The quality, *or* state, of the *inops*"; hence) 1. *Want, lack, deficiency of means.*—2. *Poverty, indigence.*

inquĭlīn-us, a, um, adj. [inquĭlīn-us, "an inhabitant of a place which does not belong to him"; hence, "a lodger"] ("Of, *or* belonging to, an *in-*

quĭlīnus"; hence) *Possessing merely a lodging;*—a term sneeringly applied by Catiline to Cicero, who was born at Arpīnum, and hence had not, as Catiline wished to insinuate, any property or house of his own in Rome.

in-sătĭā-bĭlis, bĭle, adj. [ĭn, "not"; sati(a)-o, "to satisfy"] *That cannot be satisfied, insatiable.*

insĭd-ĭæ, ĭarum, f. plur. [insĭd-ĕo, "to take up a position in a place"] ("A taking up of a position in" a place; hence) 1. Of troops: *An ambush, ambuscade, liers in wait.*—2. *Snares, plots.*—3. *Artifices, stratagems.*

insign-e, is, n. [insign-is, "remarkable"] ("That which is *insignis*"; hence) Mostly plur.: *A badge, mark,* or *ensign* of authority, power, *etc.*

in-sŏle-ns, ntis, adj. [in, "not"; sŏlĕ-o, "to be accustomed"] ("Contrary to custom"; hence) 1. With Gen.: *Unaccustomed to, not habituated to;* iii. 4.—2. ("Excessive, immoderate"; hence) *Haughty, arrogant, insolent.*

insŏlent-ĭa, ĭæ, f. [insŏlens, insolent-is, "haughty"]("The quality of the *insolens*"; hence) *Haughtiness, arrogance, insolence.*

in-sŏle-sco, no perf. nor sup., scĕre, 3. v. n. inch. [ĭn

"not "; sole-o, " to be wont
or usual "] (" To begin to be
unusual "; hence) *To grow
haughty* or *insolent; to be
elated.*

in-sŏlĭtus, sŏlĭta, sŏlĭtum,
adj. [ĭn, "not "; sŏlĭtus,
"customary "] (" Not *solitus*"; hence) *Unusual, un-
common.*

in-somn-ĭum, ĭi, n. [ĭn,
"not "; somn-us, " sleep "]
(" A not having sleep";
hence) *Want of sleep, de-
privation of sleep, sleeplessness ;*—at xxvii. 2 in plur.

in-sons, sontis, adj. [ĭn,
"not "; sons, "guilty "]
(" Not *sons*"; hence) *Guiltless.*—As Subst.: insons, ntis,
m. " *A guiltless person*";
hence) *One who gives no offence
by his conduct; an inoffensive,
harmless person ; one who
does no harm.*

in-stĭtŭo, stĭtŭi, stĭtūtum,
stĭtŭĕre, 3. v. a. [for in-
stătŭo; fr. in, "without
force "; stătŭo, "to set "]
1. *To put, set, place, etc.*—2.
Of troops : *To levy, raise;*
lvi. 1.—3. Of life, etc. : *To
regulate.*

instĭtŭ-tum, ti, n. [instĭtŭ-
o, in force of " to make a rule
for one's self," also, " to regulate"] 1. (" That which is
made a rule for one's self";
hence) *Custom, habit, usage,
mode of life, etc.*—2. (" That

which regulates"; hence) *A
regulation, institution, ordinance, etc.*

in-sto, stĭti, stātum, stāre,
1. v. n. [in "upon "; sto, "to
stand "] (" To stand upon ";
hence) 1. *To press hard, assail vigorously, assault, make
an assault.*—2. *To be close at
hand; to be close* or *very near.*

instructus, a, um, P. perf.
pass. of instruo.

instrŭ-mentum, mĕnti, n.
[instrŭ-o, " to build *or* construct "] (" The building, *or*
constructing, thing "; hence,
an " implement " of any kind;
hence) *Means to an end, aid,
furtherance, instrument, etc.*

in-strŭo, struxi, structum,
strŭĕre, 3. v. a. [in, " without
force "; strŭo, " to build "]
1. *To build.*—2. Of troops,
etc. : *To arrange, draw up,
form, etc.*—3. *To equip, furnish, provide, supply.*—Pass.:
in-strŭor, structus sum, strŭi.

in-sŭesco, sŭēvi, sŭētum,
sŭescĕre, 3. v. n. [ĭn, "without force"; suesco, "to become
accustomed "] *To become accustomed* or *habituated; to
accustom* or *habituate one's
self*, etc.

insŭēvi, perf. ind. of in-
suesco.

in-sum, fŭi, esse, v. n. [ĭn,
"in "; sum, "to be "] *To be
in;*—at xv. 5 strengthened by
in c. Abl.;—at xl. 6 folld. by

Dat. [§ 106, *a*].—N.B. The construction of the clause multæ facetiæ multusque lepos inerat, xxv. 5, deserves attention from the verb being in the sing. while it has a composite subject. The rule is this :—when of any number of subjects, *denoting things*, one at least is in the plur., the verb is also in the plur., unless particular emphasis attaches to one of them in the sing. number ; in which case the verb assumes the sing. number, and is placed nearest to such singular subject, thus bringing it prominently forward. In the present instance therefore lepos is that which Sallust proposes to bring more particularly before the reader's notice.

in-super, adv. [ĭn, " on *or* upon "; sŭper, " above "] (" On and above "; hence) *On the top, overhead, above.*

in-tĕg-er, ra, rum, adj. [for in-tăg-er; fr. in, " not "; tango, " to touch," through root TAG] (" Untouched "; hence) *Sound, fresh, vigorous.* —As Subst. : integri, ōrum, m. plur. Of soldiers : *Fresh, or untired men;* lx. 4.

intĕgr-ĭtas, ĭtātis, f. [intĕger, integr-i, in force of "upright "] (" The quality of the *integer*"; hence) *Uprightness, blamelessness, integrity.*

Sallust.

intellego, ĕre; see intellĭgo.

intellexi, perf. ind. of intellĭgo.

intel-lĭgo (intel-lĕgo), lexi, lectum, lĭgĕre, 3. v. a. [for inter-lego; fr. inter, "between "; lĕgo, " to choose "] (" To choose between "; hence) *To see, perceive, comprehend, understand.*

in-tempes-tus, ta, tum, adj. [for in-tempor-tus; fr. ĭn, " not "; tempus, tempŏr-is, " time "; hence, " the right time *or* season "] (" Not having *tempus* "; hence) *Unseasonable :*—intempestā nocte, (*in the unseasonable part of the night;* i. e.) *in the dead of the night;* Abl. of time " when " [§ 120].

in-tendo, tendi, tensum *and* tentum, tendĕre, 3. v. a. [ĭn, "without force "; tendo, " to stretch out "] (" To stretch out "; hence) Of the mind : *To direct, apply*, etc. ; — at li. intendĕris (2. pers. sing. perf. subj.) is used in an indefinite force ; see cerno.

intentus, a, um : 1. P. perf. pass. of intendo. — 2. Pa. : (" Bent "; hence) a. *Eager, watching* or *observing attentively, alert, intent.*—b. With Dat. : *Attentive to, watching attentively.*—c. With Abl. : *Bent upon* something; ii. 9; —so, also, with Gerund in do, iv. 1.

L

inter, prep. gov. acc. : 1. *Between, among :*—inter se, *among themselves,* i.e. *mutually, one with another.*—2. Of things : *Among, in the midst of.*—3. Of time : *During,* etc.

inter-dum, adv. [inter, "at intervals"; dum, prob. = dium, acc. of obsol. dius (whence diu) = dies, "a day"] ("At intervals during the day"; hence) *Sometimes, occasionally.*

intĕr-ĕā, adv. [for intĕr-ĕam; fr. inter, "between"; ĕam, acc. sing. fem. of is] (" Between that" and something else; hence) Of time : *Meanwhile, in the mean time.*

intĕr-ĕo, īvi or ĭi, ĭtum, īre, v. n. [inter, "among"; eo, "to go"] ("To go among" other things, etc., so as to be no longer perceived; hence) *To perish.*

inter-fĭcĭo, fēci, fectum, fĭcĕre, 3. v. a. [for inter-facio; fr. inter, "between"; făcĭo, "to make"] ("To make" something to be "between" the parts of a thing; hence) 1. *To kill, murder, put to death.*—2. Of troops, etc.: *To slaughter, slay,* etc.

interrŏgātus, a, um, P. perf. pass. of interrŏgo.

inter-rŏgo, rŏgāvi, rŏgātum, rŏgāre, 1. v. a. [inter, in a slightly "augmentative" force; rŏgo, "to ask, question"] 1. *To question, interrogate.*—2. Law t. t.: a. *To question, interrogate, examine* a witness, etc.—b. *To bring an action against, sue, prosecute.* — Pass. : **inter-rŏgor**, rŏgātus sum, rŏgāri.

intes-tīnus, tīna, tīnum, adj. [for intus-tīnus; fr. intus, "within"] ("Pertaining to *intus*"; hence, "internal, inside"; hence) Of war : *Intestine, domestic, civil.*

in-tŏlĕrandus, tŏlĕranda, tŏlĕrandum, adj. [ĭn, "not"; tolerandus, "to be borne"] ("Not *tolerandus*"; hence) *Not to be borne* or *endured, intolerable, insupportable.*

intrā, prep. gov. acc. [contr. fr. intĕrā, abl. sing. fem. of obsol. intĕrus, "within"] 1. Of place : *Within, inside of.*—2. Of time: *Within, before the expiration of.*

intrŏ-duco, duxi, ductum, dūcĕre, 3. v. a. [intro, "within"; duco, "to lead"] *To lead,* or *bring, within* or *into* a place, etc.

intrŏ-ĕo, īvi or ĭi, ĭtum, īre, v. n. [intro, "within, inside"; ĕo, "to go or come"] *To go,* or *come, inside; to enter.*

ĭn-ul-tus, ta, tum, adj. [for in-ulc-tus; fr. in, "not"; ulc-iscor, "to avenge"] *Unavenged, unpunished.*

in-vādo, vāsi, vāsum, vādĕre, 3. v. a. *and* n. [ĭn,

"against"; vādo, "to go"] ("To go against"; hence) 1. Act.: a. *To attack, seize upon, take possession of.*—b. Of a disease: *To fall upon, attack.* —2. Neut.: *To make an attack,* etc.

invāsĕram, invāsi, pluperf. and perf. ind. of invado.

in-vĕnĭo, vēni, ventum, vĕn-īre, 4. v. a. [in, "upon"; vĕnĭo, "to come"] ("To come upon"; hence) *To find, meet with,* etc.—Pass.: **in-vĕnĭor, ventus sum, vĕnīri.**

in-vĭdĕo, vīdi, vīsum, vĭd-ēre, 2. v. n. [ĭn, "towards"; video, "to see *or* look"] ("To look towards"; hence) With accessory notion of ill-will, etc.: With Dat. [§ 106, *a*]: *To envy; to feel envy at or towards; to be envious of.*

invĭd-ĭa, ĭæ, f. [invid-us, "envious"] ("The quality of the *invidus*"; hence) 1. *Envy, jealousy, grudge, hatred, ill-will.*—2. *Odium* resulting from something.

invī-sus, sa, sum, adj. [for invid-sus; fr. invĭd-ĕo, in force of "to hate"] With Dat. [§ 106, (3)]: *Hateful to, hated by.*

in-vī-tus, ta, tum, adj. ("Not desiring"; hence) 1. *Unwilling, reluctant, against one's will.*—2. In adverbial force: *Unwillingly, reluctantly,* etc. [ĭn, "not"; Sans. root vĭ, "to desire"].

i-pse, psa, psum, pron. dem. [for is-pse; fr. is; suffix pse] *Self, very, identical.* — As Subst.: m.: a. Sing.: *Himself.*—b. Plur.: (a) *Themselves.* — (b) *We ourselves;* xx. 6.

Ira, æ, f. *Wrath, anger.*

Irācund-ĭa, ĭæ, f. [iracund-us, "wrathful"] ("The quality of the *iracundus*"; hence) 1. *Wrathfulness, proneness to anger, irascibility.*—2. *Anger, wrath, rage, passion.*

Ir-ascor, ātus sum, asci, 3. v. dep. [īr-a, "anger"] *To be angry or in a rage.*

irātus, a, um: 1. P. perf. of īrascor. — 2. Pa.: *Angry, angered, enraged.*

Ire, pres. inf. of eo.

Irem, imperf. subj. of eo.

Ir-rumpo, rūpi, ruptum, rumpĕre, 3. v. n. [for in-rumpo; fr. ĭn, "into"; rumpo, "to break *or* burst"] Folld. by in with Acc.: *To break or burst into, to force one's way into* a place;—*i. e.* at l. 2 into the temple of Concord to which Cethegus and his fellow-conspirators had been taken; see xlvi. 4.

is, ea, id, pron. dem. [pronominal root ɪ] 1. *This, that,* person or thing just mentioned; —at vii. 6 eas, eam refer to the things specified in preceding clause, but are respectively in the gender of divitias and

L 2

VOCABULARY.

famam;—at liii. 4 eo refers to preceding clause and depends on factum, with which supply esse;—at ii. 1 id refers to reges and is in attribution to nomen; —at x. 3 ea refers to pecuniae . . . imperii cupido, and as a complex notion is there brought forward respecting things without life, the demonstrative pron. is put in nom. neut. plur. [§ 92, 2, *a*];— at lviii. 16 ea refers to preceding clause and is in concord with dementia;—at xiv. 1 id quod is used for quod alone, and refers to following clause omnium . . . . habebat. It is to be observed that id quod is employed only when a clause is the antecedent, and further that the clause beginning with id quod precedes that to which it relates. In grammatical strictness id is in apposition to the clause referred to, while quod relates to id.— As Subst.: a. Sing.: (a) Masc.: *He.* — (b) Fem.: *She.* — (c) Neut.: *It, that thing, that :*— sometimes with a follg. Gen.: ad id loci, *to that place* or *spot;* xlv. 3.—b. Plur.: (a) Masc.: *Those* just mentioned, *they.*— (b) Neut.: *Those things.*— 2. *Of such a nature* or *kind, such.*—3. Abl. neut. sing. as Abl. of measure [§ 118] after comparative words: *By so much, so much, all the, the :*

—eo magis, *by so much the more;* lii. 16 :—but in eoque magis properaret, xlviii. 4, eo is an adv. and magis belongs to properaret; see also, 3 eo, no. 2, b.—4. Particular constructions: a. Sometimes a subject is emphasized and brought prominently forward by the addition of the demonstr. pron. is; so that, in fact, the pron. becomes the actual grammatical Subject of the verb, while the original Subject stands as a Nom. Abs.:—urbana plebes, ea verò præceps ierat, xxxvii. 4.—b. When a clause (or a word) is explained by a subst. in connexion with sum (also dico *or* dicor, voco *or* vocor, and other similar verbs), the demonstr. (*or* rel.) pron. is usually in concord with such explanatory subst.: so, idem velle atque idem nolle, ea demum firma est amicitia, xx. 4. Here the pron. refers to the substantival clause idem velle atque idem nolle [§ 156, (3)]; but, instead of being in the neut. according to grammatical strictness, it is in the fem. in concord with amicitia. Moreover the foregoing clause stands as a Nom. Abs.; cf. above, no. 4. a.

Ita, adv.: 1. *Thus, in this way* or *manner, so.*—2. *In the following way* or *manner.*—3. *In such a way, so.*—4. *By this*

means, so.—5. *Accordingly.*—
6. a. Of extent or degree : *So,
so very; to such a degree.*—
b. In a restrictive force : *So
little, so slightly,* etc.—7. *On
this account, hence* [akin to
Sans. *iti*, " thus "].

Ĭtăl-ĭa, ĭæ, f. *Italy;* a country of Southern Europe [either
ἰταλός, "a bull," *or* a man
named Italus].

Ĭtem, adv. : 1. *So, even so,
in like manner.*—2. *Also, likewise.*—3. *Moreover, besides*
[akin to Sans. *ittham,* " so "].

Ĭ-ter, tĭnĕris, n. [ĕo, " to go,"
through root ɪ] (" A going ";
hence) 1. Of troops : *A march.*
—2. *A journey.*—3. *A route.*—
4. *A road, way.*

Ĭtĕr-um, adv. (" Beyond
this, further "; hence) *Anew,
afresh, a second time, again*
[akin to Sans. *itar-a*, " the
other "].

Ĭtūrus, a, um, P. fut. of eo.

jam, adv. [prob. for eam, fr.
is, "this"] 1. *At this time;
now.* — 2. a. *Already:* —jam
antea, *already before:*—jam
pridem, *already for this long
time.*—b. *At that time, then:*
—jam primum, *then in the
first place,* i. e. *before any-
thing and everything else;*
also, *at the very beginning,*
etc.:—jam tum, *then at that
time = at that very time.*—
3. To denote the all but im-

mediate arrival of that which
is to happen : *Now, presently,
immediately, forthwith,* etc.

jănŭa, æ, f. *The* outer *door*
of a house, *the street-door.*

Jănŭ-ārĭus, ārĭa, ārĭum,
adj. [fr. Jănŏ-ārĭus; fr. Janus,
uncontr. Gen. Jano-i, "Janus,"
the sun-god of ancient Italy,
represented with two faces,
one before and one behind]
(" Of, *or* belonging to, Janus";
hence, as Subst., **Jannarius,**
ĭi, m. " The month dedicated
to Janus," *i.e.* "January";
hence, as adj.) *Of January.*

jŏcus, i, m. (plur. jŏci, m.,
jŏca, n.) *A jest, joke.*

jŭ-bĕo, jussi, jussum, jŭbēre,
2. v. a. *To order, command, bid.*

jūdĭc-ĭum, ĭi, n. (" A judg-
ing "; hence) 1. *A trial.*—2.
Jurisdiction, legal authority
in civil matters, opp. to imperium in military affairs; xxix.
3.—3. *Judgment, opinion, de-
cision.*

jŭ-dĭc-o, āvi, ātum, āre, 1.
v. a. [for jur-dĭc-o; fr. jus,
jūr-is, "law"; dĭc-o, "to point
out "] (" To point out what
is law "; hence, "to pass judgment about"; hence) 1. *To
decide, determine.*—2. With
second Acc.: *To pronounce,
declare, proclaim* a person,
etc., to be that which is represented by the second Acc.:
—Pass.: jŭ-dĭcor, ātus sum,
āri.

jŭgŭlandi, Gerund in di fr. jŭgŭlo.

jŭgŭl-o, āvi, ātum, āre, 1. v. a. [jŭgŭl-um, "the throat"] *To cut the throat of; to kill, murder.* — Pass.: jŭgŭl-or, ātus sum, āri.

Julĭus, ĭi, m. *Julius;* a Roman name.

ju(n)g-o, junxi, junctum, jung-ĕre, 3. v. a.: 1. *To join, unite.*—2. *To bind, or fasten, together.* — Pass.: jungor, junctus sum, jungi [akin to Gr. ζυγ, root of ζεύγνυμι; and to Sans. root YUJ].

Junĭus, ĭi, m. *Junius;* a Roman name; see Silanus.

jurg-ĭum, ĭi, n. [jurg-o, "to take proceedings at law"; also, "to strive, *or* quarrel"] 1. ("A taking proceedings at law"; hence) *Law proceedings; a dispute, suit.*—2. ("A striving," *etc.;* hence) *Strife, a quarrel, dispute,* etc.

jū-s, ris, n. ("That which binds" morally; hence) 1. *Law; right, authority, power resulting from law.*—2. *A right, privilege,* etc, based upon law [akin to Sans. root YU, "to bind"].

jus-jūra-ndŭm, ndi, n. (Gen. jurisjurandi, n.) [jus, "a right"; jur(a)-o, "to swear"] ("A right to be sworn to"; hence) *An oath.*

jŭssĕrim, jussi, perf. subj. and ind. of jubeo.

1. jus-sus, sūs (only in Abl. sing.), m. [for jub-sus; fr. jub-eo, "to command"] *Command, order.*

2. jussus, a, um, P. perf. pass. of jubeo.

justissĭmus, a, um; see justus.

jŭst-ĭtĭa, ĭtĭæ, f. [just-us, "just"] ("The quality of the *justus*"; hence) *Justice.*

jus-tus, ta, tum, adj. [for jur-tus; fr. jus, jur-is, "law"] ("Provided with *jus*"; hence, "in accordance with law"; hence) *Just.* ☞ (Comp.: just-ĭor); Sup.: just-issĭmus.

jŭven-tus, tūtis, f. [jŭvĕn-is, "young"] ("The state of the *jŭvĕnis*"; hence) 1. *Youth,* i.e. *early years.* — 2. *The youth,* i.e. *young men.*

juxta, adv. [prob. for jug-sta; fr. JUG, root of jungo, "to join"; STA, root of sto, "to stand"] ("Standing joined" on to; hence) *Equally, alike,* etc.:—juxta ac, *Equally as, equally with.*

Kăl-endæ (Căl-endæ), end-ārum, f. plur. [căl-o, "to call out"] ("Things to be called out *or* proclaimed"; referring to the Nones, whether they were to be on the fifth or seventh day of the month. This proclamation was always made by the pontifices on the first day of each month, which thence obtained the name of) *The Kalends* or *Calends.*

L., abbrev. of Lucius.
lăbor (lăbos), ōris, m. ("The act of obtaining *or* getting"; hence) *Toil, exertion, labour* [akin to Sans. root LABH (whence also λαβ, root of λα(μ)β-άνω, "to take"), "to obtain *or* get"].

lăbōrans, ntis, P. pres. of laboro.—As Subst.: **lăbōrant-es,** ĭum, m. plur.: Of soldiers: *Those who are, etc., hard pressed* in battle; lx. 4.

lăbōr-o, āvi, ātum, āre, 1. v. n. [labor, "labour"] 1. *To labour, toil.*—2. Of soldiers, etc.: *To be hard pressed; to be in difficulty* or *danger.*

lăbos; see lăbor.

(**Lăcĕdæmŏn-ĭus,** ĭa, ĭum, adj. [Lăcĕdæmon, Lacedæmŏnis, "Lacedæmon," otherwise "Sparta" (now Misitra); a city of Southern Greece or the Peloponnesus (now the Morēa), which was long the rival and enemy of Athens] *Of,* or *belonging to, Lacedæmon; Lacedæmonian.*—As Subst.) **Lăcĕdæmŏnĭi,** ōrum, m. plur. *The people of Lacedæmon, the Lacedæmonians.*

lăcĕr-o, āvi, ātum, āre, 1. v. a. [lăcer, "mangled"] ("To make *lacer*"; hence, "to mangle"; hence) Of property: *To dissipate, waste, squander.*

lăcessītus, a, um, P. perf. pass. of lacesso.

lăc-esso, essīvi *or* essĭi *or* essi, essītum, essĕre, 3. v. a. intens. ("To bite eagerly"; hence) *To provoke, irritate, exasperate.*—Pass.: **lăc-essor,** essītus sum, essi [akin to δάκνω; Sans. root DAÇ, "to bite"].

Læca, æ, m. *Læca (Marcus Porcius);* a Roman senator, one of Catiline's accomplices; xvii. 3; xxvii. 3.

læt-ĭtĭa, ĭtĭæ, f. [læt-us, "joyful"] ("The quality, *or* condition, of the *lætus*"; hence) *Joy, joyousness;*—a stronger word than gaudium.

læt-or, ātus sum, āri, 1. v. dep. [id.] ("To be *lætus*"; hence) 1. *To be joyful* or *joyous, to be very glad, to rejoice.*—2. With Acc. of neut. pron.: *To rejoice at,* etc.

lætus, a, um, adj. *Glad, joyful, joyous* [prob. akin to Sans. root LAS, "to be bright"; also, "to delight"].

læv-a, æ, f. [læv-us, "left," i. e. "on the left side"] *The left hand:*—ad lævam, *towards the left hand,* or *on the left-hand side;* lv. 3.

lancĕa, æ, f. *A* light *spear* with a leathern thong attached to it; *a lance.*

languens, ntis, P. pres. of langueo.

lang-uĕo (trisyll.), ŭi, no sup., uēre, 2. v. n. ("To be weak *or* languid"; hence) *To be inert, inactive, faint-hearted,* etc. [akin to Sans. *dergh-a,* "long"; Gr. λαγγ-ά(ω, "to slacken"].

lăpĭd-ĕus, ĕa, ĕum, adj. [lăpis, lapid-is, "a stone"] ("Of, *or* belonging to, *lapis*"; hence) *Made,* or *consisting, of stones; stone-*.

lăqu-ĕus (trisyll.), ĕi, m. ("That which is hollowed out"; hence) *A rope* with a noose in it, *a halter* [akin to Gr. λάκ-κος, "a hole *or* pit"].

lăr, lăris; see Lares.

(Lăr-es (Lăs-es), um *and* ĭum, m. plur. ("The bright *or* shining ones") *The Lares,* tutelar deities of a house whose images were placed in a little shrine by the hearth, or in a small chapel in the interior of the house.—Sing.: Lar, Laris, m. *One of the Lares, a Lar;* hence) *A hearth, dwelling, home* [akin to Sans. root LAS, "to shine"].

larg-e, adv. [larg-us, "abundant"] 1. *Abundantly.*— 2. Comp.: *Too abundantly or lavishly; too freely or profusely.* ☞ Comp.: larg-ĭus; (Sup.: larg-issĭme).

larg-ĭor, ītus sum, īri, 4. v. dep. [larg-us, "large"; hence, "bountiful"] 1. *To give bountifully.*—2. *To give larg-*

esses, to bribe.—3. With Acc.: *To lavish,* in a figurative sense; lii. 12.

largī-tĭo, tĭōnis, f. [largĭ-or, "to give bountifully"] 1. *A giving bountifully* or *freely; a lavish* or *prodigal expenditure.*—2. *Bribery, corruption.*

largĭundo (largĭendo), Gerund in do fr. largĭor.

largĭus, comp. adv.; see large.

lascīv-ĭa, ĭœ, f. [lascīv-us, "sportive"] ("The quality of the *lascīvus*"; hence) *Sportiveness, mirth,* etc.

lass-ĭtūdo, ĭtūdĭnis, f. [lass-us, "weary"] ("The state, *or* condition, of the *lassus*"; hence) *Weariness.*

Lăt-īnus, īna, īnum, adj. [contr. fr. Lătĭ-īnus; fr. Lătĭ-um, "Latium"; a country of Italy in which Rome was situate (now "Campagna di Roma" and a part of the "Terra di Lavoro")] *Of,* or *belonging to, Latium; Latin.*

latr-o, ōnis, m. ("A hired servant"; hence) *A robber, bandit* [λατρ-εύω, "to work for hire"; whence λάτρ-ις, "a hired servant"].

1. **lătus,** a, um, P. perf. pass. of fero.

2. **lătus,** ĕris, n. [prob. akin to lātus, "wide"] ("The extended thing"; hence) 1. *A side.*—2. Of an army: *The flank.*

laud-o, ăvi, ātum, āre, 1. v. a. [laus, laud-is, "praise"] *To praise.*—Pass.: laud-or, ātus sum, āri.

laus, laudis, f. *Praise, commendation.*

lectus, a, um, P. perf. pass. of lego.

lēgā-tus, ti, m. [lēg(a)-o, "to send on an embassy"] ("One sent on an embassy"; hence) 1. *An ambassador.*—2. Milit. t. t.: *A lieutenant-general; a lieutenant.*

lěg-ĭo, ĭōnis, f. [lěg-o, "to levy *or* enlist"] ("A levying *or* enlisting"; hence, "a body of troops levied," *etc.;* hence) 1. *A* Roman *legion,* consisting of 10 cohorts of infantry, and a squadron of 300 cavalry; xxxii. 1.—2. Of foreign nations: Plur.: *Troops, armies, legions;* liii. 3.

lēg-ĭtĭmus, ĭtĭma, ĭtĭmum, adj. [lex, lēg-is, "law"] ("Of *or* belonging to *lex*"; hence) 1. *Lawful, legal, legitimate.*—2. *Fixed, prescribed,* or *appointed by law.*

lěgo, lēgi, lectum, lěgěre, 3. v. a. ("To lay, *or* put, together"; hence) 1. *To choose,* or *pick, out; to select.*—2. *To read, read of* [λέγω].

lēn-io, īvi *or* ĭi, ītum, īre, 4. v. a. [lēn-is, "soft"] ("To make *lenis*"; hence) Of ill-will, *etc.*: *To soften down, mitigate, appease,* etc.

lēnĭundus (= lēnĭendus), a, um, Gerundive of lēnĭo.

Lentŭl-us, i, m. [lentŭl-us, "rather slow"] ("One rather slow") *Lentŭlus (Publius Cornelius),* with the agnomen of Sura, a Roman patrician, who had been consul. He was one of Catiline's accomplices, and was strangled in prison by order of Cicero; xvii. 3; lv. 5, 6, *etc.;* see Sura.

Lěpĭd-us, i, m. ["charming, agreeable"] ("Charming *or* Agreeable One") *Lepidus (Marcus),* whose full name was Marcus Æmilius Lepidus. He was the colleague of Lucius Tullus in the consulate; xviii. 2. During his quæstorship, B.C. 77, he had the Sublician bridge built of stone.

lěpor (lěpos), ōris, m. *Agreeableness, pleasantness, attractiveness.*

lěpos; see lepor.

lěvĭor, us; see levis.

lěv-is, e, adj. *Light,* whether actually *or* figuratively. ☞ Comp.: lěv-ĭor; (Sup.: lěv-issĭmus) [akin to Gr. ἐ-λαχ-ύς; also to Sans. *lagh-u*].

lex, lēgis, f. [for leg-s; fr. lěg-o, "to read"] ("That which is read"; hence, "a bill," *i.e.* a proposition reduced to writing and read (to the people) with a view to its being passed into law; hence) *A law* or *enactment,* lībĕo, ĕre; see lŭbĕo.

1. līb-er, ĕra, ĕrum, adj. ("Doing as one desires"; hence) *Free, possessing freedom* or *liberty* [akin to Sans. root LUBH, "to desire"; whence, also, Gr. ἐ-λευθ-ερός, "free"].

2. lī-ber, bri, m. ("The inner bark" of a tree; hence) *A book* as written upon prepared bark.

lībĕr-ālis, āle, adj. [liber, "a free man"] ("Of, *or* belonging to, a *liber*"; hence) 1. *Liberal, bountiful, generous.* —2. With Gen.: *Bountiful, or generous with; liberal of.*

lībĕrāl-ĭtas, ĭtātis, f. [lībĕrāl-is, "liberal"] ("The quality of the *liberalis*"; hence) *Liberality.*

lībĕrāl-ĭter, adv. [id.] ("After the manner of the *liberalis*"; hence) *Bountifully, generously, liberally.*

līb-ĕri, ĕrōrum, m. plur. (the sing. only in late Lat.) ("The desired *or* loved ones"; hence) *Children* [akin to Sans. root LUBH, "to desire *or* love"].

lībĕr-o, āvi, ātum, āre, 1. v. n. [līber, "free"] With Acc. and Abl.: *To free* one, etc., or *set* one *free from; to release* or *rescue* one *from.*

līber-tas, tātis, f. [id.] ("The state *or* condition of the *liber*"; hence) *Freedom,*

liberty as opposed to slavery: —jus libertatis imminūtum erat, (*whose*) *right of liberty had been lessened*, xxxvii. 9. Any loss of the rights of Roman citizens was called deminutio capĭtis, *or*, as above, jus libertatis imminūtum. Sallust here alludes to the law entitled "De proscriptione et proscriptis," enacted when Sulla was Dictator, which declared the children of proscribed parents incapable of holding any public office.

lībĕr-tus, ti, m. [lībĕr-o, "to set free"] ("He that has been set free"; hence) *A freedman,* with respect to the person manumitted.

līcent-ĭa, ĭæ, f. [licens, licentis, "acting according to one's own will"] ("The condition *or* state of the *licens*"; hence) 1. *The acting according to one's own will* or *pleasure; freedom, liberty.*—2. *Boldness, unruliness, presumption, licence.*

līc-ĕo, ŭi, ĭtum, ēre (usually only in 3rd pers. sing. and inf. mood), 2. v. n. *To be allowable; to be permitted* or *lawful.*

Līcĭnĭus, ĭi, m. *Licinius;* a Roman name; see Crassus.

līcuisset; see liceo.

ling-ua (dissyll.), uæ, f. [ling-o, "to lick"] ("The licking thing"; hence) 1. *A tongue.*—2. *A language* or *tongue.*

lĭtera, æ, f.: 1. Sing.: *A letter* or *character* of the alphabet. — 2. Plur.: a. *A letter, epistle.*—b. *Learning, literature, letters.*

lŏc-o, āvi, ātum, āre, 1. v. a. [loc-us, "a place"] *To place, post, station, set.*

lŏcŭ-plē-s, tis, adj. [for loco-ple-ts; fr. locus, (uncontr. gen.) loco-i, "landed property"; ple-o, "to fill"] ("Full of landed property"; hence) 1. *Rich in lands.*—2. *Rich, wealthy, opulent.*—As Subst.: locuplētes, ĭum *and* um, m. plur. *The wealthy* or *rich.*

lŏc-us, i, m. (Plur. lŏc-i, m., *and* lŏc-a, n.) ("That which is put, placed, *or* situate"; hence) 1. *A place, spot, locality.*—2. Of a soldier: *A post.*—3. *Room, occasion, place,* etc.—4. Of birth, *etc.: Place, position, degree, rank* [prob. akin to Gr. root λεχ, "to put"].

long-e, adv. [long-us, "long"; hence, "far off"] 1. Pos.: a. *Far off, at a distance.*—b. With Comparative and Superlative words: *By far, very much, greatly.*—2. Comp.: *Too far.* ☞ Comp.: long-ius; (Sup.: long-issime).

Long-īnus, īni, m. [longus, "long"] ("One pertaining to *longus*") *Longinus* (*Lucius Cassius*); a Roman senator, who was a candidate for the consulship together with Catiline, and having failed in his object became an accomplice in the conspiracy. The part assigned to him was the firing of the city. In conjunction with Lentulus, Cethegus, and Statilius, he carried on negotiations with the ambassadors of the Allobroges, but avoided giving them, as the others had done, any written document. He quitted Rome before the ambassadors and so escaped being seized. He was, however, condemned to death in his absence; but whether he was afterwards taken and executed is not known.

long-us, a, um, adj. *Long,* whether in time or space [probably akin to Sans. *dirgha*, "long"].

lŏqu-or, ūtus sum, i, 3. v. dep. *To speak, talk* [akin to Sans. root LAP, "to speak"].

lŏquūtus, a, um, P. perf. of lŏquor.

lŭb-ĕo (lĭb-ĕo), ŭi, ĭtum, ēre, 2. v. n.: 1. *To please.*— 2. Impers.: lubuit, *It has pleased; it has been (my) will* or *pleasure;*—at liii. 2 lubuit has for its Subject the clause adtendere . . . sustinuisset [§ 157] [akin to Sans. root LUBH, "to desire"].

lŭbĭdĭnōs-e, adv.[lŭbĭdĭnōs

us, "acting according to one's own will, capricious"] ("After the manner of the *lubidinosus*"; hence) *According to one's own will and pleasure; wantonly, capriciously.*

lŭb-īdo (lĭb-īdo), īdĭnis, f. [lŭb-ĕo, "to please"] ("A pleasing of one's self"; hence) 1. *Desire, eagerness, longing.* —2. *Caprice, self-will.* —3. *Fancy,inclination.*—4.*Sensual desire, sensuality, passion, lust.*

lubuit; see lubeo.

Lūc-ĭus, ĭi, m. [lux, lūc-is, "light"; hence, "the day"] ("One belonging to the day," *i.e.* prob. "one born at break of day") *Lucius;* a Roman name.

luctŭ-ōsus, ōsa, ōsum, adj. [luctus, uncontr. Gen. luctŭ-is, "sorrow, grief"] ("Full of *luctus*"; hence) *Causing sorrow* or *grief; mournful, sorrowful, grievous.*

luc-tus, tūs, m. [for lug-tus; fr. lūg-ĕo, "to grieve"] 1. *Grief, sorrow.*—2. *Mourning, bewailing, lamentation.*

lūc-ŭlentus, ŭlenta, ŭlentum, adj. [lux, lūc-is, "light"] ("Full of *lux*"; hence) *Clear, perspicuous, lucid.*

lūd-ĭbrĭum, ĭbrĭi, n. [lūd-o, 'to mock"] ("That which brings about the mocking"; hence, "mockery, derision"; hence) *A laughing-stock; a butt, jest, sport.*

luxŭr-ĭa, ĭæ, f. [luxus, "luxury," through obsol. adj. luxŭr-is, "of, *or* belonging too, *luxus*"] ("The quality of the *luxuris*"; hence) *Luxury, luxurious style of living, extravagance,* etc.

luxŭrĭōs-e, adv. [luxŭrĭōsus, "luxurious"] ("After the manner of the *luxuriosus*"; hence) *Luxuriously, voluptuously, in a debauched way.*

lux-us, ūs, m. [lux-us, "dislocated"] ("A being *luxus*"; hence, "a dislocation"; hence, in a figurative sense) *Excess, extravagance* in eating and drinking; *luxury, debauchery.*

M., abbrev. of Marcus.

Măcĕdŏn-ĭcus, ĭca, ĭcum, adj. [Măcĕdŏn-es, "the Macedonians"] *Of,* or *belonging to, the Macedonians; Macedonian:* — bellum Macedonicum, *the Macedonian war,* i. e. the war with Perses *or* Perseus, the last king of Macedonia, which was brought to a favourable issue for the Romans by L. Æmilius Paulus, at the battle of Pydna, June 22, B.C. 168.

măchĭnātus, a, um, P. perf. of măchĭnor.

măchĭn-or, ātus sum, ari, v. dep. [măchĭn-a, "a contrivance"] 1. *To contrive, plot, scheme, devise;* xviii. 7. —2. Part. perf. in pass. force:

Contrived, schemed, devised ; xlviii. 7, where supply *esse* with machinatum.

mær-or, ōris, m. [mær-ĕo, "to be sad"] *Sadness, sorrow, grief.*

măg-is, comp. adv. [akin to mag-nus] *More, in a greater degree :* — magis magisque, *more and more :*—for eo magis, see is, no. 3.

măgistr-ātus,ātūs,m.[magister, magistr-i, "a master, superior," *etc.*] ("The office *or* rank of a *magister* "; hence) 1. *A magisterial office, a magistracy.*—2. *A magistrate.*

magnĭfĭc-e, adv. [magnĭfĭc-us, "magnificent," *etc.*] ("After the manner of the *magnificus*"; hence) 1. *Magnificently, splendidly,* etc. — 2. *Excellently, admirably, famously.*—3. *Boastfully, in a boastful or bragging way.*—4. *In lofty or glowing terms.*

magn-ĭ-fĭc-us, a, um, adj. [for magn-i-fac-us; fr. magnus, "great"; (i) connecting vowel; fac-io, "to do"] ("Doing great things"; hence) 1. Of persons : a. *Noble, distinguished, eminent.* — b. *Magnificent, grand, fond of show or pomp.*—2. Of things : *Noble, glorious, magnificent,splendid.*

magn-ĭtūdo, ĭtūdĭnis, f. [magn-us] ("The quality of the *magnus*"; hence) 1. *Greatness, vastness. magni-*

tude.—2. Of degree : *Greatness, extent,magnitude;* xxxiii. 3.—3.*Rank,dignity,authority.*

mag-nus, na, num, adj. : 1. Of size : *Great, large.*—2. In number : *Great, large, numerous.* — 3. Of degree *or* extent: *Great, large,* etc. ; *long.* — 4. Of value, importance, etc.: *Great, high, important.* —5. In estimation, etc.: a. *Of high consideration, of weight, weighty.* — b. *Grand, noble.* —6. *Mighty, powerful.* — 7. *Great* in mind.—8. Of age : *Great, advanced, old.* ☞ Comp.: mājor (= măg-ĭor); Sup.: maxĭmus (= mag-s-imus) [root MAG, akin to Gr. μέγ-ας, Sans. *mah-a,* "great"; fr. Sans. root MAH, originally MAGH,"to be great, powerful," *etc.*].

mājor, us, comp. adj.; see magnus.—As Subst.: **mājōres,** um, m. plur. *Ancestors, forefathers.*

mājōres, um ; see major.

măl-e, adv. [măl-us, "bad"] ("After the manner of the *malus*"; hence) *Badly, in a bad way, not well.*

mălēdic-tum, ti, n.[mălēdĭc-o, "to revile," *etc.*] ("That which reviles"; hence) *Reviling, abuse, foul language.*

mălĕ-făc-tum, ti (also as two words male factum), n. [male, "badly"; făc-io, "to do"] ("That which is done

badly, a doing evil"; hence)
An evil deed.

mălĕ-fĭo-ĭum, ĭi, n. [for
male-fac-ĭum; fr. mălĕ, "badly"; făcĭo, "to do"] ("A
doing badly *or* evil"; hence)
1. *An evil deed, wickedness,
offence, crime, bad action.*—2.
Mischief, hurt, harm.

mălĕvŏlent-ĭa, ĭæ, f. [mălĕ-
vŏlens, malevolent-is, "male-
volent"] ("The quality of the
malevolens"; hence) *Ill-will,
evil disposition, malevolence.*

mālo, mālŭi, malle, v. a.
irreg. [contr. fr. mag-vŏlo; fr.
root MAG (see magnus); vŏlo,
"to have a desire for"] ("To
have a great desire for";
hence) 1. *To choose rather, to
prefer.*—In comparisons folld.
by quam; viii. 5.—2. Folld. by
pro: *To prefer before, above,*
or *to; xvii. 6; where, also, in
one clause the use of quàm
occurs; see above, no. 1.—3.
With Objective clause: *To prefer that;* xxxvii. 10; where
quàm is also found; see above,
no. 1.

1. măl-us, a, um, adj.
("Dirty, black"; hence) 1.
Bad of its kind.—2. Morally
bad; evil, wicked.—As Subst.:
mălus, i, m. *A bad,* or *wicked,*
person.—Plur.: *The bad, evil,*
etc. — 3. *Mischievous.* — As
Subst.: mălum, i, n. *Mischief,
harm, hurt, injury.*—4. *Bad,
pernicious, destructive.* — 5.

*Adverse, unfortunate, calam-
itous.*—As Subst.: a. Sing.:
mălum, i, n. *An adverse* or
*unfortunate thing; a calamity,
misfortune, evil.*—b. Plur.:
mala, ōrum, n. *Misfortunes,* etc.
[akin to Sans. *mal-as,* "dirty";
Gr. μέλ-as, "black"].

2. mălus, i; see 1. malus.

mandandus, a, um, Gerund-
ive of mando.

mandā-tum, ti, n. [mand(a)-o]
("A thing enjoined"; hence)
*A command, order, charge,
injunction,* etc.

man-do, dāvi, dātum, dāre,
1. v. a. [măn-us, "hand"; do,
"to put"] ("To put into
one's hand"; hence) 1. *To
enjoin, order, command;*—at
xxxii. 2 folld. by Dat. of person and simple subj. [§§ 106,
(4); 154]. — 2. *To commit,
entrust.*

măn-ĭ-fes-tus, ta, tum, adj.
[for măn-ĭ-fend-tus; fr. manus, "a hand"; (i) connecting
vowel; obsol. fend-o, "to
dash"] ("Dashed by the
hand"; hence) 1. *Palpable,
clear, plain, manifest.* — 2.
Convicted, caught.—3. With
Gen.: *Convicted of, manifestly*
or *palpably caught in* or *guilty
of.*

Manlianus, a, um; see
Manlius.

Manlĭus, ĭi, m. *Manlius
(Caius);* the commander of
Catiline's forces in Etruria.

—Hence, **Manlĭ-ānus**, āna, ānum, adj. *Of,* or *belonging to, Manlius; Manlian.*

mansŭē-tūdo, tūdĭnis, f. [for mansuet-tūdo, fr. mansŭētus, "mild"] ("The quality of the *mansuetus*"; hence) *Mildness* of character, *gentleness, clemency.*

mă-nus, nūs, f. ("The measuring thing"; hence) 1. *A hand:*—mănūs dare, (*to give hands,* i. e.) *to submit, yield.*— Phrase: in manibus esse, *to be near* or *close at hand.*—2. a. *An* armed *force, a body* or *corps of soldiers.*—b. *A body, number, company, multitude* of persons.—3. *Power :* — in manu (esse), *to be within one's power* or *grasp* [akin to Sans. root MÂ, "to measure"].

Marc-ĭus, ĭi, m. [marc-us; see Marcus] ("One belonging to a *marcus;* Hammerer") *Marcius (Quintus);* see Rex.

Marcus, i, m. *Marcus* (usually written, by abbreviation, M.)*;* a Roman praenomen [marcus, "a crushing thing"; hence, "a large hammer"; akin to Sans. root MṚID, "to crush"].

mărе, is (Abl. mari), n. *The sea:*—mari atque terrā, *by sea and land* [akin to Sans. *vâri,* "water"].

măr-ĭtĭmus, ĭtĭma, ĭtĭmum, adj. [măr-e] *Of,* or *belonging to, the sea; sea-, on the sea-* coast, *maritime:*—bellum maritimum, *the maritime war,* otherwise called *the war with the pirates.* The Cilician pirates swarmed in almost every sea, and extended their depredations to the coasts of Italy and the mouth of the Tiber. Pompey was sent against them, B.C. 66, and brought the war to a conclusion within forty days.

Măr-ĭus, ĭi, m. [mas, măris, "a male"] ("One pertaining to *mas;* Manly or Bold One") *Marius (Caius);* the conqueror of Jugurtha, and who was seven times consul; see Cimbrĭcus.

Massĭlĭa, æ, f. *Massilia* (now *Marseilles);* a celebrated sea-port town in Gallia Narbonensis.

mă-ter, tris, f. *A mother:* —mater familias (old gen. of familia), or as one word materfamilias, *the mother of a family, the mistress of a household* [akin to Gr. μή-τηρ; Sans. *mâ-tri,* fr. root MÂ, in meaning of "to produce," and so, "the producer"].

materfamilias, æ; see mater.

mătĕr-ĭes, ĭēi, f. [mater, mat(e)r-is, in the force of "a producing cause"] ("That which belongs to a *mater*"; hence) *A cause, occasion, source, origin* of a thing; x. 3.

mātūrandus, a, um, Gerundive of maturo.

mātūr-e, adv. [matur-us, in the force of "speedy, quick"] ("After the manner of the *maturus*"; hence) *Speedily, quickly,* etc.

mātūr-o, āvi, ātum, āre, 1. v. a. [id.] 1. *To hasten, accelerate* a thing.—2. With Inf.: *To make haste,* or *hasten, to do,* etc.—3. With Inf.: *To make too much haste to do,* etc.; *to be precipitate in* doing, etc.

Maur-ĭtānĭa, ĭtānĭæ, f. [Maur-i, "the Mauri *or* Moors"] *The country of the Mauri, Mauritania* (now *Fez and Morocco*); a country of Africa on the shores of the Mediterranean.

maxŭm-e (maxĭm-e), sup. adv. [maxim-us, "greatest"] 1. *In the greatest* or *highest degree; especially:* — quam maxume longam, *as long as possible,* i. 3; — sometimes joined with positive adjectives. —2. *Very greatly, exceedingly.* ☞ Comp.: măgis; see măgis.

maxŭmus (maxĭmus), a, um, sup. adj.; see magnus.

1. **me,** acc. *and* abl. sing. of ĕgo.

2. **me,** a particle used in the expression me dius fidius, mehercule; see fidius [Gr. μα, ⁴icle used in strong pro-

testations and oaths, followed by the name of the deity or thing appealed to].

mē-cum = cum me.

měd-ĭus, ĭa, ĭum, adj. 1. *That is in the middle* or *midst; middle,* etc.—Phrase: in medio rem relinquere, *to leave a matter* (*in the midst;* i.e.) *open* or *undecided.*—2. *The middle of* that denoted by its subst. [Gr. μέσ-ος; Sans. *madh-yas*].

me-hercŭle, adv. [2. me; Hercules, "Hercules"; the god of strength, etc.] *By Hercules;* a form of oath.

měmĭněrim, perf. subj. of memini.

mě-mĭn-i, isse, v. defect. *To bear in mind, remember, recollect* [for men-men-i; reduplicated fr. root MEN, akin to Sans. root MAN, "to think"; cf. Lat. men-s, "the mind" as "the thinking thing"].

měm-or, ŏris, adj. [akin to memini, "to remember"] With Gen. [§ 133]: *Remembering, bearing in mind, mindful of.*

měmŏrā-bĭlis, bĭle, adj. [měmŏr(a)-o, "to call to remembrance"] ("Worthy of being called to remembrance"; hence) *Worthy of mention, memorable.*

měmŏrandi, Gerund in di fr. memoro.

měmŏrātu, Supine in u fr. memoro.

měmŏ--ĭa, ĭæ, f. [memor, "mindful"] ("The quality, or state, of the *memor*"; hence) *Memory, remembrance, recollection :*—memoriā meā (nostrā), *within my (our) recollection.*

měmŏr-o, āvi, ātum, āre, 1. v. a. *and* n. [id.] 1. Act.: ("To make (another) mindful of" something; hence) *To mention, make mention of; to relate, describe, state, narrate.* —2. Neut.: With de: *To speak,* or *make mention, about.*

men-s, tis, f. ("The thinking"; hence) *The mind,* as being the seat of thought [Lat. root MEN; akin to Sans. *mdn-as,* "mind"; fr. root ̣MAN, "to think"; cf., also, Gr. μέν-ος].

ment-ĭor, ītus sum, īri, 4 v. dep. [mens, ment-is, "the mind"] ("To think, *or* form, in the mind"; hence, in a bad sense, "to lie"; hence) With Acc.: *To lie,* or *speak falsely, about; to assert falsely.*

mentītus, a, um, P. perf. of mentior.

mer-ce-s, mercēdis, f. [for merc-ced-s; fr. merx, merc-is, "gain": cēd-o, "to come"] ("That which comes as, *or* for, gain"; hence) 1. *Hire, pay, wages.*—2. *Gain, advantage.*

merc-or, ātus sum, āri, 1. v. dep. [merx, merc-is, "merch-

andise"] ("To deal in merchandise; to traffic"; hence) *To buy, purchase.*

měrĭt-o, adv. [měrĭt-us, "deserved"] ("After the manner of the *meritus*"; hence) *Deservedly.*

Metellus, i, m. *Metellus;* a Roman name: 1. Quintus Metellus; see Creticus.—2. Quintus Metellus, with the cognomen of Celer; a Roman prætor; xlii. 3.

mētĭor, mensus sum, mētīri, 4. v. dep. ("To measure, measure out"; hence) Mentally: *To measure, estimate* [root MET or MEN, akin to Sans. root MÀ, "to measure"].

mětŭ-o, metŭi, mětūtum, mětŭĕre, 3. v. a. [metus, uncontr. gen. metŭ-is, "fear"] *To fear, dread, be afraid of.*

mětus, ūs, m. *Fear, dread.*

mě-us, a, um, pron. possess. [me] *Of,* or *belonging to, me; my, mine.*

mīles, ĭtis, comm. gen.: 1. *A soldier.*—2. Plur.: *The soldiers, the soldiery.*

mīlĭt-āris, āre, adj. [miles, mīlĭt-is, "a soldier"] 1. *Of,* or *belonging to, a soldier; military.*—2. *Of,* or *relating to, war; military :*—equus militaris, *a war-horse :*—res militaris, *military affairs.*—3. *Experienced in military affairs, of military experience.*

mīlĭt-ĭa, ĭæ, f. [mīlĭt-o.

"to serve as a soldier"]
(" The serving as a soldier ";
hence) **1. a.** *Military service.*
—**b.** Adverbial expression :
militiæ, *on service, abroad,
in the field* [§ 121, B, b].—
2. *Warfare.*

militiæ; see militia.

mill-e, num. adj. indecl. *A
thousand.*—As Subst. : **mill-
ia,** ĭum, n. plur. *A thousand*
[akin to χίλιοι].

mĭnĭm-e (mĭnŭm-e), sup.
adv. [mĭnŭm-us, " least "] *In
the least degree, least of all,
by no means.*

minimus (minumus), a, um,
sup. adj. ; see parvus.

mĭn-ĭtor, ĭtātus sum, ĭtāri,
1. v. dep. freg. [mĭn-or, " to
threaten "] With Dat. [§ 106,
(3)] : *To keep threatening* or
menacing ; to menace, etc.,
frequently or *very much.*

1. mĭ-nor, nātus sum, nāri,
1. v. dep. (" To jut forth, project " ; hence) *To threaten,
menace* [akin to Sans. root MÎ,
" to hurt "].

2. mĭnor, us, comp. adj. ;
see parvus.

minume; see minime.

minumus, a, um; see minimus.

mĭn-ŭo, ŭi, ūtum, ŭĕre, 3.
v. a. *To make less ; to lessen,
diminish.* — Pass. : **mĭn-ŭor,**
ūtus sum, ŭi [root MIN, akin
to mĭn-or, and μιν-ύθω].

mĭnus, comp. adv. [adverbial
neut. of mĭnor, " less "] **1.**
Less ; in a less, or *smaller, degree,* etc.; *not so much.*—**2.** To
make an emphatic negation :
*Not at all ; by no means, in
no degree.*

mirandus, a, um, Gerundive
of mīror.

mĭ-ror, rātus sum, rāri, 1.
v. dep. (" To smile upon " in
indication of approval ; hence)
1. *To admire.*—**2.** *To wonder
at ; to be amazed* [akin to
Sans. root SMI, " to smile "].

mīr-us, a, um, adj. [mīr-or,
"to wonder"] *To be wondered
at, wonderful.* — As Subst. :
mirum, i, n. *A wonder, marvel.*

miscĕo, miscŭi, mistum *and*
mixtum; miscēre, 2. v. a. (" To
mix, mingle"; hence) *To
throw into confusion, to disturb.*—Pass. : **miscĕor,** mistus
and mixtus sum, miscēri [akin
to Sans. *miçra,* "mixed";
whence, also, μίσγω, μίγνῡμι].

mĭs-er, ĕra, ĕrum, adj. [prob.
akin to mær-ĕo, " to be sad " ;
mæs-tus, " sad "] *Wretched,
miserable.*—As Subst. : **mĭs-
ĕri,** ōrum, m. plur. *The
wretched.*

mĭsĕrā-bĭlis, bĭle, adj.
[miser(a)-or, " to pity "] *To
be pitied, deserving of pity,
deplorable.*

mĭsĕrātus, a, um, P. perf.
of miseror.

mĭsĕrĕămĭni, 2. pers. plur.
pres. subj. of misereor.

mĭsĕr-ĕor, ītus sum, ēri, 2. v. dep. [mĭser, "wretched"] ("To feel *miser* about"; hence) 1. *To pity, show pity or compassion.*—2. With Gen. [§ 135]: *To pity, have pity on, compassionate.*

mĭsĕr-ĭa, ĭæ, f. [id.] ("The state of the *miser*"; hence) *Wretchedness, misery.*

mĭsĕrĭcord-ĭa, ĭæ, f. [misericors, misericord-is, "compassionate"] ("The quality of the *misericors*"; hence) *Compassion, pity.*

mĭsĕr-ĭ-cor-s, dis, adj. [for mĭsĕr-ĭ-cord-s; fr. mĭsĕr-ĕor, "to pity"; (i) connecting vowel; cor, cord-is, "a heart"] *Having a pitying heart; tender-hearted, pitiful, compassionate.*

mĭsĕrĭtus, a, um, P. perf. of misereor.

mĭsĕr-or, ātus sum, āri, 1. v. dep. [miser, "wretched"] ("To feel *miser* for *or* on account of"; hence) 1. *To lament, deplore, bewail.*—2. *To pity, compassionate.*

1. missus, a, um, P. perf. pass. of mitto.

2. mis-sus, sūs, m. [for mitt-sus, fr. mitt-o, "to send"] A *sending, despatching.*

Mĭthrĭdăt-ĭcus, ĭca, ĭcum, adj. [Mĭthrĭdăt-es, "Mithridates"; a king of Pontus in Asia, surnamed the Great. He waged war with the Romans, and on being conquered by Pompey stabbed himself] *Of,* or *belonging to, Mithridates; Mithridatic :*— bellum Mithridaticum, *the war with Mithridates;* see above.

mitto, mīsi, missum, mittĕre, 3. v. a.: 1. *To let, suffer,* or *allow to go.*—2. *To cause to go; to send.*—Pass. : mitt-or, missus sum, mitti.

mōbĭl-ĭtas, ĭtātis, f. [mōbĭl-is, in sense of "fickle"] ("The quality of the *mobilis*"; hence) *Fickleness, changeableness.*—N.B. At xlix. 4 mobilitate is the reading of modern editions; in some editions nobilitate (*nobleness, generous impulse*) is given.

mŏdĕrātus, a, um: 1. P. perf. of moderor. — 2. Pa.: *Kept within bounds* or *limits, moderate.*

mŏd-ĕror, ĕrātus sum, ĕrāri, 1. v. dep. [mŏd-us, "a bound"] ("To set bounds to"; hence) 1. *To restrict, control, impose restrictions.* — 2. With Dat. [§ 106, 4]: *To rule, sway.*

mŏdest-ĭa, ĭæ, f. [mŏdest-us, "keeping one's self within bounds"] ("The quality of the *modestus*"; hence) 1. *Self-restraint, sobriety of behaviour, moderation.* — 2. *Honour, sense* or *feeling of honour.*

mŏd-estus, esta, estum, adj. [mod-us, "bounds, limit"]

("Having *or* with *modus*"; hence) *Modest, chaste, virtuous, moral.*—As Subst.: **modestus, i,** m. *A modest or virtuous man.*

mŏdo, adv.: 1. *Only, merely.* —2. In restrictive clause: *On condition that, provided that.* —3. Of time : *Now, just now :* —modo . . . modo, *now . . . now; at one time . . . at another time.*

mŏ-dus, di, m. ("The measuring thing"; hence, "measure, measurement"; hence) 1. *A manner, method, way, mode.*—2. *Limit, bound,* etc. : —modum facere, *to set bound.* —3. With Gen. of pron., either separately or as one word : *Sort, kind :*—hujusmodi, *of this sort* or *kind ;* hujuscemodi, *of this sort here, of this very kind;* cujusquemodi, *of each sort* or *kind* [akin to Sans. root MÂ, " to measure"; whence also μέτρον, " a measure "].

mœn-ĭa, ĭum, n. plur. ("The things that ward off "; hence) 1. *Walls* of a city, *ramparts, bulwarks.*—2. *A walled town* or *city* [akin to ἀ-μῡν-ω, "to ward off"].

mōl-ĭor, ĭtus sum, īri, 4. v. dep. [mōl-es, "power, might"] (" To put forth *moles* about a thing; hence) *To undertake, engage in, employ one's self* ⸢out.*

moll-ĭo, īvi *and* **ĭi, ĭtum, īre,** 4. v. a. [moll-is, "soft"] (" To render *mollis*"; hence) Morally, etc.: *To soften, render effeminate* or *unmanly.*

mol-lis, le, adj.: 1. *Soft.*—2. *Agreeable, pleasant,* etc.—3. *Tender* in manner or tone [akin to Sans. mṛid-u, "soft"; fr. root MRID, "to rub, to crush"].

moll-ĭter, adv. [moll-is, "soft, effeminate"] (" After the manner of the *mollis*"; hence) *Softly, effeminately, voluptuously.*

moll-ĭtĭa, ĭtĭæ, f. [moll-is, "soft, weak"] (" The quality of the *mollis*"; hence) Of the mind : *Softness, weakness, timidity, irresolution.*

mŏn-ĕo, ŭi, ĭtum, ēre, 2. v. a. (" To cause to think"; hence, "to remind"; hence) 1. *To warn, admonish, advise;* —at l. 3 without nearer Object; moreover, as the composite subject res atque tempus form but one notion, the verb, monebat, is put in the sing. [Notes to Syntax, p. 133, *F*, 2];—also, at lii. 3 without nearer Object and folld. by Inf.—2. With Acc. of person folld. by uti c. Subj.: *To warn, admonish, advise* one *to do, etc.;* lviii. 8, etc.—3. With Acc. of thing : *To give warning* or *information about; to speak of,* or *about,* by way of warning [akin to Sans. root MAN, " to think "].

mon-s, tis, m. [for min-s; fr. mĭn-ĕo, " to project "] (" That which projects *or* juts forth "; hence) *A mountain, mount.*

montĭs (= montes), acc. plur. of mons.

mŏra, æ, f. *Delay.*

mor-bus, bi, m. *Sickness, disease* [prob. akin to Gr. μόρ-Fos, " disease "].

mor-s, tis, f. [mŏr-ĭor, " to die "] (" A dying "; hence) *Death.*

1. mort-ālĭs, āle, adj. [mors, mort-is, " death "] *Of,* or *belonging to, death ; subject* or *liable to death.*—As Subst.: mortālĭs, is, m. *A mortal being, a man.*

2. mortālĭs (= mortales), acc. plur. of 1. mortalis.

m-os, ōris, m. [prob. for me-os ; fr. mĕ-o, " to go "] (" The going " one's own way ; hence, " a person's will " ; hence) 1. *Practice, usage, custom, habit :* — immutato more, Abl. Abs. [§ 125], vi. 7 : —more suo, *after its own custom* or *habit,* Abl. of manner [§ 113], xxxvii. 2.—2. Plur.: *Habits, character, conduct, morals.*

mŏ-tus, tūs, m. [for movtus ; fr. mŏv-ĕo] 1. *A moving, motion.* — 2. *A commotion, rising, rebellion.*

mŏvĕo, mōvi, mōtum, mŏv-ēre, 2. v. a.: 1. (" To cause to go "; hence) *To move, set in motion. — 2. To shake, agitate, disturb.—3. To revolve, ponder, meditate, turn over* in the mind.—4. *To originate, produce,* etc. — 5. Of war: *To stir up, rouse, excite* [akin to Sans. root MĬ, " to go "].

mŭlĭ ĕ-brĭs, bre, adj. [mŭlĭer, mŭlĭĕr-is, " a woman "] (" Brought about by a woman "; hence, " performed by a woman " ; hence) *Womanish, womanlike, unmanly.*

mŭlĭer, ĕris, f. *A woman.*

mult-ĭtūdo, ĭtūdĭnis, f. [mult-us] (" The quality of the *multus*"; hence) 1. *A great number, a multitude.— 2.* a. *The multitude, the mass of the people.* — b. Plur.: *Multitudes* or *mobs ;* l. i.

mult-um, adv. [adverbial neut. of mult-us] 1. *Much, greatly.—2. Often, frequently.*

mul-tus, ta, tum, adj.: 1. Sing.: *Much.*—As Abl. of measure [§ 118]: multo, *by much, by far.*—2. Plur.: *Many.*—Adverbial neut. plur. multa : *Much, greatly, very greatly.*—As Subst. : a. multi, ōrum, m. plur. *Many persons, many.* — b. multa, ōrum, n. plur. *Many things.* ☞ Comp. : plūs ; Sup.: plūrĭmus [perhaps akin to πολ-ύς].

Mulvĭus, a, um, adj. *Mulvian:* — Pons Mulvius, *The Mulvian Bridge ;*—a bridge built by M. Æmilius Scaurus across the Tiber, above Rome, on the Via Flaminia. It is now called *Ponte Molle.*

mūnĭcĭp-ĭum, ĭi, n. [munĭceps, mūnĭcĭp-is, ("one undertaking duties; a burgher"; *i. e.*) "an inhabitant of a free town"] ("A thing—here town —pertaining to a *municeps;*" hence) *A free town ;*—a term applied to a town, particularly in Italy, which possessed the right of Roman citizenship (together with in many cases the right of voting), but was governed by its own laws.

mūnĭfĭcent-ĭa, ĭæ, f. [obsol. mūnĭfĭcens, munificent-is = mūnĭfĭcus, "bountiful"; and whence this latter adj. obtains its comp. and sup. mūnĭfĭcent-ĭor, mūnĭfĭcent-issĭmus] ("The quality of the *munificens*"; hence) *Bountifulness, munificence.*

mūn-ĭo (old form mœn-ĭo), īvi *or* ĭi, ītum, īre, 4. v. a. [mœnĭa, "walls"] ("To wall"; hence) 1. *To build a wall,* or *raise fortifications, around; to fortify.*—2. *To defend, protect, secure, guard.*—Pass.: mūn-ĭor, ītus sum, īri.

mūnī-tus, ta, tum, adj. [munĭ-o, "to fortify"; hence,

"to protect"] *Protected, defended, safe.*

mūnus, ĕris, n. *A gift, present.*

Muræna, æ, m. [muræna, a fish of which the Romans were especially fond, supposed to be the "lamprey"] *Muræna (Caius) ;* the Roman *legatus* in Gallia Ulterior; see Gallia.

mūr-us, i, m. ("The encircling thing"; hence) *The wall* of a city [akin to Sans. root MUR, "to encircle"].

mūtātus, a, um, P. perf. pass. of muto.

mū-to, tāvi, tātum, tāre, 1. v. a. intens. [for mov-to ; fr. mŏv-ĕo, "to move"] ("To move much *or* from place to place"; hence) 1. *To change, alter.*—2. With Acc. of thing exchanged and Abl. of that for which the exchange is made: *To exchange* one thing *for* another.—Pass.: mu-tor, tātus sum, tāri.

mūt-ŭus, ŭa, ŭum, adj. [mūt-o, "to exchange"] ("Exchanged"; hence, "mutual, reciprocal"; hence) Of money: *Borrowed, taken up* or *obtained on loan.*

nactus (nanctus), a, um, P. perf. of nanciscor.

nam, conj. *For.*

nam-que, conj. [nam ; que] An emphatic confirmative partĭcle: *For, for indeed, for truly.*

na(n)c-iscor, nactus *and* nanctus sum, nancisci, 3. v. dep.: 1. *To get, obtain.*—2. *To meet with, find* [akin to Sans. root NAÇ, " to attain "].

nanctus; see nactus.

narrandi, Gerund in di fr. narro.

· nar-ro, rāvi, rātum, rāre, 1. v. a. [nār-us (= gnār-us), " known "] (" To make a thing known, *or* a person acquainted with " something; hence) *To tell, relate, describe, narrate, etc.*;—at viii. 5 the inf. narrāre has its subject (ipse) in nom. by attraction to the subject of the finite verb malēbat, inasmuch as both one and the other of them speak of the same person.

nā-scor (old form gnascor), tus sum, sci, 3. v. dep.: 1. *To be born.*—2. With Abl. of origin, *or* with ex: *To be born, sprung,* or *descended from.*—3. With Abl. of position *or* rank: *To be born in* [root GNA, another form of root GEN = γεν, akin to Sans. root JAN in intransitive force].

nā-tĭo, tĭōnis, f. [na-scor, " to be born "] (" A being born "; hence) *A nation, race* of people.

nā-tūra, tūræ, f. [id.] (" A being born "; hence, " birth "; hence) 1. *The nature,* i. e. *the natural constitution* or *property,* etc., of a thing.— Adverbial Abl.: naturā, *By nature, naturally.*—2. *Nature,* i. e. *natural disposition, temper, character.*

nātus, a, um, P. perf. of nascor.

nāv-ĭgo, ĭgāvi, ĭgātum, ĭgāre, 1. v. a. [na-vis, " a ship "] *To sail over, navigate.*

1. nē, adv. *and* conj.: 1. Adv.: a. *Not:*—nequidem, *not even.*—b. (= nedum) *Much less.*—2. Conj.: a. *That not, lest* [§ 152, 1, (2)].—b. *After* verbs of hindering: *That not, from* [prob. akin to Sans. na, " not "].

2. nē, enclitic and interrogative particle: 1. In direct questions with verb in Indic. it throws force and emphasis on the word to which it is attached, pointing it out as the principal one in the clause or sentence; in this force it has no English equivalent.— 2. In indirect questions with Subj.: *Whether:*—ne ... an, *whether ... or whether.*

3. nē (= næ), adv. *Verily, truly,* etc.; lii. 27.

nec; see neque.

nĕcātus, a, um, P. perf. pass. of nĕco.

nĕcess-ārĭus, ārĭa, ārĭum, adj. [necess-e, " unavoidable "] (" Pertaining to the *necesse;* " hence) *Needful, requisite, ne-*

cessary.—As Subst.: nĕcess-ārĭa, ōrum, n. plur. *Necessary or requisite things; the necessaries or requisites of life.*

nĕ-ces-se, neut. adj. (found only in Nom. and Acc. sing.; sometimes used as a substantive, and in connexion with *sum* or *habeo*) [for ne-ced-se; fr. ne, "not"; cēd-o, "to yield"] ("Not yielding *or* giving way"; hence) 1. *Unavoidable, inevitable, not to be avoided.—2. Needful, requisite, necessary.*

necess-ĭtūdo, ĭtūdĭnis, f. [necess-e, "necessary"] ("The state *or* condition of *necesse*"; hence) 1. *Need, want, necessity;* —at xxi. 3 in plur.—2. *Needfulness, indispensableness, necessity.*

nĕc-o, āvi, ātum, āre, 1. v. a, ("To cause to perish"; hence) *To kill, put to death, slay, destroy.*—Pass.: nĕc-or, ātus sum, āri [akin to Sans. root NAÇ, "to perish"].

nĕ-fa-ndus, nda, ndum, adj. [nĕ, "not"; f(a)-or, "to speak"] ("Not to be spoken, not to be mentioned"; hence) *Impious, abominable, wicked,* etc.

nĕfā-rĭus, rĭa, rĭum, adj. [for nefas-rius; fr. nefas, "an impiety"] ("Of, *or* belonging to, *nefas*"; hence) *Impious, execrable, abominable, nefarious.*

neglĕgent-ĭa(neglĭgent-ĭa), ĭæ, f. [neglĕgens, neglegent-is, "negligent"] ("The condition, etc., of the *neglegens*"; hence) *Negligence, neglect.*

neg-lĕgo (neg-lĭgo), lexi, lectum, lĕgĕre, 3. v. a. [for nec-lĕgo; fr. nec, "not"; lĕgo, "to gather"] ("Not to gather"; hence) 1. *To overlook, neglect.*—2. With Inf.: *To make light of doing, etc.; to take no heed,* or *neglect, to do, etc., to disregard.*—Pass.: neg-lĕgor- (neg-lĭgor), lectus sum, lĭgi.

neglexĕrim, perf. subj. of neglego.

nĕgōtĭ -or, ātus sum, āri, 1. v. dep. [nĕgōtĭ-um, "a business, occupation"] ("To carry on a *negotium*"; hence) *To trade, traffic.*

nĕgōtĭ-ōsus, ōsa, ōsum, adj. [id.] ("Full of *negotium*"; hence) *Full of business, busy.*

nĕg-ōtĭum, ōtĭi, n. [for nec-ōtĭum; fr. nec, "not"; ōtĭum, "leisure"] ("No leisure"; hence) 1. *An affair, matter, business transaction.*—2. *Business, occupation, employment.*

nēmo, mĭnis, comm. gen. [contr. fr. ne-homo; fr. ne, "not"; hŏmo, "a person"] *No person, no one, nobody.*—As Adj.: *No, not any.*

nĕ-que (contracted nec), conj. [ne, "not"; que, "and"]

And not, nor :—neque (nec) ... neque (nec), *neither ... nor.*

nĕ-quĕo, quīvi *or* quĭī, quītum, quīre, v. n. [ne, "not"; queo, "to be able"] 1. *Not to be able, to be unable.* —2. With Inf.: *I, etc., cannot.*

nĕ-quiquam, adv. [ne, "not"; quiquam, adverbial abl. of quisquam, "any"] ("Not in any way"; hence) *In vain, to no purpose, fruitlessly.*

nĕquīvĕrim, perf. subj. of nequeo.

nĕquīvisse, perf. inf. of nequeo.

Nĕro, ōnis, m. *Nero* (*Tiberius*), a Roman senator; l. 4 [a Sabine word = fortis; and akin to Sans. *nara*, "a man"].

neu; see neve.

nĕ-ve (contracted neu), conj. *And not, nor* [ne, "not"; ve, akin to Sans. *vá*, "and"].

nī (old form nei), conj. [identical with ne, "not"] As a conditional particle: *If not, unless, except.*

nĭhil; see nihilum. In adverbial force : *In no respect* or *degree; not at all.*

nĭhĭlo, nĭhĭlōmĭnus, nĭl; see nihilum.

nĭ-hĭlum, i (apocopated nĭ-hil, contr. nĭl, indecl.), n. [for nĕ-hĭlum; fr. ne, "not"; hĭlum (= fīlum), "a thread"] ("Not a thread"; hence)

Nothing: — With following Gen.: nihil reliqui, xi. 7; cf., also, xii. 2; xv. 2; xl. 3.— Nihilo minus (or as one word nihilominus, adv.), *not at all the less, nevertheless, notwithstanding.*

nimis, adv.: 1. *Too much, over-much, beyond measure, excessively.*—2. With Adv.: *Too, far too.*

nĭ-sĭ, conj. [ne, "not"; si, "if"] *If not; i. e. unless, except.*

nītor, nisus *or* nixus sum, nīti, 3. v. dep. ("To lean upon"; hence) 1. *To strive, exert one's self, make an effort* or *endeavour.*—2. *To make one's way by an effort, etc.; to advance, press forwards.*

Nōbĭlĭor, ōris, m. [nobilior (comp. of nobilis), "more, or very, noble"] *Nobilior* (*Marcus Fulvius*); a Roman knight, one of Catiline's accomplices. He is supposed to have been the M. Fulvius Nobilior, who for some crime not known was exiled B.C. 54.

nō-bĭlis, bĭle, adj. [no-sco, "to know"] ("That is, or can be, known"; hence) 1. *Famous, renowned, celebrated.*—2. *Noble, of noble birth, highborn.*—As Subst.: nōbĭlis, is m. *A noble, a nobleman.* ☞ Comp.: nōbĭl-ĭor; Sup.: nōbĭlissĭmus.

nōbĭl-ĭtas, ĭtātis, f. [nōbĭl-is, "noble"] ("The state, or quality, of the *nobilis*"; hence) 1. *Celebrity, renown.*—2. *The nobility, the nobles.*—3. *Nobleness, noble quality, excellence, superiority.*

nōbis, dat. and abl. plur. of ego.

nōbiscum = cum nobis; see cum.

noct-urnus, urna, urnum, adj. [nox, noct-is, "night"] *Of,* or *belonging to, the night; by* or *at night, nocturnal, night-.*

nolite; see nolo.

n-ōlo, ōlŭi, olle, v. irreg. [contracted fr. ne-volo: ne, "not"; vōlo, "to wish"] 1. a. *To not wish, to be unwilling.*—b. Nōlĭte (imperat.), with follg. Inf.: (*Be ye*, etc., *unwilling to do, etc.;* i. e.) *Do not do, etc.,* that denoted by the Inf.—2. With Acc. of neut. pron.: *Not to desire, not wish for :*—idem nolle, (*not to desire the same thing,* i. e.) *to hare,* or *entertain, the same dislike,* etc., for a thing that some one else has, *etc.;* xx. 4, where nolle is a Substantival Inf. [§ 156, 2].

nō-men, mĭnis, n. [no-sco, "to know"] ("That which serves for knowing" an object; hence) 1. *A name.*—2. As the name of a person against whom a demand existed was entered in some book or signed in some legal document: *A bond, security,* etc.—3. *An account, reason :*—hoc nomine, *on this account, for this reason;* Abl. of cause [§ 111], xxxv. 4.—4. *A pretence, pretext.*

nōmĭnans, ntis, P. pres. of nomino.

nōmĭn-o, āvi, ātum, āre, 1. v. a. [nomen, nōmĭn-is, "a name"] *To name, to call* or *designate by name.*—Pass.: nōmĭn-or, ātus sum, āri.

non, adv. *Not.*—Particular use. non placed before a neg-ative word forms, in connexion with it, a slight affirmative: non nunquam, *or* as one word, nonnunquam, (*not never,* i. e.) *sometimes;* non nullus, *or* as one word, nonnullus, (*not none,* i. e.) *some* [akin to Sans. *na* or *no.*]

Nōn-æ, ārum, f. plur. [nōn-us, "ninth"] ("The ninth days"; *i. e.* the ninth day before the Ides, in the several months) *The Nones;* the fifth day of each month in the year except March, May, July, October, in which it was the seventh; see Kalendæ.

non-dum, adv. [non, "not"; dum, "yet"] *Not yet.*

non-ne, interrog. adv.: 1. In direct interrogations: *Not?* —2. In indirect interrogations: *If not, whether not,* [non, "not"; ne, akin to Sans. *na,* a negative particle].

non-nullus, nulla, nullum, adj. [non, ' "not"; nullus, "none"] ("Not none"; hence) *Some.*—As Subst.: nonnulli, ōrum, m. plur. *Some persons, some.*

nos; see ego.

nō-sco (old form **gno-sco**), vi, tum, scĕre, 3. v. a.: 1. In present tense and derivatives: *To acquire a knowledge of; to become acquainted with, come to know.*—2. In perfect tense and derivatives: *To have acquired a knowledge of; to know.*—Pass.: **nō-scor,** tus sum, sci [akin to γνω, root of γι-γνώ-σκω, and Sans. root JŃÂ].

nos-met, plur. of ego with suffix met; see ego, no. 2.

nos-ter, tra, trum, pron. poss. [nos, "we"] *Our, our own, ours.*

nostri, nostrum, gen. plur. of ego.

nōtus, a, um: 1. P. perf. pass. of nosco.—2. Pa.: *Known, well known.*

nŏvandus, a, um, Gerundive of novo.

1. **Nŏvembr-is,** e, adj. [November, Novembr-is, "November," the ninth month of the old Roman year] *Of November.*

2. **Novembrīs** (= Novembrēs), masc. and fem. acc. plur. of 1. Novembris.

nōvĕram, nōvi, pluperf. and perf. ind. of nosco.

nŏvissīm-e (nŏvissŭm-e), sup. adv. [nŏvissīm-us, (of time) "most, *or* very, recent"] *Very recently.*

nŏv-ĭtas, ĭtātis, f. [nŏv-us, "new"] ("The quality of the *novus*"; hence) 1. *Newness.* —2. *Novelty, unusualness, strangeness.*

nŏv-o, āvi, ātum, āre, 1. v. a. [nŏv-us, "new"] 1. *To make new* or *anew.*—2. *To change, alter.*—Pass.: **nŏv-or,** ātus sum, āri.

nŏvus, a, um, adj.: 1. *New:* —novæ res, *a change in the state, a revolution:*—novus homo, *a new man;* a term applied by the Romans to those of their fellow-citizens who were the first of their family that had risen to any curule office, *i. e.* an office to which appertained the privilege of using a curule chair; xxiii. 6.—As Subst.: **nŏva,** orum, n. plur.: a. *New things;* xxxvii. 3.—b. *New houses, buildings,* etc.; xx. 12.—2. Of war : *New, fresh.* ☞ Sup.: nŏv-issĭmus [akin to Gr. *véos,* and Sans. *nava*].

nox, noctis, f. *Night;*—media nox, *mid-night;* cf. medius no. 2. [akin to *νύξ,* Sans. *nakta*].

nūbo, nupsi, nuptum, nūbĕre, 3. v. n. [nūb-es, "a cloud"] ("To cloud over"; hence) Of a bride : With Dat. of person [§ 107] : *To cover* or *veil her-*

self for the bridegroom ; i. e. *to marry* or *wed* a man.

Nŭcĕr-īnus, ina, inum, adj. [contr. fr. Nŭcĕrĭ-ĭnus; fr. Nŭcĕrĭ-a, "Nuceria" (now "Nocera"), a town of Campania].—As Subst.: **Nucerinus,** i, m. *A man* or *native of Nuceria.*

n-ullus, ulla, ullum, adj. [for ne-ullus; fr. nē, "not"; ullus, "any"] *Not any, none, no;*—sometimes with Gen. of "thing distributed" [§ 130].

nŭm-ĕrus, ĕri, m. ("The distributed thing"; hence) 1. *A number.*—2. *A multitude, large number; great numbers* [akin to νέμ-ω, "to distribute"].

numquam; see nunquam.

nun-c, adv. *Now, at this time* [for nun-ce; akin to νῦν (Sans. *nu* or *nú*), with demonstrative suffix ce].

n-unquam (n-umquam), adv. [for ne-unquam; fr. ne, "not"; unquam, "ever"] *Not ever* or *at any time; never.*

nuntĭātus, a, um, P. perf. pass. of nuntio.

nuntĭ-o, āvi, ātum, āre, 1. v. a. [nuntĭ-us] *To carry* or *bring intelligence about; to report, announce.*—Pass.: nuntĭ-or, ātus sum, ari.

nuntĭ-us, ĭi, m. [perhaps contracted fr. nov-ven-tĭus; fr. nŏv-us, "new"; vĕn-ĭo, "to come"] ("A person, or

thing, newly come"; hence) 1. *A bearer of news* or *tidings; a messenger, courier,* etc.—2. *News* or *tidings; a message.*

nupt-ĭæ, ĭārum, f. plur. [nupt-a, "a bride"] ("The state, *or* condition, of the *nupta"*; hence) *Marriage, nuptials.*

n-usquam, adv. [n-e, "not"; usquam, "anywhere"] *Not anywhere, nowhere.*

ob, prep. gov. acc. ("Towards, at"; hence) To indicate object *or* cause: *On account of, for* [akin to ἐπ-ί; Sans. *ap-i*].

ŏbēdĭens, ntis, P. pres. of ŏbēdĭo.

ŏbēdĭentĭa, neut. acc. plur. of obediens; i. 1.

ŏb-ēdĭo, ēdīvi *or* ēdĭi, ēdītum, ēdīre, 4. v. n. [for ŏb-audĭo; fr. ŏb, "without force"; audĭo, in force of "to listen *or* give ear to"] ("To listen *or* give ear to"; hence) With Dat. [§ 106, (4)]: *To obey, yield obedience to, submit to, serve.*

obfĕro; see offĕro.

ob-fĭcĭo (of-fĭcĭo), fĕci, fectum, fĭcĕre, 3. v. n. [for ob-tacio; fr. ŏb, denoting "opposition"; facĭo, "to act"] ("To act in opposition to *or* against"; hence) 1. With Dat.: *To stand in the way of, obstruct, thwart, hinder, prove* *detrimental to* [§ 106, (3); *or* § 106, *a*].—2. Alone: *To stand in the way, to present,* or *offer, an obstruction, hindrance,* etc.

oblātus, a, um, P. perf. pass. of offĕro.

oblītus, ta, tum, P. perf. of oblīviscor.

ob-lĭ-viscor, tus sum, visci, 3. v. dep. ("To be melted" away from the mind; hence) With Gen. [§ 133, *a*]: *To forget* [prob. ŏb, without force; root LI *or* LIV, akin to Sans. root Lĭ, "to melt"].

ob-nox-ĭus, ĭa, ĭum, adj. [ob, ın "intensive" force; nox-a, "a fault"] ("Of, *or* belonging to, *noxa*"; hence) 1. With Dat. [§ 106, (4)]: *Liable, subject,* or *addicted to* a fault, crime, *etc.*—2. *Subject, submissive, obedient, compliant;*—at xiv. 6; xxiii. 3, alone; at xx. 7 with Dat.—3. Wıth Dat. [§ 106, 3]: *Under obligation, ındebted* or *beholden to.*

obpugnātus, a, um, P. perf. pass. of obpugno.

ob-pugno, are; see oppugno.

obscūr-o, āvi, ātum, āre, 1. v. a. [obscūr-us, "obscure, unknown"] ("To make *obscurus*"; hence) *To obscure, render unknown, sink in obscurity.*

ob-scŭ-rus, ra, rum, adj. ("Covered over"; hence) 1. *Obscure, unknown. — As*

Subst.: **obscūrum,** i, n. *Obscurity.*—2. *Obscure, ignoble, low, mean* [prob. ŏb, "over"; Sans. root SKU, "to cover "].

ob-sīdo, no perf. nor sup., sīdĕre, 3. v. n. [ŏb, "over against"; sido, "to sit down"] ("To sit down over against"; hence) With accessory notion of watchıng : 1. *To ınvest, besiege, blockade.*—2. *To beset, occupy, block up,* etc.— 3. Of a door of a house, *etc.: To beset,* etc.

obstĭnā-tus, ta, tum, adj. [obstin(a)-o, "to be resolved on"] ("Resolved on"; hence) In bad sense : *Inflexible, stubborn, determıned, obstinate.*

ob-sto, stĭti, stātum, stāre, 1. v. n. [ŏb, "over against"; sto, "to stand"] ("To stand over against"; hence) 1, *To block up the way.*—2. *To oppose, present an obstacle;*—at li. 37 folld. by quomĭnus c. Subj.—3. *To be agaınst, oppose, contradıct,* etc.;—at lii. 31 with Dat. [§ 106, (3)].

ob-strĕpo, strĕpŭi, strĕpĭtum, strĕpĕre, 3. v, n. [ŏb, "without force"; strĕpo, "to make a loud noise"] ("To make a loud noise"; hence) *To shout,* or *bawl, out; to raise a loud cry* or *outcry.*

ob-testor, testātus sum, testāri, 1. v. dep. [ŏb, "without force"; testor, "to call as witness"] ("To call as a

witness; to protest, assert ";
hence) *To conjure, entreat,
beg, implore ;*—at xxxiii. 6
folld. by simple Subj. [§ 154].

obtinendus, a, um, Gerundive of obtineo.

ob-tĭnĕo, tĭnŭi, tentum, tĭnēre, 2. v. a. [for ob-tĕnĕo; fr.
ŏb, "without force"; tĕnĕo,
"to hold"] ("To hold, *or* lay
hold of," with the hands;
hence) 1. *To hold* or *occupy.*
—2. *To acquire, get possession
of, obtain.*

obtŭlĕram, pluperf. ind. of
offero.

obvĭam, adv. [adverbial
acc. fem. of obvĭus, "meeting,
in the way"] *In the way, in
order to meet :*—obviam ire,
(*to go to meet;* i. e.) With
Dat.: a. *To advance against*
or *to meet.*—b. *To encounter,
oppose, contend against.*

occā-sĭo, sĭōnis, f. [for
occad-sĭo; fr. occĭd-o, "to
fall out *or* happen," through
true root OCCAD] ("A falling
out *or* happening"; hence)
An opportunity, occasion ;—
at lvi. 4 folld. by Gerund
in di —occasionem dare, *to
give, present,* or *offer an opportunity :* — per occasionem,
*on a favourable opportunity ;
as opportunity offers* or *offered*
according to time spoken of.

occā-sus, sūs, m. [for occad-
sus; fr. occĭd-o, "to set,"
through true root OCCAD] Of

the sun, *etc. : The setting* or
going down :—occāsus solis,
the setting of the sun, sun-set,
i. e. *the west,* xxxvi. 4.

1. **oc-cĭdo,** cĭdi, cāsum,
cĭdĕre, 3. v. n. [for ob-cădo ;
fr. ŏb, "without force"; cădo,
"to fall"] ("To fall"; hence)
To fall, or *perish,* in battle.

2. **oc-cĭdo,** cĭdi, cīsum, cĭdĕre, 3. v. a. [for ob-cædo; fr.
ŏb, "against"; cædo, "to
strike," *etc.*] ("To strike
against"; hence, "to strike
to the ground"; hence) *To
cut down, kill, slay, slaughter,*
etc.—Pass. : oc-cĭdor, cīsus
sum, cĭdi.

occīsus, a, um, P. perf.
pass. of occīdo.

occult-e, adv. [occult-us,
"hidden, secret"] ("After
the manner of the *occultus*";
hence) 1. *In a hidden* or
*secret way; secretly, covert-
ly.*—2. *In secret, privately.*
☞ Comp. · occult-ĭus; (Sup.:
occult-issĭme).

occul-to, tāvi, tātum, tāre,
1. v. a. intens. [occŭl-o, "to
hide"] *To hide, conceal,
secrete.*

occul-tus, ta, tum, adj.
[occŭl-o, "to hide"] *Hidden,
concealed, secret :*—occultum
habere, *to keep secret, conceal,*
xxiii. 4.

oc-căp-o, āvi, ātum, āre,
1. v. a. [for ob-căp-o ; fr. ob,
"without force"; CAP, root

of căp-ĭo, "to take"] *To take* or *lay hold of, to seize;*—at xlvi. 2 occupavere has a composite subject, cura atque lætitia [§ 92].—Pass.: **oc-cŭp-or,** ātus sum, āri.

octo, num. adj. indecl. *Eight* [ὀκτώ].

ŏc-ŭlus, ŭli, m. ("The seeing thing"; hence) *An eye:*—in oculis, *before the eyes, in sight* [akin to Gr. ὄκ-ος, Sans. *aksh-a;* prob. fr. a lost verb AKSH (= ĪKSH), "to see"].

ŏdi, isse, v. a. defect. *To hate.*

ŏdisse, perf. inf. of odi.

ŏd-ĭum, ĭi, n. [ŏd-ı, "to hate"] 1 *Hatred, hate,* etc.—**2.** With Objective Gen.: [§ 132] *Hatred of, aversion* or *dislike to;* xxxvii. 3.

ŏd-or, ōris, m. In bad sense: *A foul smell, stink, stench* [root OD, akin to ὄζω (= ὄδ-σω), "to have, *or* emit, a smell"].

offĕro (obfĕro), obtŭli, oblātum, offerre, v. a. irreg. [for ob-fĕro; fr. ŏb, "towards"; fĕro, "to bring"] ("To bring towards"; hence) 1. *To present, offer.*—**2.** *To bring prominently forwards, to present to notice.*—Pass.: **offĕror,** oblātus sum, offerri.

of-fĭc-ĭum, ĭi, n. [for op-făc-ĭum; fr. (ops) ŏp-is, "aid"; făc-ĭo, "to perform," etc.] ("The performing, *or* ren-

dering, of aid;" hence) 1. *A service incumbent on one; a duty, office,* etc.—**2.** *An official duty; service, employment, office.*

ōmissus, a, um, P. perf. pass. of omitto.

ō-mitto, mīsi, missum, mittĕre, 3. v. a. [for ob-mitto; fr. ŏb, "without force;" mitto, "to let go"] 1. *To let go, allow to fall, drop.*—**2.** *To lay aside, give up, neglect, disregard.*—**3.** *To pass over, pass by, omit.*—Pass.: **ō-mittor,** missus sum, mitti.

omn-ĭno, adv. [omn-is, "all"] *Altogether, wholly, entirely.*

1. **omnis,** e, adj.: 1. Sing.: a. Of a class: *Every, all.*—b. Of a person, thing, *etc.,* in its entirety: *The whole of, the entire, all.*—**2.** Plur.: *All.*—As Subst.: **a. omnes,** ĭum, comm. gen. plur. *All persons, all.*—b. **omnĭa,** um, n. plur. *All things, everything.*

2. **omnĭs** (= omnes), masc. and fem. acc. plur. of 1. omnis.

ŏnus, ĕris, n. *A burden,* whether actually or figuratively [prob. akin to Sans. *anas,* "a cart"].

ŏpĕr-a, æ, f. [ŏpĕr-or, "to work"] ("A working"; hence) 1. *Pains, exertions, work, labour:*—operam dare, *to (give, i. e.) bestow pains, exert one's* *self*, etc.:—opĕræ pretium est, (*it is the reward of one's pains;* i. e.) *it is worth while.* —2. *Aid, help, assistance,* etc.

ŏpes, um, plur. of ops; see ops.

ŏpĭ-fex, fĭcis, comm. gen. [for ŏper-fac-s; fr. ŏpus, oper-is, "work"; fac-ĭo, "to do"] ("One doing work": hence) *A workman, mechanic, artizan.*

ŏpĭtŭlātus, a, um, P. perf. of ŏpĭtŭlor.

ŏp-ĭ-tŭl-or, ātus sum, āri, 1. v. dep.: With Dat. [§ 106, (3)]: *To bring aid to; to help, aid, succour, assist* [ops, op-is, "aid"; root TUL, akin to Sans. root TUL, "to bring"; cf., also, tŭl-ı, perf. of fero].

op-pĕrĭor (ob-pĕrĭor), pĕr-ītus *and* pertus sum, pĕrīri, 4. v. dep. *To wait for, await.*

opportūn-ĭtas, ĭtātıs, f. [opportūn-us, "opportune"] ("The quality, *or* condition, of the *opportunus*"; hence) *Op-portunity.*

op-port-ūnus, ūna, ūnum, adj. [for ob-port-ūnus; fr. ŏb, "over against"; port-us, "a harbour"] ("Belonging to that which ıs over against the harbour"; hence) 1. *Con-venient, suitable, seasonable, opportune.*—2. *Advantageous, serviceable.* ☞ (Comp.: opportūn-ĭor); Sup.: opportun-issĭmus.

oppressissem, pluperf. subj. of opprĭmo.

oppressus, a, um, P. perf. pass. of opprĭmo.

op-prĭmo, pressi, pressum, prĭmĕre, 3. v. a. [for ob-prĕmo; fr. ŏb, "against"; prĕmo, "to press"] ("To press against") hence) 1. *To overthrow, crush, destroy.*—2. *To weigh* or *press down, to overwhelm* with debt, slavery, *etc.*—3. *To fall upon, surprise, take by surprise, come unexpectedly upon.* — Pass.: op-prĭmor, pressus sum, prĭmi.

opprĭmendus (opprĭmund-us), a, um, Gerundive of op-prĭmo.

op-pugno (ob-pugno), pugn-āvi, pugnātum, pugnāre, 1. v. a. [for ob-pugno; fr. ŏb, "against"; pugno, "to fight"] ("To fight against"; hence) *To attack, assault, assail;*— at xlix. 2 employed respecting judicial proceedings.—Pass.: op-pugnor, pugnātus sum, pugnāri.

op-s, is (Nom. Sing. does not occur, and the Dat. Sing. is found, perhaps, only once), f. [prob. for ap-s, fr. root AP, whence ăp-iscor, "to obtain"] 1. ("The obtaining thing"; hence) *Power, mıght, strength, ability.*—2. ("The thing ob-tained"; hence) a. Mostly plur.: *Means* of any kind that one possesses; i. e. (a) *Property, substance, wealth, resources.*—

(b) Political *or* military *power, might, influence, resources,* etc. —b *Aid, help, support, assistance, succour.*

optandus, a, um, Gerundive of opto.

optĭmus (optŭmus), a, um; see bonus ;—at xxxii. 1 folld. by Supine in u [§ 141, 6].

op-to, tāvi, tātum, tāre, 1. v. a. *To desire, wish for* [akin to Sans. root ÂP, " to obtain "; in desiderative force, " to desire to obtain "].

optŭmus ; see optĭmus.

ŏpŭlent-ĭa, ĭæ, f. [opulentus, " wealthy "] (" The condition, *or* state, of the *opulentus* "; hence) 1. *Wealth, opulence.*—2. *Power* or *resources* of a people.

ŏp-ŭlentus, ulenta, ulentum, adj. [ŏp-es (plur. of ops), " wealth "] (" Abounding in *opes* "; hence) *Wealthy, rich, opulent, possessing great resources* or *means.*

ŏpus (only in Nom. and Acc.), n. indecl. *Need, necessity.*—In connexion with some part of sum used as an Adj.· *It is needful, necessary; I (thou,* etc.) *have need of, need, want.* The abl. dependent on opus [§ 119, (a), (3)] is mostly that of a subst.: at times, however, the abl. is that of a part. perf. pass. in neut. sing. : see i. 6; xliii. 3, etc.

ŏrā-tĭo, tĭōnis, f. [or(a)-o, " to speak "] (" A speaking "; hence) 1. *A speech, oration;* —at xxxi. 6 oratio means Cicero's first oration against Catiline.—2. *A mode of speech, way of speaking.*

orb-is, is, m. *A circle* or *ring;* — orbis terrarum, *the circle of lands,* i. e. *the world.*

ord-o, ĭnis, m. [ord-ĭor, " to weave·"] (" A weaving "; hence) 1. *Arrangement, order.* 2. *Consecutive,* or *due, order; regular succession,* etc. :— ordine, *in order,* i.e. *regularly, properly,* etc.—3. *A row,* or *rank,* of soldiers in battle array.—4. *An order,* i. e. *a rank, class, degree* of persons in civil life.

Orest-illa, illæ, f. [fem. dim. of Orest-es, " Orestes "] *Orestilla,* the sister of Cneius Aurelius Orestes, who was Prætor B.C. 76. Of her personal appearance and character Sallust speaks in xv.

ŏr-ĭor, tus sum, īri, 3. *and* 4. v. dep. : 1. *To rise,* in the fullest power of the word.— 2. Of origin : a. With Abl. [§ 123]: *To spring, be born,* or *descend, from.*—b. Of things : *To arise, proceed, originate, have their origin ;*—at li. 27 folld. by ex c. Abl. [prob. akin to ŏp-νῦμι, " to stir up "].

ŏr-o, āvi, ātum, āre, 1. v. a. [os, ōr-is, " the mouth "] (" To

N

use the mouth"; hence, "to speak"; hence) *To pray, beg, entreat, beseech.*

1. **ortus, a, um,** P. perf. of orior.

2. **or-tus,** tūs, m. [or-ior, "to rise"] *A rising, rise :*—ortus solis, *sun-rising, sun-rise,* i. e. *the east,* xxxvi. 4.

os-tendo, tendi, tensum, tendĕre, 3. v. a. [for obs-tendo; fr. obs. (= ŏb), "before *or* over against"; tendo, "to stretch out"] ("To stretch out, *or* spread, before" one; hence) *To show, point out,* etc.

ōtĭum, ĭi, n.: 1. *Leisure, ease.*—2. *Rest, repose,* etc.

P., abbrev. of Publius.

pac-tĭo, tĭōnis, f. [pac-iscor, "to covenant"] ("A covenanting"; hence) *An agreement, covenant, compact.*

pār, pāris, adj. *Equal, on a par ;*—sometimes with Dat. [§ 106, (3)].

părātus, a, um: 1. P. perf. pass. of păro.—2. Pa.: *Ready, prepared.*

parco, pĕperci (less frequently parsi), parcĭtum and parsum, parcĕre, 3. v. n. [parcus, "sparing"] ("To be sparing"; hence) *To spare, to abstain,* or *refrain, from ; to let alone ;*—sometimes with Dat. [§ 106, (3)].

parcus, a, um, adj. ("Sparing, scanty," etc.; hence) Of

expenditure: *Sparing, thrifty, economical.*

păr-ens, entis, m. *and* f. [either for păr-ĭens, fr. păr-ĭo, "to beget," also, "to bring forth"; or fr. an obsol. păr-o = părĭo] ("He who begets"—"she who brings forth"; hence) 1. a. *A parent.*—b. Plur.: *Parents.*—2. *A father.*

păr-ĕo, ŭi, ĭtum, ēre, 2. v. n. ("To come forth"; hence, "to appear" at a person's command; hence) *To obey ;*—sometimes with Dat. [§ 106, (4)].

păr-ĭ-es, ĕtis, m. ("The thing going around"; hence) *A wall* of a house [akin to Sans. *par-i,* Gr. περ-ί, "around"; I, root of ĕo, "to go"].

părĭo, pĕpĕri, partum, părĕre, 3. v. a. ("To bring forth"; hence) 1. Of rest, quietness, etc., as Subject : *To produce, bring about, occasion,* etc.—2. *To obtain, procure, acquire.*—Pass.: părĭor, partus sum, pări [prob akin to Gr. φέρ-ω, Lat. fer-o].

păr-o, āvi, ātum, āre, 1. v. a. and n. ("To bring *or* put"; hence, with accessory notion of readiness) 1. Act.: a. *To make,* or *get, ready ; to prepare.*—b. With Inf. : *To prepare,* or *make preparation, to do,* etc.—c. *To provide, furnish,* etc.—2. Neut. : *To* *make preparations, prepare one's self,* etc.; vi. 5, where parare is the Hist. Inf. [§ 140, 2].—Pass.: păr-or, ātus sum, āri [probably akin to φέρ-ω].

parr-ĭ-cīd-a, æ, m. [for patr-i-cæd-a; fr. păter, patr-is, "a father"; (i) connecting vowel; cædo, "to kill"] 1. *Killer,* or *murderer, of a father; a parricide;* xiv. 3. —2. *One guilty of high treason; a traitor, rebel,* as if being the murderer of his country; xxxi. 8; lii. 31;—at li. 25 with addition of reipublicæ.

par-s, tis, f.: 1. *A part, piece, portion, share,* etc.— 2. *A part,* i. e. *some* out of many :—pars ... alii, also reversely, alii ... pars, *some ...some; some ... others.*— 3. *A party, part, side;* — mostly plur.

part-ĭ-cep-s, cĭp-is, adj. [for part-i-cap-s; fr. pars, part-is, "a part"; (i) connecting vowel; căp-ĭo, "to take"] *Taking a part, sharing, partaking, participating.* — As Subst.: *A sharer, partaker, partner.*

part-im, adv. [part-ĭor, "to divide"] (" By a dividing"; hence) 1. *Partly, in part.*—2. As Subst.: *Some;*—at l. 1 used as a noun of multitude, and forming the subject of a plur. verb—exquirēbant[Notes to Syntax, p. 133, *E,* 3].

partus, a, um, P. perf. pass. of pario.

parum, adv. [akin to parvus, "little"] 1. *Too little, not enough;*—at v. 5 used substantively in connexion with Gen [§ 131].—2. With Verbs or Adjectives: *Not very, not particularly, little.*

par-vus, va, vum, adj. [prob. akin to par-s. " a part "] 1. Of size or space: *Small, little.* —2. Of degree or extent: *Small, slight, little.*— 3. Of value, consideration, *etc.:* a. *Little, small, trifling.*— b. After verbs of valuing, considering, *etc.:* Neut. Gen. Sing.: **parvi,** *Of little value, account,* or *worth* [§ 128, *a*]. ☞ Comp.: irreg. mĭnor; (Sup. irreg. mĭnĭmus).

păt-ĕ-făcĭo, fēci, factum, făcĕre, 3. v. a. [păt-ĕo, "to lie open"; (e) connecting vowel; făcĭo, "to make"] (" To make to lie open"; hence) 1. *To lay open* a matter, *etc.;* i. e. *to give information about, disclose, reveal,* etc.—2. *To detect, bring to light.*—Pass.: păt-ĕ-fĭo, factus sum, fĭĕri.

patefactus, a, um, P. perf. pass. of patefacio.

păt-ĕo, ŭi, no sup., ēre, 2. v. n.: 1. *To lie,* or *stand, open, to be open.* — 2. *To be open* or *accessible.* — 3. With Dat.: *To be at the power* or *disposal of.*—4. ᴛ

N 2

be clear, plain, evident, mani-fest, etc. ; lviii. 2 [akin to πετ-άννῡμι, " to extend "].

păt-er, tris, m. (" A pro-tector" ; also, "a nourisher") 1. *A father,* as one who pro-tects, *etc.*—2. Plur. . Patres Conscripti. — Originally the term Patres designated those who in the earliest days of Rome were appointed members of the highest council of the state, and was given to them, as Sallust states at vi. 6, either in reference to their age, or from the paternal care they exercised for the public welfare. Moreover, Conscripti (subst.) was the name prim-arily given to such Romans as were appointed members of the Senate by Brutus, after the expulsion of Tarquin the Proud, to supply the place of those whom that king had put to death. It was employed, be-cause their names were writ-ten with or enrolled among those of the old members. According to Livy, Bk. ii. ch. 1, when the Senate was convened, the PATRES and the CONSCRIPTI were sum-moned as distinctive and separate members of that body. Eventually, however, the two names came to be applied to senators generally ; and Con-scripti is now commonly re-garded and rendered as an attributive of Patres: *Con-script Fathers* [akin to Gr. πα-τήρ, Sans. *pi-tri ;* fr. root PĂ, " to protect, to nourish "].

păt-ĕra, ĕræ, f. [păt-ĕo, "to lie open" ; hence, " to spread out, extend "] (" The thing spreading out *or* extending"; hence) *A* broad flat *dish,* especially used in making offer-ings : *a bowl* for libations.

păter-nus, na, num, adj. [pater, pat(e)r-is, "a father"] (" Of, *or* pertaining to, a father "; hence) Of property : *Received* or *inherited from a father; paternal.*

pătĭens, ntis : 1. P. pres. of pătĭ-or.—2. Pa. : With Gen. [§ 132] : *Enduring, patient of,* etc.

pătĭor, passus sum, păti, 3. v. dep. : 1. *To bear, endure, support, undergo,* etc.—2. *To allow, permit, suffer* [akin to παθ, root of πάσχω].

patrĭa, æ ; see patrius.

pătr-ĭcĭus, ĭcĭa, ĭcĭum, adj. [pătr-es, "senators"] (" Of, *or* belonging to, *patres*"; hence) *Noble, patrician.—As* Subst. : patricius, ĭi. m. *A patrician.*

pătr-ĭmōnĭum, ĭmōnĭi, n. [păter, pătr-is, "a father"] (" A thing pertaining to a *pater*"; hence) *A paternal inheritance* or *estate, a patri-mony.*

pătr-ĭus, ĭa, ĭum, adj. [id.]

Of, or *belonging to, a father; a father's.*—As Subst.: **pătr-Iı, æ,** f. *Father-land, native country.*

pătr-o, āvi, ātum, āre, 1.v.a. [id.] ("To make *or* appoint as *pater*"; so, only in the phrase . pater patratus, the name given by the ancient Romans to the fetialis *or* priest who ratified a treaty with religious rites; hence) *To bring to pass, perform, achieve, accomplish,* etc.— Pass.: **patr-or,** ātus sum, āri.

pătrŏcĭn-ĭum, ĭi, n. [pătr-ōcĭn-or, "to protect"] ("A protecting"; hence) *Protection, patronage.*

pauc-ĭtas, ĭtātis, f. [paucus, "small"; see paucus] ("The quality of the *paucus*"; hence) *A small number, small numbers, fewness.*

paucus, a, um, adj : 1. Sing.: *Small,* whether in degree *or* number.—2. Plur.: *Few.*—As Subst.: **a. pauci,** ōrum, m. plur. *A few persons; few, a few;* xxx. 4, etc. —**b. pauca,** ōrum, n. plur. : *A few words :*—paucis, *in a few words, briefly;* iv. 3, etc.

paul-ātim, adv. [paul-us, "little"] *By little and little; by degrees, gradually.*

1. **paul-o,** adv. [Adverbial Abl. of paul-um, "a little"] *By a little; a little, somewhat :*—paulo post, *a little,* or *shortly, afterwards;*—paulo ante, *a little,* or *shortly, before;*—with Comp. adj.: *By a little, a little, somewhat;* li. 15.

2. **paulo;** see 1. paulus.

paulŭl-um, adv. [adverbial neut. of paulŭl-us, "very little"] *Just a little; a very little; a little or somewhat.*

1. **paulus,** a, um, adj.: 1. *Little.*—2. **paulo,** neut. abl. sing. as Abl. of measure [§ 118; —Notes to Syntax, p. 137, *E*].

2. **Paul-us,** i, m. [paul-us, "little"] ("Little") *Paulus (Lucius Æmilius Lepidus),* a brother of Lepidus the triumvir.

pauper-tas, tātis, f. [pauper, "poor"] ("The state, *or* condition, of the *pauper*"; hence) *Narrow circumstances, poverty.*

păvĕo, pāvi, no sup., păvēre, 2. v. a. [prob. akin to păvĭo, "to strike"] *To be struck with fear at; to be terrified* or *alarmed at; to fear, dread;*—at xxxi. 3 păvēre is the Hist. Inf. [§ 140, 2].

păx, pācis, f. [for pac-s; fr. root PAC, *or* PAG, whence păciscor, "to bind, to covenant"; pango, "to fasten"] ("The binding, *or* fastening, thing"; hence) 1. *Peace,* concluded between belligerents, etc.—2. *Peace, tranquillity.*

peccandi, Gerund in di fr. pecco.

peccā-tum, ti, n. [pecc(a)-o, "to do amiss"] ("That which is done amiss"; hence) *A fault, error, transgression.*

pecco, āvi, ātum, āre, 1. v.n. *To do amiss, commit a fault, act wickedly,*

pectus, ŏris, n. *The breast.*

pĕcū-nĭa, nĭæ, f. [for pĕcud-nĭa; fr. pĕcus, pĕcŭd-is, "cattle"] ("The thing pertaining to *pecus*"; hence) 1. *Property, riches, wealth.*—2. Sing. and Plur.: *Money; a sum of money.*

pĕc-us, ŏris, n. ("The thing fastened up"; hence) In collective force: Sing. and Plur.: *Cattle,* as animals tied up in stalls [akin to Sans. *paçu,* "cattle"; fr. root PAÇ, "to bind"].

1. **pĕdes**, plur. of pes.

2. **pĕdes**, ĭtis, m. [for pĕd-i-t-s; fr. pes, pĕd-is, "a foot"; I, root of ĕo, "to go," (t) epenthetic] *One that goes on foot; on foot, afoot.*

pello, pĕpŭli, pulsum, pellĕre, 3. v. a. ("To cause to go"; hence) *To rout, beat, put to flight.*—Pass.: **pellor**, pulsus sum, pelli [akin to Sans. root PAL, "to go"].

pendo, pĕpendi *and* pendi, pensum, pendĕre, 3. v. a. [prob. akin to pend-eo, "to hang"] ("To cause to hang, to suspend"; hence, "to weigh, ~~weigh out~~"; hence) 1. *To pay.*

—2. *To value, esteem, regard;* —at xii. 2 folld. by Gen. of value [§ 128, *a*].

pen-sus, sa, sum, adj. [for pend-sus; fr. pend-o, "to weigh"] ("Weighed"; hence) *Esteemed, regarded, valued, prized, dear.*—Phrases: **a.** Aliquid nihil pensi habere, *to account something as a thing of no weight* or *value; i. e. to attach no value to it,* etc.—**b.** Quidquam pensi habere, *to have any regard* or *consideration.*—**c.** Quidquam pensi est, etc., alicui, *there is any regard* or *consideration to one; i. e. one has any regard,* etc.

pĕpercĕram, pluperf. ind. of parco.

pĕpĕri, perf. ind. of pario.

pĕr, prep. gov. acc.: 1. *Through, through the midst of.*—2. *In consequence of, on account of.*—3. *Through, by, by means of:*—per se, *through, by,* or *of himself,* etc.—4. Of time: **a.** *Through, throughout, during, for.*—**b.** *During, in the course of.*

per-cello, cŭli, culsum, cellĕre, 3. v. a. [pĕr, in "augmentative" force; cello, "to urge on"] ("To urge on, *or* impel, greatly"; hence) 1. *To smite, strike, hit.*—2. *To strike with dismay, to daunt, terrify, dispirit, dishearten,* etc.—Pass.: **per-cellor**, culsus sum, celli.

perculsus, a, um, P. perf. pass. of percello.

percunctātus, a, um, P. perf. of percunctor.

percunctor (percontor), ātus sum, āri, 1. v. dep. [etym. uncertain, evidently not connected with cunctor; prob. pĕr, "through"; cunct-us, "all"] ("To go through all things *or* points" in a matter; hence, with accessory notion of enquiry) With things as Object: *To ask, or enquire, much or particularly about.*

perdendus (perdundus), Gerundive of perdo;—at xlvi. 2 perdundæ reipublicæ is the dat. dependent on esse to be supplied, *for the destruction of the state*, i. e. *a cause of destruction*, etc.

perdĭtum, Supine in um fr. perdo.

perdo, perdĭdi, perdĭtum, perdĕre, 3. v. a.: 1. *To make away with, destroy, ruin, overthrow,* etc.— 2. *To lose* [perhaps Gr. πέρθω, "to destroy"].

per-dūco, duxi, ductum, dūcĕre, 3. v. a. [pĕr, "through"; dūco, "to lead"] ("To lead through"; hence) *To bring, or conduct, to a place.*—Pass.: **per-dūcor**, ductus sum, dūci.

pĕrĕgrīnans, ntis, P. pres. of peregrinor.

pĕrĕgrīn-or, ātus sum, āri, 1. v. dep. [peregrīn-us, "for-eign"] *To be, live, or dwell in a foreign land.*

pĕr-ĕo, īvi *or* ĭi, ĭtum, īre, v. n. irreg. [pĕr, "through"; ĕo, "to go"] ("To go through"; hence) *To perish, die.*

per-fĕro, tŭli, lātum, ferre, v. a. irreg. [pĕr, "without force"; fĕro, "to bear"] *To bear, bring, carry, convey.*

perfŭg-a, æ, m. [per-fŭg-ĭo "to desert"] *A deserter* to the enemy.

per-fŭgĭo, fūgi, fŭgĭtum, fŭgĕre, 3. v. a. [pĕr, "quite"; fŭgĭo, "to flee"] ("To flee quite *or* thoroughly" somewhither; hence) *To flee for refuge, to escape.*

perfŭg-ĭum, ĭi, n. [perfŭg-ĭo, "to flee for refuge"] ("A fleeing for refuge"; hence, "that which is fled to for refuge"; hence) *A place of refuge; a refuge, shelter,* etc.

per-go, rexi, rectum, rĕgĕre, 3. v. n. [for per-rĕgo; fr. pĕr, in "intensive" force; rego, "to make straight"] ("To make quite straight"; hence) *To proceed;* i. e. *to go* or *come.*

pĕrī-cŭlum, cŭli, n. [obsol. pĕrĭ-or, "to try"] ("That which serves for trying"; hence) 1. *A trial, experiment, proof,* etc.—2. *Danger, hazard, peril.*

perjŭr-ĭum, ĭi, n. [perjŭr-o, "to swear falsely"] ("A

swearing falsely"; hence) *A false oath; perjury.*

perlectus, a, um, P. perf. pass. of perlĕgo.

per-lĕgo, lēgi, lectum, lĕgĕre, 3. v. a. [pĕr, "through"; lĕgo, "to read"] *To read through* or *throughout; to read to the end.*—Pass.: **perlĕgor,** lectus sum, lĕgi.

per-miscĕo, miscŭi, mistum *and* mixtum, miscēre, 2. v. a. [pĕr, in "augmentative" force; miscĕo, "to mix"] ("To mix thoroughly"; hence) *To mix up, mingle, commingle,* etc.

permissus, a, um, P. perf. pass. of permitto.

permistus (permixtus), a, um, P. perf. pass. of permisceo.

per-mitto, mīsi, missum, mittĕre, 3. v. a. [pĕr, "through"; mitto, "to let go"] ("To let, *or* suffer, to go through"; hence) 1. *To give up, commit, entrust.*—2. *To permit, allow, suffer, give permission to.*—Pass.: **per-mittor,** missus sum, mitti.

permixtus; see permistus.

permōtus, a, um, P. perf. pass. of permoveo.

per-mŏvĕo, mōvi, mōtum, mŏvēre, 2. v. a. [pĕr, "thoroughly"; mŏvĕo, "to move"] ("To move thoroughly"; hence) 1. *To move deeply* in mind, etc.; *to stir up, rouse, excite,*

etc.—2. *To influence, persuade, induce,* etc.—Pass.: **per-mŏvĕor,** mōtus sum, mŏvēri.

pernĭc-ĭes, ĭēi, f. [for pernĕc-ĭes; fr. pernĕc-o, "to kill utterly"] ("A killing utterly"; hence) *Destruction,* etc.

per-pello, pŭli, pulsum, pellĕre, 3. v. a. [pĕr, in "intensive" force; pello, "to drive," etc.] ("To drive utterly *or* violently"; hence) *To prevail upon, constrain,* etc.; —at xxvi. 4 folld. by ne c. Subj.

perpessus, a, um, P. perf. of perpetior.

per-pĕtĭor, pessus sum, pĕti, 3. v. dep. [for per-pătĭor; fr. pĕr, in "augmentative" force; patior, "to bear"] ("To bear completely"; hence) *To endure, put up with, suffer with patience,* etc.

perpŭlĕram, pluperf. ind. of perpello.

perpulsus, a, um, P. perf. pass. of perpello.

per-scrībo, scripsi, scriptum, scrībĕre, 3. v. a. [pĕr, "completely"; scrībo, "to write"] ("To write completely"; hence) *To write a full account of* a matter, etc.; *to write at length.*

per-sĕquor, sĕquūtus sum, sĕqui, 3. v. dep. [per, in "augmentative" force; sĕquor, "to follow"] 1. *To follow perseveringly, to continue to follow, to* *pursue.*—2. In hostile sense: *To follow after, chase, pursue.* —3. *To avenge, revenge, take vengeance for;* lii. 4 ;—at ix. 5 supply eam (= injuriam) after persequi.

Perses, is, m. *Perses* (or *Perseus*), the last king of Macedonia, conquered by L. Æmilius Paulus. He was carried to Italy, and adorned the triumph of his conqueror, B.C. 167. Afterwards he was cast into a dungeon, where he would probably have been killed; but Æmilius procured his release, and he was permitted to end his days in an honourable captivity at Alba. He survived his removal to that place for a term variously estimated at from two to five years [Πέρσης, Περσεύς].

per-solvo, solvi, sŏlūtum, solvĕre, 3. v. a. [pĕr, in "augmentative" force; solvo, "to pay"] *To pay,* or *discharge, completely* or *to the full.*

per-terrĕo, terrŭi, terrĭtum, terrēre, 2. v. a. [pĕr, "thoroughly"; terrĕo, "to frighten"] *To frighten thoroughly; to terrify greatly.*—Pass.: **perterrĕor,** terrĭtus sum, terrēri.

perterrĭtus, a, um, P. perf. pass. of perterreo.

per-tĭnĕo, tĭnŭi, tentum, tĭnēre, 2. v. n. [for per-tĕnĕo; fr. pĕr, "thoroughly"; tĕnĕo,

"to hold"] ("To hold thoroughly"; hence) *To tend,* or *lead,* to an end or result.

perturbandus, a, um, Gerundive of perturbo.

perturbātus, a, um, P. perf. pass. of perturbo.

per-turbo, turbāvi, turbātum, turbāre, 1. v. a. [pĕr, "utterly"; turbo, "to disturb"] *To disturb utterly, to throw into great confusion.* —Pass.: **per-turbor,** turbātus sum, turbāri.

per-vĕnĭo, vēni, ventum, vĕnīre, 4. v. n. [pĕr, "quite"; vĕnĭo, "to come"] ("To come quite" to a place, *etc.;* hence) *To reach* or *arrive; to come up,* etc.

pes, pĕd-is, m. ("The going thing"; hence) *A foot,* whether of persons, *etc.,* or as a measure of length:— pĕdĭbus īre in sententĭam ălĭcūjus, (*to go with the feet into the vote of some one;* i. e.) *to support a person's vote.* The phrase arose from the mode of taking a division in the Roman senate. The formula used by the senator who presided was, "Let those who are of this opinion pass over to that side; those who think otherwise, to this."—At lv. 3 duodecim pedes is Acc. of "Measure of Space" [§ 102, (2)] [akin to πούς, ποδ-ός; and to Sans. *pad,* fr. root PAD, "to go"].

186

pessĭmus (pessŭmus) a, um, sup. of mălus.

pestĭlent-ĭa, ĭæ, f. [pestĭlens, pestĭlent-is, "pestilent"] ("The state, or quality, of the pestĭlens"; hence) A plague, pestilence.

pĕtendi (pĕtundi), Gerund in di fr. peto.

pĕtens, ntis, P. pres. of peto.

pĕt-ītĭo, ītĭōnis, f. [pet-o, "to seek"; hence, "to canvass" for office] A canvassing for office, a candidature.

pĕtīvĕrim, perf. subj. of peto.

pĕt-o, īvi and ĭi, ītum, ĕre, 3. v. a. ("To fly" towards; hence) 1. To seek, seek for.— 2. To apply, or canvass, for an office; to be a candidate for office.—3. To endeavour to obtain; to pursue; to seek or strive after [akin to Sans. root PAT, "to fly"].

Pĕtrēĭus, ĭi, m. Petreius (Marcus); the lieutenant of C. Antonius in the engagement with Catiline. At a later date Petreius was the lieutenant of Pompey in Spain, and on his defeat by Cæsar joined Pompey in Greece. After the battle of Pharsalia, B.C. 48, he fled into Africa, and was present at the battle of Thapsus, B.C. 46, by the issue of which the hopes of Pompey's party in Africa were completely destroyed. After the battle Petreius fled with Julia to Zama; and as the people of that city would not receive them, they resolved, it is said, to perish by each other's hands.

pĕtŭlant-ĭa, ĭæ, f. [pĕtŭlans, petulant-is, "petulant"] ("The quality of the petulans"; hence) Sauciness, wantonness, impudence, petulance.

pĕtundi; see pĕtendi.

Pīcēn-us, a, um, adj. [Pīcēnum, "Picenum"; a district in the Eastern part of Italy] Only of things: Of, or belonging to, Picenum; Picene.

pictus, a, um, P. perf. pass. of pingo.

pĭ-ĕtas, ĕtātis, f. [pĭ-us, "pious"] ("The quality of the pius"; hence) With respect to the gods: Piety.

pī-lum, li, n. ("The grinding, or pounding, thing"; hence, "a pestle" of a mortar; hence) A heavy javelin used by the Roman infantry [akin to Sans. root PISH, "to grind or pound"].

pingo, pinxi, pictum, pingĕre, 3. v. a. To paint.—Pass.: pingor, pictus sum, pingi [akin to Sans. root PINJ, "to dye or colour"].

Pis-o, ōnis, m. [pis-o = pins-o, "to pound or bray" in a mortar] ("The Pounder, The Mortar") Piso (Cneius); a needy and unprincipled young Roman noble, who in

Catiline's first conspiracy, joined Autronius and Catiline in an attempt to murder the consuls, L. Cotta and L. Torquātus, xviii. 4, 5.

Pistŏrĭ-ensis, ense, adj. [Pistŏrĭ-um, "Pistorium" (now "Pistoia"); a town of Etruria, near which Catiline was defeated and slain] *Of*, or *belonging to, Pistorium.*

plăc-ĕo, ŭi, ĭtum, ēre, 2. v. n.: 1. With Dat. [§ 106, (3)]: **a.** *To be pleasing*, or *agreeable to; to please*, etc.— **b.** Impers.: Pres.: **placet**, *It pleases; it is one's pleasure* or *will;*—at lviii. 7 placet has for its Subject the Inf. īre [§ 157].—2. Political t. t.: **a.** *To be resolved upon; to be willed, determined, ordered.* —**b.** Impers.: **placet**, etc., *It is my*, etc., *will, order, good pleasure*, etc., *it is my opinion;*—at l. 3 placeat is the subj. (pres.) in an indirect question (or oblique interrogation) [§ 149]; quid is the acc. and forms the Subject of fieri [§ 94, (1)]; and the clause quid de his fieri, qui, *etc.*, forms the Subject of the impersonal verb placeat [§ 157].

placet; see placeo.

plăcĭd-e, adv. [plăcĭd-us, "calm"] ("After the manner of the *placidus*"; hence) *Calmly, mildly, gently.*

plān-ĭtĭes, ĭtĭēi, f. [plān-us,

"flat"] ("The quality, *or* condition, of the *planus*"; hence, "flatness"; hence) *A flat, level*, or *even surface*, etc.; *level ground, a plain.*

Plaut-ĭus, ĭa, um, adj. [Plaut-ius, "Plautius"] *Of*, or *belonging to, Plautius; Plautian:*—lex Plautia, *the Plautian* (or *Plotian*) *law* (DE VI, "Respecting violence"), was one passed B.C. 88 on the proposition of M. Plautius Silvanus, a tribune of the Commons. It enacted that all who should plot against the senate, offer violence to a magistrate, appear with a weapon in public, seize upon the higher places of the city with seditious intent, or beset with armed followers the house of any citizen, should be punished with exile. This law was subsequently put in force against all those associates of Catiline who had not been capitally punished.

plēb-s (plēb-es), is, f. *The multitude* or *mass; the populace* [akin to Gr. πλῆθ-ος, "a multitude"].

plērīque; see plērusque.

plērumque, adv. [adverbial neut. of plērusque] *For the most part, generally.*

plērusque, plērăque, plērumque, adj. [a strengthened form of plērus, "very many"] 1. Sing.: *The larger*, or *greater,* *part of :*—ju"entus plērăque, xvii. 6.—2. Plur.: *Very many, a very great part, most of.*— As Subst.: a. **plerique,** m. plur. *Most, or very many, persons ; a considerable portion, the majority.*—b. **plērăque,** n. plur. *Most things, most of the things, very many things ;*—at vi. 3 folld. by Gen.

plūrĭm-um, sup. adv. [adverbial neut. of plurim-us] *Most, very much.*

plŭ-rĭmus, rĭma, rĭmum, sup. adj. [PLE, root of plĕ-o, "to fill"; (i) connecting vowel ; sĭmus, superl. suffix : = ple-i-sĭmus; changed as follows : plei-sĭmus, plī-sĭmus, ploi-sĭmus, ploi-rŭmus, plū-rĭmus] ("Most, *or* very, full"); hence) 1. Sing.: *Very much.* —2. Plur.: *Very many, most numerous.*

1. **plūs,** plūris(Plur. **plūres,** plūra), comp. adj. [contr. and changed fr. ple-or; PLE, root of plĕ-o, "to fill"; comparative suffix, "or"] ("Fuller"; hence) 1. *More.*—2. Plur.: *Several, very many.* — As Subst.: **plūres,** ium, m. plur. *Several,* or *very many, persons.*

2. **plus,** comp. adv. [adverbial neut. of 1. plus] *More.*

pœna, æ, f. ("The purifying thing"; hence) 1. *Satisfaction* for an offence committed. —Phrase : pœnas dare, (*to give satisfaction* to another ;

i. e.) *to suffer punishment* for an injury, *etc.*, committed.— 2. *Punishment* [ποινή, akin to Sans. root PÛ, "to purify"].

polle-ns, ntis, adj. [pollĕ-o, "to be powerful"] *Powerful.*

pollĭcendo, Gerund in do fr. polliceor.

pol-lĭcĕor, lĭcĭtus sum, lĭc-ēri, 2. v. dep. [for pot-lĭcĕor; fr. inseparable prefix pŏt, "much"; lĭcĕor, "to bid" at an auction] ("To bid much *or* largely"; hence) 1. Act.: *To hold forth,* or *promise,* a thing.—2. Neut.: *To make a promise, to promise.*

pollicitando, Gerund in do fr. pollicitor.

pollĭc-ĭtor, ĭtātus sum, āri, 1. v. dep. freq. [pollĭc-ĕor, "to promise"] *To make frequent* or *great promises ; to promise frequently* or *largely.*

pollĭcĭtus, a, um, P. perf. fr. pollĭcĕor.

pollŭo, ŭi, ūtum, ŭĕre, 3. v. a.: 1. *To defile, pollute.*—2. *To violate, dishonour.*—Pass.: pollŭor, ūtus sum, ŭi.

Pompēĭus, ĭi, m. *Pompeius;* 1. Cneius Pompeius, surnamed Magnus, the Roman Triumvir. —2. Quintus Pompeius, with the cognomen of Rufus; who was one of the Roman Prætors at the date of Catiline's conspiracy ; xxx. 5.

Pomptīnus, i, m. *Pomptinus (Cneius);* a Roman Prætor

mentioned at xlv. 1 as having been sent together with L. Valerius Flaccus to seize the ambassadors of the Allobroges at the Mulvian bridge.

pōno, pŏsŭi, pŏsĭtum, pōnĕre, 3. v. a. [usually regarded as contracted fr. posĭuo (*i. e.* po, inseparable prefix with augmentative force; sĭno, "to let down "), " to let down quite "; but rather fr. a root POS] 1. *To put, place,* or *set.*—2. *To set forth, propose* a thing as a prize, *etc.;* xx. 14.

pon-s, tis, m. (" A road " as "that which serves for going" over water, *etc.;* hence) *A bridge* [akin to Sans. *pathin* for *panthan,* " a road "; fr. root PATH (= PAD), "to go"].

pontĭfĭc-ātus, ātūs, m. [pontifex, pontific-is, " a high-priest "] (" The office of a *pontifex* "; hence) *A high-priesthood.*

pŏpŭlāris, is, m. [pŏpŭlāris, in the force of " belonging to the same people "] (" One belonging to the same people; a fellow-countryman"; hence)*An accomplice, associate, partner.*

pŏ-pŭl-us, i, m. (" The many "; hence) 1. *A people.* —Plur.: *Peoples.*— 2. a. *The people.*—b *The* Roman *people,* assembled in Comitia [probably for pol-pol-us; fr. πολ-ύs ("many ") reduplicated].

1. Porc-ĭus, ĭi, m. [porc-us,

"a pig "] ("One pertaining to porcus") *Porcius;* a Roman name.—Hence, Porcĭ-us, a, um, *Of,* or *belonging to, Porcius; Porcian:*—lex Porcia, *the Porcian law.* The Porcian laws were three in number, brought forward at various, but uncertain, times by different members of the Porcian family. It is known, however, that these laws confirmed the right of appeal to the people, and forbade, under heavy penalties, that any Roman citizen should be bound, scourged, or put to death, except in the case of the wilful murder of a parent. Thus the highest punishment that could be legally inflicted in Rome, at the date of Catiline's conspiracy, was banishment. Under the dictatorship of Cæsar, however, the forfeiture of all property was added in the case of wilful murder, and of the half of it for all other offences.

2. Porcius, a, um; see 1. Porcius.

porro, adv. (" Forwards "; hence) *Farther, moreover* [πόρρω].

portā-tĭo, tĭōnis, f. [port(a)-o, " to carry "] *A carrying* or *conveyance; carriage, conveyance.*

por-tendo, tendi, tentum, tendĕre, 3. v. a. [por (= pro), "forth "; tendo, "to stretch "]

("To stretch forth"; hence) Of future events, etc.: *To predict, foretell, portend.*—Pass.: por-tendor, tentus sum, tendi.

porten-tum, ti, m. [for portend-tum; fr. portend-o, "to portend"] ("That which is portended"; hence) *A sign, omen, portent.*

por-to, tāvi, tātum, tāre, 1. v. a.: 1. *To carry, convey.*—2. With auxilium, instead of the usual fero: *To bring, render, give;* vi.5 [prob. akin to φέρ-ω].

posses-sĭo, sĭōnis, f. [for possed-sĭo; fr. possĭdĕo, "to possess," through true root POSSED] ("A possessing"; hence) *A possession.*

pos-sĭdĕo, sēdi, sessum, sĭdēre, 2. v. a. [for pot-sĕdĕo; fr. pŏt (inseparable prefix), "much"; sĕdĕo, "to sit"] ("To sit much" in a place, etc.; hence) *To possess, have* or *hold possession of*

possum, pŏtŭi, no sup., posse, v. n. irreg. [for pot-sum; fr. pŏt-is, "able"; sum, "to be"] 1. *To be able,* or *powerful; to have power* to do, etc., something; (*I, you, he,* etc.) *can,* etc.:—plus posse, *to be more powerful, to possess the greater power.*—2. *To avail,* etc.

post, adv. *and* prep. [perhaps contracted from pōne, "behind"; est, "it is"] 1. Adv.: Of time: *Afterwards, after, later,* etc.—2. Prep. gov. Acc.:

a. Of place: *After, behind.*—b. Of time: *After, subsequent to.*

post-ĕa, adv. [probably for post-eam; *i.e.* post, "after"; ĕam, acc. sing. fem. of is, "this," "that"] *After this* or *that; afterwards, subsequently.*—In combination with quam, or as one word: *After that.*

postĕā-quam; see postea.

post-ĕrus, ĕra, ĕrum, adj. [post] *Coming after, following next.* ☞ (Comp.: posterĭor); Sup.: postrēmus (for poster-ēmus).

postfŭi, perf. ind. of postsum.

post-quam, adv. (also written as two words, post quam) [post, "after"; quam, "that"] *After that, when.*

postrēm-o, adv. [postrēmus, "last"] *At last, lastly, in the last place.*

postrēmus, a, um, sup. adj. (see posterus) *Last.*—As Subst.: postrēma, ōrum, n. plur. *The last things,* i. e. the things last done; meaning at li. 15 the punishment of the conspirators.

post-sum, fŭi, esse, v. n. [post, "after *or* behind"; sum, "to be"] ("To be *post*"; hence) *To fall to the rear, to retreat;*—at xxiii. 6 postfuere has a composite Subject, viz. invidia atque superbia [§ 92].

postŭlo, āvi, ātum, āre, 1. v. a. [usually considered akin to

posco, "to require"] *To ask,
demand, request, require,* etc.

pŏtens, ntis, (P. pres. of
possum, but used only as) adj.
Powerful, mighty.

pŏtent-ĭa, ĭæ, f. [pŏtens,
pŏtent-is, "powerful"] ("The
state *or* quality of the *pot-
ens*"; hence) 1. *Power, might,
force.*—**2.** Political *power,
authority, weight, influence;*
—at xlviii. 5 summā potentiā
is Abl. of quality [§ 115].

pŏtes-tas, tātis, f. [for pŏt-
ent-tas; fr. pŏtens, pŏtent-is,
"powerful"] ("The quality
of the *pŏtens*"; hence) 1.
Power, ability of doing something.—**2.** *Power, authority*
with which a person is invested.—**3.** *Power, opportunity,
permission;* xlviii. 6; where
indicandi must be supplied;
cf. preceding section 4.

pŏt-ĭor, ītus sum, īri, 4. v.
dep. [pot-is, "powerful"] ("To
become *potis*"; hence) With
Gen.: *To become master of;
to have,* or *get, possession of;*
xlvii. 2.

pŏt-ĭus, comp. adj. [ad-
verbial neut. of potior, "preferable"] ("In a preferable
way"; hence) *Rather, by preference.*

pō-to, tāvi, tātum *or* tum,
tāre, 1. v. n. *To drink,* i. e. *to
be addicted to drinking* [Gr.
πό-ω = πί-νω, "to drink"].

præ-ăcūtus, ăcūta, ăcūtum,
adj. [præ, "before"; ăcūtus,
"sharp"]("Sharpened before";
hence) *Sharp towards,* or *at,
the end; sharp at the point.*

præ-bĕo, bŭi, bĭtum, bēre, 2.
v. a. [contr. fr. præ-hibeo; for
pɪæ-habeo; fr. præ, "before";
hăbĕo, "to have *or* hold"]
("To hold before *or* forth";
hence) *To give, provide, furnish, supply.*

præ-cep-s, cĭpĭtis, adj. [for
præ-capit-s; fr. præ, "before";
căput, căpĭt-is, "the head"]
("Head-foremost"; hence) Of
persons: *Headlong, in headlong haste, precipitate.*

præcep-tum, ti, n. [for
præcap-tum; fr. præcĭpĭo, "to
order," through true root PRÆ-
CAP] *An order, command, injunction,* etc.

præceptus, a, um, P. perf.
pass. of præcipio.

præ-cĭpĭo, cēpi, ceptum, cĭpĕre, 3. v. a. *and* n. [for præ-
căpĭo; fr. præ, "beforehand";
căpĭo, "to take"] ("To take
beforehand"; "to give rules,
or precepts, about" a thing;
hence) 1. *To enjoin, direct,
order, bid, command.*—2. Impers. Pass.: præceptum eraᵗ,
It had been enjoined or *com-
manded.*—Pass.: præ-cipior,
ceptus sum, cĭpi.

præ-clārus, clāra, clārum,
adj. [præ, in "augment-
ative" force; clārus, "bright"]
("Very bright *or* clear";

hence) *Splendid, noble, re-markable, distinguished, illustrious, famous.*

præda, æ, f.: 1. *Booty, spoil, prey, plunder, pillage.* — 2. *Gain, profit.*

prædĭcans, ntis, P. pres. of prædĭco.

præ-dĭco, dĭcāvi, dĭcātum, dĭcāre, 1. v. a. [præ, "publicly"; dĭco, "to proclaim"] *To proclaim publicly; to declare, publish, state, announce.*

præ-d-ĭtus, ĭta, ĭtum, adj. [præ "before *or* above"; d-o, "to give"] ("Gifted before *or* above" others, with something; hence) With Abl. [§ 119, *a*, (2)]: *Endued, endowed, provided with.*

præfec-tus, ti, m. [for præfac-tus; fr. præfĭcĭo, "to set before," through true root PRÆFAC] ("One set before *or* over" some persons *or* things; hence) *A commander, prefect.*

præ-fĕro, tŭli, lātum, ferre, v. a. [præ, "before"; fĕro, "to bear *or* carry"] ("To bear, *or* carry, before"; hence, "to place, *or* set, in front"; hence) *To take,* or *choose, in preference; to prefer.* — Pass.: **præ-fĕror,** lātus sum, ferri.

præ-mitto, mīsi, missum, mittĕre, 3. v. a. [præ, 'before"; mitto, "to send"] *To send before* or *forwards; to send in advance.* — Pass. : **præ-ittor,** missus sum, mitti.

præ-m-ĭum, ĭi, n. [for præ-ĕm-ĭum; fr. præ, "before"; ĕm-o, "to take"] ("A taking before *or* above" others; hence, "profit, advantage"; hence) *Reward, recompense.*

præ-s-ens, entis (abl. sing. usually præsente of persons, præsenti of things), adj. [præ, "before"; s-um, "to be"] ("That is before" one; hence) 1. In time : *Present :*—in præsenti, *at the present time.*— 2. *Prompt, ready,* etc.

præsent-ĭa, ĭæ, f. [præsens, præsent-is, "present"] *A being present, presence.*

præ-sĭdĕo, sēdi, sessum, sĭdēre, 2. v. n. [for præ-sĕdĕo; fr. præ, "before"; sĕdĕo, "to sit"] ("To sit before"; hence) 1. *To have,* or *hold, the command.*—2. *To keep guard* or *watch.*

præsĭd-ĭum, ĭi, n. [præsĭdĕo, "to sit before"; hence, "to guard"] ("A guarding"; hence) 1. *Protection, defence, aid, assistance.*—2. *A protecting force, garrison, soldiers, troops, forces,* both sing. and plur.—3. *An escort, guard.*

præ-sto, stĭti, stĭtum, stāre, 1. v. n. [præ, "before"; sto, "to stand"] ("To stand before *or* in front"; hence) 1. With Dat. [§ 106, *a*]: *To surpass, excel.*—2. Impers. : præstat, *It is preferable* or *better ;*—at xx. 9 præstat has for its Subject the clause emori per virtutem [§§ 157; 156, (3)].—3. With Abl.: *To be pre-eminent, to distinguish one's self,* etc.; xxxvii. 5.

praesŭm, fŭi, esse, v. n. [præ, "before"; sum, "to be"] ("To be before" a thing *or* person; hence) With Dat. [§§ 106, (4); 107, *b*]: 1. *To be over, rule.*—2. *To be set over, to have the command of.*—3. *To have the charge of, to preside,* or *rule, over.*

prae-ter, adv. *and* prep. [præ, "before"; demonstrative suffix ter] 1. Adv.: *Except.*—2. Prep. gov. Acc. : *Except.*

praeter-ĕā, adv. [for prætercam; fr. præter, "beyond'; cam, acc. sing. fem. of pron. is, "this"] ("Beyond this"; hence) *Besides, moreover, further.*

praetĕr-ĕo, īvi *or* ĭi, ĭtum, īre, 4. v. a. [præter, "past"; co, "to go"] ("To go past"; hence) *To pass by,* or *over,* in silence; liii. 6.

prae-tor, tōris, m. [contr. fr. præ-ĭ-tor; fr. præ, "before"; I, root of ĕo, "to go"] ("One who goes before"; hence) *A prætor.*—1. A Roman magistrate charged with the administration of justice, first chosen B.C. 366. In and after B.C. 243 there were two prætors. Of these the one administered justice between citizen and citizen, and was

Sallust.

called Prætor Urbanus; and also, as he took precedence of his colleague, Prætor Honorātus. The other Prætor administered justice between the foreigners who resided at Rome, and between citizens and foreigners; hence he was styled Prætor Peregrīnus.—2. For proprætor; an officer who after the administration of the prætorship was sent as governor to a province, or was invested with some military command; for pro prætore, see pro, no. 2. b.

praetōr-ĭus, ĭa, ĭum, adj. [prætor] *Of,* or *belonging to, a prætor; prætorian.*

praetŭlĕram, pluperf. ind. of praefero.

prāvus, a, um, adj. ("Crooked"; hence, morally) *Vicious, bad, depraved,* etc.

prĕ-tĭum, tĭi, n. ("That which buys"; hence) 1. *Money.* —2. *Worth, value, price.*—3. *Bribery* [akin to πρί-ασθαι, "to buy"].

prex, prĕc-is (Nom. and Gen. Sing. obsol.; mostly in plur.), f. [for prec-s; fr. prĕc-or, "to ask"] ("The asking thing"; hence) *A prayer, request, entreaty, petition.*

prī-dem, adv. [for prædem; fr. præ, "before"; suffix dem] *Long since, long ago, for this long time past.*

prīm-o, prīm-um, adv. [primus, "first"] *At first, in the* *first place, at the beginning, firstly :*—quàm primum, *as soon as possible:*—ubi primum (*when first,* i. e.), *as soon as.*

prīm-um; see primo.

prī-mus, ma, mum, sup. adj. [for præ-mus; fr. præ, "before"; with superlative suffix mus] ("That is most before, foremost"; hence) 1. Of order : *First, the first.*— 2. Of place : a. *First, fore, foremost.*—As Subst.: prīmi, ōrum, m. plur. (*The first men* or *soldiers,* i. e.) *The foremost ranks,* or *van,* of an army; lx. 6.—b. *The first,* or *foremost, part of* that denoted by the subst. to which it is in attribution.—3. Of time : a. *First, earliest, before others,* etc.—b. In connexion with the subject of a verb : *The first who,* etc., *does, etc.,* that of which the verb speaks.—4. Of rank, station, estimation, etc.: *The first, chief, principal, of first importance* or *considera- tion —*Adverbial expression : In primis (also written as one word, inprimis *or* imprimis), *Chiefly, especially, particular- ly ;* iii. 2; xv. 3; xxiii. 5 ;— but at lx. 6 in primis belongs to no. 2. a. above.

prin-cep-s, cĭpis, adj. [for prim-cap-s; fr. prīm-us, "first"; căp-ĭo, "to take"] ("Tak- ing the first" place, *or* "taken first"; hence) 1. *First* in time

or order.—As Subst. m.: With Gerund in di : *The first in doing* or *to do, etc.,* xxiv. 2. —2. *First, foremost, chief, most eminent* or *distinguished.* —As Subst. m. : a. *A chief, chieftain.*—b. *A head, leader* of a conspiracy, *etc.*

princĭp-ĭum, ĭi, n. [prin- ceps, princĭp-is, "first"]("That which pertains to the *prin- ceps";* hence)*A beginning, com- mencement.*

pris-tĭnus, tĭna, tĭnum, adj. [obsol. pris, "before"] (" Be- longing to *pris*"; hence) *For- mer, previous, ancient.*

prĭus, comp. adv. [adverb- ial neut. of prĭor, "before"] *Before, sooner :*—prius quam (or, as one word, priusquam), *sooner than, before that.*

priusquam; see prius.

prīv-ātim, adv. [priv-us, "single"; hence, "private"] (" By a being *privus";* hence) *In private, privately.*

1. prīvātus, a, um : 1. P. perf. pass. of privo.—2. Pa. : *Apart from the state, belong- ing to an individual person, private.*—As Subst.: prīvātus, i, m. *A private person.*

2. prīvātus, i ; see 1. priv- atus.

privignus, i, m. *A step-son.*

prīv-o, āvi, ātum, āre, 1. v. a. [priv-us, "single"] (" To make *privus";* hence) With Abl. [§ 119, 1] : *To deprive of.*

—Pass.: **prīv-or**, ātus sum, āri.

1. **pro (proh)**, interj. *O! Ah! Alas!*—at xx. 10 with Acc. [§ 138].

2. **prō**, prep. gov. abl. : 1. *Before, in front of.*—2. **a.** *Instead of, in the place of, for.*—b. In connexion with the title of any officer to denote that officer's substitute :—pro praetore, (*one acting for the praetor*, i. e.) *a propraetor;* xix. 1. Of the same kind are pro consule, *proconsul;* pro quaestore, *proquaestor,* etc. These expressions were in course of time written, respectively, as one word, viz. propraetore, proconsule, *etc.;* and in these forms they became, as it were, indeclinable nouns in apposition with the name of the person of whom they speak.—3. *For, on account of, in return for.*—4. *In proportion to, according to.*—5. *For, as.*—6. *In preference to.*—7. *For, on behalf of* [akin to Sans. *pra;* Gr. πρό].

prŏba, æ; see probus.

prŏb-ĭtas, ĭtātis, f. [probus, "good"; morally, "upright"] ("The quality of the *probus*"; hence) *Uprightness, worth, probity.*

prŏb-o, āvī, ātum, āre, 1. v. a. [prŏb-us, "good"] *To esteem,* or *regard, as good; to approve of,* etc.

prŏbrum, i, n.: 1. *Disgrace, shame, dishonour.*—2. *A disgraceful act; disgraceful,* or *shameful, conduct.*

prŏ-bus, ba, bum, adj. [pro, "before"] ("That is before" other persons or things; hence) 1. *Good.*—2. *Upright, virtuous, modest.*—As Subst.: **a.** proba, æ, f. *A virtuous,* or *modest, woman.*—b. **prŏbum**, i, n. *Uprightness, probity.*

prŏc-ax,ācis, adj. [proc-o,"to ask"] ("Prone to ask"; hence) *Bold, shameless, wanton.*

pro-cēdo, cessi, cessum, cēdĕre, 3. v. n. [pro, "forth"; cēdo, "to go"] 1. *To go forth* or *out; to go forwards, advance, proceed.*—2. *To turn out well, succeed, prosper, be advanced.*

prōcessĕram, pluperf. ind. of procēdo.

prŏcul, adv. [PROCUL, a root of procello, "to drive forwards"] ("Driven forwards"; hence) Of place : *At a distance, far off, a great way off.*

prō-dĭg-ĭum, ĭi, n. [for prodĭc-ĭum; fr. prō, "beforehand"; root DIC, "to show"] ("A showing beforehand"; hence) *A prophetic sign; an omen, prodigy.*

prō-do, dĭdi, dĭtum, dĕre, 3. v. a. [pro, "forth *or* forwards"; do, "to put"] ("To put forth *or* forwards"; hence, "to make known, disclose, *etc.*; hence) *To betray* perfidiously.

prœlĭum, ĭi, n. *A battle, engagement :*—prœlium committere, *to engage in battle.*

prŏ-fān-us, a, um, adj. [prŏ, "before *or* in front"; fān-um, "a temple"] ("Being before, *or* in front of, a temple"; *i. e.* outside of it, as opposed to the being within it; hence) *Common, unholy, profane.*

prŏ-fect-o, adv. [for pro-fact-o; fr. pro, "for"; fact-um, "a deed"] ("For a deed"; hence) *Actually, certainly, doubtless, without doubt.*

prŏfectus, a, um, P. perf. of prŏfĭciscor.

prŏ-fĭc-iscor, fec-tus sum, fĭc-isci, 3. v. dep. n. inch. [for pro-fac-iscor; fr. pro, "forward"; făc-ĭo, "to make"] ("To begin to make one's self to be forward"; hence) Of persons : *To set out, go, proceed;*—at xxxiv. 2 with Acc. of place "whither" [§ 101].

prŏ-fĭtĕor, fessus sum, fĭtēri, 2. v. dep. [for prŏ-fătĕor; fr. prŏ, "openly"; fateor "to own"] ("To own, *or* avow, openly"; hence) (Either with nomen as Object, or) alone: *To give in one's name, announce one's self* as a candidate, *etc.;* xviii. 3.

prŏ-fŭgĭo, fūgi, fŭgĭtum, fŭgĕre, 3. v. n. [pro, "forth"; fŭgĭo, "to flee"] *To flee forth or away; to escape.*

prŏfŭg-us, a, um, adj. [prŏfŭg-ĭo, "to flee forth *or* away"] ("Fleeing forth *or* away"; hence) *Fleeing from one's country, fugitive, exiled, banished,* etc.

prŏ-fundo, fūdi, fūsum, fundĕre, 3. v. a. [pro, "forth"; fundo, "to pour"] ("To pour forth *or* out"; hence) Of property, *etc.: To throw away, dissipate, squander.*

prŏfūs-e, adv. [profus-us, "immoderate"] ("After the manner of the *profusus*"; hence) *Immoderately, beyond bounds.* ☞Comp. prŏfūs-ĭus.

prŏfūsĭus, comp. adv.; see profuse.

prŏfū-sus, sa, sum, adj. [for profud-sus; fr. profundo, "to squander" through root PROFUD (*i. e.* pro; FUD, the root of fundo)] With Objective Gen.[§ 132]: *Squandering, lavish of,* etc.

. prŏ-hĭbĕo, hĭbŭi, hĭbĭtum, hĭbēre, 2. v. a. [for prŏ-hăbĕo; fr. prŏ, "before"; hăbĕo, "to hold"] ("To hold before one *or* in front"; hence) 1. *To keep off or away; to hold or keep back.*—2. With no c. Subj.: *To prevent or hinder from* doing, *etc.*—3. *To forbid, prohibit.* — Pass.: prŏ-hĭbĕor, hĭbĭtus sum, hĭbēri.

prŏhĭbĭtus, a, um, P. perf. pass. of prohibeo.

prŏ-inde, adv. [pro, "with-

out force"; inde, "hence "]
("Hence"; hence) *Just, even,
in the same manner, just so:*—
proinde quasi, *just as if,* xii. 5.

prolatando, Gerund in do
fr. prolāto.

prōlā-to, tāvi, tātum, tāre,
1. v. a. intens. [PROLA, root
of supine of prŏfĕro, in force
of "to put off"] *To put off,
defer, delay, postpone.*

pro-misc-ŭus, ŭa, ŭum,
adj. [pro, "without force";
misc-ĕo, "to mix"] ("Mixed";
hence) *Without distinction,
indiscriminate in common, pro-
miscuous.*

1. prom-ptus, ptūs, m. [prom-
o, "to bring forth"] ("A
bringing forth *or* out"; hence)
Readiness;—only in Abl. Sing.
and in connexion with some
part of the verbs sum and
habeo.

2. prom-ptus, pta, ptum,
adj. [id.] ("Brought forth *or*
out"; hence) *Ready, prompt.*

prōnus, a, um, adj. Of
things: *Inclined downwards,
bending forwards* [πρηνής].

prŏpe, adv. [adverbial neut.
of obsol. adj. propis, "near"]
1. *Near.*—Comp.: prŏp-ĭus,
Nearer;—at xi. 1 in figurative sense, and folld. by Acc.
—2. *Nearly, almost.*
Comp.: prŏp-ĭus; (Sup.: prox-
ĭme = prop-sĭme.)

prŏpĕ-dĭem, adv. [prope,
"near"; diem, acc. of dies,

"day"] ("Near, *or* nigh, the
day"; hence) *At an early day,
very soon, shortly.*

prō-pello, pŭli, pulsum,
pellĕre, 3. v. a. [prō, "forwards"; pello, "to drive"]
("To drive forwards *or* before
one's self"; hence) *To drive
away, repel, keep* or *ward off.*

prŏpĕrandus, a, um, Ger-
undive of prŏpĕro.

prŏpĕrans, ntis, P. pres. of
propero.

prŏpĕr-e, adv. [proper-us,
"hastening"] ("After the
manner of the *properus*";
hence) *Hastily, in haste, quickly, with speed.*

prŏpĕr-o, āvi, ātum, āre, 1.
v. n. [id.] ("To be *properus*";
hence) *To hasten, make haste.*

prŏp-inqu-us, a, um, adj.
[for prŏp-hinc-us; fr. prŏp-
e; hinc, "from this place"]
("Being near, *or* not far, from
this place"; hence) With Dat.
[§ 106, (1)]: *Near,* or *nigh, to.*

propius; see prope.

prō-pōno, pŏsŭi, pŏsĭtum,
pōnĕre, 3. v. a. [pro, "before";
pōno, "to put"] *To put, place,
or set before* a person; *to mention, make known, state.*

prop-ter, prep. gov. acc.
[obsolete adj. prŏp-is, "near"]
1. *Near, hard by, close to.*—
2. *On account,* or *by reason,
of; because of.*

prŏpŭlĕram, pluperf. ind.
propello.

prŏ-rĭpĭo, rĭpŭi, reptum, rĭpĕre, 3. v. a. [for prō-răpĭo; fr. prō, "forth"; răpĭo, "to snatch," *etc.*] ("To snatch, *or* hurry forth"; hence) With Personal pron. in reflexive force ("To snatch one's self forth"; *i. e.*) *To hasten or hurryforth, to rush out.*

prŏrĭpŭi, perf. ind. of pro-ripio

pro-rsus, ady. [contr. fr. prō-versus; fr. prō, "forwards"; versus, "turned"] ("Turned forwards"; hence) 1. *For-wards.—2. Utterly, altogether. —3. Truly, verily, certainly. —4. In short, in fine, in a word.*

prō-scrĭbo, scripsi, scriptum, scrĭbĕre, 3. v. a. [prō, "forth"; scrĭbo, "to write"] ("To write forth"; *i. e.* to put forth in writing; hence) *To pro-scribe, or outlaw,* by hanging up a tablet containing the person's name, the sentence of his outlawry, *etc.*—Pass.: prō-scrĭbor, scriptus sum, scrĭbi.

proscrip-tĭo, tĭōnis, f. [for proscrib-tio; fr. proscrib-o, "to proscribe"] *A proscrib-ing, proscription.*

proscriptus, a, um, P. perf. pass. of proscrībo.—As Subst. : proscriptus, i, m. *A proscribed person.*

prospĕr-e, adv. [prosper-us, "prosperous"] ("After the manner of the *prosperus*";

hence) *Prosperously, success-fully, well.*

pro-spĕ-rus, ra, rum, adj. [pro, "in accordance with"; spes, spĕ-i, "hope"] ("In ac-cordance with one's hope *or* wish"; hence) *Favourable, fortunate, prosperous.*

prō-vĕnĭo, vēni, ventum, vĕnīre, 4. v. a. [prō, "forth"; vĕnĭo, "to come"] ("To come forth"; hence) *To spring up, arise.*

prōvĭdendus, a, um, Ger-undive of provideo.

prō-vĭdĕo, vīdi, vīsum, vĭd-ēre, 2. v. n. *and* a. [prō, "before"; vĭdĕo, "to see"] 1. Neut.: *To make prepara-tion or provision; to take care beforehand ;*—at lii. 4 folld. by ne c. Subj.—2. Act. : a. *To see beforehand, to foresee.*— b. *To make provision for, to prepare or provide for;* lx. 4. —c. *To take care of, look to.*—Pass. : prō-vĭdĕor, vīsus sum, vĭdēri.

prōvincĭa, æ, f. *A pro-vince;* i. e. a territory out of Italy, acquired by the Rom-ans, chiefly by conquest, and brought under their rule;—at xxvi. 4 the province to which allusion is made is Macedonia, which had fallen to the lot of Cicero, but which, being a rich one, he yielded to his col-league in order to secure his adherence to the side of order in the dangerous emergency of the state.

proxĭmus (proxŭmus), a, um, sup. adj. [= proc-sĭmus, for prop-sĭmus; fr. obsol. prŏp-is, "near"; superlative suffix simus] 1. Of place: *Nearest, next; very near* or *close.*—2. Of time: *The next,* whether before or after; *the following; the last.*

prūdens, ntis, adj. [contracted fr. pro-videns; fr. pro, "before"; videns, "seeing"] 1. *Foreseeing, foreknowing.*—2. *Intelligent, clever, talented.*

psallo, i, no sup., ĕre, 3. v. n. *To play on a stringed instrument* [ψάλλω].

publĭcandus, a, um, Gerundive of publĭco.

publĭc-e, adv. [public-us, "public"] ("After the manner of the *publĭcus*"; hence) 1. *On account of the public* or *state; in public life.*—2. *Publicly, in public, openly.*

publĭc-o, āvi, ātum, āre, 1. v. a. [id.] ("To make public property"; hence) *To confiscate.*—Pass.: publĭc-or, ātus sum, āri.

publ-ĭcus, ĭca, ĭcum, adj. [contracted and changed fr. pŏpŭl-ĭcus; fr. popul-us, "the people"] *Pertaining to the people; public* (as opposed to "private").

Publĭus, ii, m. *Publius;* a Roman praenomen.

pŭdīc-ĭtĭa, ĭtĭæ, f. [pŭdīc-us, "chaste"] ("The quality of the *pudĭcus*"; hence) *Chastity.*

pŭd-or, ōris, m. [pud-eo, "to be ashamed"] ("A being ashamed"; hence) In a good sense: *Shame, a sense of shame, modesty.*

pŭ-er, ĕri, m. ("The nourished one"; hence) *A boy, lad* [prob. akin to Sans. root PUSH, "to nourish"; and to πόϊρ, the Spartan form of παîς].

pugnandi, pugnando, Gerunds in di and do fr. pugno.

pugnans, ntis, P. pres. of pugno.

pugn-o, āvi, ātum, āre, 1. v. n. [pugn-a] *To fight.*

pul-cher, chra, chrum, adj. [for pol-cher; fr. pŏl-ĭo, "to polish"] ("Polished"; hence, "beautiful"; hence) Morally: 1. *Honourable.*—2. *Excellent, noble, glorious.* ☞ (Comp.: pulchr-ĭor); Sup.: pulch(e)rrĭmus.

pulsus, a, um, P. perf. pass. fr. pello.

Pūn-ĭcus, ĭca, ĭcum, adj. [for Pœn-ĭcus; fr. Pœn-i, "the Phœnicians"; hence, "the Carthaginians"] ("Of, or belonging to, the *Pœni*"; hence) *Carthaginian, Punic:*—bellis Punicis omnibus, *in all the Carthaginian,* or *Punic, wars.* These were three in number. The First lasted from B.C. 264 to B.C. 241, a space of 23 years

—the Second, from B.C. 218 to B.C. 201, or 17 years—the Third, from B.C. 150 to B.C. 146, or between 3 and 4 years.

pŭt-o, āvi, ātum, āre, 1. v. a. [pŭt-us, "clean, clear"] ("To make clean *or* clear"; hence, "to clear up, *or* settle," accounts; hence, "to reckon"; hence) 1. *To deem, hold, think, consider.* — 2. With second Acc. : *To deem*, etc., some Object to be that which is denoted by the second Acc.

Q , abbrev. of Quintus.

quæro, quæsīvi, quæsītum, quærĕre, 3. v. a.: 1. *To seek, search for* or *after.*—2. *To ask about, seek to learn, enquire.*

quæs-tor, tōris, m. [quæro, "to seek," through root QUÆS] ("A seeker") *A quæstor.* — The Quæstors were Roman magistrates, originally employed in attending solely to the public revenues. At first they were two in number, and their functions were confined to Rome itself; but in B.C. 420 their number was increased to four. Of these, two remained at Rome, and were called Prætores Urbāni ; two attended the consuls, or other governors, in their provinces, and hence were named Prætores Provinciāles or Militāres. (In either case, however, the distinctive appellation is not usu-ally expressed.) The principal charge of the Quæstores Urbāni was the care of the treasury (which was kept in the temple of Saturn) and the management of all affairs connected with it. They, also, had the custody of the military standards, entertained and lodged foreign ambassadors, and arranged for the funerals of those who were buried at the public expense. To each Quæstor Provincialis or Militaris, when on service in a province, it appertained to attend to the provisioning and payment of the soldiers, to exact the tribute due to Rome, to sell spoils taken in war, and to make a return of all receipts and payments to the Treasury. Beyond this he exercised such jurisdiction as was assigned to him, and generally supplied the place of his chief, when the latter left his province.

quæs-tus, tūs, m. [quæro, "to gain"; id.] ("A gaining"; hence) *Gain, profit, advantage.*

quam, adv. [adverbial fem. acc. sing. of quis, "who, what"] 1. *In what manner, as, how, how much, as much as.*—2. After comp. words, or words containing the idea of comparison: *Than :* — magis quam, *more than;* for prius

quam, see prius; malle . . .
quam, *to desire more, to be
more desirous,* . . . *than, to
prefer* . . . *to ;* præstat . . .
quam, *it is better* . . . *than.*—
3. In comparisons : a. *As :*—
tam . . . quam, *so* . . . *as.*—b.
After supra : *Than :*—supra
quam, *more than, above* or
beyond what.—4. After post,
postea: *That.*—5. In augmentative force : a. With Superl.
words: *As much* (or *as little*)
as possible :—quam maxŭme,
as much, or *as greatly, as
possible ;* quam verissume, *as
truly as possible.* — b. With
Pos. words : *How, how very :*—
quam făcĭle, *how easily, with
how very great ease* or *readiness ;* quam magnĭfĭcum, *how,*
or *how very, magnificent* or
glorious.

quam-ŏb-rem, adv. [quam,
fem. acc. sing. of qui (relatively), "who, which"; (interrogatively), "what ?"; ŏb,
"on account of"; rem, acc.
sing. of res, "a thing"] 1.
Relatively : ("On account of
which thing"; hence) *From
which cause* or *reason ; wherefore.* — 2. Interrogatively :
("On account of what thing ?";
hence) *Wherefore? why ? for
what reason ?*

quam-prĭmum ; see primo.
quam-vis, adv. and conj.
[quam, "as"; vis, 2. pers.
pres. indic. of volo, "to wish"]

1.Adv.: *As you will.*—2. Conj.
[§ 152, I, (5)]: *However,
although, though.*

quant-um, adv. [adverbial
acc. neut. of quant-us, "how
much"] 1. *How much.*—2.
As much as, as far as.—3.
As a correlative : *As.*

qua-ntus, nta, ntum, adj.:
1. a. *How much.*—b. quanto,
neut. abl. sing. as Abl. of
measure [§ 118]: *By how
much.*—2. *How great ;*—at
xxviii. 2 the neut. nom. sing.
is folld. by periculi, Gen. of
thing measured [§ 131].—3.
As a correlative to tantus: *As.*

quā-propter, adv. [for quam-
propter ; fr. quam, fem. acc.
sing. of qui, "who, which";
propter, "on account of"]
("On account of which thing";
hence) *On which account,
wherefore.*

quā-re, adv. [fem. abl. sing.
of qui, "who, "which"; re,
abl. sing. of res, "a thing"]
("From which thing"; hence)
Wherefore, for which reason
or *cause.*

quar-tus, ta, tum, num.
adj. [contr. fr. quatuor-tus,
fr. quat-uor, "four"] (" Provided with four"; hence)
Fourth.

quā-sĭ, adv. [for quam-si ;
fr. quam, "as"; si, "if"] 1.
As if, as though.—2. *As it
were ;*—at x. 3 quasi qualifies
materies.

que, enclitic conj. *And :—* que . . . que, *both . . . and; as well . . . as; partly . . . partly* [akin to τέ].

quĕo, quīvi *or* quiī, quītum, quīre, v. n. *To be able.*

quĕror, questus sum, quĕri, 3. v. dep. : **1.** *To complain.—* **2.** *To complain of, lament, bewail* [root QUES *or* QUER, akin to Sans. root ÇVAS, "to sigh "].

questus, a, um, P. perf. of queror.

1. qui, quæ, quod, pron. : **1.** Relative : **a.** *Who, which, what, that;—*at v. 7 quæ (neut. acc. plur.) relates to the two sing. fem. substt. inopia and consciĕntia, inasmuch as they are things without life; so, at iii. 2, quæ (neut. acc. plur.) relates to virtute and gloriā.—**b.** At the beginning of a clause instead of a conj. and demonstr. pron.: *And this*, etc.—**c.** With Subj. : To point out a purpose, *etc.: For the purpose of; that; in order to* or *that; to.*—**d.** With ellipse of demonstrative pron. : *He,* or *she, who; that which.* —**e. Quo**, neut. abl. sing. as Abl. of measure [§ 118], with comparative words: *By (what, i. e.) how much :*—quo minus . . . eo magis, *by how much 'ess . . . by so much the* liv. 5.—**f.** After idem, !s *;* xlviii. 4.—**g.** Sunt,

etc., qui, (*There are,* etc., *those who;* i. e.) *Some :* = aliqui ; xiv. 4 ; cf., also, xxxix. 5 ; xlviii. 7. The mood of the verb following sunt, *etc.*, qui will depend upon whether the statement of a fact is made, or a mere conception of the mind expressed—oratio recta *or* obliqua.—**h.** Particular constructions : **(a)** When a word (or sentence) is explained by a subst. in connexion with sum, dico *or* dicor, appello *or* appellor, *etc.*, the relative is usually in the gender of such explanatory subst. ; est locus in carcere, quod Tullianum adpellatur, lv. 3. — **(b)** The relative sometimes attracts the subst. out of the demonstrative clause into its own : plerique, quæ delicta reprehendĕris, *etc.*, for plerique delicta, quæ reprehendĕris, *etc.*, iii. 2.—**(c)** For id quod, xiv. 1, see is no. 1.—**2.** Interrogative : In indirect clauses : *What, what sort of.*—**3.** Indefinite : *Any one, any.*

2. qui, adv. [adverbial neut. abl. sing. of 1. qui, "who," *etc.*] *In what manner, how.*

quĭ-a, conj. [adverbial old acc. plur. of 1. qui] [§ 152, ɪɪ, (1)] *Because.*

quĭ-cumque, quæ-cumque, quod-cumque, pron. rel. [qui ; suffix cumque] *Whoever, whatever ; whosoever, whatsoever.*

—As Subst. : **a. quicumque,** m. plur. *Whatever persons, whoever.*—**b. quæcumque,** n. plur. *Whatever things.*

1. **quid**; see 1. and 2. quis.

2. **quid,** adv. [adverbial neut. of 1. quis, "who *or* what"] *For what purpose,* etc.; *wherefore, why.*

quī-dam, quæ-dam, quod-dam (and as Subst. quiddam), pron. indef. [qui; suffix dam] *Particular, certain; some in-definite person or thing.*—As Subst. : **a.** Masc.: (a) Sing. : *A certain person.*—(b) Plur.: *Certain persons; some persons or other; some.* — **b.** Neut.: (a) Sing. : *A certain thing.* — (b) Plur. : *Certain things.*

quĭdem, adv.: 1. *Indeed :*— ne quĭdem, *not even.*—2. *At least, certainly, forsooth.*

quidquam; see quisquam.

quī-es, ētis, f. ("A lying down"; hence) *Rest, repose ;* —at xv. 4 in plur. to denote the repeated occasions on which repose was sought [akin to Sans. root çī, "to lie down"].

quĭēt-us, a, um, adj. [quĭe-sco, "to be quiet," through root QUIET] *Quiet, calm, tranquil.*—As Subst.: **quĭēta,** ōrum, n. plur. *Quiet, or calm, things;* i. e. at xxi. 1 the tranquillity of the state.

quī-lĭbet, quæ-lĭbet, quod-lĭbet (Gen. cujus-lĭbet ; Dat. cuī-lĭbet), (at v. 4 in tmesis : cujus rei libet), pron. ind. [qui, "who"; lĭbet, "it pleases"] ("Whom it pleases" you; hence) *Any one,* etc. ; *whom you will, any.*

quī-n, conj. [for qui-ne; fr. qui, abl. of relative pron. qui, "who, which"; ne = non] ("By which not") With Subj. : 1. *That not, but that, without, from.*—2. After words expressive of fear, doubt, etc.: *That.* — 3. Interrogatively : *Why not? wherefore not ?*

Quintus, i, m. [quintus, "fifth"] *Quintus;* a Roman name.

qui-ppe, conj. [for quip-te; fr. qui, abl. of relative pronoun qui, "who, which"; suffix pte] ("From which very thing" ; hence) 1. *Surely, assuredly, in fact, certainly, in good truth.*—2. In connexion with causal particles, enim, etc. : *Since in fact, for indeed, inasmuch as.*—3. In connexion with rel. pron. qui, in all cases : *As one, etc , in fact who, which, or that;* i. e. *since,* or *inasmuch as, I, thou, he,* etc.; xlviii. 2.

1. **quis,** quæ, quid, pron. interrog. : In indirect questions: *Who* or *what;* i. e. *what person or thing;* xl. 2, etc. ; —neut. with Gen. of "thing Measured" [§ 131], xx. 13:

xlvii. 1.—As Subst. n. : **quid**, *What thing, what* [τίς].

2. **quis**, quid. pron. indef. 1. *Anybody, any one; any-thing.*—2. Acc. neut. in adverbial force : **quid**, *In any-thing, in any respect.*

quis-nam, quæ-nam, quid-nam (Gen., cujus-nam ; Dat., cui-nam), pron. interrog. [1. quis; suffix nam] *Who, which, what* (person *or* thing) *pray ?*

quis-quam, quæ-quam, quic-quam *or* quid-quam, pron. indef. [2. quis, "any one"; suffix quam] *Any, any what-ever ;*—at xxxvi.5 with Gen. of "thing Distributed" [§ 130]; —neut. with Gen. of "thing Measured" [§ 131], v. 6.—As Subst. m. : *Any one, anybody.*

quis-que, quæ-que, quod-que, pron. adj. indef. [quis, "any one"; suffix que]1. *Each, every, any.*—As Subst. m. : *Each one, each.* — 2. With Superl., to express universality : *Every the most, all the most :*— prudentissimus quis-que, *every the most talented,* i. e. *all the most talented,* viii. 5.—3. Particular construction : To a plural Subject, whether expressed or understood, quis-que is often added, by way of apposition, in order to give a more special definition: cœpere ... quisque, *they began, each one of them,* vii. 1 ; cf., also, xxxvii. 6, *etc.*

quī-vis, quæ-vis, quod-vis, pron. indef. [qui, "who"; vis, 2. pers. sing. of volo, "to will"] *Who,* or *what, you please* or *will; any whoever* or *whatever.*

quo, adv. [for quo-m, old form of que-m, acc. masc. sing. of qui, "who"] ("To what" place ; hence) 1. *Whither, where.*—2. *To the end that, in order that, so that, that.*— 3. *Wherefore, for which rea-son, on which account.*

quō-cumque, adv. [quo; suffix cumque] *Whithersoever.*

quŏd, conj. [Adverbial Acc. Neut. Sing. of qui] 1. *In that, because that, inasmuch as.*— 2. *That.*

quō-mĭnus (or, as two words, quo minus), conj. [1. quo, no. 3 ; mĭnus, no. 2.] With Subj. after verbs of hindering, preventing, *etc.* : *That . . . not; but that; from* doing, *etc.*

quo-mŏdo (at xxiii. 4 in tmesis ; quōquĕ mŏdo = que quomodo), adv. [adverbial ablatives of qui, "what"; mŏdus "manner"] *In what manner, how.*

quonam, abl. sing. of quis-nam.

quŏn-Yam, adv. [for quom-jam ; fr. quom = quum, "since"; jam, "now"] *Since now, since then, since, because.*

1. **quŏque**, conj. *Also, too :*

—placed after the word to be emphasized.

2. quŏque, masc. abl. sing. of quisque.

3. quŏque modo; see quomŏdo.

quŏtīdĭ-ānus, āna, ānum, adj. [quŏtīdĭ-e, "daily"] ("Pertaining to *quŏtīdĭe*"; hence) *Daily, every day.*

quŏ-usque, adv. [for quomusque; fr. quom, old form of quem, masc. acc. sing. of qui, " who, what"; usque, "until, as far as "] (" Until, *or* as far as, that which "; hence) Of time: *Until what time, till when, how long.*

quum (old form quom), relative adv. *and* causal conj. [for quom = quem, fr. qui, " who "] 1. Relative Adv.: ("To the time which"; hence) *When.* — 2. Causal Conj.: ("To the end that *or* which"; hence) *Seeing that, since, as, inasmuch as.*

rād-ix, īcis, f. ("The increasing, *or* growing. thing "; hence, " a root " of a plant, etc.; hence) Of a mountain: *The lower part, foot* [prob. akin to Sans. root VRIDH, "to increase"].

răp-ina, ĭhæ, f. [răp-ĭo, in force of "to rob"] (" A robbing"; hence) *Robbery, plundering, pillage, rapine.*

răp-ĭo, ŭi, tum, ĕre, 3. v. a.:

1. *To seize and carry off; to snatch away.*—2. *To seize and carry off by force or with violence; to rob, plunder;*—at xi. 4 rapere is the Hist. Inf. [§ 140, 2], and has no nearer Object depending on it.—Pass.: răp-ĭor, tus sum, i [akin to ἁρπ-άζω, " to seize "].

ră-tĭo, tĭŏnis, f. [rĕor, "to reckon "; through root RA]: 1. *A reckoning, account, calculation.*—2. *A business-matter, transaction, business;* also, *a business or matter* in general.—3. *Mode, method, manner, means.*—4. *A plan, purpose.*

rătus, a, um, P. perf. of reor.

rĕceptus, a, um, P. perf. pass. of recipio.

rĕ-cĭpĭo, cēpi, ceptum, cĭpĕre, 3. v. a. [for rĕ-căpĭo; fr. rĕ, " back again "; căpĭo, "to take"] *To take or get back again; to retake, recover;*—at xi. 4 there is in receptā republicā an allusion to the final overthrow of the Marian party by Sulla.—Pass.: rĕ-cĭpĭor, ceptus sum, cĭpi.

rĕ-cĭto, cĭtāvi, cĭtātum, cĭtāre, 1. v. a. [rĕ, "without force"; cĭto, in force of "to call out, announce "] (" To announce "; hence) *To read out or aloud.*

rect-e, adv. [rect-us, "right"] (" After the manner of the *rectus*"; hence) *Rightly, properly.*

rec-tus, ta, tum, adj. [for reg-tus; fr. reg-o, " to lead straight "] (" Led straight "); hence, "straight, direct "; hence) *Right, proper,* etc. ☞ Comp.: rect-ĭor; (Sup.: rect-issĭmus).

reddĭtus, a, um, P. perf. pass. of reddo.

red-do, dĭdi, dĭtum, dĕre, 3. v. a. [red (= re, with a demonstrative), "back "; do, " to give "] 1. *To give back, return.* —2. Of a letter, *etc.,* as Object: *To give, hand,* or *deliver* to one.—Pass.: **red-dor**, dĭtus sum, di.

rĕd-ĭmo, ēmi, emptum, ĭmĕre, 3. v. a. [for rĕd-ĕmo; fr. red (see reddo) in "intensive " force; emo, " to buy "] (" To buy up "); hence) *To pay for, to make compensation* or *amends for, to compensate;* xiv. 2.

referendus (referundus), a, um, Gerundive of refero;—at l. 4 supply esse with referundum.

rĕ-fĕro, tŭli, lātum, ferre, v. a. irreg. [rĕ, "back "; fĕro, see fĕro] (" To bring *or* carry back "; hence, " to report "; hence) 1. *To refer,* or *lay,* a matter *before* the senate ; xxix. 1, *etc.*—2. Impers. pass.: **rĕfĕrātur**, *It should be referred to,* or *laid before,* them, *i. e.* that they should be consulted or their opinion should be taken,

xlviii. 5 :—cf. the Impers. Gerundive constr. at l. 4 : referundum esse, *that it must be referred to* them, *i. e.* that they must be consulted, *etc.,* [§ 144, 1].—Pass.: **rĕ-fĕror**, lātus sum, ferri.

rē-fert, tŭlit, ferre, v. n. impers. [for rem-fert; fr. rem, acc. sing. of res ; fert, 3. pers. sing. pres. indic. of fero] (" It bears one's affair *or* property "; hence) *It imports* or *concerns;* —at lii. 16 folld. by Dat. of person [§ 107], and having for its Subject the Inf. timere [§ 157; cf., also, Notes to Syntax, p. 149, *b,* (1)].

rĕ-fĭcĭo, fēci, fectum, fĭcĕre, 3. v. a. [for rĕ-făcĭo; fr. re, "again "; făcĭo, " to make "] (" To make again "; hence) Of the spirits, courage, *etc.,* *To reanimate, restore,* etc.— Pass.: **rĕ-fĭcĭor**, fectus sum, fĭci.

rĕg-ĭo, ĭōnis, f. [rĕg-o, " to direct "] (" A directing "); hence, "a direction "; hence) *A tract, district, territory, region.*

rēg-ĭus, ĭa, ĭum, adj. [rex, rēg-is, "a king "] (" Of, *or* belonging to, a *rex* "; hence) *Kingly, regal, royal.*

reg-num, ni, n. [rĕg-o, " to rule "] (" That which rules "; hence) 1. *Sovereignty, supreme* or *royal power.*—2. *A kingdom.*

rĕgrĕdĭor, gressus sum, grĕdi, 3. v. dep. [for rĕ-grădĭor; fr. rĕ, "back"; grădĭor, "to step"] ("To step back"; hence) *To return.*

regressus, a, um, P. perf. of regredior.

rĕlictus, a, um, P. perf. pass. of relinquo.

rĕlĭgĭōsissĭmus, a, um; see religiosus.

rĕlĭgĭ-ōsus, ōsa, ōsum, adj. [contr. fr. rĕlĭgĭōn-ōsus; fr. rĕlĭgĭo, rĕlĭgĭōn-is, "religion"] ("Full of *religio*"; hence) *Religious, given to religion* or *the worship of the gods.* ☞ (Comp.: rĕlĭgĭōs-ĭor); Sup.: rĕlĭgĭōs-issĭmus.

rĕ-linquo, līqui, lictum, linquĕre, 3. v. a. [rĕ, "behind"; linquo, "to leave"] 1. *To leave behind* in a place. — 2. *To allow* or *suffer to remain, to leave:*—in medio aliquid, *to leave something in the midst,* i. e. *open* or *undecided.*—3. *To leave, go away from, quit, abandon, forsake.*—Pass.: rĕlinquor, lictus sum, linqui.

1. rĕlĭqui, perf. ind. of relinquo.

2. rĕlĭqui, ōrum; see reliquus.

rĕlĭqu-us, a, um, adj. [rĕlinquo, through true root RELIQU] 1. *That is left* or *remains, remaining.*—As Subst.: rĕlĭquum, i, n. *The rest, remainder· residue:* quid reliqui habemus, *(what of a remainder have we,* i. e.) *what have we left remaining,* xx. 13.—Phrase: Nihil reliqui facere, *(to make nothing of a remainder;* i. e.) *to leave nothing remaining,* xi. 7;—so, also, in pass. constr.: nihil reliqui fit, *(nothing of a remainder is made;* i. e.) *nothing is left remaining,* lii. 4.—2. *The remaining part,* or *rest, of* that denoted by the subst. to which it is in attribution.—3. *The rest* or *remaining; the other.* —As Subst.: rĕlĭqui, ōrum, m. plur. *The rest, the others.*

rĕ-mĕd-ĭum, ĭi, n. [re, "again"; med-eor, "to heal"] ("That which heals again"; hence) *A cure, remedy.*

rĕmōtus, a, um, P. perf. pass. of removeo.

rĕ-mŏvĕo, mōvi, mōtum, mŏvēre, 2. v. a. [rĕ, "back"; mŏvĕo, "to move"] ("To move back"; hence) *To remove, withdraw, send away.*—Pass.: rĕ-mŏvĕor, mōtus sum, movēri.

rĕor, rătus sum, inf. not found, 2. v. dep.: 1. *To reckon, calculate.*—2. *To suppose, imagine, consider.*

rĕpent-e, adv. [repens, repent-is, "sudden"] *Suddenly, on a sudden.*

rĕ-pĕrĭo, pĕri, pertum, perīre, 4. v. a. (for rĕ-părĭo; fr. re, "again"; părĭo, "to produce"] ("To produce again"; hence)

To find out, discover, ascertain.
—Pass.: rĕ-pĕrĭor, pertus sum, pĕrīri.

repertus, a, um, P. perf. pass. of reperio.

rĕ-pĕto, pĕtīvi *or* petĭi, pĕt-ītum, pĕtĕre, 3. v. a. [rĕ, "back again"; pĕto, in force of "to fetch"] ("To fetch back again"; hence) 1. With reference to the memory: *To recall to mind, recollect, remember.*—2. Law t. t.: Of property, *etc.*: *To demand back,* or *reclaim,* in *or* before a court of law.

rĕpĕtundæ, undārum; see repetundus.

rĕpĕtundus, a, um, Gerundive of repeto, in force of "to demand back *or* reclaim" in a court of law.—Pecuniæ repetundæ, or simply as subst., repetundæ, ārum, f. plur. *Money* (or any other thing extorted by a provincial governor, and which was) *to be demanded back* by the aggrieved persons.—With reference to the governor, commonly translated *Extortion.* Repetundæ included not merely unjust exactions, but even the receiving of presents.

rĕ-prĕhendo, prĕhendi, prĕ-hensum, prĕhendĕre, 3. v. a. [re, "back"; prĕhendo, "to seize"] ("To seize and hold back"; hence, "to check"; hence) *To blame, censure, find fault with, reprehend.*

rĕpŭdĭ-o, āvi, ātum, āre, 1. v. a. [repudi-um, "divorce"] ("To divorce"; hence) *To refuse, reject,* etc.

rĕpul-sa, sæ, f. [rĕpello, "to drive back"; hence, "to refuse," through root REPUL; *i. e.* re and PUL, a root of pello] ("A refusing"; hence) *Refusal, denial, repulse;*—at xx. 8 in plur.

rĕ-pŭto, pŭtāvi, pŭtātum, pŭtāre, 1. v. a. [rĕ, "again"; pŭto, in force of "to think over"] *To think over again;* i. e. *to ponder, meditate,* or *reflect upon.*

rĕ-quĭes, quĭētis *and* quĭēi (Dat. Sing. and all cases in Plur. wanting), f. [rĕ, "without force"; quies, "rest"] *Rest, repose.*

rĕ-quĭesco, quĭēvi, quĭētum, quĭescĕre, 3. v. n. [rĕ, "without force"; quĭesco, "to rest"] *To rest, repose, rest one's self* or *itself,* etc.

rĕ-quīro, quīsīvi *or* quīsĭi, quīsītum, quīrĕre, 3. v. a. [for re-quæro; fr. rĕ, "again"; quæro, "to seek"] ("To seek again"; hence) *To seek out; to seek* or *search after; to ask,* or *enquire, about;*—at xl. 2 folld. by clause as Object [§ 156, (3)].

res, rĕi, f. ("That which is spoken of"; hence) 1. *A thing, matter.*—2. *An actual thing; reality, real state,* *truth, fact.*—3. *An affair, business, event, circumstance,* etc.:—res humanæ, *human affairs;*—res dubiæ, *critical circumstances;*—res asperæ, *adverse,* or *calamitous, circumstances.*—4. With or without publica: a. *The commonwealth, state, republic.*—b. *Civil,* or *public, affairs,* etc.—5. *Effects, substance, property,* etc.;—see familiaris.—6. *Benefit, profit, advantage:* —in rem, *for,* or *of, advantage, advantageous,* xx. 1.—In Law: *A suit, cause, case* [akin to ῥῆ-μα, fr. ῥέ-ω, "to speak"].

rĕ-sisto, stĭti, no sup., sistĕre, 3. v. n. [re, "against"; sisto, "to stand"] ("To stand against"; hence) *To withstand, resist; oppose; to make opposition* or *resistance;*—sometimes with Dat. [§ 106, *a*].

rĕ-spondĕo, spondi, sponsum, spondēre, 2. v. a. *and* n. [rĕ, "in return"; spondĕo, "to promise"] ("To promise in return"; hence) 1. *To answer, reply.*—2. Of priests, *etc.,* respecting some future event: With Objective clause: *To respond* or *reply* (in answer to those who consult them) *that* something will be, *etc.;* xlvii. 2.

res-publĭca, rĕi-publĭcæ, f.; see res, no. 4.

rĕ-stinguo, stinxi, stinctum, stinguĕre, 3. v. a. [re, "without force"; stinguo, "to ex-

tinguish"] Of a conflagration as Object: *To put out, extinguish.*

rĕ-stĭtŭo, stĭtŭi, stĭtūtum, stĭtŭĕre, 3. v. a. [for re-statuo; fr. re, "again"; statuo, "to set up"] 1. *To set up again, to replace.*—2. *To restore.*—Pass.: **rĕ-stĭtŭor,** stĭtūtus sum, stĭtŭi.

rĕ-tĭcĕo, tĭcŭi, no sup., tĭcēre, 2. v. a. [for rĕ-tăcĕo; fr. re, "without force"; taceo, "to be silent about"] *To be silent about, to keep silent,* or *preserve silence, respecting;*—at xxiii. 2 reticere, quæ audierat = reticere ea, quæ audierat.

rĕtĭnendus, a, um, Gerundive of retineo.

rĕtĭnens, ntis, P. pres. of retineo.

rĕ-tĭnĕo, tĭnŭi, tentum, tĭnēre, 2. v. a. [for rĕ-tĕnĕo; fr. rĕ, "back"; tĕnĕo, "to hold"] 1. *To hold,* or *keep, back; to detain, retain.*—2. *To preserve, keep, maintain.*—Pass.: **rĕ-tĭnĕor,** tentus sum, tĭnēri.

retractus, a, um, P. perf. pass. of retraho.

rĕ-trăho, traxi, tractum, trahĕre, 3. v. a. [rĕ, "back"; traho, "to drag"] *To drag back, bring back by force,* etc.—Pass.: **rĕ-trăhor,** tractus sum, trăhi.

rĕ-us, i m. [res, rĕ-i, in force of Law t. t., "a suit *or* action "] (" One pertaining to a *res* "; hence, "a party to an action "; hence) Of a defendant and with Gen.: **1.** *A defendant with respect to.—* **2.** *One guilty of.*

rĕvertĕram, pluperf. ind. of reverto; see revertor.

rĕ-vertor, versus sum, verti, 3. v. dep. [rĕ, "back "; vertor, "to turn one's self "] (" To turn one's self back "; hence) *To return.—*N.B. In the ante-Augustan age the perfect and its derivatives are commonly taken from a form **reverto**; e. g. rĕvertĕram, xxxvii. 11. The present tense of **re-verto** is critically certain in only two passages in two old Latin authors.

rĕvŏcātus, a, um, P. perf. pass. of revoco.

rĕ-vŏco, vŏcāvi, vŏcātum, vŏcāre, 1. v. a. [re, "back "; vŏco, " to call "] *To call back, recall.—*Pass.: rĕ-vŏcor, vŏc-ātus sum, vŏcāri.

1. rex, rēgis, m. [for reg-s; fr. reg-o, "to rule "] (" He who rules "; hence) *A king.*

2. Rex, Rēgis, m. [1. rex, "a king "] *Rex (Quintus Marcius);* a Roman procon-sul, who at the time of the conspiracy had just returned from Cilicia, where he had gain-ed such successes, as caused him to claim a triumph; xxx. 3.—*Rex* was a cognomen in the

Marcian family, which was de-scended from Ancus Marcius, the fourth king (*rex*) of Rome.

Rhŏdii, orum; see Rhodus.

Rhŏdus (Rhŏdos), i, f. *Rhod-us* or *Rhodos* (now *Rhodes*) an island off the coast of Car-ia, in Asia Minor, celebrated for its Colossus and the skill of its people in navigation.— Hence, **Rhŏd-ius,** ĭa, ĭum, adj. *Of,* or *belonging to, Rhodes; Rhodian.—*As Subst.: **Rhodii,** ōrum, m. plur. *The people of Rhodes, the Rhodians.* Up to the time of the Macedon-ian war the Rhodians had maintained the most friend-ly relations with Rome, and (by Roman aid, according to Sallust, li. 5) had extended their power not only over several of the adjacent islands, but also over a portion of the opposite mainland. During that war, however, they ap-peared to the Romans to waver in fidelity, and to be more inclined to take part with their adversary, Perses;— whence Sallust's words, *civitas . . infida atque advorsa nobis.* In consequence of this, when Perses had been defeated, the Romans at first deprived the Rhodians of a great part of their territory; but afterwards they were propitiated, and re-stored what they had taken away. Hence Sallust says,

(*Rhodios*) *impunitos dimisere* (*Romani*). See Perses ['Ρόδος; prob. fr. ῥόδον, "a rose," and so, "a thing—here, island— with roses, Rose-island"].

rŏg-ĭto, ĭtāvi, ĭtātum, ĭtāre, 1. v. a. intens. [rŏg-o, "to ask"] *To ask much* or *eagerly; to put eager* or *repeated questions; to ask* or *enquire with eagerness;*—at xxxi. 3 without nearer Object.

rŏgo, āvi, ātum, āre, 1. v. a.: 1. *To ask, beg, request,* etc. —2. Political t. t. : a. Rogare aliquem sententiam : *To ask one his opinion.*—b. In Pass. : With sententiam alone : *To be asked one's opinion.*

Rōma, æ, f. *Rome;* a city of central Italy, on the banks of the Tiber, the capital of the Roman Empire.—Romæ, *at Rome,* Gen. of place "where" [§ 121, B. *a*], xxvii. 2, *etc.;* but at xxxi. 7 Romæ is in apposition to urbis [§ 90] :— Romam, *to Rome,* Acc. of place "whither" [§ 101].— Hence, Rōm-ānus, a, um, adj. *Of,* or *belonging to, Rome; Roman.*—As Subst.: Romāni, ōrum, m. plur. *The Romans* [usually considered akin to ῥώμη, "strength"; but perhaps connected with ῥέ-ω, "to flow"; ῥεῦ-μα, "a stream *or* river"; akin to Sans. root SRU, "to flow"; and so, "The stream- *or* river-city"].

Rūfus, i, m. [rūfus, "red; red-haired"] ("Red-haired One"] *Rufus* (*Quintus Pompeius*), a Roman prætor; xxx. 5.

rŭ-ĭna, īnæ, f. [rŭ-o, "to fall down"] ("A falling down"; hence) *Downfall, overthrow, destruction, ruin.*

rūmor, ōris, m. *Report, common talk, rumour.*

rup-es, is, f. [ru(m)p-o, "to break," through root RUP] ("The broken, *or* rent, thing"; hence) *A cliff, steep rock.*

rursus, adv. [contr. fr. revorsus, "turned back"] ("Turned back"; hence, "backwards"; hence) *Again.*

S. = salutem (dicit); see salus.

săc-er, ra, rum, adj. *Sacred, consecrated, dedicated, holy.* —As Subst.: săcrum, i, n.: a. *A sacred,* or *holy, thing.*— b. *A religious rite* or *solemnity* [root SAC; akin to ἅγ-ιος, "holy," and Sans. root YAJ, "to sacrifice, to worship (deities) by sacrifices"].

săcer-dō-s, tis, comm. gen. [for sacer-da-(t)s; fr. săcer, sac(e)r-i, "sacred"; DA, root of do, "to give"] ("One giving himself, *etc.,* to sacred things"; hence) 1. *A priest.* —2. *A priestess :*—sacerdos Vestæ, *a priestess of Vesta,* i. e. a Vestal Virgin. The sacerdos mentioned at xv. 1

was Fabia Terentia, the sister of Terentia, the wife of Cicero. When brought to trial by Clodius she was acquitted, and her prosecutor compelled to flee from Rome; see Vesta.

săcerdōt-ĭum, ĭi, n. [săcer-dos, săcerdōt-is, "a priest"] ("The office of a *sacerdos*"; hence) *A priesthood.*

săcr-ĭ-lĕg-us, a, um, adj. [săcr-um, "a sacred thing"; (i) connecting vowel; lĕg-o, in force of "to steal"] *That steals sacred things* or *robs a temple; sacrilegious.*—As Subst.: **sacrileg-us,** i, m. *A sacrilegious person; an impious* or *wicked man.*

săcrum, i; see sacer.

Sænius, ĭi, m. *Sænius (Lucius);* a Roman senator; xxx. 1.

saep-e, adv. [obsol. saep-is, "frequent"] 1. *Frequently, often.*—2. In connexion with nŭmĕro (abl. of numerus, "number"), or as one word, saepenumero: ("Often in number"; *i. e.*) *Oftentimes, over and over again, very often* or *frequently.*

saepe-nŭmĕro; see saepe.

saev-ĭo, ĭi, ĭtum, īre, 4. v. n. [saev-us, "fierce"] *To be fierce; to rage; to be furious, angry,* or *wrathful.*

saev-ĭtĭa, ĭtĭae, f. [id.] ("The quality of the *saevus*"; hence) ~~Fierceness, cruelty, barbarity, ~~ess, etc.

saevus, a, um, adj. *Fierce, cruel, harsh, severe.*

Sallustĭus (Salustius), ĭi, m. *Sallustius (Caius),* with cognomen of Crispus, was born B.C. 86 at Amiternum (now S. Vittorino), a very ancient town of the Sabines. In B.C. 50 the censors, Appius Claudius Pulcher and Lucius Calpurnius Piso, ejected him from the senate for some immorality; but on becoming Praetor elect in B.C. 47 he was restored to his rank. He accompanied Caesar to Africa in B.C. 46, where he was subsequently appointed governor of Numidia. On his return to Rome he was accused of mal-administration; and, though he was never brought to trial, the charge is supposed to have been founded on facts, for he became immensely rich, as was shown by the expensive gardens (Horti Sallustiani) which he formed on the Quirinal. Most probably it was not till he returned from Africa that he wrote his historical works:—Bellum Catilinarium, Bellum Jugurthinum, and Historiarum Libri Quinque. Of these the two former have come down to us complete; of the Histories some fragments alone remain. Other works are by some attributed to Sallust, but the more general opinion is that they are not his production. With regard to the Bellum Catilinarium, the introduction to it, though admired by some, is but a feeble attempt to support the part of a philosopher and moralist. The speeches are held to be his own undoubted composition; though it is considered tolerably certain that the one Cæsar delivered was actually extant at the time when Sallust wrote, and it is known that Cato's words were taken down in the Senate-house by short-hand writers.

sal-to, tāvi, tātum, tāre, 1. v. n. intens. [săl-ĭo, " to leap "] (" To leap much "; hence) *To dance.*

sălū-s, tis, f. [for salv-ts; fr. salv-ĕo, " to be well *or* in good health "] (" A being well," etc.; hence, " health "; hence) 1. *Safety, preservation.* —2. *A wish for one's welfare,* whether verbal or written; *a greeting, salutation, salute:* —salutem alicui dicere, (*to speak a greeting,* etc., *to some one;* i. e.) *to greet, salute some one.*—At the commencement of a letter the formula employed was salutem dicit (with sometimes the name of the person to whom the letter was sent in the Dat.). This was commonly abbreviated to

the letters s.D., or even, as at xxxv. 1, to s. alone.

sălūtātum, Supine in um fr. saluto;—at xxviii. 1 dependent on introīre [§ 141, 5].

sălūt-o, āvi, ātum, āre, 1. v. a. [sălus, sălūt-is, " health "] (" To wish health to "; hence) 1. *To salute, greet.*—2. *To visit out of compliment, to pay one's respects to, to wait upon* a person;—at xxviii. 1 without nearer Object.

Samnītes, ĭum, m. plur. *The Samnites;* i. e. the inhabitants of Samnium, one of the principal districts of central Italy.

săn-e, adv. [san-us, " sound in mind "] (" Soundly "; hence) *Well, truly, of a truth.*

Sanga, æ, m. *Sanga (Quintus Fabius);* a Roman noble, the patron of the Allobroges, to whom the ambassadors of that nation communicated the treasonable designs of Catiline; see xli. 3—5.

sangu-is, is, m. *Blood* [akin to Sans. *asan* or *asanj,* " blood "].

săpĭ-ens, entis, adj. [sapi-o, " to be wise "] *Wise, sensible, discreet, judicious.*—As Subst. m.: *A wise man.*

săpĭent-ĭa, ĭæ, f. [sapiens, sapient-is] (" The quality of the *sapiens* "; hence) 1. *Wisdom.*—2. *Good sense, discretion, discreetness, prudence.*

săt-is, adj. *and* adv.: 1. Adj. indecl.: *Sufficient, enough;* — at v. 5 with Gen. of "thing measured" [§ 131].—2. Adv.: a. *Sufficiently, enough.*—b. *Moderately, tolerably.*

sătisfac-tĭo, tĭōnis, f. [sătis-făc-ĭo, in force of "to make au excuse, to apologize"] ("A making au excuse," *etc.*; hence) *An excuse, apology.*

sаucĭus, a, um, adj. *Wounded.*—As Subst. m.: *A wounded man.*

scĕlĕrā-tus, ta, tum, adj. [sceler(a)-o, "to pollute"] *Polluted, profaned* by crime; lii. 36.

scĕles-tus, ta, tum, adj. [for sceler-tus; fr. scelus, scĕlĕr-is, "wickedness"] ("Having *scelus*"; hence) *Wicked, guilty.*

scĕlus, ĕris, n. *A wicked deed; wickedness, guilt.*

scī-lĭcet, adv. [contr. fr. scire licet, "it is permitted to know"] 1. *Indeed, in truth, certainly.*—2. Ironically: *In good truth, forsooth.*

scĭo, scīvi and scĭi, scĭtum, scīrc, 4. v. a. *To know.*

scortum, i, n. *A courtezan, harlot.*

scrībo, scripsi, scriptum, scrībĕre, 3. v. a.: 1. *To write,* in the fullest sense of the term.—2. Military t. t.: *To enlist, enrol, levy* soldiers.— Pass.: **scrīb-or**, scriptus sum, scrībi [akin to γράφ-ω].

scrī-nĭum, nĭi, n. [for scrib-nĭum; fr. scrīb-a, "a scribe"] ("A thing pertaining to a *scriba*"; hence) *A letter-case, letter-box; a box for papers, letters,* etc.

scrip-tor, tōris, m. [for scrīb-tor; fr. scrīb-o, "to write *or* compose"] *A writer* of history, *etc.*;—at viii. 3 scriptorum magua ingenia, (*great talents of writers*) = scriptores magno ingenio *or* magni ingenii (abl. *or* gen. of quality), *writers of great talent or ability.*

scriptus, a, um, P. perf. pass. of scrībo.

se (reduplicated **sese**), acc. *and* abl. of pron. sui.

sē-cēdo, cessi, cessum, cēdĕre, 3. v. n. [sē, "apart, aside"; cēdo, "to go"] ("To go apart *or* aside"; hence) 1. *To withdraw, retire.*—2. Political t. t.: *To revolt, secede.*

sēcum = cum se; see cum.

sĕc-undus, unda, undum, adj. [for sequ-undus; fr. sĕquor] ("Following"; hence, Nautical t. t., of the wind, *etc.*, "favourable, fair"; hence, in fig. sense) *Favourable, propitious, fortunate:*—secundæ res, *prosperous circumstances, prosperity*, xi. 8.

sĕd, conj. [same word as sed = sine, "without"] *But.*

sĕd-es, f. [sĕd-ĕo, "to sit"; hence] ("That on which one sits"; hence) *A dwelling-place, habitation, abode.*

sēd-ĭ-tĭo, tĭōnis, *or* se-d-ĭtĭo, ĭtĭōnis, f. [acc. to some sēd (= sine, in force of) "apart"; I, root of ĕo, "to go"; and so, "a going apart":—acc. to others, sē (= sine), "apart"; d-o, "to put"; and so, "a putting apart, a separation"] *An insurrectionary movement, whether political or military; insurrection, mutiny, sedition.*

sēd-o, āvi, ātum, āre, 1. v. a. [akin to sĕd-ĕo] ("To cause to sit, to seat"; hence) *To appease, allay, calm.*—Pass.: sēd-or, ātus sum, āri.

sēmet; see sui.

sem-per, adv. *Always* [akin to Gr. ὁμ-ος, ὁμ-οῖος, "like"; Sans. *sam-a*, "same," also, "all, entire"].

Semprōnĭa, æ, f. *Sempronia,* the wife of Decimus Junius Brutus. She was a person of great personal attractions and highly accomplished, but very profligate. She engaged in Catiline's conspiracy without the knowledge of her husband, who was in no way privy to it.

sĕn-ātor, ātōris, m. [senex, sen-is, "an old man"] ("One who has become *senex*"; hence) *A senator,* as one originally appointed from among the older men.

sĕnātŏr-ĭus, ĭa, ĭum, adj. [sĕnātŏr. sĕnātōr-is, "a sen-ator"] *Of, or belonging to, a senator* or *the senators; senatorian;*—at xvii. 3 senatorii ordinis is the Gen. of quality [§ 128].

sĕn-ātus, ātūs (*and* senati, xxx. 3), m. [senex, sĕn-is, "old man"] ("The office of a *senex*"; hence) *The Senate;* i. e. *the council,* or *assembly, of elders.*

sentent-ĭa, ĭæ, f. [for senti-ent-ĭa; fr. sentiens, sentĭent-is, "thinking"] *A way of thinking, an opinion, sentiment.*

sentīna, æ, f. ("Bilge-water"; hence) *The hold* of a ship.

sentĭo, sensi, sensum, sent-īre, 4. v. a.: 1. With Objective clause: *To feel, perceive, observe, notice.* — 2. Political (and Law) t. t.: *To give one's opinion* concerning a matter; *to vote,*—3. *To hold views, cherish sentiments;*—at xxvi. 4. without Acc. of nearer Object.

sēpără-tim, adv. [separ(a)-o, "to separate"] ("By a separating"; hence) *Separately.*

Septĭmĭus, ĭi, m. *Septimius;* a man of Camerinum, who was one of the leaders in Catiline's conspiracy; xxvii. 1.

sĕqu-or, ūtus sum, i, 3. v. dep.: 1. *To follow.*—2. *To follow in pursuit of, pursue,* whether actually or figuratively [akin to Gr. ἕπ-ομαι, Sans. root SACH].

sĕquūtus, a, um, P. perf. of sĕquor.

Ser., abbrev. of Servius.

ser-mo, mōnis, m. [commonly referred to sĕr-o, "to connect"] ("The connected thing"; hence) *Conversation, discourse,* etc.

serv-īlis, īle, adj. [serv-us, "a slave"] *Of,* or *belonging to, a slave* or *slaves ; servile, slavish.*

serv-ĭo, īvi *or* ĭi, ītum, īre, 4. v. n. [id.] ("To be a slave"; hence) 1. *To be a slave.*—2. With Dat. [§ 106, (4)]: *To be the slave of ; to have regard* or *care for ; to be devoted* or *subject to.*

servītĭa, ōrum; see serv-itium, no. 2.

serv-ĭtĭum, ĭtĭi, n. [serv-us, "a slave"] ("The thing pertaining to a *servus*"; hence) 1. *Slavery.*—2. Plur. : *Slaves.* —3. *Servitude* or *subjection* of any kind.

serv-ĭtus, ĭtūtis, f. [serv-us, "a slave"] ("The state, *or* condition, of the *servus*"; hence) *Slavery, servitude.*

Servĭus, ĭi, m. *Servius ;* a Roman prænomen : 1. Servius Cornelius Sulla, the brother of the Dictator. — 2. Servius Sulla, the son of no. 1, and one of the co-conspirators of Catiline ; xvii. 3 ; xlvii. 1.

serv-o, āvi, ātum, āre, 1. v. a. ("To drag away" from an enemy, *etc. ;* hence) *To protect, preserve* [from same source as servus; see servus].

serv-us, i, m. ("One dragged away or taken captive"; in war, *etc.;* hence) *A slave, servant* [prob. akin to Gr. ἐρύω, "to drag"].

sese, reduplication of se, acc. of pron. sui.

sestertĭum, ĭi; see sestertius.

(ses-tertĭus, tertĭa, tertĭum, adj. [contr. fr. semistertius, fr. semis, "a half"; tertĭus ; "third"] ("With a third half"; i. e.) *Containing two and a half;* in this meaning perhaps only with nummus.—As Subst.) **sestertĭus** (written also in the characters HS. *i. e.* II = duo ; and Semis), ĭi, m. *A sesterce ;* a small silver coin, equal to two and a half *asses,* or one fourth part of a *denarius.* Up to the time of Augustus its value was about two pence and half a farthing English ; afterwards about ⅛ less. It was the coin in ordinary use among the Romans, and by it the largest sums were reckoned. From the frequent employment of *sestertiûm* (= *sestertiōrum*) in designating numbers above *mille,* "a thousand," there very early arose a distinct substantive ; viz. **ses-tertĭum,** ĭi, n. (= mille sestertiûm *or* sestertĭōrum) *A· sestertium=* *a thousand* sestertĭi, or *sesterces.* This sum up to the time of Augustus was equal to about £8 17*s.* 1*d.* English; afterwards to ⅛ less : ducenta sestertia (xxx. 6), *two hundred sestertia,* or *two hundred thousand sesterces,* would therefore represent a sum of £1770 16*s.* 8*d.* English.

seu ; see sive.

sĕvēr-ĭtas, ĭtātis, f. [sĕvēr-us, "serious"] ("The quality of the *severus*"; hence) *Seriousness* of character, *etc.; sternness, gravity, severity.*

sĕv-ērus, ēra, ērum, adj. ("Reverenced"; hence, "serious, grave"; hence) Of punishment, *etc.:* 1. *Severe, harsh, rigid.*—2. Comp.: To denote a too high degree : *Too severe,* etc.; li. 15 ; see also 1. paulo.

sex-tus, ta, tum, num. ord. adj. [sex, "six"] ("Provided with *sex*" ; hence) *sixth.*

si, conj.[§ 152,III,(2)]*If*[*eĭ*].

Sĭbyll-īnus, īna, īnum, adj. [Sibyll-a, "a Sibyll *or* prophetess"; but esp. "*the* Sibyll," who came to Tarquinius Superbus, and offered to sell nine books of oracles. On his refusing to buy them, she went away, burnt three of them, and then returned and asked the same price for the remaining six. Being ridiculed by the king, she burnt three more, and then demanded the same price, again, for the three now alone remaining. Hereupon Tarquin consulted the augurs, and at their advice gave the sum required. The Sibyll having received it, delivered the three books, and after having desired that they might be carefully kept, disappeared] *Of,* or *belonging to, the Sibyll; Sibylline.*—Lĭbri Sĭbyllīni, *The Sibylline books,* were supposed to contain the fates of the Roman state ; and hence in seasons of emergency the keepers of them (who varied in number at different times) were ordered by the Senate to inspect them. Originally they were kept in a stone chest, underground, in the temple of Jupiter Capitolinus. But when the Capitol was burnt· in the wars of Marĭus and Sulla, the Sibylline books perished in the conflagration, B.C. 83. In consequence of this loss, ambassadors were sent far and wide to collect the oracles of other Sibylls.

sīc-ut (sīc-ŭti), adv. [sic, "so"; ut, "as"] 1. *So as, just as.*—2. *As if, just as if.*

signā-tor, tōris, m. [sign(a)-o, "to seal, affix a seal"] ("One who seals *or* affixes a seal"; hence) *A witness to a will,* who attests it by affixing his seal.

signātus, a, um, P. perf. pass. of signo.

sign-o, āvi, ātum, āre, 1. v. a. [sign-um, "a mark"] ("To set a mark upon": hence) To seal, attach a seal to.—Pass.: sign-or, ātus sum, āri.

signum, i, n. ("A mark, sign," etc.; hence) 1. a. A military standard or ensign, whether of a legion, cohort, or maniple.—b. A cohort, a maniple.—2. A sign or signal for battle, etc.—3. A statue.—4. A seal, signet, etc.

Sīlānus, i, m. Silanus (Decimus Junius); consul elect at the date of Catiline's conspiracy; 1. 4.

sīlent-ĭum, ĭi, n. [silens, silent-is, "silent"] 1. A being silent; silence, stillness.—2. Inaction, repose.

sĭl-ĕo, ŭi, no sup., ēre, 2. v. n.: 1. To be silent.—2. Impers. Pass.: sĭlētur, Silence is kept or preserved, there is silence, i. e. there is no mention made; ii. 8.

sĭlētur; see sileo.

sĭm-ĭlis, ĭle, adj. With Dat. [§ 106, (1)]: Like, similar [akin to Gr. ὅμ-οιος; and Sans. sam-a, in force of "like"].

sĭmĭl-ĭtŭdo, ĭtūdĭnis, f. [sĭmĭl-is, "like"] ("The quality of the similis"; hence) Likeness, resemblance, similitude.

sĭm-ŭl, adv.: 1. Together, at once, at the same time.—2. (= simul ac), As soon as [akin to Gr. ὅμ-οιος, "like"; Sans. sam-a, "same"].

sĭmŭlans, ntis, P. pres. of simulo.

sĭmŭlā-tor, tōris, m. [simul(a)-o, "to feign"] ("One who feigns"; hence) A feigner, pretender, simulator.

sĭmŭl-o, āvi, ātum, āre, 1. v. a. [for sĭmĭl-o; fr. sĭmĭl-is, "like"] ("To make like"; hence) To feign, pretend, simulate.

sĭmul-tas, tātis, f. [simul, "together"] ("The state, or condition, of being simul"; hence, "an encounter"; hence) Of two persons or parties: Dissension, animosity; jealousy, enmity.

sī-n, conj. [shortened fr. sine; fr. si, "if"; ne, "not"] If on the contrary, if however, but if.

sĭne, prep. gov. abl. [akin to se, "apart; without"] Without.

singŭl-ātim, adv. [singŭlus, "individual"] Individually, one by one, singly.

sin-gŭli, gŭlæ, gŭla (rare in sing.), num. distrib. adj. Separate, single, individual.—As Subst.: singŭli, ōrum, m. plur. Individual persons, individuals, persons individually; xvii. 1 [akin to εἷς, ἑνός, "one"].

sĭnister, tra, trum, adj. *On the left* or *left-hand (side), left.*

sĭnus, ūs, m. ("A bent surface, a curve"; hence, "the hanging fold" of a toga; hence, "the bosom" of a person; hence) *The interior, inside, inmost part* of a thing; lii. 35.

sĭ-tis, tis (Acc. sĭtim; Abl. sĭtī), f. ("A becoming exhausted"; hence, "exhaustion"; hence) *Thirst* [akin to Sans. root KSHI, "to destroy"; pass., "to become exhausted"].

Sittĭus, ĭi, m. *Sittius(Publicus)*; a native of Nuceria, and a member of the equestrian order, who shortly before the outbreak of the conspiracy had taken service with the king of Mauritania, then at war against the neighbouring princes. Catiline claimed him as an accomplice probably for the mere purpose of raising the spirits of his associates, but had no ground for reckoning him as one of the conspirators. Cicero in his oration for Sulla speaks of him as a man of high character, a friend of his own, and as having gone to Mauritania solely in consequence of an agreement of long standing.

sĭ-tus, ta, tum, adj. [sĭ-no, "to place"} *Placed, lying, situate;*—at xx. 14 sita (neut.

nom. plur.) is predicated of divitiæ, decus, gloria [§ 92, 2, a].

sī-ve (contr. seu), conj. (sī, "if"; vě, "or"] *Or if:*—sive (seu) ... sive (seu), *whether ... or.*

sŏcĭ-ĕtas, ĕtātis, f. [socius, "a companion"] ("The state, *or* condition, of a *socius*"; hence) 1. With Gen.: *A participation in.*—2. *League, alliance, confederacy.*

sŏcĭus, ĭi, m.: 1. *A comrade, companion.*—2. *A confederate, accomplice.*—3. *An ally, confederate* [akin to Sans. *sakhi,* "an associate, a friend"].

sŏcord-ĭa, ĭæ, f. [sŏcors, socord-is, "careless, lazy"] ("The state, *or* quality, of the *socors*"; hence) *Carelessness, negligence, laziness, indolence, inactivity.*

sōl, sōlis, m. *The sun* [akin to Gr. ἥλ-ιος Sans. *svar*].

sŏl-ĕo, ĭtus sum, ēre, 2. v. n. semi-dep. *To be wont* or *accustomed; to be customary* or *usual.*

sŏlĭtus, a, um, P. perf. of soleo.

soll-enn-is, e, adj. [for sollann-is; fr. soll-us (= totus), "whole, complete"; ann-us, "a year"] ("That takes place when the year is complete"; hence, of religious rites, "yearly, annual"; hence, with the religious notion predominant) *Religious, solemn.*

sollĭcĭtātus, a, um, P. perf. pass. of sollicito.

sollĭcĭt-o, āvi, ātum, āre, 1. v. a. [sollĭcĭt-us, " greatly moved *or* tossed "] (" To make *sollicitus*"; hence, "to agitate," *etc.*; hence) In a bad sense: *To stir up, instigate,* to something bad, *tamper with,* etc.—Pass.: **sollĭcĭt-or, ātus sum, āri.**

sōl-um, adv.[adverbial neut. of sol-us, "alone"] *Alone, only.*

sōlus, a, um (Gen., solīus; Dat., soli), adj.: 1. *Alone, only, sole.*—2. With the Subject of a verb: *The only one,* etc., *that* does, *etc.,* the act denoted by the verb.

sōlūtus, a, um: 1. P. perf. pass. of solvo.—2. Pa.: *Free, unfettered, unshackled, exempt from control,* etc.

so-lvo, lvi, lūtum, lvĕre, 3. v. a. [for se-luo; fr. se, "apart"; lŭo, " to loosen "] (" To loosen apart "; hence, "to untie, unbind"; hence, with reference to an obligation for goods, *etc.,* obtained) *To pay.* — Pass.: **so-lvor, lūtus sum, lvi.**

som-nus, ni, m. *Sleep* [akin to Gr. ὕπ-νος, Sans. *svap-na,* fr. root SVAP, " to sleep "].

sons, sontis, adj. (" Hurtful, noxious"; hence) *Guilty, criminal.*—As Subst. m. (" A ~uilty person, a criminal";

hence) *One that gives offence by his conduct; an offensive person.*

spărus, i, m. *A hunting-spear* (a small missile weapon with a curved blade).

spătĭum, ĭi, n.: Of time: *A space, interval;*—at lvi. 2 brevi spatio is the Abl. of time "when" [§ 120] [στάδιον, Æolic form of στάδιον, " a stadium "=about 606 feet English.

spĕcĭ-es, ēi, f. [spĕcĭ-o, " to see "] (" That which is seen "; hence, " a shape, form, figure"; hence) *Appearance, semblance, pretence,* etc.

spectā-tus, ta, tum, adj. [spect(a)-o, in force of " to try, test "] With Dat. of person: *Tried, proved, tested by* one;—at xx. 2 spectata neut. nom. plur. is predicated of the two fem. sing. substt. virtus and fides [§ 92, 2, *a*].

spēr-o, āvi, ātum, āre, 1. v. a. *To hope, expect, hope for;*—at xxxvii. 6 with Dat. of person [§ 107] [akin to Sans. root SPRIH, " to desire, long for "].

spē-s, ĕi (Gen. Dat. and Abl. Plur. only in post-classical writers), f. [for spēr-s, fr. sper-o; as seen by *spēr-es,* an old Acc. Plur. in one of the earliest Roman writers] *Hope, expectation;* — at xxxvii. 8 maxumā spe is the Abl. of quality [§ 115].

Spinther, ĕris, m. *Spinther;* an agnomen of Publius Cornelius Lentulus, given to him in consequence of his likeness to an actor named Spinther. He was ædile at the time of Catiline's conspiracy, and it was to his keeping that Lentulus the conspirator was entrusted; xlvii. 4.

spīrans, ntis, P. pres. of spīro.

spīro, āvi, ātum, āre, 1. v. n. *To breathe.*

spŏliandi, Gerund in di fr. spolio.

spŏli-o, āvi, ātum, āre, 1. v. a. [spoli-um, "that which is stripped off"] ("To strip, *or* deprive, of covering"; hence) 1. *To rob, plunder, pillage, spoil.*—2. *To strip or spoil* the slain;—at lxi. 8 without nearer Object.

spŏl-ium, ĭi, n. ("That which is stripped off"; hence, "arms, armour," *etc.*, stripped off a fallen foe; hence) *Spoil, booty, plunder, prey.*

Statilius, ĭi, m. *Statilius* (*Lucius*); a Roman knight, one of Catiline's accomplices; xvii. 4. In conjunction with Gabinius he was ordered to fire the city in twelve places simultaneously; xliii. 2. He was strangled in prison at the same time as Lentulus; lv. 6.

stătŭo, stătŭi, stătūtum, stătŭĕre, 3. v. a. [stătus, un- contr. gen. stătŭ-is, "a standing position"] (In causative force: "To make to be in a standing position"; hence, "to put, place," *etc.;* hence) 1. *To resolve, determine.*—2. *To appoint, fix, set.*—3. *To settle, decide, enact,* etc.;—at lii. 31 statuatis is Subj. (pres.) in an indirect question or oblique interrogation [§ 149].

stă-tus, tūs, m. [st(a)-o, "to stand"] ("A standing"; hence) 1. *Condition, state, circumstances.*— 2. Of dignity, *etc.* : *Condition, station, position, rank.*

stĭmŭl-o, āvi, ātum, āre, 1. v. a. [stĭmŭl-us, "a goad"] ("To goad"; hence) *To urge, urge or spur on, incite, stimulate.*

stĭpā-tor, tōris, m. [stip(a)-o, in force of "to attend"] *An attendant.*—Plur.: *Attendants, suite, train, retinue.*

stĭ-pend-ium, ĭi, n. [for stippend-ium; fr. stips, stip-is, in original force of "small coin" heaped up; pendo, "to pay"] "A paying of *stips*"; hence) *Tribute, impost, tax,* payable in money, as distinguished from vectīgal, which was paid in kind.

stirps, is, f. (rarely m.) ("The lower part of the trunk" of a tree, *etc.*, including the roots; hence) *A root:*—ab stirpe interire, *to perish from* the root, i. e. *utterly* or *entirely*, x. 1.

strēnŭissĭmus, a, um; see strēnŭus.

strēn-ŭus, ŭa, ŭum, adj. *Prompt, energetic, strenuous.* —As Subst.: strēnŭus, ŭi, m. *One who is prompt,* etc.; *an energetic man.* ☞ (Comp.: strēnu-ĭor); Sup.: strenuissĭmus [akin to στρην-ής].

stŭd-ĕo, ŭi, no sup., ēre, 2. v. n. *and* a. ("To be in haste" to do, etc., a thing; hence) 1. Neut.: *To favour, show favour;* li. 13.—2. Act.: With Objective clause: *To be eager, very desirous,* etc., that something should take place, etc.; i.1; xxxvii. 3 [akin to σπουδ-ή, "haste"].

stŭd-ĭum, ĭi, n. [stŭd-ĕo, "to be eager"] 1. *Eagerness, eager desire.*—2. *Zeal, ardour, energy.*—3. *Application to learning, study.*

stul-tus, ta, tum, adj. [akin to stol-idus, "dull"] *Foolish, silly, stupid.*

stŭprum, i, n. *Debauchery.*

sŭa, sŭămet; see suus.

sŭb, prep. gov. acc. *and* abl.: 1. With Acc.: a. *Under, below, beneath.*—b.*Near, close to.*—c. Of time: *At the approach of, towards, about.*— 2. With Abl.: a. *Under, beneath.*—b. Of lofty things, *or* in a high situation: *beneath, at the foot*

of [akin to Gr. ὑπ-ό, Sans. up-a].

sŭbactus, a, um, P. perf. pass. of subĭgo.

sub-dŏl-us, a, um, adj. [sŭb, "somewhat, slightly"; dŏl-us, "craft"] ("Having *dolus* slightly"; hence) *Somewhat crafty, cunning, sly, deceptive.*

sub-dūco, duxi, ductum, dūcĕre, 3. v. a. [sŭb, "from below"; dūco, "to draw"] ("To draw from below"; hence) Military t. t.: Of soldiers, etc.: *To draw off* from one post to another.—Pass.: sub-dūcor, ductus sum, dūci.

sŭbēgi, perf. ind. of subigo.

sŭb-ĭgo, ēgi, actum, ĭgĕre, 3. v. a. [for sŭb-ăgo; fr. sŭb; ăgo, "to put in motion"] 1. [sŭb, "under"] ("To put in motion under"; hence, "to bring, *or* get, under"; hence) *To overcome, conquer, subjugate, subdue.*—2.[sŭb,"from beneath"] ("To put in motion from beneath"; hence, "to impel, push on," a vessel, *etc.;* hence) Mentally: *To compel, force, constrain.*

sublātus, a, um, P. perf. pass. of tollo.

sublĕvando, Gerund in do fr. sublĕvo;—at liv. 3 without nearer Object.

sub-lĕvo, lĕvāvi, lĕvātum, lĕvāre, 1. v. a. [sŭb; lĕvo] 1. [sŭb, "from beneath"; lĕvo, "to lift up"] ("To lift up from beneath "; hence) *To console, support, assist*, etc.— **2.** [sŭb, "without force"; lĕvo, "to make light, to lighten"] *To lighten, lessen, alleviate.*

sub-sĭd-ĭum, ĭi, n. [for sub-sĕd-ĭum; fr. sub, "behind"; sĕd-ĕo, "to sit"] ("A sitting behind"—"that which sits behind"; hence, "a body of reserve"; hence) **1.** *Aid, assistance, succour.* — **2.** Military term: *A support*, i. e. a body of soldiers rendering aid to those hard pressed by the enemy; *a reserve.*

subversus, a, um, P. perf. pass. of subverto.

sub-verto, verti, versum, vertĕre, 3. v. a. [sŭb, "beneath"; verto, "to turn"] ("To turn beneath"; hence) **1.** *To overturn, overthrow, upset.*—**2.** *To overthrow, ruin, destroy, subvert.*—Pass.: **subvertor,** versus sum, verti.

suc-curro, curri *and* cŭcurri, cursum, currĕre, 3. v. a. [for sub-curro; fr. sub, "towards"; curro, "to run"] ("To run towards"; hence) With Dat. [§ 106, *a*]: *To run* or *hasten to the aid of* a person; *to help, assist, relieve, succour.*

sŭdes (Nom. not found), is, f. *A stake, pile.*

1. sŭi, sĭbi, se (reduplicated sese), pron. pers. sing. *and* plur. *Of*, etc., *himself, herself, itself, themselves;*—sometimes strengthened by the addition of suffix met; *e.g.* se-met, acc. sing., xliv. 2.

2. sŭi, ōrum; see suus.

Sulla, æ, m. *Sulla;* the cognomen of a patrician family of the Gens Cornelia: **1.** Lucius Cornelius Sulla, with agnomen of Felix, was born B.C. 138. He served at first under Marĭus in the war with Jugurtha, which his soldier-like qualities and great address mainly brought to a successful issue. Marĭus became jealous of Sulla's merit, and hence arose that quarrel between them which was productive of enormous cruelties on either side, and finally led to the extinction of Roman liberty. In B.C. 82 he was appointed Dictator, and in the early part of B.C. 79 resigned his power. After this he retired to his estate at Puteŏli, where he died in the following year, B.C. 78, in the 60th year of his age. The immediate cause of his death was the rupture of a blood-vessel, though for some time previous he had been suffering from a loathsome disease known at the present day by the name of Morbus Pediculosus *or* Phthīrĭāsis.—Hence, **Sull-ānus,** āna, ānum, adj. *Of*, or *pertaining to, Sulla.*— **2.** Servius Cornelius Sulla, the brother of the dictator and father of no. 3.—3. Publius Cornelius Sulla and Servius Cornelius Sulla, sons of no. 2, and accomplices of Catiline; —at xvii. 3 Sullæ, nom. plur., is used as specifying both Publius Cornelius, and Servius Cornelius, Sulla.

Sullānus, a, um; see Sulla.

sum, fŭi, esse, v. n.: **1.** *To be;* for sunt quí, *etc.,* see qui. —**2.** With Dat.: *To belong* or *appertain to;* or, rendering the Dat. as Subject of the verb: *To have* [§ 107, *c*).—**3.** With Double Dat. [§ 108]: *To be* (for, *i.e.* a cause of) something *to* some ·one.—**4.** With Gen. [§ 127, *b*]: *To be the property of; to belong to, to appertain to* [in pres. tenses akin to ἐσ-μί = εἰ-μί, and to Sans. root AS, "to exist, to be "; in Perf. tenses akin to φύ-ω, φῦ-μι, and Sans. root BHÛ, "to be"].

sŭmendus (sŭmundus), a, um, Gerundive of sūmo.

summus, a, um; see superus.

sŭ-mo, mpsi, mptum, mĕre, 3. v. a. [contr. fr. sŭb-ĕmo; fr. sŭb, "up"; ĕmo, "to take"] **1.** *To take up, take, lay hold of.*—**2.** Of punishment: With de and Abl. of person: (*To take* punishment *from* another, as that which he has to yield; hence) *To inflict* punishment *upon.*— Pass.: **sŭ-mor,** mptus sum, mi.

1. sumptus, a, um, P. pe. pass. of sumo.

2. sum-ptus, ptūs, m. [sum-o, "to spend "] ("A spending"; hence) *Expense, cost,* etc.

sŭmundus, a, um; see sumendus.

sŭperb-ĭa, ĭæ, f. [superb-us, "proud "] ["The quality of the *superbus*"; hence) *Pride.*

sŭper-bus, ba, bum, adj. [sŭper, "above "] ("That is above" others; hence) *Proud, haughty, arrogant.*

sŭpērior, us; see sŭpĕrus.

sŭpĕr-o, āvi, ātum, āre, 1. v. n. *and* a. [sŭper, "above "] ("To rise above"; hence) **1.** Neut.: Of wealth as Subject: Folld. by Dat. of person [§ 107]: *To abound, be abundant,* etc.; xx. 11.—**2.** Act.: *To surpass, excel* in any quality, *prove superior to;* liii. 4. — Pass.: **sŭpĕr-or,** ātus sum, āri.

sŭper-us, a, um, adj. [super, "above "] (1. Pos.: "That is above; on high").—**2.** Comp.: **sŭpērior,** us: **a.** Of locality: *Higher, upper.*—**b.** In arrangement, etc.: *Former, preceding, above-named.*—**c.** *Superior,* etc.—**3.** Sup.: **summus,** a, um: **a.** Of locality: (a) *Highest.* —(b) *The highest part of* that denoted by the substantive to which it is in attribution.—**b.** Of degree, etc.: *Highest, utmost, greatest, very great, consummate.*

cantum-mŏdo, adv. [tant-
m, "only"; strengthened by
1ŏdo, "only"] *Only, merely.*

tant-us, a, um, adj. : 1. a.
o *much.*—b. tanto, *By so
uch;* Abl. of measure [§ 118].
-2. *So great.*—3. *Of such con-
quence* or *importance; so
nportant, so great* [akin to
ans. *tâvant,* "so much"].

tard-e, adv. [tardus, "slow"]
Slowly.—2. Comp.: *Too
owly.* ☞ Comp.: tardĭus.

tardĭus; see tarde.

tar-dus, da, dum, adj.
prob. for trah-dus ; fr. trăh-o,
to draw"] ("Drawing one's
lf along"; hence) *Slow,
rdy.*

Tarquĭnĭus, ĭi, m. *Tarquin-
us* (*Lucius*); a man who,
nder a promise from the
enate that he should be held
armless, gave such informa-
on as he possessed respecting
atiline's conspiracy, xlviii. 3,

Tarrăcĭn-ensis, ense, adj.
Tarracīn-a, "Tarracina," for-
erly called "Anxur"; a town
? Latium] *Of,* or *belonging
), Tarracina.* — As Subst.:
arrăcĭnensis, is, m. *A man,
r native, of Tarracina.*

tĕgo, texi, tectum, tĕgĕre,
v. a.: 1. *To cover.*—2. *To
rotect, defend.*—Pass. : tĕg-
r, tectus sum, tĕgi [akin to
τέγω, "to cover"].

tēlum, i, n. *A weapon,*
whether for hurling or for
close quarters [commonly referred to τῆλε, "afar off";
but rather for tend-lum, fr.
tend-o, "to hurl *or* launch";
and so, "that which is hurled
or launched"].

tĕmĕr-e, adv. [obsol. tĕmĕr-
us, "despising"] ("After the
manner of the *temerus*"; hence)
Rashly, inconsiderately.

tempĕr-o, āvi, ātum, āre,
1. v. n. [prob. akin to tempus,
tempĕr-is, in its etymological
force; see tempus and tempes-
tas] ("To observe a proper
measure ;" hence) With Dat.
[§ 106, (4)]: *To moderate, use
with moderation; to be moderate* or *temperate in;* xi. 8.

tempes-tas, tātis, f. [for
temper-tas; fr. tempus, old
gen. tempĕr-is, as proved by
existing adverbial abl. tempĕr-
i] ("The state, *or* condition,
of *tempus*"; hence) *A* particular *time* or *season :*—eā tem-
pestāte, Abl. of time "when"
[§ 120].

tem-plum, pli, n. ("A piece
cut off"; hence, "an open
space" marked by the augur
for taking auspices; hence) *A
temple,* as a place dedicated to
some deity [akin to τέμ-νω,
"to cut"].

tem-pus, pŏris, n. ("That
which is cut off; a section,
portion," *etc.; hence, "a portion of time; a time"; hence)

1. *Time* in general. — 2. *A particular time; an occasion, season,* etc.—3. *The time,* i. e. *the right* or *fitting time, the right season, opportunity* [root TEM, akin to τέμ-νω, "to cut"].

tendo, tĕtendi, tensum or tentum, tendĕre, 3. v. a. and n.: 1. Act.: a. *To stretch out* or *forth; to extend.*—b. Of snares: *To lay.*—2. Neut.: ("To direct one's self *or* one's course"; hence) *To exert one's self,* etc.; *to strive, contend* [akin to τεν, root of τείνω].

tĕn-ĕbræ, ĕbrārum, f. plur. *Darkness* [akin to Sans. *tamas,* "darkness"].

tĕn-ĕo, ŭi, tum, ĕre, 2. v. a. [akin to ten-do]: 1. *To hold, keep, have, lay hold of.*—2. Mentally *or* morally : *To take hold,* or *possession, of* one or one's mind.—3. Of a public office, *etc.: To have, hold, possess, be in possession of.* —4. Pass.: *To be stayed, controlled,* or *influenced;* iii. 4. —Pass.: tĕn-ĕor, tus sum, ĕri.

ten-to, tāvi, tātum, tāre, 1. v. a. intens. [tĕn-ĕo, "to hold"] ("To hold greatly"; hence, "to handle, feel," *etc.;* hence) 1. *To try, make trial of.*—2. *To attack, assail, harass.*—3. *To attempt, essay, endeavour.* —4. *To tamper with.*

Tĕrentĭus, ĭi, m. *Terentius* (*Cneius*), a Roman senator. to whose charge Cæparius was entrusted by the Senate; xlvii. 4.

ter-ra, ræ, f. ("The dry thing"; hence, "the earth" as such ; hence) 1. *Land* as opposed to water, *etc. :*—terrā mărīque, *by land and by sea;* xiii. 3.—2. Plur. : *The lands, countries,* i. e. *the earth;* ii. 1, *etc.* [prob. akin to Gr. τέρσομαι, "to be, *or* become, dry"; Sans. root TRISH (TARSH), "to thirst"].

terr-ĕo, ŭi, ĭtum, ēre, 2. v. a. *To frighten, terrify, alarm:*— metu terrere, *to frighten with fear,* i. e. *to cause immense alarm to;* li. 30; so Cæsar B. G., Bk. v. ch. 6, metu territare [akin to Sans. root TRAS, "to tremble"; in causative force, "to cause to tremble"].

terr-ĭbĭlis, ĭbĭle, adj. [terr-ĕo, "to frighten"] ("That may, *or* can, frighten"; hence) *Causing fright* or *terror; terrible, fearful, dreadful;*— at lv. 4 with Abl. of cause [§ 111].

ter-tĭus, tĭa, tĭum, adj. [tres, tr-ĭum (with e inserted), "three"] ("Pertaining to *tres*"; hence) *The third.*

testis, is, comm. gen. *A witness.*

test-or, ātus sum, āri, 1. v. dep. [test-is, "a witness"] *To call upon,* or *invoke, as witness; to call to witness;* xxxiii. 2.

tŏ-ter (tæ-), tra, trum, adj. [for tæd-ter; fr. tæd-et, "it disgusts"] ("Effecting disgust or loathing"; hence) *Foul, offensive, disgusting, loathsome.*

tĕtrarcha (tĕtraches), æ, m. *A tetrarch*—i. e. a ruler over a fourth part of a kingdom; but used as a term for "a prince" in general without reference to the extent of his territory [τετράρχης].

texĕrim, perf. subj. of tego.

Ti., abbrev. of Titus.

Tib., abbrev. of Tiberius.

Tĭber-ĭus, ĭi (-ĭ, l. 4), m. [Tĭber-is, "the Tiber" (now "Tevere"), the river running through Rome] ("One belonging to *Tiberis*") *Tiberius;* a Roman name.

tĭmens, ntis, P. pres. of tĭmĕo.

tĭmĕo, ŭi, no sup.,ēre, 2. v. a. and n.: 1. Act. *To be afraid of; to fear.*—2. Neut.: *To fear; to be afraid; to be in fear or terror.*

tĭm-ĭdus, ĭda, ĭdum, adj. [tĭm-ĕo, "to fear"] 1. *Timid, fearing, in fear.*—2. *Cowardly, faint-hearted.*

tĭm-or, ōris, m. [tĭm-ĕo, "to fear"] ("A fearing"; hence) *Fear, dread, terror.*

Tĭtus, i, m. *Titus;* a Roman name.

tŏl-ĕro, ĕrāvi, ĕrātum, ĕrāre, 1. v. a. [root TOL; see tollo] *To bear, endure, support.*

tollo, sustŭli, sublātum, tollĕre [root TOL, whence tŭli; see fĕro] 1. *To lift up, raise:* —tollere ad cœlum, (*to lift up to heaven*, i. e.) *to extol to the skies ;*—at xlviii. 1 tollere is Hist. Inf. [§ 140, 2].—2. ("To take away"; hence) *To hide* or *conceal* the name of; xxiii. 4.—Pass.: tollor, sublātus sum, tolli.

tŏreuma, ătis, n. *Work executed in relief, embossed work, embossed plate* [τόρευμα].

torpesco, torpŭi, no sup., torpescĕre, 3. v. n. inch. [torpĕo, "to be dull or inactive"] *To become dull* or *inactive.*

Torqu-ātus, ăti, m. [torquis, "a collar" for the neck] ("One provided with a *torquis;* Collar-wearer") *Torquatus;* the name of a family belonging to the Manlian house: 1. Titus Manlius Imperiosus, who obtained, and handed down to his descendants, the name of Torquatus, from his having spoiled a Gaul, whom he had slain in single combat, of his *torquis* or twisted neck-chain or collar. So rigid a disciplinarian was he that he caused his own son to be put to death for having engaged in combat with a Latin contrary to his command. Sallust is in error at lii. 30 when he states that the son engaged a Gaul.—2. Lucius Manlius Torquatus, who was consul with Lucius AureliusCotta, B.C.65; xviii.5.

tŏ-tus, ta, tum, adj. ("Increased"; hence) *All, all the, the whole, the whole of* (denoting a thing in its entirety) [akin to Sans. root TU, "to increase"].

trāc-to, tāvi, tātum, tāre, 1. v. a. intens. [for trah-to; fr. trăh-o, "to draw *or* drag"] ("To draw *or* drag much" to one; hence, "to take in hand, handle"; hence, in figurative meaning) *To handle, manage, control,* etc., persons.

trādĭdĕrim, perf. subj. of trādo.

trādĭtus, a, um, P. perf. pass. of trādo.

trā-do, dĭdi, dĭtum, dĕre, 3. v. a. [tra (= trans), "across"; do, "to give"] ("To give across"; hence) 1. *To give up, hand over, deliver, surrender.* —2. *To commit, entrust, confide, give over.*—3. With Personal pron. in reflexive force: *To give up, surrender,* etc., *one's self,* etc.;—at lii. 29 tradideris, 2. pers. sing. (perf.) subj., is used in indefinite force. —Pass.: trā-dor, dĭtus sum, di.

trāho, traxi, tractum, trăh-ĕre, 3. v. a.: 1. *To draw, drag, drag along,* etc.—2. *To drag away violently, carry off by force.*—3. Of money, *etc.: To*

make away with, squander, dissipate. — Pass. : **trăhor,** tractus sum, trăhi.

trām-es, ĭtis, m. [for trame-(t)-s; fr. tramĕ-o, "to go across"] ("That which goes across"; hence) *A cross-way, by-path.*

tranquillus, a, um, adj. *Calm, quiet, still.*

trans-ĕo, īvi or ĭi, ĭtum, īre, v. a. irreg. [trans, "across"; ĕo, "to go"] ("To go across"; hence) Of life: *To pass through, spend.*

trans-fĕro, tŭli, lātum, ferre, v. a. irreg. [trans, "beyond"; fĕro, "to bear *or* carry"] ("To bear, *or* carry, beyond"; hence) 1. *To transfer.*—2. *To put off, defer, postpone.*— Pass.: trans-fĕror, lātus sum, ferri.

trans-ĭgo, ēgi, actum, ĭgĕre, 3. v. a. [for trans-ăgo; fr. trans, "through," from beginning to end; ăgo, in force of "to do"] ("To do from beginning to end"; hence) Of time as Object: *To lead, pass, spend.*

Trans-păd-ānus, āna, ānum, adj. [trans, "beyond"; Păd-us, the "Padus" (now "Po," the principal river of Italy] *That is beyond the Padus.*—As Subst.: **Transpădānus,** i, m. *A dweller beyond the Padus.*

transtŭlĕram, pluperf. ind. of transfero.

trĕpĭd-o, āvi, ātum, āre, 1. v. n. [trĕpĭd-us, "alarmed"] ("To be *trĕpidus*"; hence) *To be in a state of alarm or trepidation; to hurry about in alarm, to run hither and thither in anxiety.*

tres, trĭa (Gen. trium), num. adj. *Three* [τρεῖς, τρία].

trĭbūn-ĭtĭus, ĭtĭa, ĭtĭum, adj. [trĭbun-us, "a tribune" of the people] *Of,* or *belonging to, a tribune* or *the tribunes; tribunitian.*

trĭb-ūnus, ūni, m. [trĭb-us, ' a tribe"] ("One pertaining to a *tribus*"; hence) *A tribune,* whether of the people (xliii. 1) or of the soldiers (lix. 6).

trĭb-ŭo, ŭi, ūtum, ŭĕre, 3. v. a. *To give, bestow, grant,* etc.

trī-ginta, num. adj. indecl. "Three tens"; hence) *Thirty* tres, trĭ-um, "three"; ginta = κοντα = "ten"].

trist-ĭtĭa, ĭtĭæ, f. [trist-is, ' sad"] (" The quality of the *ristis*"; hence) *Sadness, grief, sorrow.*

trĭumph-o, āvi, ātum, āre, . v. n. [trĭumph-us, "a triumph"] *To have,* or *enjoy, a triumph; to triumph.*

trĭum-vir, vĭri, m. [tres, rĭum, "three"; vir, "a man"] "A man of three"; *i. e.* one f three men) *A triumvir;* one f a board of three persons associated together in some public office.—Plur.: *Triumvirs;*—at lv. 1 the triumviri mentioned are the triumviri capitales, who were the superintendents of the prisons.

Trōja (= Tro-ia), æ, f. [Trōs, Trō-is, "Tros," an ancient king of Phrygia] ("The city of Tros") *Troy;*—the taking of Troy by the Greeks is said to have occurred B.C. 1184.— Hence, Trōj-ānus, āna, ānum, adj. *Of,* or *belonging to, Troy; Trojan.*—As Subst.: Trōjāni, ōrum, m. plur. *The Trojans,* who, under Æneas, settled in Latium, and were the ancestors of the Roman nation.

Trōjāni, ōrum; see Trōja.

trŭ-cīdo, cīdāvi, cīdātum, cīdāre, 1. v. a. [for truc-cædo; fr. trux, trŭc-is, "fierce"; cædo, "to slay"] ("To slay fiercely"; hence) *To hew* or *cut to pieces cruelly; to slaughter, slay, butcher, massacre.*

tu (Gen., tŭi; Dat., tĭbi), pron. pers. *Thou, you* [τύ, Doric form of σύ].

tŭb-a, æ, f. [akin to tŭb-us, "a tube"] *A* straight *trumpet* used by the infantry.

tŭ-ĕor, ĭtus sum, ēri, 2. v. dep. ("To look upon, behold"; hence) With accessory notion of care *or* protection: *To protect, defend.*

Tullĭ-ānum, āni; see Tullius.

Tullĭus, ĭi, m. *Tullius;* a

Roman name;—at li. 35 for Cicero. — Hence, **Tullĭ-ānus,** āna, ānum, adj. *Of,* or *belonging to, a Tullius.* — Subst.: **Tullĭānum,** i, n. *The Tullianum; a cell in the state-prison on the Capitol at Rome,* built by king Servius Tullius.

Tullus, i, m. *Tullus (Lucius Volcatius); consul* with Marcus Æmilius Lepidus, B.C. 77.

tum, adv. *At that time; then* [prob. akin to a demonstr. root TO; Gr. τό].

tŭm-ultus, ultūs (Gen. tumulti, lix. 5), m. [prob. akin to tum-eo, "to swell"] ("A swelling"; hence) 1. *Tumult, confusion.* — 2. *Insurrection, rising, rebellion, civil war.*

tun-c, adv. [apocopated and changed from tum-ce; fr. tum, "at that time"; demonstr. suffix ce] *At the very time, at that time, then.*

turba, æ, f. *Disorder, disturbance* [akin to τύρβη].

turp-ĭtūdo, ĭtūdĭnis, f. [turpis, "base"] ("The quality of the *turpis*"; hence) *Baseness, dishonour, infamy, turpitude.*

Tusci, ōrum, m. *The Tusci,* i. e. *the Tuscans, Etruscans,* or *Etrurians;* the inhabitants of Etruria.

tŭ-tus, ta, tum, adj. [tŭ-eor, "to protect"] ("Protected, guarded"; hence) *Safe,* ''re.

tŭ-us, a, um, pron. poss. [tu, "thou *or* you"] *Thy, thine, your, yours.*

ŭ-bi, adv. [akin to qui] 1. *In which place, where.*—2. Of time: *At what time, when.*

1. **ŭbīque** = que ubi.

2. **ŭbī-que,** adv. [ŭbi, "where"; with indef. suffix que] 1. *Wherever, wheresoever.* —2. *In any place whatever, anywhere, everywhere.*

ulciscor, ultus sum, ulcisci, 3. v. dep. *To take vengeance for, to avenge.*

ul-lus, la, lum (Gen. ullīus; Dat. ulli), adj. [for un-lus; fr. un-us, "one"] *Any one, any.*

ulter-ĭor, ĭus, comp. adj. [obsol. ulter, "beyond"] ("More beyond") *Further.*

ultr-a, adv. *and* prep. [obsol. ulter, ultr-i, "beyond"] 1. Adv.: *Beyond, further, longer.* —2. Prep. gov. acc.: *Beyond.*

ultus, a, um, P. perf. of ulciscor.

Umbrēnus, i, m. *Umbrenus (Publius);* a trader, whom Lentulus employed to tamper with the Allobroges.

ūn-ā, adv. [Adverbial Abl. of ūn-us, "one"] *In company, at the same time, together.*

u-nde, adv. [for cu-nde (= qu-nde), fr. qu-i] *From which place, whence.*

und-ĭ-que, adv. [und-e; (i) connecting vowel; que, in-

definite suffix] ("Whenceso-
ever"; hence) *From all parts
or every quarter; on all sides.*

ūn-ĭ-versus, versa, versum,
adj. [un-us, "one"; (i) connecting vowel; versus, "turned"] ("Turned into one";
hence) *All together, or colectively; the whole,* etc.—
As Subst.: **ūnĭversi,** ōrum,
n. plur. *All, the whole* of a
body of persons.

un-quam (um-quam), adv.
ūn-us, "one"] *At any (one)
time, ever.*

ūn-us, a, um (Gen., unīus;
Dat., uni), adj.: 1. *One;*—at
i. 2 in plur. in attribution
o mœnia.—Adverbial expres-
ion: In unum, *Into,* or *to,
ne place; together;* xvii. 2.—
3. In connexion with some part
f quisque (or as one word
unusquisque, *etc.) Each one.*
—As Subst.: *Each one, each
ndividual person, each* [akin
o εἷς, ἑν-ός].

ūnus-quisque; see unus.

urb-ānus, āna, ānum, adj.
urbs, urb-is, "the city"; see
urbs, no. 2] *Of,* or *belonging
o, the city,* i. e. to Rome; *in
he city; city-.*

urb-s, is, f. [probably urb-o,
"to mark out by a plough"]
"That which is marked out
by a plough"; hence) 1. *A
walled town, a city.*—2. THE
City; i. e. Rome.—Phrase: Ad
urbem esse, *To be near to* or

by the city. When a general
returned home and claimed a
triumph, he did not enter the
city at once, but gave an account of his exploits to the
Senate assembled in the temple
of Bellōna, the goddess of war,
or in some other outside the
walls. Till the matter was
decided, he remained near the
city (whence he was said ad
urbem esse), and retained his
title of Imperator; xxx. 3. The
same expression was also applied to provincial magistrates
on the point of departing for
their provinces.

urgeo, ursi, no sup., urgēre,
2. v. a. ("To press upon";
hence) *To press hard* or *close;
to beset closely;* — at lii. 35
without nearer Object; so
Horace, Sat. 2, 2, 64, hac urget
lupus.

u-s-que, adv. [akin to qui;
with s epenthetic; que, indefinite suffix] *Even:*—usque eo,
even to such a degree, xlix. 4.

ūsūrus, a, um, P. fut. of utor.

1. **ū-sus,** ūs, m. [for ut-
sus, fr. ūt-or] 1. *A using* or
making use.—2. *Intercourse,
familiarity, intimacy.*—3. *Experience, practice.*—4. *Service,
advantage, benefit:*—usui esse,
to be serviceable.

2. **ūsus,** a, um, P. perf. of ūtor.

ut (originally ŭti), adv. *and*
conj. [prob. akin to qui] 1.
Adv.: **a.** *As, just as.*—**b.**

How.—2. Conj.: a. *That =
to* with English Inf.—b. *So
that.*—c. For ita ut : *In such
a way that.*—d. *To the end
that, in order that.*

ūtendus, a, um, Gerundive
of utor.

ŭter-que, utră-que, utrumque (Gen., utrius-que ; Dat.,
utri-que), pron. adj. [uter,
" which" of two ; " one *or* the
other " ; que, " and "] *Both
one and the other ; both, each
of two ;*—at v. 7 utraque is
neut. acc. plur.—As Subst. :
a. uterque, m. *Both one and
the other, both, each.*—b. Plur. :
utrique, m. *Both; both parties*
or *sides;* xxxviii. 3.

1. ŭti ; see ut.

2. ūti, pres. inf. of utor.

ūt-ĭlis, ĭle, adj. [ūt-or, " to
use"] (" That may, *or* can,
be used "; hence) With Dat.
[§ 106, (3)]: *Useful, beneficial,
advantageous to.*

ūtor, ūsus sum, ūti, 3. v.
dep.: 1. With Abl. [§ 119, (a)]:
*To use, make use of, employ,
avail one's self of, enjoy,* etc.
—2. With second Abl. : *To
use, employ, make use of* one,
etc., as that which is denoted
by the second Abl.; xx. 16.

ut-pŏt-e, adv. [ut, " as ";
pŏt-is, "able "] (" As being
able "; hence) *Inasmuch as,
as being, seeing that, as,* etc.:
—ut pote qui, *inasmuch as he
was one who,* lvii. 4.

utr-ăm-que, adv. [uterque
(" both one and the other "),
utr-(ius)-que ; with adverbial
suffix im inserted between que
and the theme of the first portion of this compound word]
On both sides, on each side.

văc-ŭus, ŭa, ŭum, adj. [văc-
o, " to be empty "] (" Empty,
void," etc.; hence) 1. With ab:
Free from, devoid of.—2. Of
places, etc. : With Dat.: *Free,
open, accessible to;* xv. 2.

văg-or, ātus sum, āri, 1. v.
dep. [vag-us, " wandering "]
To wander, roam at large, etc.

văl-ĕo, ŭi, ĭtum, ēre, 2. v. n. :
1. *To be strong* or *powerful,*
whether actually or figuratively.—2. *To avail, prevail,
have force* or *power.*—3. Of
things : *To possess weight,
have influence;*—at xxxvii. 10
the change of construction
from the Objective clause,
rempublicam conturbari, to
the simple Inf. *valere,* after
malebant should be noticed.
The rule is as follows. When
malo is folld. by an Inf.
having a different subject from
itself, then such Inf. requires
an Acc. as its subject, the two
together being an Objectival
clause. But when *malo* and
its Inf. have the same subject,
then the Inf. at times takes
before it an acc. of a pronoun
of the same person as that

which *malo*, etc., has (Objective clause) ; or, more frequently, as here, it is followed immediately by the Inf. (prolate, Inf. [§ 140, 4]). Further, when a pronoun is in this last-named construction added to the Inf. for further definition or emphasis, it is put in the case of the subject of *malo;* or, in other words, the subject, which in regular construction would be in the acc., is attracted to the case of the finite verb, *i. e.* to the nominative ; thus here *ipsi* is found in the place of *ipsos* (= *se ipsos*). Render, *They desired that the commonwealth should be thrown into utter confusion, rather than to be without power themselves;* or, more freely, *They preferred the convulsion of the state to their own exclusion from power.* Observe also, that quam refers to the magis in malo (= magis volo) ; and that minus= non ; —at ix. 1 valebat has for its subject jus bonumque. This arises from the two nouns colectively forming a single idea prob. akin to Sans. *bal-a,* ' strength "].

Vălĕrĭus, ĭi, m. *Valerius;* a Roman name ; see Flaccus.

văl-ĭdus, ĭda, ĭdum, adj. [văl-o, " to be strong "] *Strong, powerful.*

văn-ĭtas, ĭtātis, f. [văn-us,

in force of " vain, vain-glorious "] ("The state, *or* quality, of the *vanus";* hence) *Vanity, vain-glory.*

vănus, a, um, adj. ("Empty"; hence) 1. *Vain, ineffectual, of no avail, fruitless,* etc.—2. *False, deceptive, delusive,* etc.

Vargunteĭus, ĭi, m. *Vargunteius (Lucius),* a Roman senator, one of Catiline's accomplices ; xvii. 3. In conjunction with Caius Cornelius he undertook to attempt the assassination of Cicero; xxviii.1.

vărĭ-e, adv. [vărĭ-us, "various "] ("After the manner of the *varius";* hence) *Variously, in different ways.*

văr-ĭus, ĭa, ĭum, adj. ("Party-coloured, spotted "; hence) 1. *Various, different.* — 2. *Changeable, mutable, fickle* [akin to βαλ-ιός].

vas, vāsis, n. *A vessel,* or *utensil,* of any kind.

vast-o, āvi, ātum, āre, 1. v. a. [vast-us, " waste "] (" To lay waste "; hence) *To harass, perplex, distress;*—at xv. 4 the imperf. vastabat denotes a continued action.

vastus. a, um, adj.: 1. *Vast, huge, immense.* — 2. Of the mind : *Insatiable,* as grasping at vast things; v. 5.

vĕcord-ĭa, ĭæ, f. [vēcors, vĕcord-is, "mad"] ("The quality of the *vecors";* hence) *Madness, insanity.*

vect-ĭgal, īgālis, n. [vect-is, in etymological force of "a carrying "] (" That which pertains to *vectis*"; i. e. for carrying, *or* bringing, goods into a country; hence) *A tax, impost,* paid to the state; see stipendium.

vectĭgāl-is, e, adj. [vect-ĭgul, "tribute"] *Of,* or *belonging to, tribute; tributary.*

vĕhĕ-mens, mentis, adj. [prob. lengthened from ve-mens; fr. ve, negative insepar-able particle; mens, "mind"] (" Not having *mens*"; hence, " unreasonable"; hence) *Vio-lent, impetuous, ardent, vehe-ment.*

vĕhĕmen-ter, adv. [for vĕhĕ-ment-ter, fr. vĕhĕmens, vĕhĕ-ment-is, "eager"] (" After the manner of the *vehemens*"; hence) *Eagerly, ardently, vehe-mently.*

vel, conj. [akin to vŏl-o, vel-le, " to wish "] (" Wish *or* choose"; hence) *Or if you will, or :*—vel . . . vel, *either . . . or.*

vĕl-ut (vĕl-ŭti), adv. [vĕl, "even"; ut (ŭti), "as "] 1. *Even as, just as.*—2. *Just as if, just as though, as if, as though.*

vĕn-ālis, āle, adj. [vēn-um, "sale "] (" Of *or* belonging to sale; for sale "; hence) *That is to be bought by bribes, that can be bribed, venal.*

vĕnando, Gerund in do fr. vēnor.

ven-do, dĭdi, dĭtum, dĕre, 3. v. a. [vēn-um, "sale "; do, " to place "] (" To place, *or* expose, for sale "; hence) *To sell, vend.*

vĕ-nĕ-num, ni, n. [for vĕ-nec-num; fr. vĕ, inseparable particle in " intensive " force; nĕc-o, "to kill "] (" Power-ful, *or* mighty, killing thing"; hence, " poison, a potion" that destroys life; hence) *A drug, potion;*—at xi. 3 with attrib-utive adj. malis.

vĕnĭo, vēni, ventum, vĕnīre, 4. v. n.: 1. *To come.*—2. Im-pers. Pass.: ventum est, (*it was come;* i. e.) a. *They came;* lx. 2.—b. *It came;* l. 5 [Oscan root BEN; akin to Gr. βα(ί)ν-ω, " to go "; Sans. root GA, " to go, to come "].

vēnor, ātus sum, āri, 1. v. dep. *To hunt.*

venter, tris, m.: 1. *The belly.*—2. With accessory notion of gormandizing: *The paunch, the maw* [prob. Γέντερ-ον, " the entrails "].

ventum est; see venio.

ventūrus, a, um, P. fut. of venio.

verber, ĕris (Nom., Dat., and Acc. Sing. do not occur), n. [prob. for fer-ber; fr. fĕr-ĭo, " to beat "] (" That which brings about the beating"; hence, " a lash, whip, scourge";

hence) *A stripe, blow*, etc. :— verberibus in aliquem anim- advertere, *to inflict punish- ment on one by stripes*, i. e. *to scourge;* alluding to scourging with the rods of the lictors; i. 21.

verbĕr-o, āvi, ātum, āre, 1. *r. a.* [verber, "a lash"] *To 'ash, beat, strike.*—Pass.: ver-)ĕr-or, ·ātus sum, āri.

verbum, i. n. *A word.*

vēr-e, adv. [vēr-us, "true"] *i. Truly.*—**2.** Sup.: *Most truly:* —quam verissume, *as truly as possible.* 📖 (Comp.: vērĭus); Sup.: vēr-issĭme *or* verissŭme.

vĕr-ĕor, ĭtus sum, ēri, 2. *r. dep. To fear, dread, be 'fraid of.*

verissĭme (verissŭme); see 'ere.

vēr-o, adv. [vēr-us, "true"] *.. In truth, in fact, assuredly. -2. But in fact, but indeed, · owever.*

ver-so, sāvi, sātum, sāre, *. v. a.* intens. [for vert-so; *r.* vert-o, "to turn"] *To turn such or often.*—Pass.: ver- or, sātus sum, sāri; In re- exive·force: ("To keep turn- ig one's self about"; hence) *'o occupy,* or *busy, one's self,* tc.; *to engage* or *be engaged s.*

ver-sus, sūs, m. [for vert- 1s, fr. vert-o] ("A turning"; *·* ence, of that in which the çt of turning takes place, "a

furrow"; hence, "a row, line," *etc.;* hence) 1. *A line* in writ- ing.—2. In poetry: *A verse, line:*—versūs facere, *to make,* or *compose, verses*, xxv. 5.

1. vēr-um, adv. [vēr-us, "true"] ("Truly"; hence) In adversative force: *But.*

2. vērum, i; see verus.

vērus, a, um, adj.: 1. *True.*— As Subst.: vērum, i, n. *That which is true, truth.*—2. *Right, proper, fitting, suitable.*

vescendi, Gerund in di fr. vescor.

vesc-or, no perfect, vesci, 3. v. dep. *To take* something *as food, to eat, feed* [akin to esc-a, "food"; or perhaps Gr. βόσκ-ω, "to feed"].

Ves-ta, tæ, f. *Vesta;* one of the principal Roman deities, in whose temple were said to be preserved the Penates and the sacred fire which Æneas had brought from Troy. No statue was erected in it, but the sacred fire was kept burn- ing, night and day, on the altar. The goddess, herself, was regarded as pure and chaste, and her priestesses (the Vestal virgins, originally four, afterwards six, in number, taken from the noblest families of Rome) were bound by a vow of chastity. If any one of them violated this vow, she was to be buried alive in the Campus Sceleratus, and her paramour scourged to death in the Forum :—sacerdos Vestæ, *a priestess of Vesta,* i. e. *a Vestal virgin,* xv. 1 [akin to Sans. root VAS, "to dwell"; hence, "The Dweller" in households, as their presiding deity].

vestǐ-mentum, menti, n. [vestǐ-o, "to clothe"] ("That which clothes"; hence) *A garment, vestment, clothing,* etc

vestrum, gen. plur. of tu.

vĕtĕr-ānus, āna, ānum, adj. [vĕt-us, vĕtĕr-is, "old"] ("Pertaining to *vetus*"; hence, " of long standing, old "; hence, of troops, *etc.*) *Having served for a long time, veteran;* lix. 5. —As Subst.: **veterāni,** ōrum, m. plur. *Veteran soldiers, veterans;* lx. 3.

vĕt-o, ǔi, ǐtum, āre, 1. v. a. *To forbid, prohibit.*

vĕt-us, ĕris, adj. ("That has existed for years"; hence) *Old, ancient, of long standing, etc.*—As Subst.: **vĕtĕra,** um, n. plur. *Old things;* xxxvii. 3 [prob. akin to Fέτ-ος, "a year"].

vexo, āvi, ātum, āre, 1. v. a. intens. [= veh-so; fr. veh-o] ("To carry much *or* frequently"; hence, of the result of such carrying; "to move violently"; hence) 1. *To harass, trouble, disquiet.*— 2. Of wealth, *etc.: To use to*

a wrong end or purpose; to abuse, lavish shamefully, etc.

VI. = sextus, *etc.;* see sextus.

vǐa (old form vĕ-a), æ, f. [for ve-ha; fr. vĕ-ho, " to carry "] (" That which carries *or* conveys"; hence) 1. *A way, road.*—2. *A way, method,* etc.

vǐcīn-ǐtas, ǐtātis, f. [vǐcīnus, "neighbouring"] ("The state, *or* condition, of the *vicinus*"; hence, "neighbourhood, vicinity"; hence) *The neighbourhood, the neighbours.*

vic-tor, tōris, m. [vi(n)c-o, " to conquer "] *A conqueror, victor.*

victor-ǐa, ǐæ, f. [victor, victōr-is, " a conqueror "] (" The thing pertaining to a *victor*"; hence) *Victory.*

1. **victus,** a, um, P. perf. pass. of vinco.—As Subst.: **victi,** ōrum, m. plur. *The conquered* or *vanquished.*

2. **vic-tus,** tūs, m. [for vigv-tus; fr. VIGV, root of vīv-o, "to live"] 1. *A living, mode of living, way of life.*—2. *Food, sustenance,* etc.

vic-us, i, m. *A street* [akin to Folκ-ος, " a house."]

vǐdē-lǐcet, adv. [contr. fr. vǐdēre, "to see"; lǐcet, "it is permitted"] ("It is permitted to see"; hence) 1. *Plainly, clearly, manifestly.* —2. In ironical force: *Of course, forsooth.*

vĭdeo, vīdi, vīsum, vĭdēre, 2. v. a.: 1. Act.: a. *To see.—* 2. Pass.: a. *To be seen.—*b. *To seem, appear.—*3. With Objective clause: *To perceive, note, mark, observe that;* xl. 3;—at xxxvii. 6 the Objective clause is alios (esse) senatores. —4. a. *To seem good, appear right.—*b.Impers.Pass.: vīsum est, *It seemed good,* etc. — Pass.: vĭdeor, vīsus sum, vĭdēri [akin to Sans. root VID, in original force of "to see"].

vĭg-ĕo, no perf. nor sup., ēre, 2. v. n. *To be vigorous, to flourish.*

vĭgĭlando, Gerund in do fr. vigilo.

vĭgĭl-ĭa, ĭæ, f. [vĭgĭl-o,"to be watchful"] 1. *A being watchful; a being,*or *keeping, awake.* —2. *Wakefulness, sleeplessness.*—3. Plur.: *The watch;* i.e. *watchmen, sentinels.*

vĭgĭl-o, āvi, ātum, āre, 1. v. n. [vigil, "watchful"] *To be watchful* or *vigilant, to watch.*

vilis, e, adj. ("Of small price"; hence) *Poor, paltry, vile; of no account* or *value.*

vil-la, læ, f. [probably for vic-la; fr. vic-us, "a village"] ("A thing pertaining to a *vicus*"; hence) *A country house, country seat, villa.*

vinco, vīci, victum, vincĕre, 3. v. a. *and* n. ("To conquer"; hence) 1. Act.: a. *To conquer,*

vanquish enemies, *etc.—*b. Of riches as Object: *To overcome, get the better of,* i. e. *to get rid of, dissipate,* etc.; xx. 12. 2.—Neut.: *To prevail, carry the day, gain the victory.—* Pass.: vincor, victus sum, vinci.

vinc-ŭlum, ŭli, n. [vinc-ĭo, "to bind"] ("The binding thing"; hence) 1. *A chain, bond, fetter.—*2. Plur.: *Chains, fetters,* i. e. (sometimes)*prison.*

vindex, ĭcis, comm. gen. [for vindic-s; fr. vĭndĭco, in force of "to avenge"] *An avenger, punisher.*

vindĭcātum est; see vindico.

vindĭc-o, āvi, ātum, āre, 1. v. a.: 1. *To lay legal claim to* a person, *etc.:*—vindicare aliquem in libertatem, *to lay legal claim to one for liberty,* i. e. to demand or require that one who is held as a slave should be set, or pronounced, free;—at xx. 6 Catiline uses this phrase as if he and those whom he addressed were held in actual slavery through the necessitous circumstances in which they had involved themselves.—2. a. *To avenge, revenge, punish* a wrong.—b. Impers. Pass.: vindĭcātum est, *Punishment was inflicted.*

vine = vi, abl. sing. of vis; ne; i. 5.

vīnum, i, n. *Wine* [Folvos].

vĭŏlent-ĭa, ĭæ, f. [vĭŏlens,

vĭŏlent-is, "violent"] ("The quality of the *violens* "; hence) *Violence*.

vĭr, vĭri, m.: 1. *A man.*—2. *A husband;*—at xxv. 2 vir (of Sempronia) means Decimus Junius Brutus [akin to Gr. ἥρ-ως; Sans. *vir-a*, "a hero"].

vĭres, ĭum, plur. of vis.

virgo, ĭnis, f. *A maiden, virgin.*

vĭr-ĭlis, ĭle, adj. [vir, "a man"] 1. *Of,* or *belonging to, a man.* - 2. *Manlike, manly ;*—at xxv. 1. virilis audaciæ is Gen. of quality [§ 128].

vir-tus, tūtis, f. [vir, "a man"] ("The quality of the *vir*"; hence) 1. *Courage, bravery, valour.*—2. *Merit, worth, excellence ;*—at liii. 6 ingenti virtute is Abl. of quality [§ 115].—3. *Virtue, moral worth.*—4. *Vigour, strength, energy* of mind, *etc.*

vis, vis (plur. vĭres, ĭum), f. : 1. *Strength, might.*—2. *Power :*—tanta vis hominis, (*so great power of a man;* i.e.) *so powerful a man,* xlviii. 5.—3. *Force, violence, impetuosity* [*Vis*].

visendi (visundi), Gerund in di fr. viso.

vi-so, si, sum, sĕre, 3. v. n. *and* a. intens. [for vid-so ; fr. vĭd-ĕo, "to see"] ("To look at attentively"; hence) 1. Neut.: *To look on, behold, take a look* or *view.*—2. Act.: *To go to see, to visit.*

visum est ; see video.

visundi ; see visendi.

vī-tă, tæ, f. [for viv-ta ; fr. vīv-o, "to live"] ("That which is lived"; hence) *Life :*—vitam habēre, (*to have,* i. e.) *to pass,* or *spend, life.*

vĭtĭum, ĭi, n.: 1. *A fault, defect, etc.*—2. *A* moral *fault, crime, vice.*

vīvens, ntis, P. pres. of vivo.

vīvo, vixi, victum, vīvĕre, 3. v. n. *To live* [akin to Sans. root JĬV, whence also βιϝ-όω].

vīv-us, a, um, adj. [vīv-o, "to live"] *Living, alive.*

vix, adv. *With difficulty, hardly, scarcely, barely.*

vŏbiscum = cum vobis; see cum.

vŏcă-bŭlum, bŭli, n. [voc(a)-o, "to call"] ("That which serves for calling"; hence) *An appellation, designation, name.*

vŏc-o, āvi, ātum, āre, 1. v. a.: 1. *To call.*—2. *To call, summon, cite.*—3. a. With second Acc.: *To call* an Object that which is denoted by second Acc.—b. Pass. folld. by nom.: *To be called* something.— Pass.: vŏc-or, ātus sum, āri [akin to Sans. root VACH, "to speak, say"].

vŏlens, ntis, P. pres. of volo.

volgus, i; volnĕrātus, a, um; volnus, eris; voltis; voltus, ūs; see vul-.

vŏlo, vŏlŭi, velle, v. irreg :
1. *To be willing.*—2. *To wish,
desire;*—at xvii. 2 supply ex-
plorare after voluit [akin to
Gr. βολ, root of βόλ-ομαι =
Βο(ύ)λ-ομαι, "to wish"; and
Sans. root VRI, "to choose"].

Volturcius, ĭi, m. *Volturcius
(Titus)*, a man of Crotona, one
of Catiline's accomplices who
accompanied the Allobroges on
their pretended departure from
Rome. After vainly endeavour-
ing to defend himself at the
Mulvian bridge, he surrendered
to Caius Pomptinus, the Prae-
tor ; xlv. 3, 4. When brought
before the Senate he makes dis-
closures respecting the conspiracy and conspirators; xlvii.
, 2.

vŏlunt-ārĭus, arĭa, arĭum,
adj. [for vŏluntāt-ārĭŭs; fr.
vŏluntas, vŏluntāt-is, "free-
will "] (" Of, *or* belonging to,
oluntas"; hence) *Of one's,
etc., own free will, voluntary.*
-As Subst.: **vŏluntārĭus**, ĭi,
1. *A volunteer.*

vŏlun-tas, tātis, f. [for
olent-tas ; fr. vŏlens, vŏlent-
i, "willing"] (" The quality
f the *volens* "; hence) *Will,
inclination, wish, desire :*—ex
oluntate, *according to his
will,* i. e. *just as he liked,*
xvi. 1.

vŏlupt-ārĭus, ārĭa, ārĭum,
adj. [contr. fr. vŏluptat-ārĭus;
. vŏluptas, vŏluptāt-is, "plea-

sure "] (" Of, *or* belonging to,
voluptas"; hence) *Of* places:
Full of pleasures, etc.

vŏlup-tas, tātis, f. [volup,
"pleasant"] (" The quality of
the *volup*"; hence) *Pleasure,
delight,* etc., whether of mind
or body;—at lii. 23 in plur.

volvens, ntis, P. pres. of
volvo.

volvo, volvi, vŏlūtum, volv-
ĕre, 3. v. a.: 1. *To roll, roll
along.*—2. *To revolve, or turn
over, in the mind; to ponder,
meditate upon.*—3. Of corpses
on the field of battle: *To turn,
turn over,* etc.; lxi. 8 [akin to
Fελύ-ω, "to roll "].

vorsus (versus), adv. [for
vort-sus (vert-sus); fr. vort-o
= vert-o, "to turn "] *Turned
in the direction of, towards ;
*—generally found after a word
denoting a place, and frequently in connexion with in
c. Acc. or ad; cf. lvi. 4.

vorto (old form of **verto**),
vorti, vorsum, vortĕre, 3. v. a.
To turn [akin to Sans. root
VRIT, "to turn "].

vos-ter (old form of **ves-ter**),
tra, trum, pron. poss. [vos, plur.
of tu, "you "] *Of, or belonging
to, you; your, yours.*

vostrum ; see vestrum.

vō-tum, ti, n. [for vov-tum;
fr. vŏv-ĕo, "to vow "] (" That
which is vowed"; hence) *A
vow.*

vox, vōcis, f. [for voc-s ; f

Sallust.   R

vŏc-o, "to call"] ("That which calls *or* calls out"; hence) *A voice.*

vulgus (old form **volgus**), ı, m. *and* n. *The multitude* or *mass; the common people, mob, populace* [prob. akin to Ὄχλος, "a crowd"].

vulnĕrātus (old form **volnĕrātus**), a, um, P. perf. pass. of vulnero.

vulnĕr-o (old form **volnĕr-o**), āvi, ātum, āre, 1. v. a. [vulnus, vulnĕr-is, "a wound"] *To wound.*—Pass.: **vulnĕr-or**, ātus sum, āri.

vuln-us (old form **voln-us**), ĕris, n. *A wound* [akin to Sans. *vran-a,* " a wound"; fr. root VRAN, "to wound"].

vultis (old form **voltis**), 2. pers. plur. pres. ind. of volo.

vultus (old form **vol-tus**), tūs, m. [prob. vŏl-o, "to wish"] ("The wishing, *or* expressing one's wish" by the looks; hence) 1. *Expression of countenance;* often to be translated by *features, looks, air, mien.* —2. *Face, countenance.*—3. Of things : *Look, appearance.*

GILBERT AND RIVINGTON, LIMITED, ST. JOHN'S SQUARE. LONDON.

LATIN TEXTS:—

CÆSAR, Gallic War. Books I. II. V. VI. 1s. each.

CÆSAR, Gallic War. Book I. Text only. 3d.

CÆSAR, Gallic War. Books III. and IV. 9d. each.

CÆSAR, Gallic War. Book VII. 1s. 6d.

CICERO, Cato Major (Old Age). 1s. 6d.

CICERO, Lælius (Friendship). 1s. 6d.

EUTROPIUS, Books I. and II. of Roman History. 1s.

EUTROPIUS, Books III. and IV. of Roman History. 1s.

HORACE, Odes. Books I. II. and IV. 1s. each.

HORACE, Odes. Book III. 1s. 6d.

HORACE, Epodes and Carmen Seculare. 1s.

NEPOS, Miltiades, Cimon, Pausanias, and Aristides. 9d.

OVID, Selections from the Epistles and Fasti. 1s.

OVID, Select Myths from the Metamorphoses. 9d.

PHÆDRUS, Select Fables. 9d.

PHÆDRUS, Fables. Books I. and II. 1s.

SALLUST, Bellum Catilinarium. 1s. 6d.

VIRGIL, Georgics. Book IV. 1s.

VIRGIL, Æneid. Books I. to VI. 1s. each.

VIRGIL, Æneid. Book I. Text only. 3d.

VIRGIL, Æneid. Books VII. VIII. X. XI. and XII. 1s 6d. each.

LIVY, Books XXI. and XXIII.
The Latin Text with English Explanatory and Grammatical Notes, and a Vocabulary of Proper Names. Edited by JOHN T. WHITE, D.D. Oxon. 12mo, price 2s. 6d. each BOOK.

London : LONGMANS, GREEN, & CO.

CLASSICAL SCHOOL BOOKS,

EDITED BY THE REV. JOHN T. WHITE, D.D

BRADLEY'S *EUTROPIUS*, newly edited by the Rev. Dr. WHITE, with a Vocabulary and Notes adapted to the Public School Latin Primer. Price 2s. 6d.

BRADLEY'S *CORNELIUS NEPOS*, newly edited by the Rev. Dr. WHITE, with English Notes adapted to the Public School Latin Primer. Price 3s. 6d.

BRADLEY'S OVID'S METAMORPHOSES, newly edited by the Rev. Dr. WHITE, with English Notes adapted to the Public School Latin Primer. Price 4s. 6d.

BRADLEY'S *PHÆDRUS*, newly edited by the Rev. Dr. WHITE, with English Grammatical Notes adapted to the Public School Latin Primer. Price 2s. 6d.

The Rev. Dr. WHITE'S FIRST LATIN PARSING BOOK, adapted to the SYNTAX of the Public School Latin Primer. Price 2s.

The Rev. Dr. WHITE'S FIRST LATIN EXERCISE BOOK, adapted to the Public School Latin Primer. Price 2s. 6d.—KEY, 2s. 6d.

VALPY'S LATIN DELECTUS, newly edited by the Rev. Dr. WHITE, with Grammatical Notes adapted to the Public School Latin Primer. Price 2s. 6d.—KEY, 3s. 6d.

VALPY'S GREEK DELECTUS, newly edited by the Rev. Dr. WHITE, with Notes adapted to Parry's Greek Grammar, and with a new Lexicon. Price 2s. 6d.—KEY, 2s. 6d.

XENOPHON'S EXPEDITION of CYRUS into UPPER ASIA; principally from the Text of SCHNEIDER With English Notes. By the Rev. Dr. WHITE. Sixth Edition. Price 7s. 6d.

London : LONGMANS, GREEN, & CO.

Lightning Source UK Ltd.
Milton Keynes UK
UKHW021445270219
338010UK00005B/711/P